LIFE IN THE
OCEANS

Written by **Lucy Baker**

Consultant Roger Hammond
Director of Living Earth

Created and published by
Two-Can Publishing Ltd
346 Old Street
London
EC1V 9NQ

This edition published by Two-Can Publishing Ltd in 1997.

Hardback ISBN   1-85434-584-2
Paperback ISBN   1-85434-043-3

Hardback 2 4 6 8 10 9 7 5 3 1
Paperback 6 8 10 9 7 5

A catalogue record for this book is available from the British Library.

Photograph Credits:
p.4 Greenpeace/Morgan p.5 Ardea/Francois Gohier p.7 Ardea/Ron & Valerie Taylor p.8-9 ZEFA/Dr D. James p.10 Planet Earth/Robert Arnold p.11 (top) Oxford Scientific Films/Peter Parks(bottom) Oxford Scientific Films/Peter Parks p.12 (top) Ardea/J-M Labat (bottom) Oxford Scientific Films/G.I. Bernard p.13 (top left) Planet Earth/Peter David (top right) Planet Earth/Gillian Lythgoe (bottom) Planet Earth/Peter Scoones p.14 Ardea/Ron & Valerie Taylor p.15 Planet Earth/Peter David p.16 Ardea/Clem Haagner p.17 (top) Planet Earth/Jim Brandenburg (bottom) Ardea/Francois Gohier p.18-19 B. & C. Alexander p.20 Ardea/Richard Vaughan p.21 ZEFA p.22-23 Ardea/Francois Gohier
Front cover: Ardea/Francois Gohier. Back cover: Tony Stone Worldwide/Mike Smith
Illustrations by Francis Mosley. Artworking by Claire Legemah.

Printed in Hong Kong

CONTENTS

Looking at the oceans   4
Dividing the seas   6
Moving waves   8
Food for life   10
All shapes and sizes   12
The hunter and the hunted   14
Taking to the water   16
Ocean resources   18
Making the sea sick   20
Save the oceans   22
Dakuwaca fights for his life 24
True or false?   29
Glossary   30
Index   32

LOOKING AT THE OCEANS

Over two-thirds of the world's surface is covered by vast oceans. The oceans are the oldest and largest living **environments**. Life began here more than 3,500 million years ago. Without the fertile oceans, the Earth would be dry, barren and devoid of life.

Beneath the world's oceans lie rugged mountains, active volcanoes, vast plateaux and almost bottomless **trenches**. The deepest ocean trenches could easily swallow up the tallest mountains on land.

Seen from above, the oceans appear empty and unchanging but beneath the surface hides a unique world where water takes the place of air. A fantastic and rich assortment of plants and animals lives in these waters, from the microscopic **plankton** to the giant blue whale.

DID YOU KNOW?

● Salt is not the only substance found in sea water. There are also tiny traces of gold, silver, uranium and other valuable **minerals**.

● Sound travels through water five times faster than through air. Some sea animals such as dolphins navigate through the oceans by bouncing sounds off their surroundings and listening to their **echoes**.

● Although oceans dominate the world map, we have only just begun to explore their hidden depths. The deepest part of the ocean was first visited in 1960.

▶ There are no boundaries in the ocean. Animals can travel freely through the water. Most sea animals breathe underwater but some, such as dolphins and whales, need to come up for air every few minutes.

◀ In the Tropics the oceans are warm and clear, but around the North and South **Poles** it is very cold; here, parts of the ocean are frozen all year long. Huge chunks of ice, called icebergs, float in these seas.

DIVIDING THE SEAS

In truth there is only one ocean. It stretches from the North Pole to the South Pole and encircles the globe. However, because the **continents** loosely divide the water, four separate oceans are recognised – the Pacific, the Atlantic, the Indian and the Arctic. Within these oceans there are smaller bodies of water called seas, **bays** and **gulfs** that are cut off from the open oceans by land formations.

The Pacific is the largest and deepest of the four great oceans. It covers more of the world's surface than all of the continents put together. The word *pacific* means peaceful but the water can be rough. Waves over 35 m (112 feet) tall have been recorded in the Pacific Ocean.

The Atlantic is the second biggest ocean and the busiest. Boats regularly cross the Atlantic waters carrying cargo between the Americas, Africa and countries in Europe.

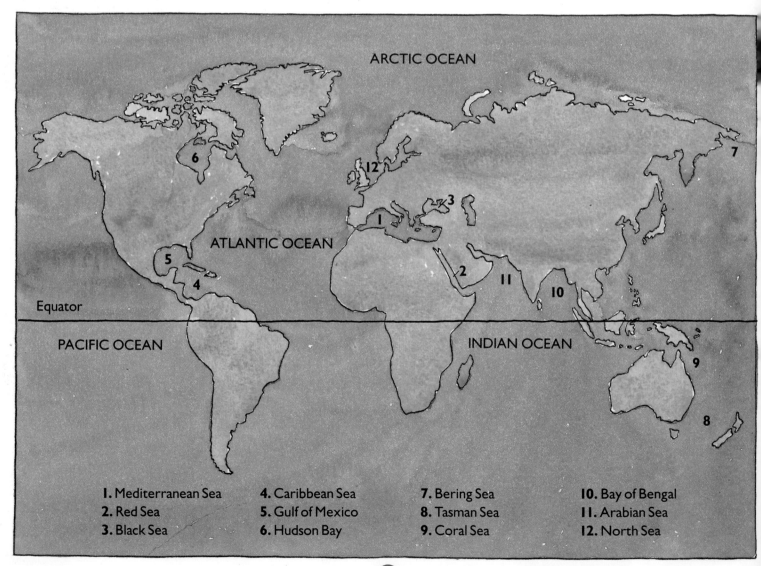

ARCTIC OCEAN

ATLANTIC OCEAN

Equator

PACIFIC OCEAN

INDIAN OCEAN

1. Mediterranean Sea
2. Red Sea
3. Black Sea
4. Caribbean Sea
5. Gulf of Mexico
6. Hudson Bay
7. Bering Sea
8. Tasman Sea
9. Coral Sea
10. Bay of Bengal
11. Arabian Sea
12. North Sea

DID YOU KNOW?

● One drop of seawater may travel through all the world's oceans in 5,000 years.

● The Atlantic Ocean is growing and the Pacific Ocean is shrinking. The world's continents move a few centimetres each year. This means that the relative sizes of the oceans are always changing.

● Greek divers are known to have reached depths of 22–30.5 m (75–100 feet) in search of sponges, coral and other treasures. When a diver ran short of breath, he would poke his head into a special weighted diving bell, filled with air from the surface.

● In several countries around the world the legend is told of a lost continent called Atlantis. This land is supposed to have lain in the Atlantic Ocean and was swallowed up by the sea after earthquakes and floods.

▲ In warm, tropical seas where the water is shallow and clear, there are vast, rocky structures known as **coral reefs**. These are formed by small sea animals called polyps. Coral reefs are the **marine** equivalent of the rainforests. They hold a greater variety of life than any other part of the oceans.

MOVING WAVES

The world's oceans are always on the move. They travel in well-defined circular patterns called ocean **currents**. The currents flow like rivers, carrying warm water from the Tropics and cold water from the poles. Where two currents meet, the colder water sinks pushing warmer water up to the surface.

Besides the ocean currents, there is also the regular movement of the **tides**. Twice a day, all around the world, the oceans rise and fall along the coastlines. Scientists do not fully understand how the tides work but they know that they are linked to the pull on the Earth by the Moon and the Sun. The continual movement of the oceans is important to marine life. The tides and currents carry food from one part of the ocean to another. They stir up the water and produce small bubbles of oxygen which the ocean animals need to breathe.

In the northern hemisphere the ocean currents travel in a clockwise direction. In the southern hemisphere they travel anti-clockwise. The wind is the driving force behind the ocean's currents.

OCEAN POWER

Giant whirlpools or maelstroms can occur where two rushing currents are forced through narrow channels. These turbulent waters can wreck small sailing vessels.

Earthquakes and volcanic eruptions under the surface of the ocean can cause huge waves to speed through the water and explode on the shore. These giant waves are often called tidal waves but their proper name is tsunamis.

FOOD FOR LIFE

Plants provide the basic food for life in the ocean, just as they do on land. Plants that grow underwater are called algae and there are two main groups found in the oceans.

The most familiar ocean algae are the seaweeds found around our coastlines. Limpets, periwinkles and other shoreline creatures graze on seaweeds but these are not available to the animals of the open ocean.

The most important marine plants are called phytoplankton. These tiny, floating plants grow wherever sunlight penetrates the water. Huge clouds of phytoplankton drift in the upper layers of the ocean but they are too small to be seen with the naked eye.

Floating alongside and feeding upon the phytoplankton are tiny animals called zooplankton. This rich mix of plant and animal life, called plankton, is the foundation of all marine life.

PLANKTON FACTS

● Sailors crossing the ocean at night often see a soft glow on the water's surface. This is because some plankton produce flashes of blue-green light when they are disturbed.

● The very first lifeforms probably looked similar to today's phytoplankton.

● The largest animal in the world feeds on plankton. A blue whale can weigh over 90 metric tonnes and be over 30.48 m (100 feet) long. It sieves krill, tiny plankton animals, from the ocean waters through a curtain of whalebone inside its mouth.

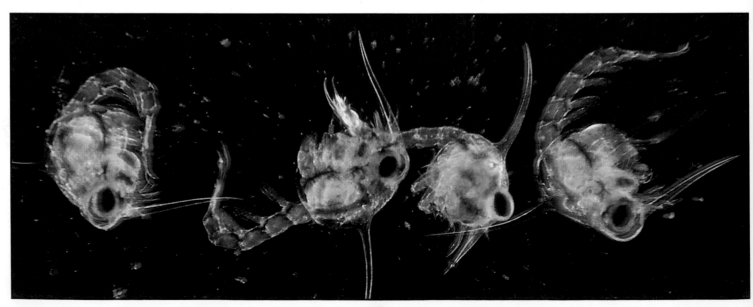

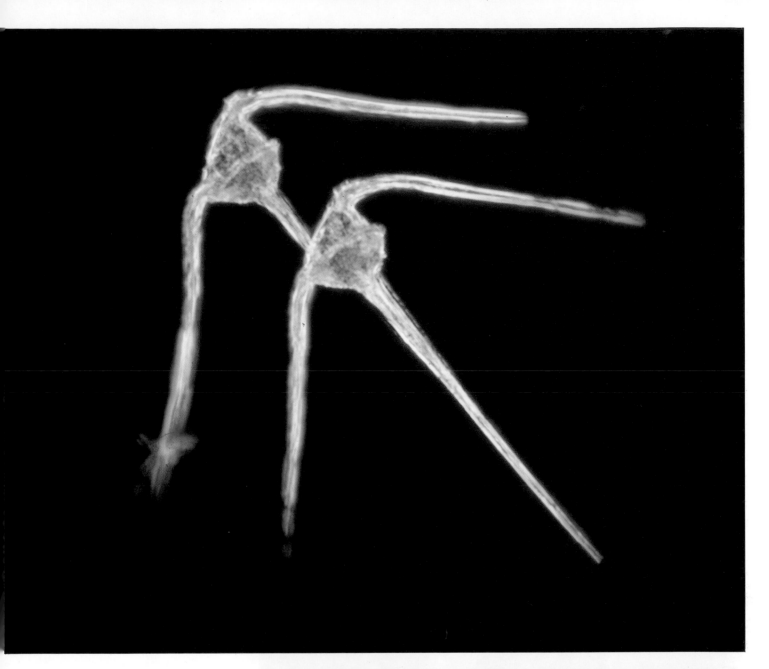

▲ ▶ Many of the tiny floating plants that make up the phytoplankton join together to make chains and bracelets. Others float alone and look like small pill boxes, sea shells, pencils, ice picks or ribbons.

◀ Some members of the zooplankton are simple, single-celled lifeforms but many are the tiny larvae of fish, crabs, starfish and other sea animals.

ALL SHAPES AND SIZES

There is a staggering variety of animals living in the world's oceans. They differ from each other enormously in size, shape and colour. To some extent, the appearance of each marine animal depends on the way it lives and where in the ocean it lives. Sea anemones and sponges, for instance, stay rooted to the ocean floor for their entire lives and look more like plants than animals.

Fishes are the most familiar marine creatures but appearances can be deceptive. Some species, like eels and pipefish, look more like worms or snakes than fish. Others, like the delicate sea horse, seem like a different sort of animal altogether.

▲ Many sea animals are transparent or a silvery-blue colour, but some have bright, bold markings. The most colourful animals live in clear tropical waters. Their striking appearance helps them to establish territory and frighten off would-be attackers.

◄ The octopus is one of many curious sea animals. It has eight arms and a short, rounded body. Many octopuses live on the ocean floor where they hide among rocks and grab passing animals with their long suckered arms. To swim, octopuses squirt water from a special siphon in their bodies.

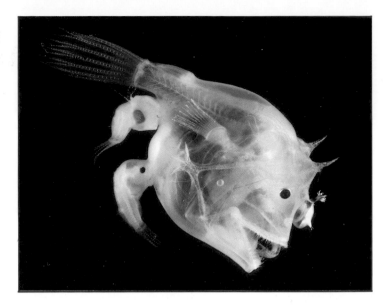

▲ It is cold, black and very still in the deepest parts of the ocean. Many animals living there have a light on their bodies that they use to attract prey. The deep-sea angler fish, above, is very strange. If the male of the species meets his mate, he attaches himself to her body. After a time, his body breaks down and he becomes no more than a sperm bag used to fertilise the female's eggs.

▲ Sponges encrust rocks, corals and vegetation on the sea floor, from the shallowest coastlines to the deepest trenches. There are over 3,500 marine sponges. Some form fleshy sheets, others upright chimney stacks. Sponges sieve dead and decaying matter from the water around them.

▶ The blue-spotted sting ray is a close relative of the shark. It floats over the surface of the sea bed feeding on slugs, worms and other sea animals.

THE HUNTER AND THE HUNTED

Many marine animals spend their entire lives sifting the water for plankton, but they, in turn, are hunted by other animals. It is estimated that for every ten plankton-feeders at least one hunter lurks nearby.

One of the most notorious marine hunters is the shark. Sharks have a reputation as man-eaters but of the 200 varieties only 25 are dangerous to people. Sharks are perfect killing machines. Their bodies are streamlined for a fast-moving, hunting life and their mouths are lined with razor-sharp teeth.

Not all marine hunters are as fearsome as the sharks. The pretty sea anemone looks harmless but it traps animals in its feathery tentacles and injects poison into its victim's body.

DEFENCE FACTS

Octopuses and cuttlefish squirt ink into the face of their attacker. This gives them time to get away.

Flying fish leap out of the water to escape their enemies.

Many sea animals, like clams and oysters, live in shells. The shells provide a home and act as armour, protecting the animals' soft bodies.

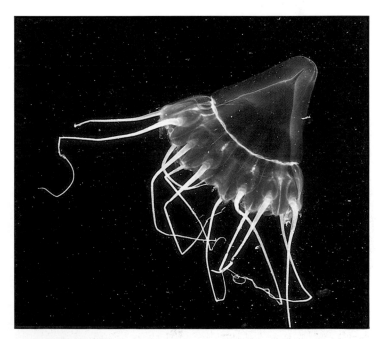

▲ Jellyfish, like sea anemones, catch animals in their trailing tentacles and then poison them. Some of the most powerful poisons in the natural world are produced by jellyfish.

◄ Sharks race through the water, chasing their prey of fish, seals, turtles, small whales, other sharks and even sea birds. Even when they are not chasing their next meal, sharks must keep moving all the time or they begin to sink.

TAKING TO THE WATER

During the long passage of time, a small procession of land animals has turned to the ocean for survival. Reptiles, mammals and even birds have braved the deep, salty waters to take advantage of the rich bounty of sea life.

Whales, seals, turtles and penguins are some of the animals that have left dry land to colonise the oceans. These creatures cannot breathe underwater like true sea animals so they regularly visit the water's surface for air.

Whales are the most successful ocean colonisers. People often mistake them for fish. Whales spend their entire lives in the water but most animals that have taken to the water must come ashore to **reproduce**.

▼ Many birds are called sea birds because they live on coastlines or on remote islands and rely on the oceans for their food. However, one bird in particular has mastered life in the oceans. The penguin spends most of its time swimming in cold waters, chasing fish and other sea animals.

▲ Animals are still turning to the world's oceans. Polar bears are considered to be marine mammals because they spend most of their time on or in the frozen Arctic Ocean hunting seals. They are expert swimmers and their wide, furry paws are webbed to help them move through the water.

▶ Sea reptiles such as turtles are restricted to warm parts of the world's oceans. They leave the water to lay their eggs on sandy beaches.

OCEAN RESOURCES

People cannot live in the world's oceans but they have always harvested the rich waters. As the human population has increased, people have turned to the oceans more and more for food and raw materials. Today over 70 billion kg (70 million tons) of fish are caught each year and one-fifth of the world's oil and gas is mined from the sea bed.

Modern fishing methods are often so intensive that they devastate fish communities and upset the balance of ocean life. Many of yesterday's most fertile seas are no longer able to support large fishing fleets because the fish stocks are so low.

The nets used by many of today's fishermen can also cause problems. They are made of nylon and do not rot underwater. If they are lost overboard, these nets become death traps to seals, dolphins and other marine creatures that cannot detect them.

Fish are not the only animals people take from the ocean. Crabs and lobsters are two of our many seafood products. Sponges are chipped off the ocean floor and end up in bathrooms all over the world. Some seals and whales have been hunted to **extinction** for their meat, fur and oil.

▼ Fishing is big business. Every day thousands of boats drag nets through the oceans to catch fish and other sea animals. This North Sea trawler is small compared to the largest fishing vessels. The world's supertrawlers can be over 90 m (295 feet) long.

OCEAN PRODUCTS

● Fish oils are used to make glue, soap, and margarine.

● A rare gem called a **pearl** is formed inside the shells of certain oysters.

● Big nodules of iron, copper and manganese are lifted from the sea bed using special suction pumps or are raked into nets by dredging machines.

● In dry lands, seawater is sometimes treated to create a fresh water supply.

● Seaweed can be eaten like a vegetable and is also used to help make ice cream, toothpaste, paint, medicine and other everyday products.

MAKING THE SEA SICK

Although we rely on the oceans for food, we treat them like rubbish bins and sewers. Waste is pumped and dumped into the water and man-made **pollutants** such as **pesticides** are washed into the ocean by rivers and streams.

The pollution of the world's oceans is harmful. Many sea animals are injured, strangled or suffocated each year because of floating debris called flotsam. The high level of **toxic** wastes in a few seas is poisoning some animals and driving others away.

Land-locked seas such as the Mediterranean are among the most polluted, but coastal waters everywhere are affected by the waste.

▶ Busy ports can become virtual deserts of the ocean world. The oil, sewage and litter spilled into the water make a harbour unfit for sea life.

▲ Oil spills threaten marine life. This sea bird will probably die unless the oil is cleaned from its feathers.

POLLUTION PROBLEMS

● Sealed barrels of dangerous radioactive and chemical waste have been dumped in some oceans, but no one knows if the containers are safe in the watery conditions.

● In some places around the world the local seafood is unfit to eat.

SAVE THE OCEANS

Countries around the world are beginning to realise the importance of the oceans. International laws have been made to restrict the amount of waste put into the water and some marine mammals are now protected. Countries on the shores of the dirtiest seas have started major clean-up programmes.

There is still a lot to be done. We need to understand patterns of marine life if we are to avoid over-fishing and preserve future fish stocks. In recent years, enormous damage has been caused in some oceans by oil tankers spilling their deadly cargo. Oil blocks out light from the ocean, upsetting plankton production and so affecting all marine life. Through public pressure, oil companies could be persuaded to buy safer boats that would not leak in an accident.

Seemingly harmless activities in the oceans have now been found to have damaging effects on marine life. The electric cables that criss-cross the ocean floor disturb some sea bed creatures and confuse many fish. Sharks bite into the cables, mistaking them for prey. The noise from boats, busy coastal resorts and ocean-based industries frightens away seals, dolphins and other animals from their traditional breeding grounds.

Whales have become a strong international symbol of ocean conservation. These extraordinary creatures have lived in the oceans far longer than people have lived on land. They are giants of the natural world.

Whales have been hunted for their oils and meat for so long that they are now difficult to find.

Most people agree that we must not kill any more whales and laws have been made to protect the largest species. A few countries, however, continue to hunt whales and eat their meat as an expensive delicacy.

DAKUWACA FIGHTS FOR HIS LIFE

For thousands of years people have told stories about the world around them. Often these stories try to explain something that people do not really understand, such as how the world began, or where light comes from. This tale is told by the people of Fiji, who depend on the ocean which surrounds them for food and transport.

Long ago the sharks were the rulers of the islands that make up Fiji in the Pacific Ocean. Each island had its own particular shark who lived beside the reef entrance of the island. These sharks patrolled the waters of their territory, challenging anyone who dared to come near. They allowed friends in but fought with hostile sharks until they paid a tribute.

Dakuwaca thought himself the greatest of all the sharks. He was big and fierce and enjoyed nothing better than a fight with another shark. He had never lost a fight and he was quite sure he never would. He cared nothing for the terrible storms which his fights caused, whipping up the waters so that the islanders were tossed about in their boats. Often island houses were swept away by massive waves from the ocean.

Dakuwaca was patrolling his reef one day when he came across a shark called Masilaca. Masilaca was the mischief maker among the sharks. He did not fight much himself but, with his wily ways, he had caused more fights than most sharks had fought!

"Good day, Dakuwaca," he said. "I suppose you're off for another fight. It's amazing, the way you always beat the other sharks. I wish I were as good a fighter as you."

"No other shark is as good a fighter as I am," said Dakuwaca. "Hardly anyone bothers to challenge me any more. They all know that I am so much stronger than them. In fact it's getting very dull around here."

"Perhaps if you want a really good fight, you should go over to Kandavu Island. I hear there's a creature well worth fighting there, a mighty monster which guards the reef so that it is impossible to go near it. But no one ever goes there because they are much too afraid of the creature," said Masilaca, with a sly glint in his eye. "Of course, I'm not suggesting that you're frightened, you're much too brave and strong. And I'm sure none of the other sharks think that you're afraid either."

Dakuwaca thrashed his tail through the water. Of course he wasn't afraid, what a suggestion! But if the other sharks thought he was afraid, he had better do something at once. Almost before Masilaca had finished speaking, Dakuwaca set off towards Kandavu, determined to challenge the fearsome monster.

As Dakuwaca approached Kandavu, he heard a deep, powerful voice calling from the shore. Dakuwaca had never heard anything like it before, and he found himself trembling a little.

"How foolish," he told himself. "Nothing on the shore can harm me." And he swam on.

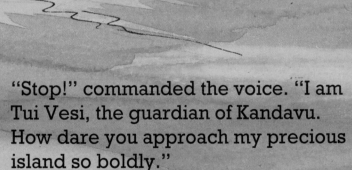

"Stop!" commanded the voice. "I am Tui Vesi, the guardian of Kandavu. How dare you approach my precious island so boldly."

Dakuwaca was rather frightened, but determined not to show it.

"And I am Dakuwaca, the greatest of all sharks. Come out and fight to defend your island."

"I am a land guardian and so cannot come into the water to fight you," said Tui Vesi. "I shall send one of my servants to fight you instead. But be warned! It is a great and terrible monster, and it would be much better if you left now."

"No one is braver or stronger than I," said Dakuwaca. "I am not afraid of anything. I will fight your servant."

He swam around the mouth of the reef, watching and waiting for his opponent. His body was strong and quick and his teeth were sharp.

Suddenly a giant arm appeared from the reef and grabbed him. A giant octopus! This wasn't what Dakuwaca was expecting at all! He thrashed and twisted to rid himself of the arm. His sharp teeth were quite useless because he could not bend his body to bite at the arm. The arm loosened as he twisted and, for a moment, Dakuwaca thought he was free. But no, two more arms whipped round, so that he could no longer move at all. And the arms began to squeeze, tighter and tighter until Dakuwaca could bear it no longer.

"Have mercy!" he gasped. "Forgive my terrible presumption, Tui Vesi."

The arms of the octopus loosened slightly, and Tui Vesi's mighty voice boomed out into the waters once more.

"I will release you, Dakuwaca, providing that you promise to guard the people of my island from sharks which might attack them when they go out in their canoes."

"Yes, yes! Of course I will," Dakuwaca agreed.

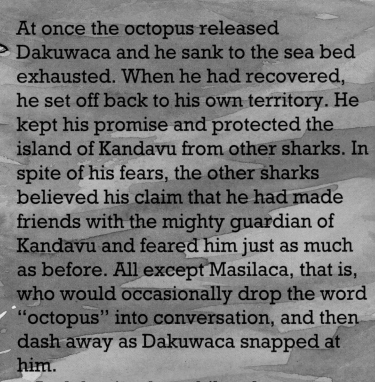

At once the octopus released Dakuwaca and he sank to the sea bed exhausted. When he had recovered, he set off back to his own territory. He kept his promise and protected the island of Kandavu from other sharks. In spite of his fears, the other sharks believed his claim that he had made friends with the mighty guardian of Kandavu and feared him just as much as before. All except Masilaca, that is, who would occasionally drop the word "octopus" into conversation, and then dash away as Dakuwaca snapped at him.

And that is why, while other fishermen of the Fiji islands fear for their lives because of the sharks, the men of Kandavu ride happily in their canoes.

TRUE OR FALSE?

Which of these facts are true and which ones are false? If you have read this book carefully, you will know the answers.

1. Almost one-third of the world's surface is covered by oceans.

2. Dolphins and whales can stay underwater for several hours.

3. Sound travels through water five times faster than through air.

4. The world's four oceans are the Pacific, the Atlantic, the Mediterranean and the Aegean.

5. It takes 5,000 years for one drop of seawater to travel through all the world's oceans.

6. Tsunamis are caused by underwater volcanic eruptions and earthquakes.

7. Plankton is a rich mixture made up of debris from seaweed.

8. Blue whales are the largest animals in the world.

9. Octopuses have 12 arms and feed mainly on seals.

10. Sharks must keep moving all the time or they will sink.

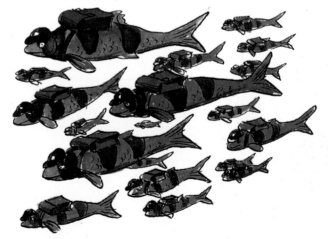

11. Fish travel in schools until they have learnt how to protect themselves.

12. The paws of a polar bear are webbed.

13. Seaweed is used to help make ice cream.

ANSWERS: 1. False 2. False 3. True 4. False 5. True 6. True 7. False 8. True 9. False 10. True 11. False 12. True 13. True

GLOSSARY

● **Bay** is a part of an ocean or other large body of water that forms a curve in the shoreline. It is bordered on the coastline by headlands or capes.

● **Continent** is a large piece of land, or mainland. It is larger than a normal island and is usually divided into several countries (except for the continent of Australia). Two or more continents may be joined together by a narrow neck of land.

● **Current** or stream is the movement of a body of water in a particular direction. Ocean currents may be very strong and extend over great distances.

● **Echo** is the repetition of a noise caused by the bouncing back of sound waves from a solid object. Marine mammals such as dolphins use echoes to locate food and to avoid obstacles.

● **Coral reef** is a colourful ridge formation, usually underwater. It is made up of the hard outer casing produced by a colony of millions of tiny animals known as polyps.

● **Environment** is the set of conditions in the area where an animal lives. The animal's survival depends on how well it can respond to these conditions.

● **Extinction** occurs when the last member of a species dies out. This may be due to overhunting by humans, the arrival of a rival animal or plant or changes in the species' environment.

● **Gulf** is a part of a sea or ocean that loops into the neighbouring coastline. It is narrower at its mouth than a bay.

● **Land-locked** means surrounded by land.

● **Marine** means connected with the sea. Marine animals are those that live in the sea.

● **Minerals** are chemical compounds found in rocks. Some of them are useful to humans and are mined.

● **Pearl** is a small gem, usually round and white, cream or bluish-grey. It slowly forms as a protective layer around a grain of sand or other object that irritates the soft flesh inside an oyster's shell.

● **Pesticides** are chemicals used to kill pests that feed on crops. Pesticides may sometimes be dangerous to creatures other than the pests they control.

● **Plankton** is the rich soup made up of many types of microscopic life. A large variety of sea animals feeds on it.

● **Poles** are found at the exact north and south ends of the Earth. Day and night each last six months here.

● **Pollutant** is a dirty and poisonous product such as car fumes that damages the environment.

● **Reproduction** is when adult creatures produce new, young individuals for the continuation of their species.

● **Tide** is the regular rise and fall of the sea. It is caused by the pull of the Moon and the Sun.

● **Toxic** means poisonous and harmful to life.

● **Trench** is a deep furrow. The Mariana Trench near Guam is the deepest known place in any ocean.

INDEX

Arctic Ocean   6, 17
Atlantic Ocean   6, 7

coral reef   7
current   8

deep-sea angler fish   13

exploration   4

fishing   18, 19

iceberg   4
Indian Ocean   6

jellyfish   15

krill   10

maelstrom   9
mineral   4

octopus   12, 15
oil spill   20

Pacific Ocean   6, 7, 24
pearl   19
penguin   16
phytoplankton   10, 11
plankton   4, 10, 14, 22
polar bear   17
Pole, North   4, 6
Pole, South   4, 6
pollution   20

salt   4
sea turtle   17
seaweed   10, 19
shark   13, 14, 15, 23
sound   4
sponge   7, 12, 13, 19
sting ray   13

tides   8
trench   4, 13
tsunami   9

whale   4, 15, 16, 19, 22, 23
   blue whale   10
whirlpool   9

zooplankton   10, 11

Revision Guide

Electrical Installations

Levels 2 and 3

2330 Technical Certificate and 2356 NVQ

Author Team:

Brian Clements

Steve Thompson

Nigel Harman

Electrical Assessment Services UK Ltd

www.heinemann.co.uk

✓ Free online support
✓ Useful weblinks
✓ 24 hour online ordering

01865 888118

Heinemann

Heinemann is an imprint of Pearson Education Limited, a company incorporated in England and Wales, having its registered office at Edinburgh Gate, Harlow, Essex, CM20 2JE. Registered company number: 872828

www.heinemann.co.uk

Heinemann is a registered trademark of Pearson Education Limited

Text © Pearson Education Ltd, 2008

First published 2008

12 11 10 09 08

10 9 8 7 6 5 4 3 2 1

British Library Cataloguing in Publication Data is available from the British Library on request.

ISBN 978 0435402 57 0

Copyright notice

Typeset by HL Studios

Original illustrations © Pearson Education Limited, 2007

Illustrated by HL Studios

Cover photo/illustration © Getty Images/Stone

Printed in the UK by Scotprint

Websites

The websites used in this book were correct and up-to-date at the time of publication. It is essential for tutors to preview each website before using it in class so as to ensure that the URL is still accurate, relevant and appropriate. We suggest that tutors bookmark useful websites and consider enabling students to access them through the school/college intranet.

Contents

Acknowledgements   iv

Introduction   v

Chapter 1   Industry and communication   1

Chapter 2   Health and safety   37

Chapter 3   Electrical science   65

Chapter 4   Craft theory   101

Chapter 5   Statutory regulations and codes of practice   139

Chapter 6   Earthing and protection   161

Chapter 7   Lighting   185

Chapter 8   Circuits and systems   199

Chapter 9   Inspection, testing and commissioning   221

Chapter 10   Fault diagnosis and rectification   261

Chapter 11   Electrical machines and motors   291

Chapter 12   Electronics   317

Answers to the end-of-chapter questions   351

Index   367

Acknowledgements

The authors and publishers would like to thank the following individuals and organisations for permission to reproduce photos.

Alamy Images – 168

Art Directors and Trip – 206, 325, 326, 333

Corbis/Roger Ressmeyer – 223

Ginny Stroud-Lewis – 204, 206 (sounder)

JTL/Dave Allan – 51 (foam)

Pearson Education Ltd/Jules Selmes – 45

Photographers Direct/Malcolm Furrow – 335

All other photos © Pearson Education Ltd/Gareth Boden

The publishers would also like to thank Andrew Jeffery for his technical proof read of this title.

Introduction

The aim of the guide is to:

- Complement Level 2 Electrical Installations 2330 Technical Certificate and Level 3 Electrical Installations 2330 Technical Certificate and 2356 NVQ
- Complement Electrical Installations NVQ and Technical Certificate Book 1 and Electrical Installations NVQ and Technical Certificate Book 2.
- Provide essential revision support and preparations to electricians who are taking the examinations for the 2330 Technical Certificate and the 2356 NVQ.

The guide is structured on a topic-by-topic basis, rather than split between levels. Each chapter contains the essential job knowledge needed for each topic in a condensed yet easy to read format. Each chapter can be read either independently, or in relation with the other chapters of the book. Where useful cross references have been inserted to help you use the book more effectively.

The end of each chapter contains a number of short answer and multiple choice questions to test your knowledge of the contents and learning of the chapter. You are encouraged to complete these as you progress through the book as they will both serve as a check on your progress and confirm your understanding of the chapter.

The last section of the guide contains the answers to the revision questions, providing further details with the short answers questions. This should again help your learning.

More in depth feedback and details of all the topics in this book can be found in the booked described above.

Good luck with your examination preparations!

01 Industry and communication

By the end of this chapter, you should be able to demonstrate your knowledge and understanding of the structure of the industry, the way communication takes place and the legal framework that you will be working within. This guide will cover the following:

- The world of work
  - Employment legislation
  - Discrimination
  - Quality systems
  - Changing demand
- The construction industry
- The electrotechnical industry
  - Building services
  - Specialist areas
  - Electrical contracting industry support organisations
  - Electrical contractors and employer structure
- Project roles and responsibilities
  - People involved in the design stage
  - The tendering process
  - Construction stage
- Drawings, diagrams and symbols
- Site documentation
  - Job sheets
  - Variation orders
  - Day work sheets
  - Timesheets
  - Purchase orders
  - Delivery notes
  - Completion order
  - Manufacturer's data and service manuals
  - Site reports and memos

- Storage, use and retrieval of information
- Working with documentation, drawings and specifications
  - Scaled drawings
  - Data sheets and charts
  - Bar charts (Gantt charts)
  - Critical path analysis (CPA)
- Project management
- Relationships and team working
  - Customer relationships
  - Relationships with other contractors
  - Communication
  - Team working

The world of work

No matter where we find ourselves working, whether it is in contracting or working as an administrator in an office, our working lives are governed by laws passed by Parliament. In the main, these laws are designed to protect the workforce from excessive demands that may be placed upon them by employers. They also serve to protect the employer against outrageous claims for unfair dismissal, etc.

Employment legislation

In the UK, the principal rights and obligations imposed on employers and employees arise from three sources:

- common law, which governs any contract of employment between the employer and employee, and includes historical practice and decisions made in the courts
- UK legislation
- European legislation.

Employment Rights Act 1996 and the Employment Act 2002

The Employment Rights Act 1996 was amended by the Employment Act 2002. It covers all areas of employment, including statutory (i.e. enacted by law) minimum rights as follows:

- statement of employment (contract of employment)
- statement of pay (wage slip including details of deductions)
- no unauthorised deductions from pay
- minimum wage
- minimum holidays
- disciplinary procedures
- maximum working hours (exemption by agreement permitted)
- maternity/paternity/adoption leave and pay
- access to an industrial tribunal for resolving disputes
- redundancy pay.

Data Protection Act 1998

This Act covers the problems that can arise from data (personal information) being held by an individual or organisation that is shared with others without permission.

The Act is based on eight principles, stating that data must be:

- fairly and lawfully processed
- processed for limited purposes
- adequate, relevant and not excessive

- accurate
- not kept for longer than necessary
- processed in line with your rights
- secure
- not transferred to other countries without adequate protection.

Disability Discrimination Act 1995

This act gives people with disabilities rights in the areas of work. Employers are *not* allowed to discriminate in the selection process between able-bodied and disabled applicants; all employees should be treated fairly, and selected on merit.

Other areas covered by the Act are also applicable outside work. These are:

- equal opportunity in employment
- access to goods
- access to facilities
- access to services
- access to buildings
- access to transport.

Race Relations Act 1976 amended 2000

This Act makes it illegal to discriminate on racial grounds in relation to training, employment, the provision of goods, facilities and services and other specified activities.

The Act also imposes a liability on employers for acts of racial discrimination committed by their employees, subject to the defence that the employer had taken all reasonable steps to prevent the employee discriminating.

In 2000 the Race Relations Act was extended to cover all public services and authorities. Duties were placed upon local authorities to work towards the elimination of racial discrimination and to promote equal opportunity and good relations between different racial groups.

Sex Discrimination Act 1975 amended 2003

In the areas of employment, education and training, discrimination on the grounds of gender and/or marital status is unlawful. The enforcing authority is the Equal Opportunities Commission (EOC). The amendment in 2003 included police forces within the scope of the Act.

The Human Rights Act 1998 (European legislation)

This Act covers many areas of discrimination, some not covered in the Acts previously mentioned. The main articles of the Act apply to public authorities, such as police or local councils, and not to private companies.

Main articles within the Act are:

- the right to life
- the prohibition of torture
- the prohibition of slavery and forced labour
- the right to liberty and security
- no punishment without law
- the right to respect for private and family life
- freedom of thought, conscience and religion
- freedom of expression
- freedom of assembly and association
- the right to marry
- prohibition of discrimination
- restrictions on the political activity of aliens
- prohibition of abuse of rights
- limitation on the use of restrictions on rights.

Discrimination

This includes either direct or indirect discrimination. It can also take the form of positive discrimination or positive action.

Direct discrimination

This is where somebody is treated less favourably than another person because of the colour of their skin, their gender, disability or age. An example could be where a disabled person, with more experience and qualifications, is overlooked for a position within a company for somebody who has less experience and qualifications.

Also, an employer seeking to employ an administrative assistant in an office situation could not refuse to give the job to somebody in a wheelchair on the basis that their movement about the office would be restricted by stairs and space between desks. It is not a defence recognised by the Act, which, in fact, places a duty on the employer to make premises accessible to people with disabilities.

Indirect discrimination

This can occur, where the requirements or conditions of a particular type of employment may have an adverse affect on an individual or group of individuals, thereby preventing them from being given an employment opportunity.

However, this is more difficult to define in law. For example, someone may be prevented from taking up employment as a fireman because they have a beard, which would prevent their facemask from fitting properly, so it could be argued that men with beards are being discriminated against indirectly.

Alternatively, a company, whose business is to care for elderly women, may seek to employ a female care worker at the exclusion of male care workers, so that male care workers would appear to be indirectly discriminated against. However, in either case a court of law is likely to rule in favour of the organisation, as this would be seen as an operational requirement, rather than one of discrimination.

Positive discrimination and positive action

These cover the selection for employment on the basis of race or gender, not on the ability to do the job. Both the Sex Discrimination Act and Race Relations Act make this unlawful except where there is a 'genuine occupational requirement', such as the example of the female care worker working with elderly female clients above. This would be acceptable as positive discrimination.

Also, both the Sex Discrimination Act and Race Relations Act require employers to make their workforce reflect the community from which selection takes place. Therefore, if an organisation wishes to increase its proportion of female employees, then it is permissible for the company to take positive action and advertise for female workers.

Did you know?

An organisation would have to be prepared to defend its position on positive discrimination in court should it be challenged.

Victimisation

Victimisation is a specific form of discrimination where somebody is selected for unfair treatment, or is treated differently from others, without legitimate cause. This can be either by an employer or fellow employees.

If, for example, someone reports a dangerous activity to a trade union representative and is then singled out by the employer for unfair treatment, this would be victimisation. Another example would be a person within a group of workers, who perhaps looks different or has a different religion, who is treated by the group in an unfair manner, such as giving them the dirty work to do.

Quality systems

These cover a system or standard adopted by organisations to demonstrate to potential users that they are efficient and effective companies.

They turn to outside organisations to verify their policies, procedures and processes. If they meet the requirements they are then allowed to display a logo to show compliance.

Did you know?

ISO 9001/2, Investors in People and BS EN ISO 14001 are examples of quality assurance and management systems.

ISO 9001/2

In a competitive world, one way of ensuring that an organisation is able to compete with others is to convey to its potential clients the quality of its products and processes.

ISO 9001/2 is a paper trail system, which ensures a product can be tracked through the organisation's processes, avoiding duplication and waste of time or money. An effective management system is one that sets objectives that are clearly demonstrable and measurable, resulting in an improved use of time and resources. Improved communications, both internally and externally, reduce wastage and produce a greater consistency of products and services, which in turn leads to improved staff morale, motivation and production.

Investors in People (IiP)

This is a national quality standard, which recognises good practice within organisations in the opportunities provided to staff for continued professional development (training). This, in turn, allows the business to achieve its goals.

It is based on four key principles:

- commitment to investing in people to achieve business goals
- planning how skills, individuals and teams are to be developed to achieve these goals
- taking action to develop and use necessary skills in a well defined and continuous programme directly tied to the business objectives
- evaluating the outcomes of training and development and an individual's progress towards defined goals, the value achieved and future needs.

BS EN ISO 14001

Did you know?

Contractors wishing to do work for local government or central government must be in possession of BS EN ISO 14001.

Environmental management systems (EMS), meeting the requirements of BS EN 14001, demonstrate to clients and the public that an organisation takes seriously the impact that their activities or products have on the environment. For many organisations, it is a prerequisite for gaining access to preferred contract lists.

For an organisation to achieve the standards, it must take action on environmental issues that relate to its business. This includes training staff to make them aware of their environmental responsibilities.

The advantages of improved environmental management can be divided into two broad categories:

- Improved environmental management is good for our planet and a fundamental requirement of global sustainability.
- An effective EMS could benefit an organisation by saving costs in meeting environmental targets, having procedures that ensure legislative compliance, improved public image and increased market opportunities, and be viewed more favourably by sector regulators and the financial sector in general.

Organisations seeking certification from the accreditation body will need to prove that all aspects of design, installation and disposal of waste materials during the construction process have been considered for their impact upon the environment and, where necessary, alternative methods, materials, etc. have been used.

Compliance with BS EN ISO 14001 will mean taking into account the following pieces of legislation:

- **Environmental Protection Act 1990** – This controls pollution released to the air. It also places a duty of care on all those involved in the management of waste, be it collecting, disposing or treating controlled waste.
- **Pollution Prevention and Control Act 1999** – This ensures the use of the best available techniques to prevent and, where that is not practicable, to reduce to acceptable levels, pollution of the air, land and water from industrial activities.
- **Clean Air Act 1993** – Industrial locations may generate smoke, dust, heavy metals, carbon or other fibres, along with many other general emissions. This Act places a duty on organisations to reduce, and keep to a minimum, pollutants released into the air, such as concrete and brick dust when chasing walls to install cables.
- **Radioactive Substances Act 1993** – This applies to any organisation that is involved in the handling, storing and transportation of radioactive materials. There is a requirement for only qualified experts to be employed. They will need relevant expertise, training and knowledge. They must also be provided with the appropriate safety equipment/PPE and wear a dosimeter to register exposure levels.
- **Controlled Waste Regulations 1998** – All waste removed from site falls under the remit of controlled waste, and as such can only be removed in vehicles licensed for such activity. For example, the taking down and removal of fluorescent luminaires, a common task, falls under the umbrella of these Regulations. It places a duty upon the organisation to manage the disposal of waste effectively and efficiently with due regard to current legislation.
- **Dangerous Substances and Preparations and Chemical Regulations 2000** – These Regulations place duties of care on organisations involved in the design and installation of products within buildings to ensure that the materials used are not dangerous and harmful to those that will live in, work in or pass through such installations.

Did you know?

For waste disposal, materials must have been disposed of in the appropriate registered sites.

Changing demand

The electrotechnical industry, as with all other industries, is prone to changes in demand, and the major factor that affects demand is the economy. A buoyant healthy economy generally results in lots of investment into construction and engineering projects.

Increase in demand

An increase in demand can mean:

- recruitment of additional staff
- training of new and existing staff
- opportunities for promotion
- opportunities for increased earnings (overtime).

If caused by winning more contracts, this could be the result of:

- **Effective marketing** – Companies use a range of marketing styles; e.g. telephone sales, cold calls, leaflets, letters and advertising in the local press.
- **Competitive tendering** – Identifying new ways and new materials, which can result in an increase in profit margins, plus a combination of doing deals with wholesalers/suppliers to get the best prices, can all result in lower tender prices.
- **Completion of existing projects on time and within budget** – If installations are completed on time, within budget and to the required standards of the customer, a good reputation is built up as a company that is fit for purpose and one that regularly meets its agreed completion dates. This, in itself, can lead to further work through personal recommendation, and the inclusion on architects' preferred contractor lists.
- **Extending the range of work offered** – Contractors that look to the future and keep abreast of changing technologies will always be in a favourable position to win new contracts. For example, changes in technology have seen building contractors involving themselves in the installation of data systems, computer networks, audiovisual equipment and use of fibre optics.
- **Being flexible to the demands of the client** – With the demand today for fast turn around and shorter contract times, it is essential that the workforce is flexible regarding hours required to meet the contract. Shop fitting, maintenance, installing additional socket outlets and lightings may all need to be completed out of hours. There is always a need to respond swiftly to emergency callouts, such as customers losing their supply to light and heating.

Decrease in demand

This could result from a down turn in the economy or increased competition, with more contractors competing for the same work.

It may result in the need for a company to reduce its staff. Those employees that had taken the opportunities for training/retraining and developing transferable skills may find themselves in the best position either to retain their job with their current employer, as they have the skills and experience that are needed, or can transfer more easily to other employers.

Career development, to help employees to remain employable, is shown in Table 1.01.

Occupation	Qualifications needed
JIB recognised Electrician	NVQ Level 3 + Technical certificate
JIB recognised Approved Electrician	As above + C&G 2391 + two years' experience
Electrical Supervisor	Approved Electrician + additional experience
Contract/Site Engineer	Supervised + BTEC HNC in Building Services or Foundation degree
Contract Manager	Contract engineer + BTEC HNC in Building Services or Foundation degree
Consultant	Contract Manager + Degree + Experience

Table 1.01 Industry progression route

The construction industry

This is one of the largest industries in the UK, employing over a million people. Organisations range from sole traders (one man operations) to large employers employing thousands of workers.

Broadly, they break down into the following three sectors:

- **Building services and structural engineering** – Construction and installation of the services for buildings, including shops, offices, factories and domestic dwellings, as well as public buildings such as schools and hospitals.
- **Civil engineering** – Construction of large public works such as roads, bridges, etc.
- **Maintenance** – The everyday running and repair of existing buildings.

The electrotechnical industry

This ranges from the initial installation of electrical services into buildings, to the maintenance and servicing of the installations. Electricians may be employed within the electrical contracting industry or directly by other organisations needing their skills. Employment areas include:

- factories
- commercial buildings, shops and offices
- transport, e.g. railways and automotive
- the armed forces.

Building services

- **Lighting and power installations** – Installation within houses, shops, offices, hospitals, warehouses, etc. covering installation of supplies to machines through to socket outlets.
- **Alarm, security and emergency installations** – Including emergency lighting, burglar alarms, fire alarms and CCTV. (See also Chapter 8 on circuits and systems.)
- **Building management and control installations** – As the demand for buildings to become more efficient and cost-effective increases, so the demand to be able to control the heating, lighting and machinery increases. Control can be central through computers, or local through sensor controlled switching. Much is also being made of heat reclamation systems, which use the heat output from electrical or mechanical equipment to heat water and reduce heating costs.
- **Communication data and computer installations** – Communications are essential to the effective running of any organisation, whether internally (within the building) or externally, with others perhaps on the other side of the world. Computers may be interconnected within a building or site using a local area network (LAN) or over a wide area network (WAN). LANs are created with structured cable systems, using Cat 5, Cat 5e, Cat 6 and fibre optic cables (see Chapter 4 on cables).

Specialist areas

It is easy to focus on electrical installation within buildings. However, the electrotechnical sector also includes the following:

- **Cable jointing** – Working on high or low voltage installations.
- **Street lighting and equipment** – Installation of street lighting, traffic control systems and illuminated road signs.
- **Electrical machine drives** – Soft start, electronic control of motors and drives used in industry.
- **Motor rewinds** – Repair, maintenance and sometimes installation of motors used by industry.
- **Panel building** – Construction and wiring of panels used to control anything within industry, such as motor control panels, complex heating control panels and computer-controlled panels.
- **Instrumentation** – Widely used as a control mechanism in the process and production industries, this involves installation of flow meters, pressure and temperature gauges, valves, level switches and pumps.
- **Electrical maintenance** – This includes preventative and reactive maintenance (i.e. dealing with problems as they arise). Electricians may deal with electrical and mechanical repair or replacement. They are employed in hospitals, factories, schools, universities, refineries and power stations.

Electrical contracting industry support organisations

There are several organisations that help in the control and efficient functioning of the industry, including:

- **Electrical Contractors Association** – ECA is an organisation that represents the electrical contractors' views and opinions in negotiations with government and with trade unions. Founded in 1901, it has over 2000 member companies. Potential members are vetted to ensure they have the procedures, staff and systems in place to ensure work produced is of the highest standard.

- **National Inspection Council for Electrical Installation Contracting** – NICEIC is an accredited certification body, designed to promote and guarantee quality assurance to users of electricity. Companies registered with this organisation, for a fee, have their work inspected regularly to ensure standards are met. It can arbitrate in disputes between a customer and contractor and, if a failure to agree is reached, the NICEIC can appoint another contractor to complete work. Membership of the NICEIC is often a prerequisite to the tendering process for local council work.

- **Amicus** – Formerly known as the Amalgamated Engineering and Electrical Union (AEEU) and, prior to that, the Electrical, Electronic, Telecommunications and Plumbers Union (EETPU). It has approximately 730,000 members and their role is to represent the views and interests of members to government over issues of proposed legislation and employment, as well as negotiating with employers over terms and conditions of employment, and representing individuals in disciplinary hearings.

- **Joint Industry Board for the Electrical Contracting Industry** – JIB was formed in 1968 by partnership of the ECA and EETPU (now Amicus). Its main role is to reach agreement on national working rules, conditions, wages and training.

- **Health and Safety Executive** – The Health and Safety Commission (HSC) and the Health and Safety Executive (HSE) are responsible for the regulation of risks to the health and safety of people at work. HSE also takes the role of enforcer, with powers to enter and seize, take photos, statements and issue enforcement notices, such as improvement notices or, in severe cases, prohibition notices.

- **SummitSkills** – This is the Sector Skills Council for the building services engineering sector. It is an employer led organisation, with the task of identifying skills shortages and devising plans to overcome them. SummitSkills also develops the National Training Standards for the industry.

- **Institute of Lighting Engineers** – ILE, as its name suggests, is dedicated to excellence in lighting. Founded in 1924, it now includes lighting designers, architects, consultants and engineers among its 2500 members.

- **Institute of Engineering and Technology** – IET was formerly the Institute of Electrical Engineers (IEE), an organisation founded in 1871 with around 130,000 members worldwide. Its roles include setting standards for electrical installations, as well as the qualifications required for professional electrical engineers. Its remit also covers electronics, software, and systems and manufacturing engineers. It produces BS 7671, the Requirements for Electrical Installation, also known as the *IEE Wiring Regulations*, 17th Edition. (As publications are updated they will be produced under the IET banner, but remain valid under the IEE name until superseded.)

Electrical contractors and employer structure

Approximately 21,000 electrical installation companies are registered in the UK, with the vast majority employing fewer than 10 people. An electrical contractor has to deal with the following areas of work:

- handling initial enquiries
- estimating
- producing quotations
- negotiating with suppliers and subcontractors
- project management
- installation
- financial control
- settlement of the final account.

In large companies, specialists are employed in each of those areas. However, a sole trader will have to deal with them all. Examples of organisational flowcharts for both large and small firms are shown in Figures 1.01 and 1.02.

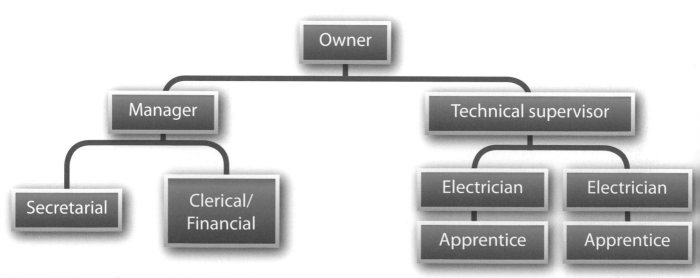

Figure 1.01 Large firm organisational chart

Figure 1.02 Small firm organisational chart

Project roles and responsibilities

There are three stages to a construction project: design, tendering and construction. The key roles and responsibilities for each stage are as follows.

People involved in the design stage

These are shown in Table 1.02.

Client	• Person/organisation that wants the work done and is paying for it. • Specifies the building purpose. • Gives an idea of number of rooms, size, design, etc., and any specific wants. • Gives an idea of the price they are willing to pay.
Architect	• Designs the appearance and construction of the building in order to fulfil the proper function. • Advises the client on the practicality of their wishes. • Ideally provides a design solution that satisfies the client and also complies with the appropriate rules and regulations. • For small projects, an architect may draw up a complete plan. For larger more complex buildings they will consult specialist design engineers about technical details.
Consulting engineers (Design engineers)	• Act on behalf of an architect, advising on and designing specific services such as electrical installation, heating and ventilation, etc. • Create a design that satisfies the client and architect, the supply company and regulations. • Ensure that cable sizes have been calculated properly, that the capacities of any cable trunking and conduit are adequate, and that protective devices are rated correctly. • Produce drawings, schedules and specifications for the project that will be sent out to the companies tendering for the contract. • Answer any questions that may arise from this. • Once the contract has been placed, they will produce additional drawings to show any amendments. • Act as a link between the client, the main contractor and the electrical contractor.

Quantity surveyor (QS)	• Responsible for taking the plans and preparing an initial bill of quantities for a project; contractors who are tendering for the project use this information to prepare their estimates. • During construction, the quantity surveyor monitors the actual quantities used, and also checks on claims for additional work and material.
Clerk of works	• Checks the quantity of materials, equipment and workmanship used on a project meet the standards laid down in the specifications and drawings. • On big contracts there may be several clerks of work, each responsible for one aspect, such as electrical, heating and ventilation. • Effectively employed by the client. • Inspects the job at different stages. • Is also present to check any tests carried out. • May also be given the authority by the architect to sign day worksheets and to issue architect's instructions for alterations or additional work.

Table 1.02 Design stage

The tendering process

Key elements involved in this process are as follows:

Contractors

Contractors, invited to tender for a project, are provided with drawings, plans and specifications from which they have to provide a price to complete the work. This has to be received by a fixed deadline. The winning tender that matches the main requirements is then awarded the contract.

Main contractors may duplicate this process to invite other companies to take on elements of the work as subcontractors.

Estimator

The estimator produces the quotation price, based on the drawings, plans and specification provided in the tender document. The estimator has to quantify the amounts of material such as cable, conduit, trunking, etc. as well as the labour needed to complete the job. The price also has to include nominal sums that allow for the costs of plant or access equipment that may be needed, as well as overhead costs such as office administration, tax and profit.

> **Did you know?**
>
> For very large projects several contractors may form a consortium to bid for the work, usually with one contractor acting as lead and coordinator.

Project engineer	*Role definitions vary within the industry but generally the role is similar to that of a contracts engineer.* • Responsible for day-to-day management of on-site operations relative to a specific project. • Often based on the site.
Site supervisor	• Contractor's representative on site. • Oversees normal day-to-day operations on site. • Experienced in electrical installation work, normally an Approved Electrician. • Responsible for the supervision of the approved electricians, apprentices and labourers. • Uses the drawings and specification to direct the day-to-day aspects of the installation. • Liaises with contracts engineer to ensure that the installation is as the estimator originally planned it. Ensures materials are available on site when required. • Liaises with the contracts engineer where plans are changed or amended to ensure additional costs and labour/materials are acceptable and quoted for.
Electricians, apprentices and labourers	• The people who actually carry out the installation work. • Work to the supervisor's instructions.
Electrical fitter	• Usually someone with mechanical experience. • Involved in varied work including panel building and panel wiring and the maintenance and servicing of equipment.
Electrical technician	*Job definition varies from company to company.* • Can involve carrying out surveys of electrical systems, updating electrical drawings and maintaining records, obtaining costs, and assisting in the inspection, commissioning, testing and maintenance of electrical systems and services. • May also be involved in recommending corrective action to solve electrical problems.
Service manager	*Similar role to contracts manager (and in some cases the roles are combined) but focuses on customer satisfaction rather than contractual obligations.* • Monitors the quality of the service delivered under contract. • Checks that contract targets (e.g. performance, cost and quality) are met. • Ensures customer remains fully satisfied with the service received.

Maintenance manager	*Once the building has been completed.*
	● Keeps installed electrotechnical plant working efficiently.
	● May issue specifications and organise contracts for a programme of routine and preventive maintenance.
	● Responsible for fixing faults and breakdowns.
	● Ensures legal requirements are met.
	● Carries out maintenance audits.

Table 1.03 People involved in the construction stage

Drawings, diagrams and symbols

Drawings, diagrams and symbols provide a major source of technical information for any project. A technical diagram conveys information to an installer or user, but has to be in a standard format to avoid misunderstanding and confusion. All electrical symbols used should comply with BS EN 60617, with drawings being able to be read in one direction.

Switches

Switch general symbol	Switch with pilot light	Period limiting switch, single-pole	Two-pole switch	Multiposition single-pole switch. For example: different degrees of lighting
Two-way single-pole switch	Intermediate switch	Dimmer	One-way switch	

Lighting outlets and fittings

Lighting outlet position. Shown with wiring	Lighting outlet on a wall. Shown with wiring from the left	Lamp, general symbol	Luminaire and fluorescent lamp, general symbol	Luminaire with three fluorescent tubes
Luminaire with five fluorescent tubes	Projector, general symbol	Spotlight	Floodlight	Pull-cord single-pole switch
Push-button	Push-button with indicator lamp		Push-button protected against unintentional operation: by means of a break-glass cover	
Timer switch	Timer period lighting equipment		Key-operated switch Watchman's systems device	

Connections

Wiring going upwards. *If the arrow is pointing towards the top of the drawing sheet, the wiring goes upwards.*	Wiring going downwards	Wiring passing through vertically	Box, general symbol
Connection box Junction box	Consumer's terminal service entrance equipment. *This symbol is shown with wiring.*	Distribution centre/board. *The symbol is shown with five wirings.*	

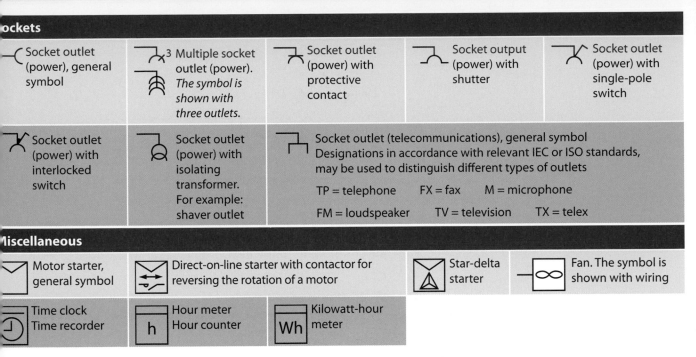

ockets

Socket outlet (power), general symbol	3 Multiple socket outlet (power). *The symbol is shown with three outlets.*	Socket outlet (power) with protective contact	Socket output (power) with shutter	Socket outlet (power) with single-pole switch
Socket outlet (power) with interlocked switch	Socket outlet (power) with isolating transformer. For example: shaver outlet	Socket outlet (telecommunications), general symbol. Designations in accordance with relevant IEC or ISO standards, may be used to distinguish different types of outlets TP = telephone FX = fax M = microphone FM = loudspeaker TV = television TX = telex		

Miscellaneous

Motor starter, general symbol	Direct-on-line starter with contactor for reversing the rotation of a motor	Star-delta starter	Fan. The symbol is shown with wiring
Time clock Time recorder	h Hour meter Hour counter	Wh Kilowatt-hour meter	

Figure 1.03 BS EN 60617 lists the standard symbols for use in installation drawings

Diagrams that are in common use are illustrated below. They are supplemented by manufacturers' data and service manuals, which are discussed further in the next section.

Block diagrams provide information on sequence of control.

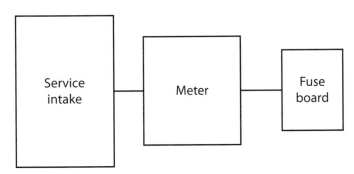

Figure 1.04 A block diagram

A circuit diagram shows how a circuit is connected; it does not show how it is physically wired.

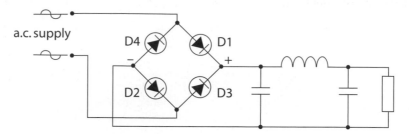

Figure 1.05 A circuit diagram

Wiring diagrams show how the circuit is actually wired and how the cables are routed from one component to the next.

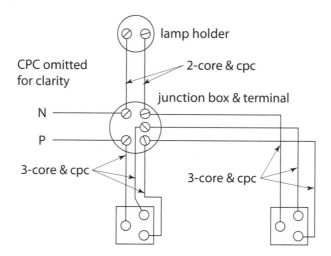

Figure 1.06 A wiring diagram

Schematic diagrams show how a circuit works, not how it is actually wired. They are mainly used to show control diagrams.

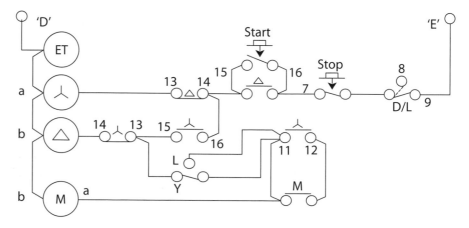

Figure 1.07 A schematic diagram

Assembly drawings show how individual components are put together to make a complete unit.

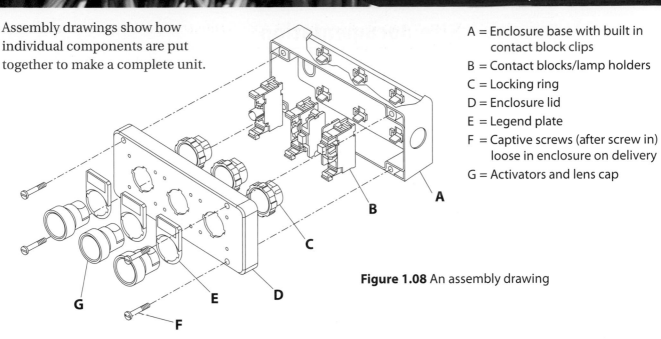

A = Enclosure base with built in contact block clips
B = Contact blocks/lamp holders
C = Locking ring
D = Enclosure lid
E = Legend plate
F = Captive screws (after screw in) loose in enclosure on delivery
G = Activators and lens cap

Figure 1.08 An assembly drawing

'As fitted' drawings show exactly where and what equipment has been located and installed. These drawings are provided to the client on completion of the job.

Layout diagrams are scaled drawings, providing details of the location of equipment to be installed, and are considered to be working drawings.

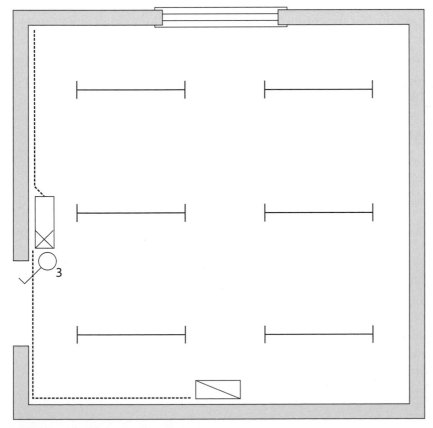

Legend
Warehouse lighting (scale 1:50)
-------- 50 × 50 mm trunking run
⌀3 3-gang 1-way switch
▨ lighting distribution board
▱ main control
├────┤ fluorescent luminaire

Figure 1.09 A layout diagram

Site documentation

In addition to the drawings and diagrams described above, other documentation will be found on site to ensure that tasks can be completed correctly, to time and with the necessary information for management control and payment.

Job Sheet

Evan Dimmer
Electrical contractors

Customer   Dave Wilkins

Address   2 The Avenue
               Townsville
               Droopshire

Work to be carried out
               Install 1 x additional 1200 mm
               fitting to rear of garage

Special conditions/instructions
               Exact location to be specified
               by client

Figure 1.10 A typical job sheet

Job sheets

Not all employers use them but those that do use them to pass details of jobs to their employees. Some can be complex and contain the work for the week, while others will only refer to one job at a time. Typical details on a job sheet could be:

- customer's name and address
- description of the work to be done
- any special conditions or instructions.

Variation orders

A variation order is issued by the main contractor for work completed that falls outside the scope of the original project estimate. The variation order gives permission for the contractor to start the additional work and ensures payment. An example of such work may be where additional walls are put in place that were not originally shown on the plans or tender documents; therefore, additional switch drops or socket outlets installed in these walls will not have been priced.

Day work sheets

These provide a record of work done outside the original contract that will need to be invoiced for payment. This is usually done on a day work basis, at the original contract rates agreed for this type of work.

Day work sheets will normally detail the following:

- customer's name and address
- job number
- date
- amount of labour used
- start and finish times
- quantities and description of materials used
- customer's signature.

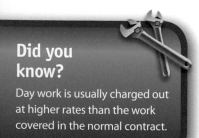

Did you know?

Day work is usually charged out at higher rates than the work covered in the normal contract.

Timesheets

These provide a method of recording the hours and work done. Commonly, a timesheet is used to record the following on a daily basis:

- details of the job
- travelling time
- start and finish times
- overtime
- expenses.

Purchase orders

These are used to order materials from a supplier. Initially, a 'materials requisition sheet' is completed. When this is returned to the office, the order is then written out on a purchase order, giving details of the delivery address, the job number and a list of the materials required.

Delivery notes

These accompany the materials when delivered to site. The materials delivered are checked off against the delivery note to verify a full or partial delivery and to note any damage or discrepancies. The delivery note is then passed back to the office, making them aware that the delivery has been made and to initialise payment.

Completion order

This signifies complete delivery of the original order.

Manufacturer's data and service manuals

Almost all equipment delivered to site and installed will be accompanied by the manufacturer's information on the product in the form of data sheets and service manuals. These should be read, to ensure knowledge about how to install/connect the product. When finished with they should be collected together and passed to the contracts manager, who will place them in the project file for passing on to the client.

Site reports and memos

Most companies will require a site diary to be kept and regular reports sent back to the office detailing progress, details of delays and problems, reports of meetings, etc. A site diary provides a chronological record of all events that take place on site that can be used to make reports back to the office. Such reports may be used to:

- identify problems that keep reoccurring, such as attendance problems with staff, or problems with deliveries of materials
- take action to avoid any difficulties or delays that may be apparent

- provide written evidence to support claims for progress payments
- provide written evidence to support appeals against the imposition of a penalty clause.

Reports need to be factual and to the point. They should contain any recommendations and be signed and dated by the creator of the report.

Storage, use and retrieval of information

Information is stored and can be retrieved in a variety of formats. However, with modern communications, particularly email, it is no longer necessary to have information locally available. It can be stored centrally and accessed remotely by many different users, or transmitted to where it is required very quickly; and either viewed electronically or printed out locally for use.

The Internet provides access to vast quantities of data, which again can be accessed only when required and downloaded if necessary for local use. For example, it is seen as a vital tool in the modern design office, as it is possible to view manufacturer's catalogues and installation details, as well as providing access to the services of specialists. These might be in the field of lighting design, construction and power distribution systems, or advice from safety specialists such as the Health and Safety Executive (HSE).

Storage and dissemination methods include:

- **Paper** – Paper remains a key method of storing information and disseminating it to those who need it. It can include hand written notes and memos, printed letters and other documents, drawings and diagrams, as well as catalogues, data sheets or reference manuals. Large drawings and plans are still easier to view this way than on a computer screen, even though they may have been originated electronically. However, paper is bulky and heavy and takes up a lot of storage space.
- **Microfilm/microfiche** – These use photographic techniques to record miniaturised images of paper records on to rolls of polyester film. Microfilm uses 25 mm wide rolls; microfiche uses 150×100 mm tiles. They can be used to store copies of technical data, drawings, photos and letters, which are viewed through a simple magnifying device with a screen. They are intended to provide storage of data for 500 years.
- **Computers** – These are now universally used in offices, but increasingly on site and able to be linked by telephone to a base computer. Very large amounts of text and graphics information can be stored and viewed locally on the computer, or accessed via a network. Information should always be backed up on other storage media for long term storage.
- **Electronic file servers** – These enable information to be stored on a central server, allowing access to users from more than one location. This can be through a local area network, wide area network or through the World Wide Web.

- **Computer storage media** – CD-ROM and DVDs are widely used. They can store many megabytes of information, are relatively cheap and robust, making transportation of data easy. New methods are appearing all the time, storing increasingly large amounts of information, which can be video, photographs, drawings, diagrams, charts, text, etc. Unlike paper, users must have a computer with the necessary facilities to view the data. There is a risk for long term storage unless re-recorded on to new media as technology advances, otherwise data may be available but unable to be read.
- **Email** – Although not a storage medium, email is widely used to disseminate information, either as text within the email or as attachments, such as photographs or drawings. It has speeded up communication and is used extensively throughout the industry, although still resisted as a formal method of communication between parties.

Working with documentation, drawings and specifications

A wide range of documentation is used within the industry, including drawings, diagrams and specifications. It must be easily interpreted by all users without risk of ambiguity.

Scaled drawings

Layout drawings, location drawings and 'as fitted' drawings used within the industry use common scaling to avoid confusion and misunderstanding. Typical scales are:

- 1:200 for site layout plans
- 1:100 or 1:50 for layout drawings
- 1:25 or less for detailed work, where equipment has to be specifically sited to fit in with tile layouts, etc.

Scaled rules are available, marked with typical scales. They can be used to read actual measurements directly off a diagram. Alternatively, any ruler can be used to measure lengths on the diagram and actual measurements obtained by simple calculation. For example:

- If a desired dimension measures 10 mm on a diagram drawn to scale 1:200, then the actual dimension would be $10 \times 200 = 2000$ mm $= 2$ m.
- If a desired dimension measures 20 mm on a diagram drawn to scale 1:25, then the actual dimension would be $20 \times 25 = 500$ mm $= 0.5$ m.

Data sheets and charts

Did you know?

Data sheets and charts will probably need to be handed to customers on completion of a contract.

These are frequently provided with materials or equipment and can contain information vital to their use. This may cover assembly, installation, fixing or connecting with other equipment. They may well contain safety information. Care must be taken to ensure such data is not lost.

Bar charts (Gantt charts)

These are key tools in the management of a project. The project is broken down into specialisms, such as plumbing, electrical, groundwork, etc., and to specific activities (also known as tasks or work packages). These are listed down the left hand side of the chart, which is divided across the top into months, weeks or days as appropriate for the project. Lines are then drawn across the chart for each activity, showing the planned start and finish times. From the chart it is possible to see where and when each section of the project should be by a particular date and to assess the probable impact of any delayed start or over run.

Note from the chart that Activity A is scheduled to last one day, Activity B will last four days, and the whole job will take seven days. The overlapping of activities can indicate the labour required at any point. For example, if we look at Activities B, C and E, and assume each requires one man, then we can see that, for Week 2, three men will be required. It can also be seen when each task requires materials, so that a delivery schedule can be prepared, avoiding the need to have all the materials delivered at the beginning of the job.

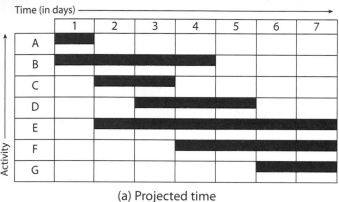

(a) Projected time

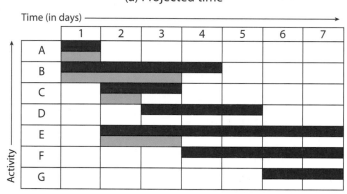

(b) Projected time and actual time

Figure 1.11 A bar chart

Critical path analysis (CPA)

CPA is a method to establish how long it will take to complete a project and to manage change effectively. It uses a network diagram consisting of circles and arrows to indicate activity, how long each will take and which are dependent on which for them to start and finish. It also shows activities that can be undertaken simultaneously and indicates when resources will be needed, such as materials, specialist tools or manpower.

Figure 1.12 Critical path diagram

Most tasks will have some leeway on their start and finish times, known as 'float'. There will be one path through the network with no float, so that any slippage on any one activity will cause the whole project to be late. This is the critical path. CPA is now usually done using computer packages, which draw the diagrams and automatically identify the critical path, and the events that lie on it. They allow 'what if?' questions to be asked, to see what would happen if other events were allowed to slip. The critical path may well change to include different activities.

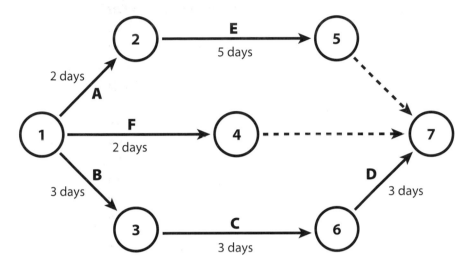

This may need a little careful study to see how it all fits together.

The minimum time for project completion is taken as the longest time path through the network. In this example it is through points 1, 3, 6 and 7, giving us a project time of nine days.

Figure 1.13 Critical path network

The components of a critical path diagram are:

- **Activities** – Each is represented by an arrow, with the base attached to the event showing the commencement of the task and the head attached to the completion event.
- **Events** – These show the time when an activity starts or finishes and are represented by circles. On more complex diagrams they will show the earliest and latest start and finish times.
- **Dummy activities** – For the diagram to work, no activity can start and finish on the same event. Hence, dummy activities are included as dotted lines that do not represent time; they just show a logical link between events.
- **Float time** – The leeway that may exist on start and finish times for individual activities.
- **Critical path** – The sequence of activities with zero float that fix the duration of the project.

The information from the Critical Path Analysis is often used to create a bar chart, as described above, which is easier to read and interpret on site.

Project management

Any project must be managed efficiently, if it is to be completed on time and within budget. Some of the tools to assist in this have been described above, including bar charts and Critical Path Analysis.

The following summarises the roles and tasks that need to be undertaken by project managers:

- Drawings and specifications must be checked to ensure that they meet the requirements of the client.
- The work area must be checked to see that it is suitably prepared and ready for work to begin; including checking that the work area is safe.
- The sequence of operations must be determined using Critical Path Analysis and bar charts.
- The tools, equipment, plant and materials that are required must be identified and delivery arranged to reach the site at appropriate times.
- The correct levels and types of labour required to complete the job must be determined and their availability confirmed.
- The installation process must be coordinated with other contractors on site, to avoid clashes and delays.
- Risks must be continually assessed, monitoring that the work is being completed in a safe manner.
- Checks must be completed to ensure that work complies with standards, particularly BS 7671, the job specification and client requirements.

The size of the project, and/or the size of the company will determine whether all of the above is undertaken by one person or by a team of people.

Relationships and team working

How we interact with our work colleagues, other contractors on site, our customers and visitors to a site is important.

Customer relationships

Customer relationships are dictated by the way we interact with them. Delivering the product on time, to the required standard and cost effectively will always result in good customer relationships and is likely to result in further contracts. Much of the work of an electrical contractor is obtained through customer referrals. Some dos and don'ts when dealing with customers are listed in Table 1.04.

Did you know?

However good we are at our job, if we are perceived to be casual, rude or uncooperative this reflects not just on ourselves but also on the organisation we work for.

DO:	DON'T:
• be honest	• 'bad mouth' your employer
• be neat and tidy in your personal appearance, and look after your personal hygiene	• use company property and materials to do favours for others
• learn how to put people at ease, and be pleasant and cheerful	• speak for your employer when you have no authority to do so
• show enthusiasm for the job	• use bad language
• try to maintain friendly relationships with customers, but don't get over-familiar	• smoke on customer premises
	• gossip about the customer or anyone else
• know your job and do it well – good knowledge of the installation and keeping to relevant standards gives the customer confidence in you and your company	• tell lies – the customer will find out eventually if he or she is being misled or ripped off
	• assume that you know what your employer wants without bothering to ask.
• explain what you are going to do, and how long it will take	
• if you are not sure about something – ask!	

Table 1.04 Some dos and don'ts to improve customer relations

Did you know?

A happy, satisfied customer will be ready and willing to recommend the services of a contractor to other people, if the experience they had of the contractor was a good one. Hence, future work and continuity of employment all depend upon the relationships created with the customer.

In addition:

- Always take care not to damage the customer's property.
- Clear up mess as you work.
- Use dust sheets.
- Remove objects that are liable to cause damage.
- Ask for pets and children to be restrained from entering the work area.
- Always keep the customer informed of anything that may be dangerous.
- Make suggestions that may save costs.
- Always answer questions if you know the answer, or refer to your supervisor if not; never try to bluff.
- Stick to agreed start and finish times, or discuss changes with the customer if circumstances outside your control make this impossible.

Relationships with other contractors

It is equally important to maintain good relationships with other contractors on site. You will generally need their co-operation to avoid problems with the progress of a project. Some dos and don'ts for dealing with other contractors are listed in Figure 1.14.

- ✔ cooperate with other trades – it's always better than conflict
- ✔ be patient and tolerant with others
- ✔ attend site meetings regularly – this helps liaison with other trades
- ✔ keep to the agreed work programme
- ✔ do your work in a professional manner
- ✔ finish your work on time; don't hold others up if you can help it
- ✔ respond cheerfully to reasonable requests from colleagues
- ✔ don't leave the site for long periods of time
- ✔ don't borrow tools and materials unless it is necessary, and return them promptly and in good condition if you do
- ✔ tell your employer if you have personal or work difficulties – don't be too proud
- ✔ take good care of your and others' property
- ✔ keep noise down, especially from your radio
- ✔ show respect for everyone on site – make an effort to learn their names
- ✔ make sure everyone, including visitors to the site, has the right PPE
- ✔ report any breakdown in discipline or disputes between co-contractors promptly to the site supervisor
- ✔ keep a current edition of the Wiring Regulations or the Amicus guide book with you on site
- ✔ always do your best to answer questions from visitors or other tradespeople
- ✔ never play practical jokes on colleagues (for example hiding tools, lunch boxes, car keys). This can cause bad feeling and may result in injury or accident.

Figure 1.14 Promoting good relationships with fellow workers

Team working

Unless you are a sole trader or working on a very small task, you are likely to be part of a team. There are four stages to good teamwork:

- **Forming** – There cannot be a team, unless one is formed. Initially, roles and responsibilities within the team can be unclear. Therefore, the role of team leader becomes important. The team leader will need to establish the purpose and objectives of the team and relationships with others outside the team.
- **Storming** – During this stage, the hierarchy within the group is established. The team leader may be challenged, as the purpose of the team becomes clear, and there may be small groups that struggle to establish their own power base. If the team is to be successful, the leader needs to assert authority and keep the group focused, and promote compromise within the team.
- **Norming** – During this stage things settle down within the team and team members are able to reach agreement on the way forward over various issues. The roles and responsibilities have become clear, and the team has formed a cohesive unit. Team members establish their preferred communication styles and fun activities may start to appear. The leader is now a guide.
- **Performing** – This is the final stage in team development, when the team knows what it is doing, why it is doing it and shares the aspirations of the group. Team members look after each other and work towards a common goal. The leader is now able to delegate and resort to overseeing projects. Instruction and assistance is no longer required except for personal development.

Communication

Communication is an important element in good relationships and team working. It can be verbal, written or non verbal, such as gestures, etc. It can even include your appearance, attitude and behaviour. It is particularly important that written communications are clear, concise and unambiguous.

The writing process

There are four steps that should be followed in writing anything, whether it is a simple memo or a formal report:

- **Step 1** – Think about what you want to say.
- **Step 2** – Get all the information together.
- **Step 3** – Plan a logical order for the document.
- **Step 4** – Start writing!

Above all, keep it simple, keep it interesting and check it before sending!

Report writing

The structure of any report is important, so that the recipient knows where to look for the information and important information is not left out. They will vary widely, depending on the type of report and many organisations will have standard formats for different report functions, or even standard forms to be completed. Use them where they exist.

A business report should contain at least the following:

- name of the author
- date when the report was completed
- the subject
- job number if applicable
- a summary outlining the problem/project and the purpose of the report
- background, what has happened to create the reported position, etc.
- evidence, information that has been gathered to support the views of the report
- conclusions, and recommendations if applicable.

Technical reports may require more structure and further details such as:

- title page
- technical acknowledgements
- history of the project
- list of contents
- report summary
- introduction
- technical chapters
- conclusions and recommendations
- references
- appendices containing specialist information.

Short answer questions

1. Describe why it is important always to deal with customers in a polite and professional manner.
2. What is a variation order?
3. Briefly, describe two laws that protect our environment.
4. Briefly, describe two laws that protect people's legal rights.
5. Briefly describe the roles of the client and architect.
6. Describe the difference between a circuit diagram and a wiring diagram.
7. Who on site checks the quality of materials and workmanship of the installation?
8. What is a block diagram?
9. When are 'as fitted' drawings used?
10. What is meant by discrimination?
11. Briefly explain two areas where the 'Investors in People' award can benefit an organisation or company.
12. Briefly explain what is meant by changes in demand for the electrical installation industry.
13. Why is it necessary for a company to be flexible to the demands of the customer?
14. What is a contract?
15. What should clearly be stated within a contract?
16. The JIB consists of two parties; who are they and what is the role of the JIB?
17. What is meant by the tendering process and who produces the quotation?
18. What is a job specification?
19. List four things that can promote good working relations with the customer?
20. What qualifications are required to be a JIB graded approved electrician?

Multiple-choice test

1. Who is the person that funds a building project?
   a. client
   b. main contractor
   c. subcontractor
   d. architect

2. Who interprets the client's requirements?
   a. main contractor
   b. subcontractor
   c. architect
   d. client

3. The electrical contractor is also known as the …?
   a. architect
   b. main contractor
   c. client
   d. subcontractor

4. A scale drawing showing the position of equipment using graphical symbols is a …?
   a. block diagram
   b. layout diagram
   c. wiring diagram
   d. circuit diagram

5. A diagram, which shows the detailed connections between individual items of equipment, is a …?
   a. block diagram
   b. layout diagram
   c. wiring diagram
   d. circuit diagram

6. A diagram which shows how a circuit works is a …?
   a. block diagram
   b. layout diagram
   c. wiring diagram
   d. circuit diagram

7. A record of works done, outside the scope of the original contract, would be recorded on a …?
   a. *memo*
   b. *day work sheet*
   c. *timesheet*
   d *delivery note*

8. An employer who only employs male full-time employees and only part-time female workers believes that only full-time employees should be promoted. What piece of legislation does this contravene?
   a. *Sex Discrimination Act 1975/2003*
   b. *Disability Discrimination Act 1995*
   c. *Race Relations Act 1976/2000*
   d. *The Human Rights Act 1998*

9. Which of the following is not a stage in the development of teamwork?
   a. *storming*
   b. *norming*
   c. *performing*
   d. *creating*

10. Where can employers look for additional advice on health and safety in the workplace?
   a. *the project manual*
   b. *the local council*
   c. *trade union*
   d. *HSE*

11. Where employees work with ionising radioactive substances, they must …?
   a. *wear a garment that covers the whole body*
   b. *wear a dosimeter pocket card*
   c. *not wear metal watches and jewellery*
   d. *not wear spectacles with glass lenses*

12. Who, on site, checks the quality of materials and workmanship of the project?
   a. *the QA*
   b. *the electrician*
   c. *the clerk of the works*
   d. *the customer*

13. What organisation represents the employers in the electrotechnical sector?
   a. *JIB*
   b. *ECA*
   c. *Amicus*
   d. *Institute of Engineering and Technology*

14. When materials are delivered to site, they should be accompanied by …?
   a. *a delivery advice note*
   b. *a job sheet*
   c. *a variation order*
   d. *the original order*

15. The most appropriate means of communication with other trades on a contract is to …?
   a *hold regular site meetings*
   b. *write them a letter*
   c. *send them a text message*
   d. *send them an email*

16. The purpose of an installation specification is to inform the …
   a. *electrician on how to install the wiring*
   b. *client on how to use the installation*
   c. *architect of the type of equipment to use*
   d. *contractor of the client's requirements*

17. One item of information, not illustrated on a bar chart used to show the work schedule for a project, is …?
   a. *start and finish dates*
   b. *hours worked per day*
   c. *plant/equipment delivery dates*
   d. *labour requirements for each stage of the project*

18. The main purpose of 'as fitted drawings' is to form part of the …?
   a. *tender documents*
   b. *installation drawings the electrician works with*
   c. *network diagrams*
   d. *project manual passed to the customer on completion*

19. Day work is work carried out …?
   a. *at the employer's shop in connection with site work*
   b. *in addition to the specified contract work*
   c. *on a daily basis by on-site, casual labour*
   d. *by an outside contractor employed by the main contractor*

20. Lack of co-operation with other trades and contractors during an electrical installation can lead to …?
   a. *good working relationships*
   b. *fewer site meetings*
   c. *risks to the safety of personnel*
   d. *completion of the job on time*

21. The disposal of waste packaging and materials should be:
   a. *left to the client*
   b. *carried out by the site agent*
   c. *the responsibility of the contractor that creates the waste*
   d. *left for the new occupier to deal with*

22. In an accident report, photographs and videos of the accident scene are:
   a. *considered as supporting evidence*
   b. *considered as non essential material*
   c. *not permissible as evidence*
   d. *not considered as reliable evidence*

23. With the changes in demand and ever improving technology, there is a need for employees to …?
   a. *possess a hydraulic platform certificate*
   b. *have transferable skills*
   c. *move to less demanding jobs*
   d. *be assessed in the work place*

24. The right to maternity and paternity leave, and the minimum wage; all come under what?
   a. *Human Rights Act*
   b. *Employment Rights Act*
   c. *Health and Safety at Work Act*
   d. *Electricity at Work Regulations*

25. The role of the contracts manager within the company would normally be within the …?
   a. *company secretary's department*
   b. *supplies department*
   c. *design department*
   d. *marketing department*

26. The tender quotation for work, is usually completed by the …?
   a. *design engineer*
   b. *technician*
   c. *estimator*
   d. *supervisor*

27. The body that represents employees in the electrotechnical sector is …?
   a. *JIB*
   b. *NICEIC*
   c. *ECA*
   d. *Amicus*

28. The sequence of control for a large installation can be simply shown using …?
   a. *a wiring diagram*
   b. *a layout diagram*
   c. *a block diagram*
   d. *a circuit diagram*

29. A recognised method of storing a lot of technical information in a limited space is by …?
   a. *microfilm*
   b. *duplication*
   c. *reprographics*
   d. *drawings*

30. Fitting instructions for electrical equipment can normally be found where?
   a. *British Standards*
   b. *manufacturers' data*
   c. *codes of practice*
   d. *block diagrams*

31. A location drawing shows a proposed cable route. If the scale of the drawing is 1:50 and the length on the drawing is measured at 85 mm, what will be the actual length of cable?
a. 4.25 m
b. 17 m
c. 42.5 m
d. 58.9 m

32. In order to complete a materials requisition list, the most appropriate drawing to work with would be a …?
a. block diagram
b. wall chart
c. layout drawing
d. assembly drawing

33. Which of the following types of information would not be required when compiling a job specification?
a. clients' needs
b. location of equipment
c. test result sheets
d. types of equipment

34. The main source for electrical symbols used in drawings is?
a. BS 7671
b. Electricity at Work Regulations
c. Electricity Supply Regulations
d. BS EN 60617

35. On a drawing an area of 2 km × 4 km is shown as 100 mm × 200 mm. What is the scale?
a. 1:1000
b. 2:100
c. 1:20000
d. 1:200

The answer section is at the back of the book.

Health and safety

By the end of this chapter you should be able to demonstrate your knowledge and understanding of health and safety issues and the Regulations relative to the electrical construction environment. This guide will cover the following:

- Safety signs
- Personal protective equipment (PPE)
- Legislation
  - Health and Safety at Work Act 1974 (HASAWA)
  - Electricity at Work Regulations 1989 (EAWR)
  - Construction (Design and Management) Regulations 1994 (CDM)
  - Workplace (Health, Safety and Welfare) Regulations 1992
  - Electricity Safety, Quality and Continuity Regulations 2002
  - Management of Health and Safety at Work Regulations 1999
  - Provision and Use of Work Equipment Regulations 1998 (PUWER)
  - Control of Substances Hazardous to Health Regulations 2002 (COSHH)
  - Control of Major Accidents and Hazards Regulations 1999 (COMAH)
  - Noise at Work Regulations 1989
  - Health and Safety (First Aid) Regulations 1981
  - Manual Handling Operations Regulations 1992
  - Health and Safety Information for Employees Regulations 1989
  - Dangerous Substances and Explosive Atmospheres Regulations 2002 (DSEAR)
  - Reporting of Injuries, Diseases, and Dangerous Occurrences Regulations 1995
- Implementing and controlling health and safety
  - Health and safety responsibility of organisations

- Health and safety responsibility of the authorities
- Penalties for health and safety offences
- Approved codes of practice (ACOPs)
- Risk assessment
- Fire safety
  - Fire triangle
  - Classes of fire
  - Fire legislation
  - Fire extinguishers
- Site safety
  - Working at height
  - Working in excavations
  - Manual handling
  - Tools and equipment
- Electrical safety
  - Reducing hazards
  - Safe isolation of electrical supplies
  - Test equipment
- First aid
- Other safety topics
  - Working in isolation
  - Environmental issues
  - Environmental management systems (EMS)
  - Portable appliance testing (PAT)
  - Insurance
- General hazards
  - General electrical hazards
  - LPG (liquid petroleum gas)
  - Chemical hazards

Safety signs

There are four types of safety signs.

- prohibition
- mandatory
- warning
- information or safe condition.

	Prohibition signs	Mandatory signs
Shape:	Circular	Circular
Colour:	Red borders and cross bar. Black symbol on white background	White symbol on blue background
Meaning:	Shows what must NOT be done	Shows what must be done
Example:	No smoking	Wear eye protection

	Warning signs	Information or safe condition signs
Shape:	Triangular	Square or rectangular
Colour:	Yellow background with black border and symbol	White symbols on green background
Meaning:	Warns of hazard or danger	Indicates or gives information on safety provision
Example:	Danger: electric shock risk	First aid post

Figure 2.01 Saftey signs

Personal protective equipment (PPE)

PPE is designed to protect against risks to health and safety. Employers must provide this free of charge and employees must use it.

Employers	Employees
Must train employees and give information on maintaining, cleaning and replacing damaged PPE	Must use PPE provided by their employer, in accordance with any training in the use of the PPE concerned
Must provide storage for PPE	Must inform employer of any defects in PPE
Must ensure that PPE is maintained in an efficient state and in good repair	Must comply with safety rules
Must ensure that PPE is properly used	Must use safety equipment as directed

Table 2.01 PPE responsibilities of employer and employees

- **Eye protection** – There are different types of eye protection, each designed to give a specific type of protection; for example safety spectacles, safety box goggles, cup goggles, face shields, welding goggles or welding mask.
- **Foot and leg protection** – This gives protection against injury to legs, ankles and feet and, where appropriate, against electric shock.
- **Hand protection** – Gloves provide protection against cuts, heat, or crushing injuries, and also against dermatitis.
- **Head protection** – It is most important to protect the most vital organ, the brain. Safety helmets have a 'use by' date stamped on them. Their effectiveness can be seriously reduced by stickers, sticky tape, dymo tape, paint or felt pens applied to them.
- **Ear protection** – There are two types: ear plugs that fit inside and ear defenders that fit outside the ears.
- **Lung protection** – This is designed to protect against fumes, dust, smells, gases, etc. Protective devices range from a simple dust mask to full face breathing equipment.
- **Whole body protection** – This can provide protection against the environment, such as adverse weather. Overalls provide general protection against minor abrasions and contamination by irritating substances.

Table 2.02 gives some guidance on when PPE should be worn. It must always be worn if a risk assessment indicates that it is required.

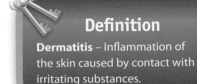

Definition

Dermatitis – Inflammation of the skin caused by contact with irritating substances.

Did you know?

80 per cent of all head injuries happen to people who are NOT wearing a safety helmet!

Safety tip

High visibility clothing ensures that you can be seen by moving traffic.

PPE	When worn
Hard hats	• where there is a risk of you either striking your head or being hit by falling objects
Eye protection	• when drilling or chiselling masonry surfaces • when grinding or using grinding equipment • when driving nails into masonry • when using cartridge-operated fixing tools • when drilling or chiselling metal • when drilling any material that is above your head
Ear protection	• when working close to noisy machinery or work operations
Gloves	• whenever there is risk to the hands from sharp objects or surfaces • when handling bulky objects, to prevent splinters, cuts or abrasions • when working with corrosive or other chemical substances

Breathing protection	<ul><li>when working in dusty environments</li><li>when working with asbestos</li><li>when working where noxious odours are present</li><li>when working where certain gases are present</li></ul>

Table 2.02 When to wear PPE

Figure 2.02 gives some guidelines for working safely.

Here are some guidelines for safe working. Take a minute to look at these and think about how you work. Are you taking any unnecessary risks?

Work tidily and cleanly. Do not leave objects lying on the floor where they may cause accidents. Clean all materials and debris away from the site at the end of the working day and ensure that when working overhead on scaffolds, trestles, ladders and steps, you do not lay anything down in such a position that it may fall on anyone or anything below.

Observe all rules and work instructions provided. When you start work your employer will make you aware of the company's rules and expectations with regard to safety. Most employers will have a health and safety policy or statement and it is part of your job to acquaint yourself with the contents and to ensure that all of your activities comply with the stated requirements.

Running or hurrying can cause accidents. Never run or take short cuts, even if you are in a hurry. You may collide with someone, trip over an obstruction or run into a protruding object causing an injury. It is always better to walk and arrive safely. Construction sites are particularly dangerous places to work if you do not take common-sense precautions.

Keep all machinery and equipment well maintained and in good condition. Never use damaged machinery, tools or equipment, and make sure that any damage that you may cause is reported or repaired promptly so that it does not endanger the next user.

Secure all loose clothing and repair any torn articles immediately. Overalls should always be fastened, with no flaps or torn pieces hanging off that may become tangled with rotating machinery, etc. If your hair is long, it should be covered by a 'snood' cap (hair net) or tied up so that it is not a hazard, and all jewellery should be removed where a safety hazard exists.

Advise supervisors immediately if you observe any unsafe practices or notice any defects in any of the equipment that is provided for use by yourself and others.

Follow all manufacturers' instructions and recommendations when using items of equipment.

Examine all electrical tools and equipment very carefully before use to ensure that they are in good working order and show signs of having been recently inspected.

Let others know when you are working overhead or nearby when your activities may pose a particular danger to them.

You are responsible for the safety of yourself and others with whom you work or who may be affected by your work. Don't leave things lying around. Everything that you do must be of the very highest commercial and safety standards so that it DOES NOT present any significant danger to you or other people who may be affected by your actions.

Figure 2.02 Working safely

Definition

Risk assessment – The careful examination of what, during working activities, could cause harm to people. The employer must take sufficient precautions to minimise that risk, including the provision of PPE. Table 2.02 provides guidance on when it should be worn.

Legislation

There are several pieces of legislation that, directly or indirectly, impact on safety in the work place. Statutory legislation results from the passing of an Act of Parliament. It may then be interpreted by the courts as the result of test cases brought before them. Such Acts are supported by Regulations which, although not in themselves statutory, amplify the law.

When interpreting these Acts and Regulations the following definitions apply:

- **Employer** – A person or body that employs one or more persons under a contract of employment.
- **Employee** – A person employed by an employer under a contract of employment.
- **Self-employed** – This covers anyone who works for gain or reward other than under a contract of employment.
- **Statutory** – This means that it is binding in law and is a criminal act to contravene it.

Did you know?

Unless specifically stated otherwise, employers, employees and the self-employed should always abide by legislation.

Health and Safety at Work Act 1974 (HASAWA)

This legislation is statutory and is an enabling Act, which means that it allows other Acts or Regulations to be introduced and enforced by this Act.

All employers, employees and the self-employed are covered by it. Duties and responsibilities are placed upon them and must be adhered to. The main coverage of each section of the Act is as follows:

- **Section 1** – The general purposes of the Act, which are to maintain and improve standards of health and safety at work, protect other people from risks due to work activities, control the storage and use of dangerous substances, and to control certain emissions into the air.
- **Section 2** – The duties imposed on employers regarding their employees.
- **Section 3** – The duties imposed on employers and the self-employed to protect other people from the effects of their activities.
- **Section 4** – This requires work premises to be maintained in a state that does not present a danger to those who work there.
- **Section 5** – This requires certain work premises not to allow harmful emissions into the atmosphere.
- **Section 6** – The duties imposed on manufacturers, suppliers, designers, etc. to ensure that the goods they supply are safe.
- **Section 7** – The general duties of employees at work relating to health and safety.
- **Section 8** – The responsibility on everyone not to interfere with safety equipment.
- **Section 9** – The duty of the employer not to charge for any safety equipment or procedure provided for under health and safety legislation.

Electricity at Work Regulations 1989 (EAWR)

EAWR are enabled by the HASAWA and came into force on 1st April 1990. Every person, be they employer, employee or self-employed, must comply with these Regulations on any matters within their control.

They require a 'duty holder' to be appointed to ensure compliance with the Regulations, but each duty holder is only responsible for parts of the electrical system within their control.

If a Regulation uses the word '*must*' or '*shall*' and avoids the use of the phrase '*so far as is reasonably practicable*' then the requirements MUST be met regardless of cost or other problems. This is an *absolute* duty.

If the phrase '*so far as is reasonably practicable*' is used then this allows decisions to be made regarding safety that are reasonable considering the risk involved.

EAWR are discussed further in Chapter 9 under Electrical Regulations.

Construction (Design and Management) Regulations 1994 (CDM)

The CDM Regulations are statutory and place duties on people who can contribute to the health and safety of a construction project.

During design and start of construction the duty holder is the planning supervisor appointed by the client who has ordered the work, with the role of coordinating and managing health and safety on site. The principal contractor is then responsible for health and safety during the construction phase.

Exceptions to these Regulations are:

- construction work (not demolition) lasting less than 30 days and employing less than four people
- construction work for a domestic client
- construction work carried out in a shop or office that does not interfere with normal work activities
- removal of insulation from pipes, boilers or other parts of a heating system.

Workplace (Health, Safety and Welfare) Regulations 1992

These Regulations apply to ALL workplaces except: ships, aircraft, locomotive or rolling stock, permanent and temporary construction sites, forestry and agricultural sites, or places where minerals are extracted.

There are **three main categories** covered:

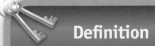

Definition

Workplace – Any part of the premises where work takes place; the exception being domestic premises.

- **Working environment**
  - ventilation to provide plenty of fresh air
  - temperature to be a minimum 16°C in an office or 13°C where manual work takes place
  - lighting must be sufficient for people to see clearly
  - all surfaces, furnishings must be kept clean
  - sufficient space to work, minimum 11 cubic metres per person
  - ergonomics of workstations should be suitable for anyone
  - outdoor protection from adverse weather including UVA and UVB rays from the sun.
- **Safety**
  - floors and surfaces should be suitable and not slippery
  - protection from falling hazards
  - pedestrian and vehicle traffic must be separated
  - escalators must have safety devices fitted, including more than one stop button.
- **Facilities**
  - sufficient toilets provided in accessible places
  - water supplies must include hot and cold water with soap and towels provided, and clean drinking water.

Electricity Safety, Quality and Continuity Regulations 2002

This Regulation replaced the Electricity Supply Regulations 1988. It is designed to protect the public and consumers from electrical danger and to ensure the continuity and quality of the electrical supply.

Duty holders with responsibility under the Regulations are:

- generators of electricity
- distributors
- suppliers
- meter operators.

Management of Health and Safety at Work Regulations 1999

These place a duty on employers to manage health and safety as enabled by the Health and Safety at Work Act 1974 (HASAWA).

If an employer has more than five employees then written health and safety (H&S) policy and risk assessments must be done.

Besides carrying out risk assessments, employers are required to:

- arrange for the H&S measures identified in the risk assessment to be carried out
- appoint competent people to help implement the arrangements
- set up emergency procedures
- provide training and information to employees
- work with other employers sharing the same workplace.

Provision and Use of Work Equipment Regulations 1998 (PUWER)

This set of Regulations requires that risks to people from equipment being used are either prevented or controlled. Equipment provided for use at work should be:

- suitable for the intended use
- safe to use and maintained in a safe condition
- used only by people who have had adequate training in its use.

Control of Substances Hazardous to Health Regulations 2002 (COSHH)

This set of Regulations requires the employer to control the exposure of employees and the public to hazardous substances used or created during work activities. The employer must:

- assess the risk of using a hazardous substance
- decide what precautions are needed
- remove or control the exposure
- maintain controls and equipment used to deal with the hazard
- monitor the level of exposure to the substance
- monitor employees' health
- prepare procedures to deal with accidents and emergencies
- ensure employees are adequately informed, trained and supervised.

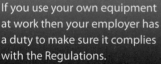

Did you know?

If you use your own equipment at work then your employer has a duty to make sure it complies with the Regulations.

Control of Major Accidents and Hazards Regulations 1999 (COMAH)

This set of Regulations applies to hazardous work environments, such as chemical, nuclear, petroleum or explosive. The main aim is to prevent or mitigate the effects of a major incident, such as a chemical leak or petroleum fire.

Noise at Work Regulations 1989

These Regulations impose a duty on employers to minimise the exposure to high noise levels and to keep the noise level at the lowest possible level.

There are two levels of noise that require action:

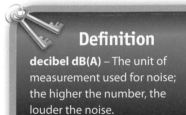

Definition

decibel dB(A) – The unit of measurement used for noise; the higher the number, the louder the noise.

- When 85 decibels (dB(A)) is exceeded then an assessment needs to be carried out and employees issued with ear protectors.
- When the noise level reaches 90 decibels (dB(A)) then the employer must limit the exposure of the employee to that noise (other than provision of ear protectors).

Health and Safety (First Aid) Regulations 1981

These Regulations impose a duty on employers to provide adequate first aid equipment and facilities; and suitable training to personnel to enable basic first aid to be given to an injured or ill person.

This applies to ALL workplaces including those with less than five employees and also the self-employed.

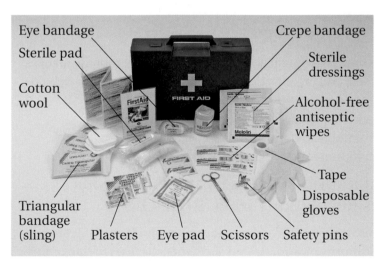

Figure 2.03 A typical first aid kit

Manual Handling Operations Regulations 1992

These Regulations are an attempt to reduce the number of accidents and injuries caused by manually handling loads.

There are three basic rules that should be considered when manually handling loads:

- Avoid manual handling of loads that involve a risk of injury whenever possible.
- Assess and then provide a safe system of work to manually handle a load.
- Reduce the risks to the lowest possible level by use of training and use of mechanical equipment.

Health and Safety Information for Employees Regulations 1989

These Regulations impose a duty on employers to provide their employees with basic health and safety information.

The employer has two ways to achieve compliance:

- Display the H&S poster or issue a copy to each employee.
- Provide details of a local enforcing authority and local HSE (Health and Safety Executive) office.

Dangerous Substances and Explosive Atmospheres Regulations 2002 (DSEAR)

These Regulations impose a duty on employers to protect workers from fire and explosions arising from using dangerous substances.

To enable compliance, employers and the self-employed must:

- carry out a risk assessment on activities that use dangerous substances
- provide technical and organisational measures to eliminate or reduce the risk
- provide equipment and procedures to deal with emergencies
- provide information and training to employees
- classify and mark zones where explosive atmospheres may occur.

Reporting of Injuries, Diseases, and Dangerous Occurrences Regulations 1995 (RIDDOR)

These Regulations impose a duty on employers to inform the HSE or local enforcing authority of work related accidents, diseases or dangerous occurrences. This can now be done by telephone via a national Incident Control Centre.

The following must be reported:

- deaths
- injuries where the person is absent for more than three days
- injuries to members of the public where they are taken to hospital
- work related diseases
- dangerous occurrences where a person could have been injured but was not.

Employers must keep a record of all injuries, disease or dangerous occurrences. These can be any form but the HSE has issued an Accident Book, which can be used. Records must contain the following:

- date and method of reporting
- date/time/place of event
- personal details of all involved
- description of event plus supporting evidence (including photographs, etc.).

Implementing and controlling health and safety

Health and safety is the responsibility of companies (or other organisations) and individuals within the rules and guidelines laid down by authorities and enforced, if necessary, by the courts.

Health and safety responsibility of organisations

Under Management of Health and Safety at Work Regulations 1999 employers MUST comply with the following:

- Assess work related risks for employees and others not employed by them.
- Provide effective arrangements for planning, organising, controlling, monitoring and reviewing preventative and protective measures.
- Appoint one or more competent persons to help comply with H&S law.
- Provide employees with comprehensive and relevant information on the risks at work and on the measures in place to remove or reduce them.
- Companies employing five or more employees MUST have a written H&S policy which details how they will implement the policy.

H&S officers are employed by the company and manage the implementation of H&S law. H&S representatives are elected by the workforce to represent the employees' interests with regard to H&S law, as per Section 15 of HASAWA 1974.

Health and safety responsibility of the authorities

The Health and Safety Commission (HSC) and the Health and Safety Executive (HSE) are responsible for health and safety in all work places.

HSE inspectors can enter work premises without warning and have a range of legal powers at their disposal, including instigating legal action. Initial action may be to issue:

- **An improvement notice** – This stipulates what must be rectified and allows 21 days for that to happen or for the company to appeal against it.
- **A prohibition notice** – This closes down a work place or activity and does not allowing reopening until the problem is resolved.

Environmental Health Officers, appointed and employed by the local authority, inspect commercial premises such as shops and offices and have a right of entry to any such building without warning.

Penalties for health and safety offences

Failure to comply with an improvement or prohibition notice incurs the following:

- **Lower court** – maximum £20,000 and/or 6 months imprisonment
- **High court** – unlimited fine and/or 2 years imprisonment.

Breaches of Sections 2 to 6 in the HASAWA 1974 (general duties) can result in:

- **Lower court** – maximum £20,000
- **High court** – unlimited fine.

Other breaches of HASAWA:

- **Lower court** – maximum £5,000
- **High court** – unlimited fine.

Approved codes of practice (ACOPs)

ACOPs give practical advice on how to comply with H&S law and are approved by the HSC. They are not mandatory but, if an employer was in court for a H&S offence and had not abided by an existing ACOP, proof would need to be provided of using another appropriate method or system.

Did you know?

The HSC is appointed by the appropriate Secretary of State, who in turn appoints members of the HSE. Responsibility is delegated to local authorities for H&S in offices, shops and other parts of the service sector.

Risk assessment

A risk assessment is a careful examination of what, during work activities, could cause harm to any persons. The important things to decide are:

- What are the hazards?
- Are they significant?
- Are the hazards covered by suitable precautions to minimise the risk?

There are five steps to completing a risk assessment:

- **Step 1** – Look for the hazard.
- **Step 2** – Decide who might be harmed and how.
- **Step 3** – Evaluate the risks and decide whether more precautions are needed.
- **Step 4** – Review the assessment and revise if necessary.
- **Step 5** – Record your findings.

Two sample forms that can assist in carrying out an assessment are shown here:

Definition

Hazard – Anything that can cause harm.

Risk – The chance of a hazard causing harm.

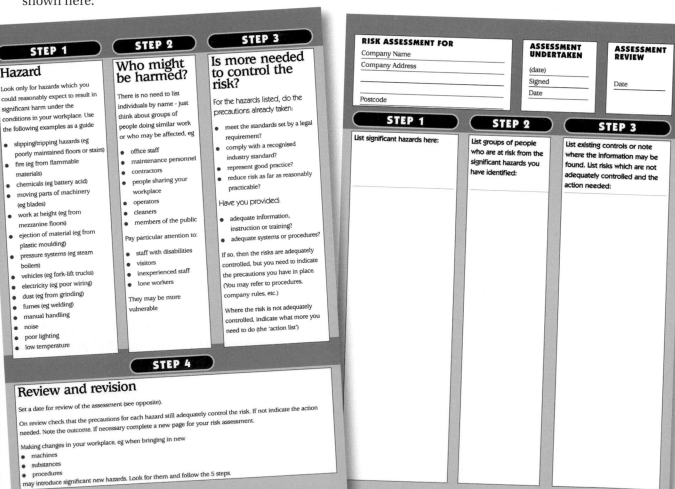

Figure 2.04 Sample form for completing risk assessment   **Figure 2.05** Alternative form for completing risk assessment

Fire safety

Fire is always a risk when dealing with electricity and electricians may also work in explosive atmospheres. Hence, it is important to understand what causes fire and how to deal with it safely.

Fire triangle

Three things are needed for a fire to happen:

- fuel
- oxygen
- heat.

If any of these is missing a fire cannot start. If any of them is removed from a fire then it will go out.

Classes of fire

Fire is divided into five classes (do not confuse these with types of extinguisher):

- **Class A** – organic solids such as paper or wood
- **Class B** – flammable liquids
- **Class C** – flammable gases
- **Class D** – metals
- **Class E** – cooking oils.

Electricity has no classification as a fire. It is a source of ignition (like matches).

Fire legislation

There are six main pieces of legislation relating to fire safety:

- Fire Precautions Act 1971 (due to be replaced)
- Fire Safety and Safety of Places of Sport Act 1987
- Construction (Health Safety and Welfare) Regulations 1996
- Health and Safety (Safety Signs and Signals) Regulations 1996
- Fire Precautions (Workplace) Regulations 1997 (due to be replaced)
- Fire Precautions (Workplace) Amendments Regulations 1999.

New legislation will place a duty on employers to ensure fire safety in the workplace and appoint appropriate people to ensure compliance. Fire authorities will assume the role of enforcement and not that of certificate issuing.

Fire extinguishers

Fire extinguishers are now all coloured RED and have a coloured band on them to indicate what type of fire they are to be used on. There are four types of extinguisher, as shown in Figure 2.06.

Dry powder fire extinguisher

Water fire extinguisher

Carbon dioxide fire extinguisher

Foam fire extinguisher

Figure 2.06 Some fire extinguisher types

Some key points to remember:

- Fire fighting is a job for professionals. A fire extinguisher is only a first response measure when a fire is small or is blocking the means of exit.
- Never use a fire extinguisher unless trained to do so.
- Do not use water extinguishers on electric fires due to the risk of electric shock or explosion.
- Do not use water extinguishers on oils or fats as this too can cause an explosion.
- Do not touch the horn of CO_2 extinguishers, as this can freeze burn the skin.
- Do not use CO_2 extinguishers in a small enclosed space, as this can cause suffocation.
- Read the operating instructions on a fire extinguisher before use.

Site safety

Site safety is the responsibility of all those working on a site. It includes:

- working at height
- working in excavations
- manual handling
- tools and equipment.

Working at height

The risks from working at height are sustaining injury by falling or causing injury by dropping something on to someone below. Ladders, step-ladders and trestles are the most commonly used access equipment on site and probably the most misused. Mobile towers are also widely used but a frequent cause of accidents through improper use. Scissor and boom lifts provide safe, flexible platforms, providing they are used correctly but are the most expensive. All equipment for working at height should be checked annually and before use.

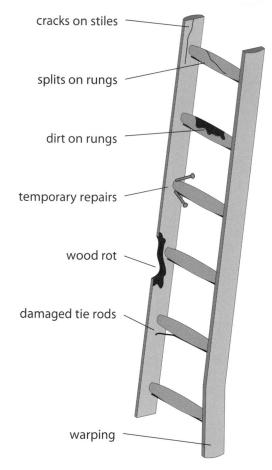

cracks on stiles

splits on rungs

dirt on rungs

temporary repairs

wood rot

damaged tie rods

warping

Figure 2.07 Ladder with defects

Ladders and step-ladders

Figure 2.07 shows faults that can occur on ladders. Similar problems can appear on step-ladders.

Some key rules for using ladders are:

- They should be on firm, level ground, away from excavations and not where they can be knocked or cause a hazard.
- They should be at approximately 75 degrees to a building (i.e. one metre out for every four metres up).
- They should be secured at the top by the stiles and, as necessary, at the bottom; or by someone holding the stiles and with one foot on the bottom.
- Extension ladders should have at least four or five rungs of overlap.
- Ladders attached to scaffolding should extend one metre or five rungs beyond the scaffold platform.
- The working position should be at least five rungs from the top.

Most of the rules for ladders also apply to step-ladders. In addition, ensure that all four legs are on firm level ground and fully open, and the hinge and ropes are sound. Ensure knees are below the top of the steps, only using the top if constructed as a platform.

Trestle scaffolding

Two sets of trestles (A frames) can be used with a scaffold board to provide a working platform.

Some rules for their use are:

- The platform between trestle frames must be a minimum of 600 mm wide.
- It should be no higher than 2/3 up the trestle frame.

- Scaffolding boards must be all the same length and thickness and not overhang more than 4 times their width.
- Trestle frames should be spaced 1 metre apart for 32 mm boards, 1.5 metres apart for 38 mm boards, 2.5 metres apart for 50 mm boards.
- Toe boards and rails must be fitted and a ladder provided for access if a platform is more than 2 metres above ground.
- Maximum platform height should be 4.5 metres and trestles over 3.5 metres should be tied to the building structure.

scaffold board

rope or hinged bracket

rectangular rungs

Figure 2.08 Trestle scaffold

Mobile scaffold towers

Some rules for their use are:

- They should only be erected by someone competent to do so.
- They should be on firm level ground with wheels or feet properly supported.
- In an exposed position, the height to base ratio should be no more than three times the minimum base dimension. For example, if the base is 3 m × 2 m then the maximum height of the tower would be 6 m (3×2). This could be extended to 7 m (3.5 × 2) for inside use.
- Guard rails should be a minimum of 910 mm high (with an intermediate rail at 470 mm), and toe boards a minimum of 150 mm high.
- Ensure they are away from power lines or overhead obstructions.
- Move them by pushing or pulling the base and never with someone on them.

Working in excavations

Even shallow excavations can be dangerous. Advance planning is essential and a competent person must be responsible. Once work commences:

- Wear a hard hat.
- Make sure sides are supported or cut at a safe angle.
- Never go into an unsupported excavation or work ahead of the supports.
- Store spoil where it cannot fall back into the excavation.
- Use markers and barriers to block access for people or vehicles. If more than 2 m deep then provide substantial barriers.
- Where vehicles have to tip anything into the excavation, use stop blocks.
- Provide safe ladder access.
- Plans must be available to avoiding cutting services.
- Take precautions to prevent access out of working hours.

Manual handling

This covers lifting, lowering, pushing, pulling or carrying. A load may be inanimate (e.g. a box) or animate (a person or animal). The weight that can be handled is reduced if arms are extended, or if it is low down or high up.

> **Did you know?**
> Guidelines given for weights that can be lifted safely are for 30 operations per hour.

The movement of loads requires careful planning based on a risk assessment. Table 2.03 gives guidance on the latter.

The task	Does the task involve: • holding loads away from the body? • twisting, stooping or reaching upwards? • large vertical movement? • long carrying distances? • strenuous pushing and pulling? • repetitive handling? • insufficient rest or recovery time? • a work rate imposed by a process?
The load	Is the load • heavy? • bulky, unwieldy or hard to grasp? • unstable or are the contents likely to shift? • sharp, hot or otherwise potentially damaging?
The working environment	Does the working environment have: • space constraints? • floors that are slippery or unstable? • poor lighting? • hot, cold or humid conditions?
Individual capacity	Does the individual: • have a reach problem, that restricts their physical capability? • have knowledge of and training in manual handling?
Handling aids and equipment	• is the device correct for the job? • is it well maintained? • are the wheels on the device suited to the floor surface? • do the wheels run freely? • is the handle height between waist and shoulders? • are the handle grips in good order and comfortable? • are there any brakes? If so do they work?

Table 2.03 Risk assessment of a manual handling operation

Tools and equipment

- Tools and equipment must always be well maintained and inspected for damage before use.
- Never use equipment for which you are not trained.
- Care must be taken particularly when using cartridge tools and airlines.
- Untidy work places cause accidents; and tools and equipment left lying around are a target for thieves.

Electrical safety

Electricity can kill. Even non-fatal shocks can cause severe and permanent injury. The main hazards are contact with live parts, faults which cause fires and faults where ignition of gases or vapours occurs. The risks can be enhanced by harsh conditions, such as wet environments. Out of doors equipment is at greater risk of damage or getting wet.

Reducing hazards

Hazards are reduced by using safe, well-maintained equipment suitable for the task and inspecting it regularly and before use.

Risk of injury is less if the operating voltage is reduced, particularly for power tools and temporary lighting on site. Battery operated power tools are safest but, if not, they should be run from a 110 volt centre-tapped to earth supply.

Safe isolation of electrical supplies

Before beginning work on any electrical circuit it should be isolated. The Joint Industry Board for Electrical Contractors (JIB) have provided two flow charts that show the procedures to be followed for isolating complete installations or individual items.

Safety tip

If equipment is operated at 230 volts or higher it should be protected by an RCD (residual current device).

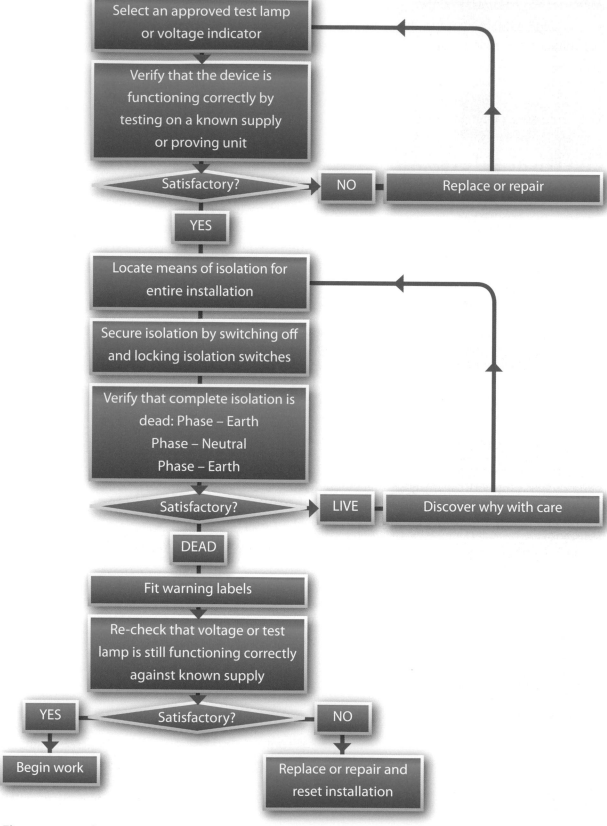

Figure 2.09 JIB flow chart for isolating a complete installation

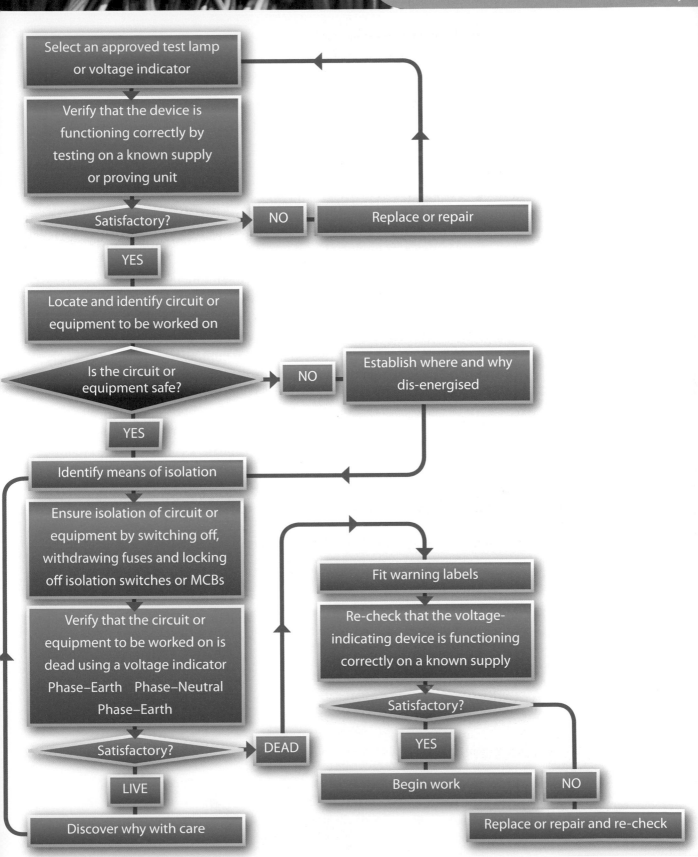

Figure 2.10 JIB flow chart for isolating individual circuit or item of fixed equipment

Test equipment

Test equipment must be regularly checked and should be calibrated. The following should be checked before use:

- damage to the casing
- batteries are in good condition and all of the same type
- leads and probes are undamaged
- operation of meters (resistance type only) by testing with leads together (should read zero) and leads apart (should read 'over range')
- a valid label shows that calibration is current.

The HSE issues Guidance note GS 38 covering testing, diagnosis and repair by electrically competent people. Advice includes:

- Test probes to be used with voltmeters, multimeters, test lamps and voltage should have finger barriers or shrouds to prevent contact with live parts; exposed conductive tip not to protrude more than 2 mm (ideally spring loaded and not exceed 1 mm); protected via 500 mA (maximum) high breaking capacity fuse or a current limiting resistor and a fuse.
- Test leads should be adequately insulated; of different colours; flexible and have sufficient capacity for the duty expected of them; sheathed against mechanical damage; sufficient length; and not have exposed conductors other than probes.

First aid

An electric shock current at 50 mA and above is likely to be fatal, as muscles contract, the heart fibrillates (beats out of sequence) and breathing stops. It may also result in other injuries such as burns at the entry and exit points of the current, or from falling.

In the event of an electric shock:

☑ First of all check for your safety to ensure that you would not put yourself at risk by helping the casualty.

☑ Then break the electrical contact to the casualty by switching off the supply, removing the plug (if it is undamaged) or wrenching the cable free (only attempt this if the cable and plug, etc. are undamaged).
If this is not possible break the contact by pushing or pulling the casualty free using a piece of non-conductive material, e.g. a piece of wood.

☑ If the casualty is conscious, guide them to the ground, making sure that further injuries are not sustained, e.g. banging their head on the way down.
If the casualty is unconscious, get help straight away, then check the casualty's response. Talk to and gently shake the casualty to gauge their level of response. If the casualty appears unharmed they should be advised to rest and see a GP.

☑ If there is no movement or any sign of breathing summon help immediately. If there is someone with you, tell them to get help, i.e. ring 999; if you are on your own with the casualty you will have to leave them for a moment while you get help yourself.

☑ As soon as you return to the casualty you need to begin CPR (cardio-pulmonary resuscitation).

If a casualty is unconscious then the first action is to find out the degree of unconsciousness by speaking to them and gently shaking them. If fully unconscious then the actions can be summarised as:

Check **A**irways, **B**reathing and **C**irculation (ABC)

Everyone should know how to carry out CPR (cardiopulmonary resuscitation) and give basic treatment for burns, shock and breaks, as well as smoke and fume inhalation.

Other safety topics

There are several other issues that relate to safety.

Working in isolation

Working in isolation always carries risks and should not be done, particularly:

- in confined spaces
- in trenches
- near, or on, live sources or equipment
- at height
- near unguarded machinery
- where there is risk of fire or other hazardous atmospheres
- with toxic or corrosive substances.

One means of reducing the risk is for someone competent to issue a Permit to Work, which specifies the work to be done, the hazards and precautions to be taken. It is active only for a set period and someone will investigate if the person working has not returned.

Environmental issues

There are strict rules on the following:

- **Storage and handling of materials**
  - Storing more than 200 litres of oil (all types) requires compliance with Control of pollution (oil storage) Regulations 2001.
  - Safety data sheets must be provided with any materials purchased or disposed of, detailing handling, storage and disposal methods.
  - Disposing of any effluents into drains, etc. requires a licence.
- **Air** – Nothing that produces dark smoke can be burnt at any premises.
- **Waste** – An employer has a duty of care to ensure all waste is handled, recovered or disposed of by individuals or businesses authorised to do so and a record must be kept via signed Waste Transfer Notes.
- **Special waste** – Any waste deemed hazardous or dangerous must be disposed of, handled, stored or treated by people or organisations with technical competence in that field.

Environmental management systems (EMS)

Concern for the environment and awareness of the need to improve management of resources is on the increase. ISO 14001 is the certification needed to show that the company uses effective environmental systems and controls.

Definition

Portable equipment – In this context, portable equipment is any equipment that is connected to the supply via a plug.

Portable appliance testing (PAT)

The Electricity at Work Regulations 1989 requires *all* electrical systems to be maintained to prevent danger. Table 2.04 lists the different categories of equipment and when they should be tested.

Equipment type	When	Class I		Class II	
		Visual only	*Visual + test*	*Visual only*	*Visual + test*
Stationary	Weekly	None	1 year	None	1 year
IT equipment	Weekly	None	1 year	None	1 year
Moveable	Before use	1 month	1 year	3 months	1 year
Portable	Before use	1 month	6 months	3 months	6 months
Hand-held	Before use	1 month	6 months	3 months	6 months

Table 2.04 Recommended frequency of equipment testing

Insurance

The Employers Liability (Compulsory insurance) Act 1969 ensures that employers have at least a minimum level of insurance relating to health and safety. Insurance normally held covers:

- **Employers liability insurance** – This is compulsory and covers the cost of compensation to employees should they have an injury or illness caused by work activities.
- **Public liability insurance** – This is voluntary and covers the employer for claims made by the public against them for damages to people or property.

General hazards

The best way to reduce the risk of accidents is to remove the cause. This requires an understanding of the hazards that can be present in the workplace.

General electrical hazards

Ensure that electrical power tools are safe before using them and that any circuit you are working on is isolated correctly.

LPG (liquid petroleum gas)

LPG changes from a liquid to a gas at −42°C and even small quantities mixed with air create an explosive mixture. It is heavier than air so will sink and rapidly form an explosive concentration that could be ignited by a spark, so is particularly dangerous in trenches or excavations. LPG bottles should be stored upright and, when not in use, the valve closed and the protective dust cap in place.

Chemical hazards

There are four types of chemical hazard: toxic agents, corrosives, flammables and reactives. They can cause injuries to eyes, skin, etc., allergies and death. Some of the effects may not appear for several years.

Toxic agents, such as hydrogen sulphide and cyanide, are specifically identified as poisons and should be labelled and handled accordingly:

- Close containers when not in use.
- Work in well ventilated areas.
- Wear correct PPE.
- Wash hands often.
- Safely dispose of contaminated clothing.
- Keep antidotes handy.

Corrosives are irritants, such as acids and alkalis, which are especially dangerous to the eyes and respiratory tracts.

- Wear correct PPE.
- Work in well ventilated areas.
- Apply water if spilt on you.
- If in the eyes then rinse with water for 15 minutes and get medical help.

Flammables are chemicals that ignite readily, giving the danger of fire or explosion resulting in burns or other injuries.

- Ensure there are no flames, sparks or cigarette lighters in the area.
- Use only small quantities.
- Store and dispose of safely.
- Call emergency services if a problem occurs.

Reactives are explosive compounds, such as nitro compounds.

- Obtain information about the chemicals you are using.
- Handle with care.
- If working in an enclosed space, at the first sign of trouble evacuate and try to contain the problem by closing doors, etc. if possible.

Asbestos dust is of particular concern as the fine fibres, if inhaled, can embed themselves in the lungs for life, creating long term health hazards.

- Know the hazards, avoid exposure and follow recommended controls.
- Wear PPE provided.
- Use special vacuums and dust-collecting equipment.
- Report any hazardous conditions to a supervisor.

Short answer questions

1. What arc employee responsibilities regarding PPE?
2. Explain what is meant by the term 'statutory' regarding a set of Regulations.
3. What is the difference between the terms 'absolute' and 'as far as is reasonably practicable'?
4. Explain what a 'hazard' and a 'risk' are.
5. Describe the five steps to carrying out a risk assessment.
6. List five things to check on a ladder before using it.
7. List the seven steps of the safe isolation procedure.
8. Describe the contents of a 'Permit to work' document.
9. Describe the visual checks you would carry out on a portable appliance.
10. What information should be contained in a visitors' book?

Multiple-choice test

1. What shape are prohibition signs?
   a. square
   b. triangular
   c. circular
   d. rectangular

2. What colour is the symbol on a mandatory sign?
   a. red
   b. white
   c. blue
   d. green

3. Who provides PPE free of charge?
   a. local authority
   b. government
   c. HSC
   d. employer

4. What item of PPE has a use by date on?
   a. gloves
   b. safety helmet
   c. safety boots
   d. safety goggles

5. Which of the following is NOT a statutory document?
   a. EAWR 1989
   b. HASAWA 1974
   c. BS7671
   d. CDM 1994

6. Which section of HASAWA imposes duties on employees?
   a. Section 1
   b. Section 9
   c. Section 7
   d. Section 2

7. What is the title of the person responsible in the EAWR 1989 Regulations?
   a. manager
   b. duty holder
   c. apprentice
   d. supervisor

8. What is the minimum office temperature allowed?
a. 13°C
b. 19°C
c. 16°C
d. 10°C

9. What is the minimum working space allowed per person?
a. 50 cubic metres
b. 20 cubic metres
c. 6 cubic metres
d. 11 cubic metres

10. What is the loudest daily noise allowed before action is taken?
a. 100 dB(A)
b. 85 dB(A)
c. 90 dB(A)
d. 75 dB(A)

11. How many days to remedy a prohibition notice?
a. 7 days
b. 28 days
c. 21 days
d. as long as it takes

12. How many steps are there in carrying out a risk assessment?
a. 5
b. 3
c. 7
d. 2

13. Which of the following is NOT a class of fire?
a. electrical
b. cooking oils
c. flammable liquids
d. metals

14. What colour is the band on CO_2 fire extinguishers?
a. red
b. black
c. white/cream
d. blue

15. What is the angle for erecting a ladder?
a. 60 degrees
b. 75 degrees
c. 72 degrees
d. 45 degrees

16. What is the minimum width of platform on a trestle?
a. 600 mm
b. 300 mm
c. 450 mm
d. 900 mm

17. What is the maximum height for an outside scaffold whose base is 3 m × 2 m?
a. 5 m
b. 10 m
c. 6 m
d. 7 m

18. GS 38 stipulates the maximum length of exposed tip, what is it?
a. 1 mm
b. 2 mm
c. 10 mm
d. 0 mm

19. What Regulations enforce PAT testing?
a. BS 7671 Regulations
b. PUWER Regulations 1998
c. EAWR 1989
d. RIDDOR Regulations 1995

20. At what temperature does LPG become a gas?
a. 40°C
b. −42°C
c. 0°C
d. −0°C

The answer section is at the back of the book.

03 Electrical science

By the end of this chapter you should be able to demonstrate your knowledge and understanding of basic electrical science:

- Mechanics
  - Mass and weight
  - Force
  - Work
  - Mechanical advantage and velocity ratio
  - Energy
  - Mechanical power
- SI units
  - Symbols
  - SI unit prefixes
- Electron theory, conductors and insulators
  - Molecules and atoms
  - Conductors
  - Insulators
- Current, voltage, resistance and power in direct current circuits
  - Current
  - Voltage, e.m.f. and potential difference
  - Resistance
  - Ohm's Law
  - Simple electrical circuits
  - Power in a d.c. circuit
- Magnetism
  - Permanent magnets
  - Electromagnets
  - Solenoids and relays

- Alternating current
  - Values of an alternating waveform
  - Frequency and period
  - Phasor representation
  - Inductors, inductance and inductive reactance
  - Capacitors, capacitance and capacitive reactance
  - Impedance
  - Power in a.c. circuits
  - The power triangle
- Instruments and measurement
  - Measuring current (ammeter)
  - Measuring voltage (voltmeter)
  - Measuring resistance
  - Loading errors
  - Meter displays
- Basic transformers
  - Laminations
  - Enclosures
  - Separate Extra Low Voltage (SELV)
  - Transmission of energy
- Electrical generators and motors
  - The effects of magnetism
  - Generators/alternators
  - Electric motors

Mechanics

All engineers need to have a clear understanding of basic mechanical principles.

Mass and weight

Mass is the amount of matter within an object. The mass of an object will stay the same wherever we are in the universe, unless it is cut or somehow changed. The SI unit of mass is the kilogram (kg).

Weight is a force and depends on how gravity pulls on a mass. This can vary according to where we are. The higher above sea level we are, the less we weigh (although this is only a very small difference). The SI unit of weight (and force in general) is the newton (N).

Force

Force is a push or pull that acts on an object (such as gravity). If the force is greater than the opposing force, the object will change motion or its shape. Force is measured in **newtons**.

The presence of a force is measured by its effect on a body. For example, a spring will stretch, if we attach a weight to it, because gravity is acting on the weight and pulling it down.

When the force of gravity acts on a mass, that mass often accelerates. It exerts a force that depends upon the mass and the acceleration due to gravity. This acceleration due to gravity is 9.81 m/s^2 at sea level and, therefore, a mass of 1 kg will exert a force of 9.81 N. In many situations this can be rounded up to 10 N.

Expressed as a formula: **Force (N) = Mass × Acceleration**

Work

If an object is moved, then work is said to have been done. The unit of work is the joule. Work done is the relationship between the effort (force) used to move an object and the distance that the object is moved.

Expressed as a formula: **Work done (J) = Force (N) × Distance (m)**

> **Remember**
>
> Mass and weight are not the same. A person would weigh less on the moon than on Earth due to the decreased gravitational force, but would still have the same mass.

> **Remember**
>
> Do not assume that the acceleration due to gravity is 10 m/s^2. It is 9.81 m/s^2. Only take it as 10 m/s^2 if you are told to do so in a question, or if you are doing a rough calculation.

Simple machines for lifting and handling

A simple machine is a device that allows work to be done more easily when a force is applied to it. A screw, wheel on an axle, and a lever are all simple machines. It allows a smaller force to overcome a larger force, change the direction of a force or work at a faster speed.

Levers

Levers let us use a small force to apply a larger force to an object. They are grouped into three classes, depending on the position of the fulcrum (the pivot).

> **Remember**
> To make any simple machine work we need to apply a force to it.

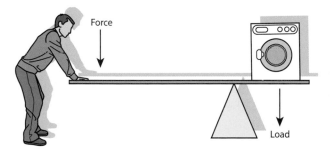

Class 1. The fulcrum is between the force and the load, like a seesaw.

> **Did you know?**
> In medieval times, siege engines were used to hurl rocks at enemy castles. A siege engine is simply a Class 1 lever.

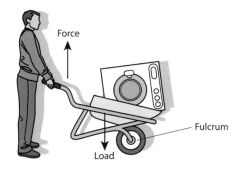

Class 2. The fulcrum is at one end, the force at the other end, and the load is in the middle. A wheelbarrow is a good example.

Class 3. The fulcrum is at one end, the load at the other end and the force in the middle, like a human forearm.

Figure 3.01 Classes of lever

Gears

Gears are wheels with teeth; these teeth fit into those close to it. They can slow down, speed up, change direction, or control several things at once. Each gear changes the direction of rotation of the previous gear. A smaller gear will always turn faster than a larger gear. This also means it turns more times.

Figure 3.02 Gears

The inclined plane

This is basically a ramp or sloping surface and is probably the simplest machine of all. It is effectively a ramp allowing us to move objects up (or down) in a straight line. A screw is an inclined plane wound around a central cylinder.

Pulleys

A pulley is made with a rope, belt or chain wrapped around a wheel and can be used to lift a heavy object (a load). There are two main types: the single fixed pulley and the moveable pulley.

A **single fixed pulley**, when attached to an immoveable object (e.g. a ceiling or wall), acts as a Class 1 lever with the fulcrum located at the axis; but the bar becomes a rope. The pulley wheel changes the direction of the force. The disadvantage of this design is that you have to apply more effort than the load as a force needs to be applied directly to the rope.

A **moveable pulley** is one that moves with the load. This allows the effort to be less than the weight of the load. The moveable pulley also acts as a Class 2 lever with the load between the fulcrum and the effort.

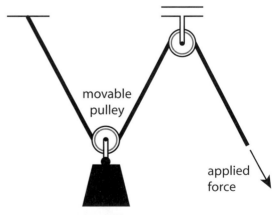

Figure 3.04 Moveable pulley

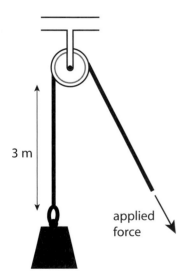

Figure 3.03 Single fixed pulley

There are many combinations of pulleys, the most common being the block and tackle. These use the two main types as their principle of operation.

Mechanical advantage and velocity ratio

The relationship between the effort needed to lift something (input) and the load itself (output) is called **mechanical advantage**. When a machine has a higher output than input, the machine is said to give a good mechanical advantage. **There are no units for mechanical advantage, it is just a number.**

$$\text{Mechanical Advantage (MA)} = \frac{\text{Load}}{\text{Effort}}$$

Sometimes machines translate a small amount of movement into a larger amount (or vice versa). For example, a small movement of a piston can cause a load to move a much greater distance. This is known as the velocity ratio. **There are no units for velocity ratio, it is just a number.**

$$\text{Velocity Ratio (VR)} = \frac{\text{Distance effort moves}}{\text{Distance load moves}}$$

In a pulley system, VR is equal to the number of pulley wheels.

Energy

Energy, measured in joules, is the ability to do work, move something, or causing change. Machines cannot work without energy and you cannot get more work out of a machine than energy put in. This is due mainly to **friction**. Friction occurs when two substances rub together, when energy is lost as heat.

Energy can be transferred from one form to another but cannot be created or destroyed. There are only two types:

* **Potential energy** (energy of position or stored energy).
* **Kinetic energy** (energy due to the motion of an object).

However, energy can appear in many forms. Some of these are: solar, electrical, heat, light, chemical, mechanical, wind, water, muscles and nuclear.

Potential energy

The amount of **potential energy** of an object depends on position and condition. A brick on the top of scaffolding has potential energy because it could fall – due to gravity.

Potential energy due to height above the Earth's surface is called gravitational potential energy, and the greater the height, the greater the potential energy.

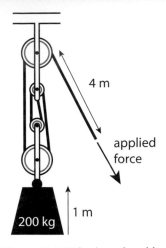

Figure 3.05 Block and tackle combination

> **Remember**
>
> Mechanical advantage and velocity ratio are just numbers. They have no units.

There is a direct relationship between gravitational potential energy and the mass of an object – objects with greater mass have greater gravitational potential energy. Also, the higher an object is above the earth, the greater its gravitational potential energy. These relationships are expressed by the following equation:

$$\textbf{PE}_{\textbf{grav}} = \text{mass of an object} \times \text{gravitational acceleration} \times \text{height} = \textbf{m} \times \textbf{g} \times \textbf{h}$$

Kinetic energy

Kinetic energy is energy in the form of motion. The greater the mass of a moving object, or the greater its velocity, the more kinetic energy it has. In fact, it is proportional to the square of the velocity, so a small object like a bullet, moving at very high speed, can have much higher kinetic energy than a very large object moving slowly.

Mechanical power

The power put into a system depends on both the amount of work we do and the speed at which we carry it out. Hence, power is the rate of doing work.

$$\text{Power (P)} = \frac{\text{Work done (W)}}{\text{Time taken to do that work (t)}} = \frac{\text{Energy used (E)}}{\text{Time taken to do that work (t)}}$$

Energy or work is measured in joules (J) and time is measured in seconds (s). Power is measured in joules per second or J/s known as watts (W). 1000 watts (W) = 1 kilowatt (kW).

Remember

Be really careful, the shorthand for work is W and the units for power are W. Do not get them confused.

SI units

In the UK and Europe an international system of units for measuring different properties is used, known as SI units. There are seven base units – the main units from which all the other units are created.

Symbols

Listed in Table 3.01 are the commonly used symbols and their units. The last column defines the unit and relates it to the fundamental principles of electro-technology.

Quantity	Symbol	Unit name	Unit symbol	Definition
Electric current	I	Ampere	A	A quantity (Q) of electricity crossing a section of a conductor in a time (t) commonly referred to as current 'flow'.
Potential difference	V	Volt	V	The cause of movement of electric charge from one point to another, or the voltage applied to a circuit.
Resistance	R	Ohm	Ω	The property of a resistor to resist the flow of charge through it, all conductors resist the 'flow' of current.
Resistivity	ρ	Ohm - metre	Ωm	The part of the resistance of a conductor that is affected by the material it is made from.
Temperature	No symbol	Kelvin	K	For practical purposes, the degree Celsius scale is used. Both have identical intervals. 1 K = 1°C, but the Kelvin scale begins at absolute zero −273°C. This means freezing point (0°C) is 273 K and boiling point (100°C) is 373 K.
Mass	No symbol	Kilogram	kg	This is a measure of the amount of material in the substance measured in kilograms (not to be confused with weight).
Force	F, f	Newton	N	The cause of mechanical displacement or motion. Force may cause stationary objects to move or bring a moving object to rest, or it can change the shape of an object.
Magnetic flux	Φ	Weber	Wb	The lines of force around magnets and conductors carrying electric currents.
Magnetic flux density	B	Tesla	T or Wb/m^2	The intensity of the lines of force around magnets and current carrying conductors.
Frequency	F	Hertz	Hz	The number of complete cycles that occur in one second in an a.c. waveform. The UK supply frequency is 50 Hz.
Power	P	Watt	W	The rate of doing work. Electrically it is the energy dissipated as a result of current flow through a load, found by the product of voltage and current.

Quantity	Symbol	Unit name	Unit symbol	Definition
Energy	W	Joule	J	The capacity to do work over a period of time. Consumers pay by the amount of energy, in kW used per hour.
Time	t	Seconds	s	The unit of time, expressed in seconds.
Length	l	Metre	m	The unit of length measured in metres.
Area	A, a	Square metre	m^2	The surface, enclosed by the sides of a two-dimensional shape (e.g. floor area).

Table 3.01 SI units

SI unit prefixes

We often deal in quantities that are much larger or smaller than the base units.

Symbols (and the quantities they represent) are altered by adding another symbol in front (a prefix). These represent base units multiplied or divided by one thousand, one million, etc.

Table 3.02 shows the most common prefixes.

Multiplier	Name	Symbol prefix	As a power of 10
1 000 000 000 000	Tera	T	1×10^{12}
1 000 000 000	Giga	G	1×10^{9}
1 000 000	Mega	M	1×10^{6}
1 000	kilo	k	1×10^{3}
1	unit		
0.001	milli	m	1×10^{-3}
0.000 001	micro	μ	1×10^{-6}
0.000 000 001	nano	n	1×10^{-9}
0.000 000 000 001	pico	p	1×10^{-12}

Table 3.02 Common prefixes

Some common examples of using the prefixes with the unit symbol are:

- km (kilometre = one thousand metres)
- mm (millimetre = one thousandth of a metre)
- MW (megawatt = one million watts)
- µs (microsecond = one millionth of a second).

Electron theory, conductors and insulators

Electrical current (measured in amperes) consists of a flow of free electrons (negatively charged particles) through a conducting material. The lower the resistance of the material, the better it is in conducting current.

Molecules and atoms

The nucleus of an atom contains neutrons and protons of about the same mass. Neutrons have zero electrical charge and protons have a positive charge. Electrons orbit around the nucleus of an atom, as shown in Figure 3.06.

- like charges repel each other (whether they are two positive or two negative charges)
- unlike charges (i.e. a positive and a negative charge) attract each other.

The neutrons hold the nucleus together and give the atom mass (as they have the same mass as the proton). Neutrons are neutral so they do not play a part in the electrical properties of atoms.

The other main particles in an atom are electrons. These orbit the nucleus in circles and have a negative charge. This negative charge equals the positive charge of a proton. All stable atoms have zero overall charge. In other words, they have the same number of electrons orbiting the nucleus as protons inside the nucleus. The negatively charged electrons are therefore neutralised by their equivalent number of positively charged protons.

However, some atoms have more than one electron shell. The more shells there are, the more chance there is of an electron orbiting further away from the nucleus. These 'free' electrons are easily 'brushed-off' an atom and the atom then becomes positively charged overall. We call this an ionised atom or simply an **ion**.

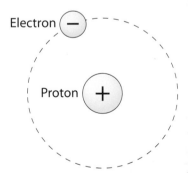

Figure 3.06 Hydrogen atom

The three states of matter

Molecules are always in a state of rapid motion, but when they are densely packed together, this movement is restricted and the substance formed by these molecules is solid. When the molecules of a substance are less tightly bound, there is a great deal of free movement and the substance is a liquid. Finally when the molecule movement is almost unrestricted, the substance can expand and contract in any direction and is a gas.

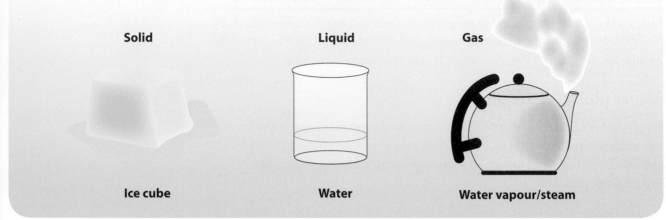

| **Solid** | **Liquid** | **Gas** |
| Ice cube | Water | Water vapour/steam |

Electrons are arranged in layers or shells at differing distances from the nucleus. The electrons in shells closer to the nucleus are held in place more strongly than those further away. These electrons can join other atoms, whose distant electrons may split away to join other atoms and so on.

It is this movement of free electrons that causes the creation of electricity flow. A material that allows the movement of free electrons is called a **conductor**. A material that does not is called an **insulator**.

Conductors

A conductor is a material that has a low resistance to the flow of free electrons. They can flow freely through the conductor, providing that there is a difference in electrical potential between one point and another. It is this difference in potential that provides the energy for the free electrons to move.

Aluminium (Al)	Low cost and weight Not very flexible Used for large power cables
Brass (alloy of Copper and Zinc)	Easily machined Corrosion resistant Used for terminals and plug pins

Carbon (C)	Hard Low friction in contact with other materials Used for machine brushes
Copper (Cu)	Good conductor Soft and ductile Used in most cables and busbar systems
Iron/Steel (Fe)	Good conductor Corrodes Used for conduit, trunking and equipment enclosures
Lead (Pb)	Flexible Corrosion resistant Used as an earth and cable sheath
Mercury (Hg)	Liquid at room temperature Quickly vaporises Used for contacts Vapour is used for lighting lamps
Sodium (Na)	Quickly vaporises Vapour used in lighting lamps
Tungsten (W)	Extremely ductile Used for filaments in light bulbs

Table 3.03 Common conductors

Insulators

Electricity is defined as the movement of free electrons along a conductor. But electricity is only useful when we can control this flow. Electricity becomes a current (like the flow of water in a pipe) if we can force it to all move in the same direction (the voltage). In direct current, or d.c. (considered here) the speed of the flow is controlled by the characteristics of the conductor. In an alternating current (a.c.) then there are additional factors that influence the speed.

Some common insulators are shown in Table 3.04.

Remember

A good insulator has high resistance. However, all insulators will eventually break down, if a high enough voltage is applied to them.

Rubber	Very flexible Easily affected by temperature Used in cable insulation
Impregnated paper	Stiff and hygroscopic Unaffected by moderate temperature Used in large cables
Magnesium oxide	Powder, therefore requires a containing sheath Very hygroscopic Resistant to high temperature Used in cables for alarms and emergency lighting
Mica	Unaffected by high temperature Used for kettle and toaster elements
Porcelain	Hard and brittle Easily cleaned Used for carriers and overhead line insulators
Rigid plastic	Less brittle and less costly than porcelain Used in manufacture of switches and sockets

Table 3.04 Common insulators

Current, voltage, resistance and power in direct current circuits

Electricity is simply the flow of free electrons along a conductor. It is only of use if we can control how and where it flows. It becomes a current (just like water in a pipe) if we can use something to force it to move in one direction (voltage). In this section we will only consider direct current (d.c.), with the current flowing in one direction. How fast it flows is then dictated by the physical characteristics of the conductor (resistance). If the current alternates, then there are additional effects that dictate current flow.

Current

Simply put, current is the number of electrons that move along the conductor. However, an electron alone is too small to be useful. We therefore use a group of electrons, known as a **coulomb**. This contains approximately 6,240,000,000,000,000,000, or 6.24×10^{18} electrons. Current is measured by the number of coulombs moving past a point every second.

Electrical current is measured in amperes. One coulomb passing along a conductor in a second is measured as one ampere. In calculations, we use the symbol **I** to indicate current. Current is the total amount of electronic

charge passing through a point on a circuit, divided by the time interval over which this takes place. This may be written as:

$$I = \frac{Q}{t}$$

Here I is the current in amperes, Q is the total electrical charge measured in coulombs and t is the time interval in seconds.

In circuit drawings we always show current moving from positive to negative. This convention is to help us understand and predict motion when designing systems. In actuality current flows from negative to positive. In many cases the key issue is the size of current not the direction of the flow. However, this is important to remember when looking at electronic components when we identify electron flow.

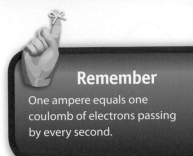

Remember

One ampere equals one coulomb of electrons passing by every second.

Voltage, e.m.f. and potential difference

These three terms are all ways of describing the force applied to the electrons to make them flow. Electrons will only flow if they can theoretically return back to where they started from. In other words unless a complete circuit is created. If there is a break in a circuit (such as a switch) then no current will flow.

The force that pushes the electrons along the conductor is called **electromotive force (e.m.f.)**. This is measured as the number of joules required to push one coulomb along the circuit. This is therefore measured in joules per coulomb. One joule per coulomb is known as **one volt**.

Potential difference is measured between any two points of a circuit or, between any point and the general mass of the Earth. For most purposes, the Earth is used as a reference point with a potential of 0 V (or no potential). So, a device with a voltage of +230 V has a potential of 230 above the potential of the Earth (which is zero).

Electromotive force comes from three principle sources:

- chemical (from a battery)
- thermal
- magnetic.

Chemical

When two dissimilar metal plates (electrodes) are placed in a chemical solution (an electrolyte) a reaction takes place causing the electrons from one plate to travel through the electrolyte and collect on the other plate. The first plate has an excess of protons, and therefore a positive charge. The second plate now has an excess of electrons, and therefore a negative charge. This is how a battery is created, with the charge varying depending on the materials used.

If each terminal of a battery has a conductor connected to it, this creates a path for the surplus electrons in the negative charged electrode to flow

Figure 3.07 A simple circuit

towards the positive charged electrode, and cancel out the positive charge. When this flow is controlled, the current can be used to flow through electrical items (such as a lamp, see Figure 3.07).

A battery converts chemical energy into electric potential energy. The charge moves from the 'high potential' terminal through the external circuit (e.g. the conductor and any electrical equipment) back to the 'low potential' terminal. The difference between the terminals is the potential difference.

In Figure 3.07 the electrons pass through the filament of the lamp, causing it to heat up and glow, before returning to the battery and completing the circuit. Breaking either of the two wires will break the circuit, preventing the electrons from moving from a high potential area to a low potential area. This will cause the lamp to go out. If a switch was inserted into one of the wires, we could break the circuit and reconnect it again whenever we chose.

Some batteries can be recharged by forcing a current through them in the opposite direction, building up the charges at the electrodes again. However most batteries can not have this chemical reaction reversed.

Thermal

In a circuit where conductors are made from different metals, a potential difference will occur if these two metals are placed at different temperatures. This effect is called the Seeback effect, after its discoverer Thomas Johann Seebeck.

It is used in the measurement of temperature with the 'hot end' placed in the equipment and the 'cold end' connected to a meter in a remote position.

Magnetic

If an electrical charge moves, it produces a radial magnetic field. The greater the charge moving (or the faster it moves), the larger the magnetic field created. As soon as the charge stops moving, the magnetic field disappears. This is called **electromagnetic induction** and will be considered when we look at alternating current.

Resistance

When a electrical current passes through a material it will produce heat. This heat is caused by the opposition the material provides to the flow of current. This property is called its **electrical resistance (R)**. Resistance varies with:

- length
- cross sectional area
- resistivity
- temperature.

Length

If two materials of equal length and the same cross sectional area are joined together and the resistance measured then the total resistance will be found to have doubled. Adding two more equal lengths of the same cross sectional area would quadruple the resistance.

The resistance of a material having a uniform cross sectional area is directly proportional to its length.

Area

If two materials of equal length and the same cross sectional area are joined side by side, this would double the cross sectional area. In this situation the resistance will have found to have halved.

The resistance of material of constant length is inversely proportional to its cross sectional area.

Resistivity

Resistivity (ρ) simply quantifies how much resistance a conductor has. The resistance will change depending on the material (e.g. copper, aluminium etc.) and its size (cross sectional area expressed as **a**), being used as a conductor. Also, the further current has to move in a circuit (the length of the conductor), the greater the resistance to its movement becomes.

All the conductors used in electrical installations have a calculated resistivity (ρ) value, which is measured in ohm metres (Ωm) but usually quoted in micro-ohm millimetres (μΩmm).

Note that the formula for the resistance of a conductor is found by:

$$R = \frac{\rho\ell}{a}$$

Conductor	Ωm	Insulator	Ωm
Silver	16.5×10^{-8}	Glass	1×10^{13}
Copper	17.8×10^{-8}	Ebonite	2×10^{14}
Aluminium	28.4×10^{-8}	Porcelain	2×10^{14}
Brass	66.0×10^{-8}	Mica	9×10^{15}

Table 3.05 Resistivity table

$$\text{Resistance} = \frac{\text{resistivity} \times \text{length}}{\text{cross sectional area}} \text{ or } R = \frac{\rho l}{a}$$

Temperature

Resistance calculations only remain true if the temperature remains constant. The majority of conductors have a positive temperature coefficient, meaning their resistance increases with their temperature. The main exception to this is carbon. This has a negative temperature coefficient, mean its resistance decreases with temperature.

Ohm's law

This states the relationship between voltage, current, resistance and circuit. Current flow is directly proportional to voltage applied to the circuit and indirectly proportional to its resistance, provided that the temperature affecting the circuit remains constant.

$$\text{Current (I)} = \frac{\text{Voltage}}{\text{Resistance}} = \frac{V}{R} \quad \text{or} \quad V = IR \quad \text{or} \quad R = \frac{V}{I}$$

Simple electrical circuits

A working circuit has:

- a source of supply (such as a battery)
- conductors through which current can flow and which must form a complete circuit
- a load (such as a lamp) that needs current to make it work
- a device (fuse/MCB) to protect the circuit, if the current is too high
- a switch to control the supply to the equipment (load).

Resistors in series

If a number of resistors are connected together end to end and then connected to a battery, the current can only take one route through the circuit. This type of connection is called a **series circuit**.

The current has the same value at every point in the circuit. Using Ohm's Law, the total circuit current (I) is the supply voltage divided by the total resistance.

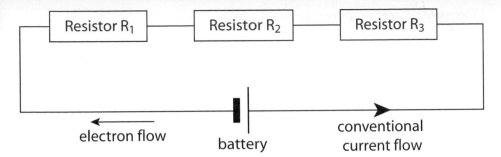

Figure 3.08 Series circuit

The total circuit resistance (R_t) is the sum of all the individual resistors = $R_1 + R_2 + R_3$.

The potential difference across each resistor is proportional to its resistance. Using Ohm's Law: $V_1 = I \times R_1$ $V_2 = I \times R_2$ $V_3 = I \times R_3$

The supply voltage (V) = the sum of the potential differences across each resistor = $V_1 + V_2 + V_3$.

Resistors in parallel

If a number of resistors are connected together so that there is more than one route for the current to flow, as shown in Figure 3.09, then they are connected in **parallel**.

The voltage is the same across each resistor. However, the current divides between them in inverse proportion to the resistance in each path. In other words, the lower the resistance, the higher the proportion of total current that will flow through it. Therefore, using Ohm's Law:

$$I_1 = \frac{V}{R_1} \text{ and } I_2 = \frac{V}{R_2}$$

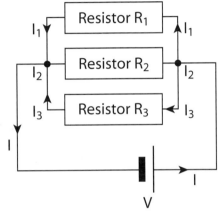

Figure 3.09 Parallel circuit

Total resistance R_t is calculated from: $\dfrac{1}{R_t} = \dfrac{1}{R_1} + \dfrac{1}{R_2} + \dfrac{1}{R_3} + \text{etc.}$

Total circuit current (I) is found by adding together the current through each of the branches:

$$I = I_1 + I_2 + I_3$$

Series/parallel circuits

Many circuits are a combination of series and parallel components. To calculate the total resistance first calculate the total resistance of each parallel group. Then add up to give us the total resistance for the whole circuit.

Power in a d.c. circuit

When current flows in a circuit, heat is produced. The amount of power used in generating this heat is proportional to both the voltage and the current. Therefore **P = VI.**

Using Ohm's Law to substitute for V and I, we can also express this as

$$P = I^2R \quad \text{or} \quad P = \frac{V^2}{R}$$

Magnetism

Magnetism is a fundamental force, just as gravity is, and it occurs either on its own or as a by-product of a moving electrical charge.

Direct currents can be converted into alternating currents through magnetic field and flux patterns of permanent magnets and current carrying conductors.

Magnetism occurs naturally in rocks such as magnetite, an iron ore. Magnetism is caused by the movement of electrical charge and can be seen whenever electrically charged particles are in motion.

Any material that is attracted to a magnet, such as iron, steel, nickel and cobalt has the ability to become magnetised. There are known as magnetic materials. The two types of magnet of interest to electricians are:

- permanent magnet
- electromagnet (temporary magnet).

Permanent magnets

A permanent magnet will exhibit a magnetic field that will exhibit a magnetic field of its own after it has been removed from a strong magnetic field. This allows the magnet to exert force (the ability to attract or repel) on other magnetic materials. The magnet will remain in this state permanently, provided it is not subject to a change in environment, such as temperature or a de-magnetising field. This retention of magnetism is called its **remanence**.

A de-magnetising field (a field in the opposite direction) can drive the magnetic force of the magnet back to zero. The amount of reverse driving field needed to revert a magnet like this is called its **coercivity**.

Magnetic fields are a series of closed loops that start at one pole of the magnet, travel to the other pole and then pass through the magnet to the original pole. Each of these lines is a line of magnetic flux and has the following properties:

- they will never cross each other
- they always try to return to their original shape

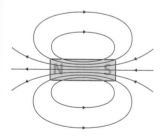

Figure 3.10 Bar magnet

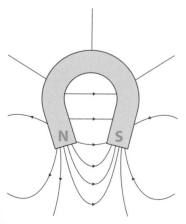

Figure 3.11 Horseshoe magnet

- they always form a closed loop (unless there is flux leakage due to a weak field)
- the magnetic polarity is north to south
- the higher the number of lines of magnetic flux, the stronger the magnetic force of the magnet.

If the lines were counted this would establish the **magnetic flux**, which is measured in **webers (Wb)**. **Flux density** is simply the amount of magnetic flux that exists over a defined cross sectional area. This is measured as Wb/m^2 or **teslas** and has the symbol B. This means that one weber of magnetic flux spread evenly over a cross sectional area of one square metre has a flux density of one tesla. The following formula defines this:

$$\text{Flux density B (tesla)} = \frac{\text{(magnetic flux)}}{\text{(csa)}} = \frac{\Phi}{A} \text{ (Webers/m}^2\text{)}$$

Electromagnets

An 'electromagnet' is simply the magnetic effect caused by an electric current flowing through a conductor. This usually disappears when the current stops, making it a temporary magnet. The only exception to this is when a current has produced a magnetic radial field around the conductor and this field is so strong that it has magnetised a magnetic material, such as a soft iron, close by. For most conductors the magnetic field appears as concentric circles around its whole length.

For an electronic charge to produce a magnetic field, it must be moving. In other words, when the charge is moving (i.e. a current is flowing in the conductor), a radial magnetic field is produced around the conductor. When the charge is not moving (the current stops flowing), no magnetic field is created. The direction of the field depends on the direction of the current.

You can visualise the direction of magnetic flux by thinking of the 'Screw Rule'. Imagine a right-hand threaded screw being screwed into a wall. The tip of the screw (going into the wall) represents the direction of the current and the clockwise direction of the turn represents the direction of the magnetic flux.

Remember
Like magnetic poles repel each other and unlike poles attract.

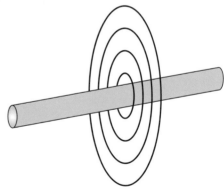

Figure 3.12 Lines of magnetic force set up around a conductor

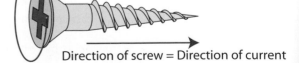

Rotation of screw = Rotation of magnetic field

Direction of screw = Direction of current

Figure 3.13 The 'Screw rule'

Solenoids and relays

A solenoid is a long hollow cylinder with a uniform coil of wire wound around it. When an electric current is flowed through this, a magnetic field is created inside the cylinder.

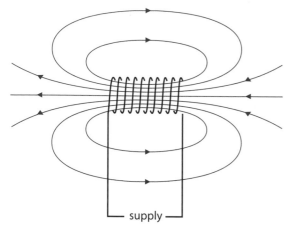

Figure 3.14 Magnetic field of a solenoid

Solenoids usually have a length several times its diameter. The magnetic field created inside the cylinder is uniform, with this uniformity increasing with the ratio of the length to the diameter.

This magnetic field is similar, in principle, to a bar magnet. The force can be used to move levers or open door latches. When used with alternating current it is most often used within door bells.

We can use the product of current flow to produce a magnetic field in the design and construction of relays and contactors which are an integeral part of switching large load circuits. Relays and contactors isolate high-current circuits from low-current circuits as in, for example, controlling lights in a sports centre via a 5 A switch in reception. When choosing a relay there are several things to consider:

- **Coil voltage** – This indicates how much voltage (230V, 24V etc) and what kind of supply (a.c. or d.c.) must be applied to energise the coil.
- **Contact rating** – This simply indicates how heavy a load the relay can control before breaking. (1 amp or 30 amps for example)
- **Contact arrangement** – Many different kinds of switch are available commercially. The geometry of the contacts indicates how many poles there are and how these are normally open (NO) and those that are normally closed (NC). Normally open or closed means when the coil of the relay or contactor is not energised. When it does become energised then the coil opens or closes the contacts from there NO or NC position.

Alternating current

Alternating current (a.c.) is a flow of electrons, which rises to a maximum value in one direction and then falls back to zero. It then repeats the process in the opposite direction. The flow of electrons alternates. This is because the voltage changes in magnitude and direction, and this drives the circuit.

This journey taken is called a cycle. The number of cycles that occur every second is the **frequency** and this is measured in hertz (Hz). This can be drawn as a **sine wave** and, if there were only resistance in the circuit, would have the same starting and finishing points for the current and voltage. They are said to be **in phase**.

Values of an alternating waveform

If we look at the graph of a sine wave, there are several values that can be measured:

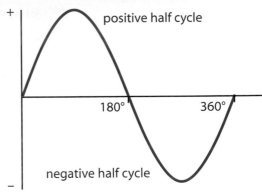

Figure 3.15 Sine wave

- Instantaneous value. This is the value at any point on the graph, varying between zero and peak value.
- Average value. Using equally spaced intervals in the cycle (say every 30 degrees) we could take a measurement of current or voltage as an instantaneous value. To find the average we would add together all the instantaneous values and then divide by the number of values used. For a sine wave only:

   Average current or voltage = Maximum (peak) current or voltage × 0.637
- Peak value. This is the highest value of current or voltage in either the positive or negative direction.
- Peak to peak value is generally of interest for the voltage, being twice the peak voltage.

In d.c. circuits, the power delivered to a resistor is given by the product of the voltage across the element and the current through it (P = VI). However, this is only true of the instantaneous power to a resistor in an a.c. circuit. In most cases the instantaneous power is of little interest, and it is the equivalent power that would create the same amount of heat as a direct current that we want to know. This is the **root mean square (r.m.s.)** value of the voltage. It is related to the peak voltage or current by:

$$\textbf{V}_{\textbf{r.m.s.}} = \textbf{V}_{\textbf{max}} \times \textbf{0.707 and } \textbf{I}_{\textbf{r.m.s.}} = \textbf{I}_{\textbf{max}} \times \textbf{0.707}$$

Alternatively $\textbf{V}_{\textbf{max}} = \textbf{V}_{\textbf{r.m.s.}} \times \textbf{1.414 and } \textbf{I}_{\textbf{max}} = \textbf{I}_{\textbf{r.m.s.}} \times \textbf{1.414}$

Frequency and period

The amount of time taken for the waveform to complete one full cycle is known as the periodic time (T) or period. Therefore, if 50 cycles are produced in one second, one cycle must be produced in a fiftieth of one second. This relationship is expressed using the following equations:

$$\textbf{Frequency (f)} = \frac{1}{\textbf{Periodic time}} = \frac{1}{\textbf{T}} \quad \text{or } \textbf{Periodic time (T)} = \frac{1}{\textbf{Frequency}} = \frac{1}{\textbf{f}}$$

Phasor representation

We can represent voltage and current by straight lines, called phasors, the length of which equate to the magnitude of the voltage or current. Only in a purely resistive circuit do the sine curves for voltage and current start and finish at the same time. Because of inductance and capacitance in a circuit, the current may either lag or lead the voltage (see below). We can represent this by drawing the phasors at different angles to represent this lead or lag.

When we use phasor diagrams, the chosen alternating quantity (current or voltage) is drawn horizontally and is known as the reference. When choosing the reference phasor, it makes sense to use a quantity that has the same value at all parts of the circuit. For example, in a series circuit the same current flows in each part of the circuit, therefore use current as the reference phasor. In a parallel circuit the voltage is the same through each branch of the circuit and therefore we use voltage as the reference phasor.

Inductors, inductance and inductive reactance

An alternating current is producing a continually changing magnetic field. If the conductor is in the form of a coil like a solenoid, this creates an e.m.f. that attempts to oppose the current that is flowing. This is called **inductance (L)**, **measured in henrys (H)** and a component designed to use inductance is called an **inductor**. All circuits contain inductance, some intentional and some of it unwanted. The filament in a light bulb is a very fine coil of wire. When it is heated by an alternating current there is both resistance and inductance.

The induction of a coil can be changed by:

- increasing or decreasing the number of turns in the reel
- altering the diameter of the coil
- altering the conductor of the coil
- altering the core material of the coil (e.g. air, iron, steel).

If we wrap a separate coil around a solenoid, so that it is also within the same magnetic field, the e.m.f driving the current in the first coil induces an e.m.f. in the secondary coil, its value dictated by the relative number of turns in each coil. We use this principle in a transformer.

With an inductive load the voltage and current become **'out of phase'** with each other. This is because the induced e.m.f., which opposes the direction of the applied voltage, is forcing the flow of electrons (current) to fall behind the force pushing them (voltage). However, over one full cycle we would see that no power is consumed. **When this happens it is known as possessing a lagging phase angle or power factor.**

The sine waves and phasor diagrams are shown here:

If we could produce a purely inductive load, the current would lag the voltage by 90° and power factor would be 1.0. However, in reality this is not possible as every coil is made of wire and that wire will have a resistance. Hence, the lag would be less than 90°.

This limiting effect to the current flow in an inductor is called **inductive reactance measured in ohms**, which we are able to calculate with the formula:

$$X_L = 2\pi fL \ (\Omega)$$

Where:

X_L = inductive reactance (ohms – Ω)
f = supply frequency (hertz – Hz)
L = circuit inductance (henrys – H)
π = 3.142

Capacitors, capacitance and capacitive reactance

A **capacitor** is a component that stores electric charge when a potential difference (p.d.) is applied across it. It is said to have **capacitance (C)**.

The simplest capacitor is two metal plates separated by a small air gap and inserted into a circuit. If inserted into a d.c. circuit, electrons will collect very rapidly on one plate and be removed from the other until the potential difference equals the supply voltage, when the current will cease. The charge will remain unless the plates are reconnected to give a circuit through which the charge can flow around to the other plate to cancel the potential difference.

When a capacitor is connected to an a.c. supply, it is continuously storing then discharging a charge as the supply moves through its positive and negative cycles. It takes time for the charge to build up in each direction and this causes the voltage to lag behind the current but the energy that is being stored is then given back to the circuit as it discharges. This means that, in a purely capacitive circuit, the current leads the voltage by a 90° phase angle but, as with the inductor, no power is consumed.

To store any worthwhile charge the surface area of the capacitor plates has to be very large. It is also improved if the plates are very close together and separated by an insulating material called a **dielectric**. Hence the plates in most capacitors are rolled up around a dielectric to give a large surface area in a small circuit component. **Capacitance is measured in farads (F)** but practical capacitors are usually in microfarads (μF), that is millionths of a farad or even smaller.

The sine wave and phasors used to represent this inductive circuit would look like this

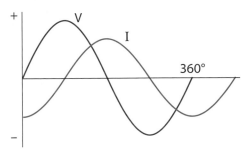

If we represented this as a phasor diagram we end up with

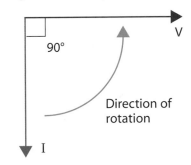

Figure 3.16 Sine wave and phasor diagrams for a purely inductive circuit

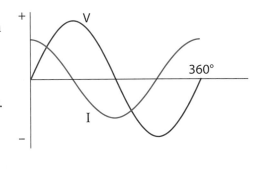

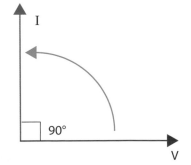

Figure 3.17 Sine wave and phasor diagrams for a purely capacitive circuit

The opposition to the flow of alternating current by a capacitor is termed **capacitive reactance**, which like inductive reactance is measured in ohms and calculated using the formula:

$$X_C = \frac{1}{2\pi fC} \ (\Omega)$$

Where:

X_C = capacitive reactance (ohms – Ω)
f = supply frequency (hertz – Hz)
C = circuit **capacitance** (farads – F)
π = 3.142

Impedance

An a.c. circuit is likely to contain components that have a mix of resistance, capacitance and inductance offering opposition to the flow of current.

- In a circuit containing only resistance, the voltage and current are in phase with each other.
- In a purely inductive circuit, inductive reactance (X_L) would cause the current to lag the voltage by 90°.
- In a purely capacitive circuit, capacitive reactance (X_C) would cause the current to lead the voltage by 90°.

In circuits containing a combination of these components the total opposition to current is called the **impedance (Z)** of the circuit. Ohm's Law then becomes V = IZ, where Z is a combination of R, X_L and X_C in the circuit. If we combine all these as phasor diagrams, including their individual lags and leads, we can calculate a magnitude for Z and the resultant lag or lead for the whole circuit. This is called the **phase angle** (usually represented by the Greek letter Φ (pronounced phi)). The calculations can either be done using Pythagoras' theorem for right angle triangles or by accurate drawing of the phasor diagrams.

If we take the cosine of this angle, we get the **power factor (PF)**. If the circuit was purely resistive then there would be no lag or lead, the phase angle would then be zero and cos Φ = 1. Therefore the power factor = 1. In a purely inductive or capacitive circuit the phase angle would be 90° and cos Φ = 0. Therefore the power factor = 0. In an actual a.c. circuit there will always be some reactance, which will give a power factor somewhere between 0 and 1.

Power in a.c. circuits

Combining all of the above, we can say that in a.c. circuits:

- The power consumed by a resistor is dissipated in heat and not returned to the source. This is called the **true power** or active power. This is measured in watts (W), and is expressed by the symbol P.
- The energy stored in the magnetic field of an **inductor**, or the plates of a **capacitor**, is called **reactive power** (also known as watt-less power)

and is returned to the source when the current changes direction. This is measured in reactive volt-amps (VAr) and is expressed by the symbol Q.

- The power in an a.c. circuit is the sum of true power and reactive power. This is called the **apparent power**. This is measured in volt-amps (VA) and is expressed by the symbol S.
- True power is equal to apparent power in a purely resistive circuit because the voltage and current are in phase. Voltage and current are also in phase in a circuit containing equal values of inductive reactance and capacitive reactance. If the voltage and current are 90° out of phase, as would be the case in a purely capacitive or purely inductive circuit, the average value of true power is equal to zero. There are high positive and negative peak values of power, which can be important, but when added together the result is zero.

Apparent power is measured in volt-amps (VA) and has the formula **P = VI**. True power is measured in watts and has the formula **P = VI cos Ø**, where Ø is the phase angle and cos Ø = power factor.

Power factor is often a number less than 1.0, and is used to represent the relationship between the apparent power of a circuit and the true power of that circuit. In other words:

$$\textbf{Power Factor (PF)} = \frac{\textbf{True Power (TP)}}{\textbf{Apparent Power (AP)}} \quad \text{or} \quad \textbf{PF} = \frac{\textbf{TP}}{\textbf{AP}}$$

Power factor has no units, it is a number. The lower the power factor of a circuit, the higher the current needed to supply the load's power requirement.

The power triangle

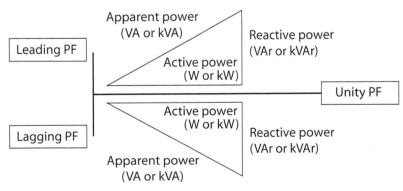

Figure 3.18 The power triangle

As for impedance, we can use Pythagoras' theorem to help us calculate the different power components within a circuit. We do so by using Pythagoras' formula as follows:

$$(VA)^2 = (W)^2 + (VAr)^2$$

Definition

True or active power – the rate at which energy is used.

Apparent power – in an a.c. circuit the sum of the true or active power and the reactive power.

Instruments and measurement

Electricians must be able to use instruments to measure electrical quantities. The most common quantities and instruments are shown in Table 3.06, though normally a multi-meter is used, which combines some or all of these instrument capabilities. If a multi-meter is used it must be set to read the correct quantity before connection to a circuit.

Property	Instrument
Current	Ammeter
Voltage	Voltmeter
Resistance	Ohmmeter
Power	Wattmeter

Table 3.06 Electrical quantities and measuring instruments

Measuring current (ammeter)

An ammeter is connected in series in a circuit, so that the current to be measured passes through it. It must have a very low resistance or it would give a false reading.

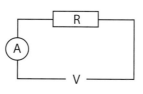

Figure 3.19 Ammeter in circuit

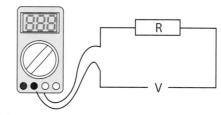

Figure 3.20 Multi-meter set to measure current

Measuring voltage (voltmeter)

A voltmeter measures the potential difference between two points (for instance, across the two connections of a resistor). The voltmeter is connected in parallel across the load or circuit to be measured. Its internal resistance must be very high to get accurate readings.

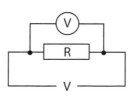

Figure 3.21 Voltmeter in circuit

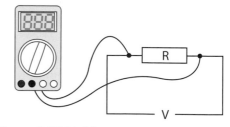

Figure 3.22 Multi-meter set to measure voltage

Measuring resistance

Measuring the resistance of part of a circuit, when it remains connected, is usually done by calculation from instrument readings (ammeter/voltmeter) or from other known resistance values. If we know the voltage across a part of the circuit and the current flowing through it, then we can apply Ohm's Law to find the resistance:

$$R = \frac{V \text{ (voltmeter)}}{I \text{ (ammeter)}}$$

An ohmmeter has its own internal supply (battery) and can be used to take a measurement directly under isolation. The current, which then flows through the meter, is dependent upon the value of the resistance under scrutiny.

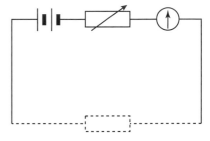

The dotted line in Figure 3.23 indicates the circuit under test. All other components are internal to the meter. In practice, we often need a long 'wandering' test lead to perform such a test. If so, we must deduct the resistance of the test lead from the circuit resistance.

Figure 3.23 Ohmmeter

Loading errors

A measuring instrument occasionally has a drastic effect on a circuit. These are known as loading errors. They can be reduced by using voltmeters with very high internal resistance. Otherwise the error may need to be calculated and readings adjusted.

Meter displays

There are two types of display, **analogue** and **digital**. Analogue meters have a needle moving around a calibrated scale, whereas digital meters show results as numeric values via a liquid crystal or LED display.

The analogue meter is still common, especially for continuity/insulation resistance testers, but are being replaced by digital meters. Most modern digital meters are based on semiconductors and consequently have very high impedance, making them ideal for accurate readings and good for use with electronic circuits. As they have no moving parts they are usually more suited to rugged site conditions than the analogue style.

Analogue meter

Digital meter

Transformers

A transformer is an electronic device that transfers energy from one circuit to another via a magnetic field, known as a magnetic coupling. It is used on an a.c. supply to transfer one level of voltage to another. A transformer is made from two or more coupled wirings around a magnetic core.

A conductor carrying a changing current creates a magnetic field. This induces an e.m.f. in the secondary coil, driving a current through the secondary coil and onto a circuit. This process is known as **mutual inductance**.

Although there are many sizes and designs of transformers they all share these basic principles.

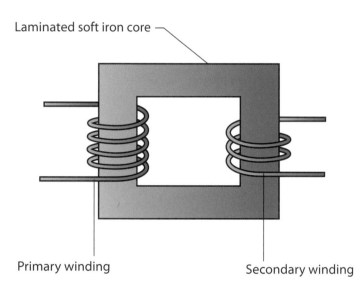

Laminated soft iron core

Primary winding

Secondary winding

Figure 3.24 Double wound transformer

There are two possible functions of a transformer. One is to step-up the input voltage (primary voltage) and the other is to step-down the input voltage. The output voltage is known as the secondary output. A transformer winding is a series of turns of copper conductor spun or wrapped around a core of some description. The transformer shown in Figure 3.24 is a step down transformer in the ratio of 2:1. This is because there is half the number of windings on the secondary winding than there is on the primary winding.

If the transformer shown had more windings on the secondary winding than on the primary winding the device would be called a step-up transformer. There is a direct relationship between transformer windings or number of turns (N), volts (V) and current (I). The following ratio is useful to remember. Note, that I_s is on top of the ratio which differs in N_p and V_p.

$$\frac{V_{Primary}}{V_{Secondary}} = \frac{N_{Primary}}{N_{Secondary}} = \frac{I_{Secondary}}{I_{Primary}}$$

There are no moving parts between the windings making the transformer very efficient. As with all systems, machines and devices there are losses

Remember

Transformers can be both step-up and step-down.

which in most cases will form heat. Losses in transformer terms are called "Copper", "Iron" and "Hysteresis". Copper losses are simply a result of current and voltage flowing in a conductor. Iron loss arises within the laminated steel core of the transformer and is due to the energy consumed in hysteresis and eddy currents within the transformer core as it goes through alternating magnetic cycles. Hysteresis is where the material of the core retains and loses flux as current in the primary windings peaks plus and minus of the sinewave. These losses can be reduced by using copper conductor of low resistivity (copper losses I^2R) and laminating the core to minimise Hysteresis losses.

Did you know?

High power transformers can also be fan cooled.

Laminations

Within the core of a transformer **eddy currents** are induced which generate heat, leading to a loss of power. This can damage the insulation on conductors. To reduce this effect, the core is constructed from insulated, laminated, soft-iron segments. The thinner these layers of lamination, the less energy is lost to eddy currents.

Enclosures

Heat losses are reduced by allowing an air gap around the windings and cooling fins. Large and high power transformers are usually encased within oil-filled steel enclosures. The oil circulates through cooling tubes to help absorb the heat and is also fire resistant.

Separate Extra Low Voltage (SELV)

BS 7671 requires that the electricians take extra precautions when there is an increased risk of electric shock to humans. Protection is provided from this by transforming the voltage to safe levels, using isolating transformers. The method is known as Separate Extra Low Voltage (SELV). This prevents the voltage from exceeding 50 V a.c. or 120 V d.c. under fault conditions. The transformer must be a safely isolating, double wound transformer complying with BS EN 61558-2-6.

Transmission of energy

Transformers are essential for the transmission of energy on the National Grid. The transformer that supplies your home is likely to be 11 kV on the primary with a 400/230 V secondary, for local distribution. That transformer will be rated in kVA.

We use a.c. current in transmitting energy because transformers allow us to step from higher to lower voltage, or vice-versa, more efficiently than d.c. Transmitting at high voltage reduces power losses and allows smaller currents to flow, so we can use smaller cables and thus reduce costs.

A.c. motor design allows us to utilise the electromagnetic induction effect more efficiently than with d.c. designs, as a.c. makes it easy to produce a magnetic field where the direction changes rapidly (i.e. 50 times per second).

Distribution of electricity

The two key points to remember are generation and transmission.

Generation

Electricity is generated by turning the shaft of an a.c. generator (the 3-phase alternator) via the kinetic energy supplied from steam turbines. The turbine energy is usually obtained from fossil fuels, such as coal, oil and gas, or nuclear power. There is also an increasing interest in wind turbines.

Transmission

The voltage generated from the average alternator supplying the National Grid system is about 25 kV. This must then be transformed for various applications, such as:

- 400 kV and 275 kV for the super grid system
- 132kV for the grid
- 66 and 33 kV for secondary transmission
- 33 k V and 11 k V for high voltage distribution
- 400 V commercial supplies
- 230 V for domestic consumers.

Electric current is transmitted through the National Grid via steel-cored aluminium conductors suspended from pylons. This is because:

- it is easier to suspend cables than lay them underground
- air is a relatively cheap insulator
- air acts as a coolant for the heat generated in the transmission line cabling.

Three-Line (phase) distribution

A three line (phase) system simply generates a three-line supply using three coils placed 120° apart on a rotating shaft. This is rotated inside a permanent magnetic field.

The advantages of three-line systems over single-phase systems include a reduction in material costs. This is because for line-to-line comparison of power transmission, three-phase systems require conductors with smaller cross-sectional areas. They also allow for a 4-wire system (star connection) where the loads are not balanced.

Delta connection

This is used when we have a balanced load (i.e. there is no need for neutral connectors, so only three wires used). Its uses include power transmission and winding connection for 3-phase motors.

Star connection

This is used when we have an unbalanced load (i.e. one in which the current in each of the phases is different). It is a neutral connection with a centre tapped earth.

Electrical generators and motors

We know that there is a magnetic field set up around any current carrying conductor. If this field is changing there is a force created, which can cause a conductor to move. This principle is used in motors and generators.

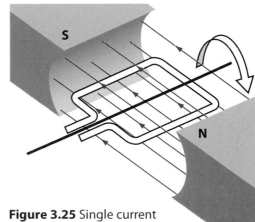

The effects of magnetism

If a conductor in the form of a loop is mounted so that it could rotate between a pair of N and S permanent magnet poles, it would look like Figure 3.25.

Figure 3.25 Single current carrying loop in a magnetic field

However, if the loop is rotated, it will start to cut through the lines of flux, which induces an e.m.f. and, if the loop is part of a circuit, a current will flow. The size of the e.m.f. (and the current, if it flows) varies from zero, to a peak value when the coil is at 90° to the magnetic field, back to zero and then repeats the process with the e.m.f. generated in the opposite direction. If this is plotted as a graph, one full 360 degree revolution (cycle) of the loop would be a sine wave.

Generators/alternators

If the coil is connected to an outside circuit via slip rings, the coil would be acting as a generator, producing an alternating output current. It is often referred to as an alternator. In practice, many coils are wound around a shaft (an armature) and there may be several 'pole pairs' creating the magnetic field. The latter may be permanent magnets, or some of the current generated may be fed back to create electromagnets. The efficiency of the machine is heavily dependent on the arrangements of the coils and the shape and materials used to form the rotating part, the armature, and the fixed part, the yoke.

If, instead of slip rings, the coils are connected to an outside circuit via a 'commutator', which reverses the contacts each time the coil goes through 180°, the current will always be in the same direction. We now have a d.c. generator, though the current is still going from zero to a peak value and back again twice every revolution, so it is a bit lumpy! However, this can be smoothed out to create a steady direct current.

A variety of sources can be used mechanically to turn the generator's coils (wound on the armature) such as steam, wind, waterfall or petrol/diesel driven motors.

Electric motors

If a current is flowing in a coil in a changing magnetic field the reverse effect occurs – there is a force on the coil which will try to rotate it. The effect is still there if it is the current that is changing and the magnetic field that is fixed, or both can be varying. In theory, any alternator can be used as a motor by driving current through it and causing the armature to rotate. In practice, various arrangements of coils and magnetic fields are used to produce motors with different capabilities, both a.c. and d.c.

Short answer questions

1. Describe the difference between mass and weight and the relationship between the two.
2. Describe the basic construction of an atom. What are the three main parts of the atom and the relationship between these three different types of particle?
3. Describe how electricity responds to:
   a. a conductor
   b. an insulator
4. State and describe in detail the three main sources of electromotive force (e.m.f.).
5. Describe the four main factors that influence the resistance of an object.
6. What is the difference between a permanent magnet and an electromagnet?
7. Explain what frequency means in relation to alternating current (a.c.).
8. What are three main types of power in an a.c. circuit and how are these measured?
9. What are different functions of a voltmeter and ammeter?
10. Describe and explain the basic function of a transformer.
11. Explain the uses of star and delta connections.
12. How does magnetism affect the function of a motor?

Multiple choice questions

1. If an object is moved then work is said to be done. Therefore, if a distribution board has a mass of 30 kg, how much work is done when it is moved 5 m (remember the force of gravity):
   a. 14.71 kJ
   b. 0.0654 J
   c. 15.29 J
   d. 1471.5 J

2. The value of resistance between the opposite faces of a 1mm cube of conductive material is known as its Resistivity. We can therefore establish the resistance (R) of a length of conductor using which of the following formulae:
   a. $R = \dfrac{\rho \times l}{a}$
   b. $R = \rho \times l \times a$
   c. $R = a\sqrt{\rho \times l}$
   d. $R = a \times l \sqrt{\rho}$

3. The rotation of a coil in a permanent magnetic field is the basis of the a.c. generator. Over the full 360° of revolution we can show the e.m.f. generated in the rotating coil as a sine wave. At 90° of rotation what value would the voltage be on the sine wave:
   a. the frequency
   b. r.m.s. value
   c. the average value
   d. peak value

4. If we know the input energy and output energy of a machine, we can therefore calculate the percentage efficiency of the machine by which formula:
   a. $Efficiency = Input\ energy \times 100 \times Output\ energy$
   b. $Efficiency = \left(\dfrac{Output\ energy}{Input\ energy}\right) \times 100$
   c. $Efficiency = Output\ energy \sqrt{Input\ energy} \times 100$
   d. $Efficiency = Input\ energy \sqrt{Input\ energy} \times 100$

5. The force that acts on a current carrying conductor within a magnetic field depends upon:
 a. *Flux density, conductor material and voltage*
 b. *Flux density, conductor material and current*
 c. *Flux density, conductor length and current*
 d. *Flux density, conductor c.s.a. and current*

6. Atoms consist of several smaller particles. Which one of these particles possesses a negative charge?
 a. *neutron*
 b. *electron*
 c. *ion*
 d. *proton*

7. Electric current is the movement or flow of:
 a. *negatively charged particles*
 b. *positively charged particles*
 c. *particles with no charge*
 d. *neutron particles*

8. A 75 W GLS filament lamp relies upon which effect of current for its operation:
 a. *movement effect*
 b. *heating effect*
 c. *magnetic effect*
 d. *chemical effect*

9. The current flowing in a circuit is directly proportional to the voltage applied and indirectly proportional to the resistance within the circuit, which formula shows this relationship:
 a. $I = R \sqrt{V}$
 b. $I = V1 \sqrt{R_2}$
 c. $I = V \sqrt{R}$
 d. $I = P \times V$

10. Electricity is transmitted at very high voltage to:
 a. *allow the installation of underground cables*
 b. *increase the size of the transmission line conductors*
 c. *assist fault diagnosis techniques in the event of a fault*
 d. *minimise power losses in the transmission system*

11. Power (Joules per second) is the rate of doing work. Therefore if a distribution board has a mass of 40 kg and is moved 20 m and it took 30 s to do this, the power would be:
 a. *261.6 W*
 b. *800 W*
 c. *7848 W*
 d. *147.15 W*

12. A single-phase transformer with 3000 primary turns and 600 secondary turns is fed from a 230 volt a.c. supply. What will the volts per turn in the secondary be ?
 a. *2.6 V*
 b. *0.077 V*
 c. *13 V*
 d. *0.38 V*

13. Two resistors, of value 7.3 W and 4.2 W are connected in series with a 24-volt battery. What is the total current flow in this circuit?
 a. *0.11 A*
 b. *9 A*
 c. *2.086 A*
 d. *0.479 A*

14. Which of the following statements is not true:
 (a) *Total circuit resistance (R_t) in a parallel connected circuit = $R_1 + R_2$*
 (c) *The current in each branch will vary according to the resistance in each branch of a parallel circuit*
 (d) *Total circuit current (I_t) in a parallel connected circuit = $I_1 + I_2$*
 (b) *The same supply voltage is applied across each branch of a parallel circuit*

15. An electric motor supplies 5 kW of power when operating at an efficiency of 75%. What must the minimum power rating be of the motor itself?
 a. *8.75 kW*
 b. *3.75 kW*
 c. *6.66 kW*
 d. *1.33 kW*

16. A 200 Ω resistor is connected in series to a 15 V d.c. supply. The power dissipated in it will be:
    a. *1.125 W*
    b. *0.075 W*
    c. *13.33 W*
    d. *3000 W*

17. A coil has a self inductance of 4 H. If the current through it changes from 0.6 A to 0.1 A in 0.02 s, the induced back e.m.f. will be:
    a. *6.25 V*
    b. *100 V*
    c. *12 V*
    d. *20 V*

18. The magnetic flux linking 1600 turns of an electromagnet changes from 0.9 mWb to 0.6 mWb in 40 ms. The value of induced back e.m.f. will be:
    a. *12 V*
    b. *120 V*
    c. *1.2 V*
    d. *1200 V*

19. A coil of 0.16 H is connected across a 100 V 50 Hz supply. The inductive reactance of the coil will be:
    a. *0.0198 Ω*
    b. *16 Ω*
    c. *50.26 Ω*
    d. *8 Ω*

20. A capacitor of 17.9 µF is connected across a 230 V 50 Hz supply. The capacitive reactance will be:
    a. *0.17 Ω*
    b. *5.62 Ω*
    c. *177.8 Ω*
    d. *5623 Ω*

21. In a capacitive circuit:
    a. *current is lagging the voltage by 90°*
    b. *current leads the voltage by 90°*
    c. *current is in phase with the voltage*
    d. *there is a lagging power factor*

22. When electrical energy is being transmitted at 400 kV it is known as:
    a. *local distribution*
    b. *the local grid*
    c. *medium voltage transmission*
    d. *the super grid*

23. Three identical loads of 40Ω resistance are connected to a 400V 3 phase supply. If the loads are delta connected, the phase current will be
    a. *0.1 A*
    b. *5.77 A*
    c. *17.32 A*
    d. *10 A*

24. Three coils of resistance 80 Ω and inductive reactance 60 Ω are connected in delta to a 400 V 50 Hz three phase supply. The total power will be:
    a. *2217 W*
    b. *3840 W*
    c. *6000 W*
    d. *1979 W*

25. A coil has a resistance of 15 Ω and an inductive reactance of 30 Ω. What is the Power Factor of this circuit arrangement:
    a. *0.45 lagging*
    b. *0.5 lagging*
    c. *0.89 lagging*
    d. *0.45 leading*

26. A transformer having a turns ratio of 3:5 is connected to a 230 V supply. The output voltage will be:
    a. *138 V*
    b. *383 V*
    c. *460 V*
    d. *60 V*

27. The voltage supplied to the primary winding of an ideal step down transformer is 1200 V and the output voltage is 230 V. If the primary current is 6 A, what will the value of the secondary current be?

a. 5.2 A

b. 31.3 A

c. 44.14 A

d. 1.15 A

28. A three line four wire system supplies a balanced load of 10 kVA with a 0.85 P.F. What is the power consumption of this system?

a. 0.085 W

b. 11.76 W

c. 8.5 W

d. 14.72

29. A 30 Ω resistor is connected in series with a capacitor with a reactance of 40 Ω. What is the Power Factor of this circuit arrangement?

a. 0.6 leading

b. 0.6 lagging

c. 0.8 lagging

d. 0.8 leading

30. A series circuit consists of a capacitor with a reactance of 20 Ω a coil with a resistance of 30 Ω and an inductive reactance of 60 Ω. What will the circuit PF be?

a. 0.6 leading

b. 0.6 lagging

c. 0.8 lagging

d. 0.8 leading

04 Craft theory

By the end of this chapter you should be able to demonstrate your knowledge and understanding of the practical skills needed to install different wiring systems, wiring enclosures and equipment safely and in accordance with industry guidelines and the appropriate Regulations. It will cover:

- Tools and equipment
  - Hand tools
  - Power tools
  - Measuring devices
  - Safety awareness for all types of tool
- Fixings
  - Screws and bolts
  - Locking devices
  - Fixing devices
- Conductors and insulators
  - Copper and aluminium
  - Other conductor materials
  - Conductor sizes
  - Insulation
- Cable types
  - PVC insulated
  - Cable with thermosetting insulation
  - LSF cable
  - PILCSWA cable
  - Trailing cables
  - Mineral insulated copper cable (MICC)
  - FP200 cable
  - Fibre optic data cable
  - Cat (Category) 5 cable

- Installation techniques
  - Rewiring an existing building
  - Protection of cables
  - Cable support and bends
  - Installing PVC/PVC cables
  - Terminating and joining cables
  - Conduit
  - Trunking
  - Cable tray and ladders
- Switching of lighting circuits
  - Wiring with single core cable
  - Wiring with multicore cable
  - Wiring using a joint/junction box
- Rings, spurs and radials
  - Ring circuits
  - Spurs
  - Radial circuits

Tools and equipment

Hand tools

Pliers and cutters

Different types of pliers are used by electricians depending on the task, such as long nosed, bent nose, needle nose and, of course, traditional electrician's pliers.

The two most common types of cutters are side cutters and insulation strippers.

Electrician's side cutters

Insulation strippers

Screwdrivers

There are three main types:

- Flared slotted, used mostly for fastening screws. They do not normally have insulated shafts so are not suitable for electrical work.
- Parallel slotted have the same head and shaft size. The shafts may be insulated and so are suitable for electrical work.
- Cross-head (Philips or Pozidrive®) provide greater grip with the screw. The shafts may be insulated and so are suitable for electrical work.

Flared slotted screwdriver

Parallel slotted screwdriver

Cross-head screwdriver

Hammers

Three main tasks using hammers are:

- Hitting fixings directly, such as nails or cable clips. Use a ball-pein, cross-pein or claw hammer depending on how large the fixing is.
- Hitting another tool such as a chisel. Use a ball-pein hammer.
- Altering the shape of material. Use a ball-pein hammer.

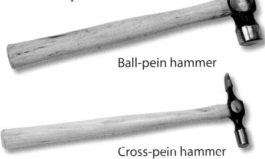

Ball-pein hammer

Cross-pein hammer

Saws

Four main types are used by electricians:

- hacksaw used for cutting metal, conduit and trunking, trayplate, etc.
- tenon saw used for cutting wood
- pad saw used for cutting a variety of materials depending on the type of blade
- flooring saw used for cutting tongues of wood flooring.

Remember

When replacing a blade the teeth must point forwards in the direction of the cutting motion.

Drills

A hand drill works by rotating the handle on the wheel.

A breast drill or carpenter's drill is a larger version of the hand drill, which allows the operator to apply pressure with the chest resting against it. It is rarely used now as effectively replaced by the power drill.

Hand drill

Wrenches, spanners and grips

These are used to loosen and tighten nuts, bolts and setscrews. They are marked with the nut size and sometimes have two ends with different sizes.

Types of spanner are:

- box spanners (square or hexagonal cylinder shape), used for recessed nuts and will grip all sides but give restricted access
- open ended spanners

Definition

Hexagon – A six sided shape.

- ring spanners with closed rings at the ends
- adjustable spanners, available for most size ranges; versatile but do not grip the nut or bolt well
- footprint wrench, used mostly for gripping conduit and conduit fittings when loosening or tightening
- vice grip, used for holding work in progress as a miniature vice
- Stillson wrench, a large version of footprint wrench.

Adjustable spanner

Vice grip

Footprint wrench

Stillson wrench

Files

These have a rough surface of hardened metal and a pointed tang to fix into a wooden or plastic handle. They are used to remove material from an object, make it smoother or change its shape. They are classified by length, cut, grade and shape.

The cut is how rough the surface is, ranging from 'bastard' (roughest) through to 'fine'; and the grade defines the hardness of the file material. Cross-sectional shape can be half-round, round, square, triangular or flat.

Surform files have a perforated blade. They are used on softer materials, such as wood and plastic, and remove material quickly without clogging.

Chisels

These are used for removing material from either wood or metal and there are a wide variety available for specific purposes. Wood chisels should only be struck with a wooden mallet. Cold chisels are used for removing metal. They are made from steel and are used by hitting them with a hammer.

Crimping tools

These are used to join conductors with special fixings. They can be hand held or, for larger conductors, can be hydraulically operated.

Power tools

There are power tools able to substitute for almost any hand tool operation. They are used where greater speed and effort is needed, but must be treated with respect and checked before using. They may be powered by mains supply, by batteries (i.e. cordless) or compressed air. On site, mains power should be via a 110 volt centre-tapped to earth transformer.

Power drills can have a hammer (percussion) action to assist in drilling into masonry, using special masonry drill bits.

Measuring devices

There are a wide range of these available. Although robust they should be handled carefully to maintain accuracy. Common types include:

- steel rules for measuring short distances
- tape measures for measuring longer distances
- laser range finders for measuring distances up to 150 metres
- spirit levels for checking horizontal and vertical alignment
- plumb bob and chalk lines to check vertical alignment and, in the case of chalk lines, mark horizontal and vertical lines.

Safety awareness for all types of tool

All tools should be treated with respect. Table 4.01 lists some basic rules for the safe use of hand and power tools.

Hand tools	Electrical tools
Always use the right tool for the job – don't make do with the nearest one.	Check that the cable is not frayed or damaged.
Keep tools clean and sharp – blunt tools are dangerous.	Check that the plug is not broken or that individual wires are not showing.
Make sure handles are secure, tight and have no splinters.	Check that mains tools (110 V or 230 V) have been properly tested (PAT tested).
Never hit a wooden handle with a hammer – use a wooden mallet.	If in doubt, don't use the tool and ask someone competent to check it out.

Table 4.01 Basic rules for safe use of tools

Some tools are particularly dangerous and should only be used if you have been taught to do so. For example, cartridge tools (nail or staple guns) and compressed air should never be pointed at anyone; and the latter should not be used to blow away dust or dirt. Compressed air can kill if it enters the body.

Fixings

There are a wide range of fixings and fastenings available. Some of the commonest are covered here.

Screws and bolts

Wood screws are used for fixing equipment to wood or, when used with rawlplugs, are used to fasten equipment to masonry.

They are specified by:

- gauge, which is the shank diameter, ranging from 12 mm to 150 mm (imperial gauges 2 to 24 are still sold)
- length up to 150 mm (6 inches), measured from the tip to the part of the head that will be flush with the surface
- type of head (Posidrive, raised head, etc.)
- type of material and finish, ferrous or non-ferrous with the former coated for rust prevention.

Clearance holes (holes larger than the screw diameter) are drilled into materials where the screw is not required to grip. Pilot holes may be drilled smaller than the screw diameter to ensure grip but reducing the danger of splitting the material.

> **Did you know?**
> Ferrous means something is made of iron or steel.

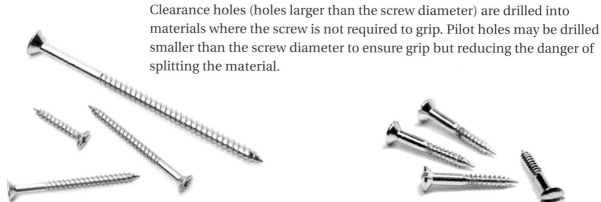

Countersunk

Raised or round head

Mirror screw head

Pan head

Self-tapping hardened steel screws are used for joining two pieces of sheet material. A hole is drilled slightly smaller than the diameter of screw, which then cuts its own thread in the material as it is screwed home.

Machine screws are threaded along the full length (unlike a bolt) and are used for fastening two pieces of metal. They are used in electrical equipment in sizes of 3.5 mm for socket fronts and 4 mm for conduit boxes.

A stud nut and washer can be used where frequent dismantling of equipment occurs. The stud is tightly fastened into a tapped hole, which remains when the nut is removed and replaced. It helps prevent stripping of threads, as can happen with machine screws.

Bolts are used in all aspects of engineering. A clearance hole must be drilled for the bolt to pass through. It is then held in place by a nut, usually with a washer.

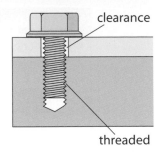

Figure 4.01 Machine screw fixing

Locking devices

These are used where vibration occurs, which would cause the fixing to become loose.

Locking device	Features and usage
Spring washer	• Similar to a coil spring. • When the nut is tightened, the washer is compressed, and because the ends of the washer are chisel-edged they dig into the nut and the component, thus preventing the nut from turning loose. • Spring washers may have either a single or double coil. • Depending on the condition, spring washers are used only once.
Locknut	• The bottom nut is tightened with a spanner. • The top nut is then tightened, and friction in the threads and between the nut faces prevents them from rotating. • Locknuts are always bevelled at the corners to ensure good setting of the faces.
Split pin	• This can be used with ordinary nuts or castle nuts (see below). • When used with ordinary nuts, ensure that the split pin is in contact with the nut when tightened. The split pin is opened out after insertion to prevent it falling out. • Split pins can be used only once. • The bolt is left 2 to 3 threads longer for drilling.
Castle nut	• The castle nut has a cylindrical extension with grooves. • The nut is tightened, the stud is drilled opposite a groove, then the split pin is passed through the nut and the stud prevents the nut from turning. The split pin is opened out after insertion to prevent it falling out. • Split pins can be used only once.

Locking device	Features and usage
Simmonds locknut	• The Simmonds nut has a nylon insert. • When the nut is screwed down the threads on the end of the stud bite into the nylon. • Friction keeps the nut tightened. • This nut can be used only once.
Serrated washer	• When the nut is tightened, the serration is flattened out, causing increased friction between the faces thus preventing rotation. • This type of washer can be used only once.
Tab washer	• This is a more positive type of locking device. • When the nut is tightened, one tab is bent up onto the flat side of the nut and the other tab is bent over the edge of the component. • Tab washers can be used only once – they tend to fracture when straightened out and re-bent.

Figure 4.02 Locking devices

Fixing devices

These are items of equipment used to help fasten components to a structure. A hole is drilled, using the correct drill size and type for the device to be used and the material into which the fixing is going. The fixing is then inserted and fastened.

Light fixings are used for fastening lightweight pieces to structures, and for partition walls and thin sheet materials.

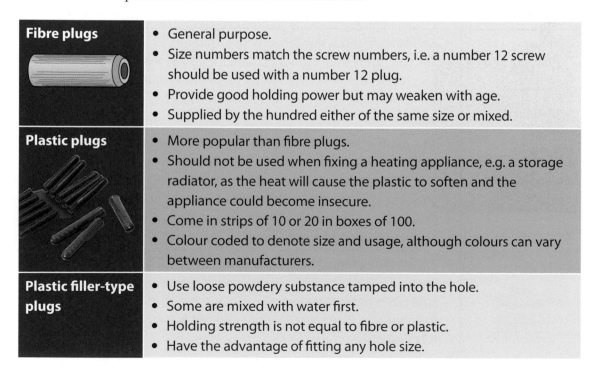

Fibre plugs	• General purpose. • Size numbers match the screw numbers, i.e. a number 12 screw should be used with a number 12 plug. • Provide good holding power but may weaken with age. • Supplied by the hundred either of the same size or mixed.
Plastic plugs	• More popular than fibre plugs. • Should not be used when fixing a heating appliance, e.g. a storage radiator, as the heat will cause the plastic to soften and the appliance could become insecure. • Come in strips of 10 or 20 in boxes of 100. • Colour coded to denote size and usage, although colours can vary between manufacturers.
Plastic filler-type plugs	• Use loose powdery substance tamped into the hole. • Some are mixed with water first. • Holding strength is not equal to fibre or plastic. • Have the advantage of fitting any hole size.

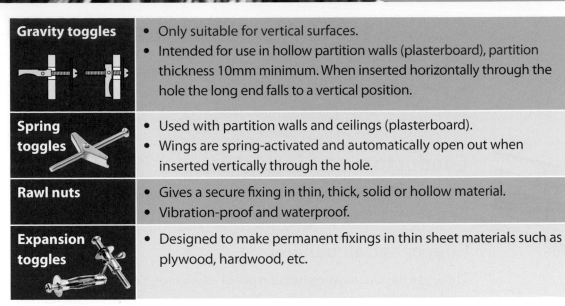

Gravity toggles	• Only suitable for vertical surfaces. • Intended for use in hollow partition walls (plasterboard), partition thickness 10mm minimum. When inserted horizontally through the hole the long end falls to a vertical position.
Spring toggles	• Used with partition walls and ceilings (plasterboard). • Wings are spring-activated and automatically open out when inserted vertically through the hole.
Rawl nuts	• Gives a secure fixing in thin, thick, solid or hollow material. • Vibration-proof and waterproof.
Expansion toggles	• Designed to make permanent fixings in thin sheet materials such as plywood, hardwood, etc.

Figure 4.03 Light fixing devices

Heavy fixing devices are used for heavier jobs, such as a large fuse board. Figure 4.04 should be seen as a guide and further information obtained on the most appropriate fixing for the task prior to use.

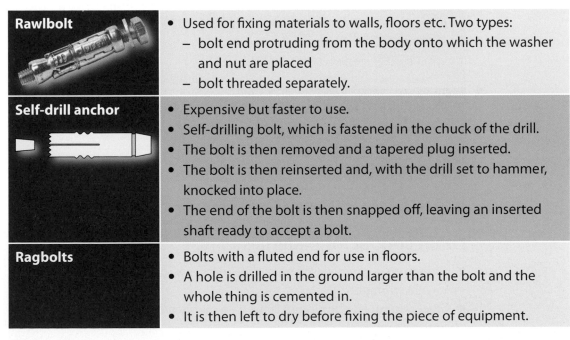

Rawlbolt	• Used for fixing materials to walls, floors etc. Two types:
	  – bolt end protruding from the body onto which the washer and nut are placed
	  – bolt threaded separately.

Self-drill anchor	• Expensive but faster to use. • Self-drilling bolt, which is fastened in the chuck of the drill. • The bolt is then removed and a tapered plug inserted. • The bolt is then reinserted and, with the drill set to hammer, knocked into place. • The end of the bolt is then snapped off, leaving an inserted shaft ready to accept a bolt.
Ragbolts	• Bolts with a fluted end for use in floors. • A hole is drilled in the ground larger than the bolt and the whole thing is cemented in. • It is then left to dry before fixing the piece of equipment.

Figure 4.04 Heavy fixing devices

Miscellaneous fixings include:

- roundhead nail for general woodwork
- oval nail for general woodwork (will not split timber)
- brad for floorboard fastening (difficult to remove)

- galvanised clout nail for fixing channelling over cables before plastering
- panel pin used with buckle clips to fasten cables or for hardboard
- masonry nail used with cable clips to fix into masonry
- rivet used to join two pieces of thin sheet metal together.

The Gripple is a suspension system used for hanging ceilings or cable trays.

Figure 4.05 Gripple supporting a basket style cable tray

Conductors and insulators

A conductor is a material with electrons loosely attached to the nucleus so they can move freely from one atom to another (see Chapter 3).

Copper and aluminium

These are the two most common types of conductor. Copper is generally used below 16 mm^2 cross section. Above that size, copper or aluminium can be used. The advantages and disadvantages are compared in Table 4.02.

Conductor	Advantages	Disadvantages
Copper	<ul><li>easier to joint and terminate</li><li>smaller cross-sectional area for given current rating</li></ul>	<ul><li>more costly</li><li>heavier</li></ul>
Aluminium	<ul><li>cheaper</li><li>lighter</li></ul>	<ul><li>bulkier for given current rating</li><li>not recommended for use in hazardous areas</li></ul>

Table 4.02 Copper and aluminium conductors compared

Other conductor materials

- Cadmium copper is used on overhead lines because of its greater tensile strength.
- Steel reinforced aluminium is used on overhead lines covering long distances.
- Silver (and even gold) is used where extremely good conductivity is required but it is very expensive.
- Copperclad (copper covered aluminium) has some properties of both (i.e. good conductivity of copper and the lightness of aluminium) but is difficult to terminate.

All conductors are either solid or stranded, stranded ones being more expensive but more flexible.

Conductor sizes

The size of conductors to be used is determined by several factors:

- current to be carried both now and possibly in the future
- ambient temperature
- grouping with other cables
- type of circuit protection (fuse, MCB, etc.)
- how installed
- voltage drop (maximum 3 per cent of the nominal supply voltage for lighting and 5 per cent for power circuits).

Insulation

An insulator is a material with electrons tightly attached to its nucleus preventing free movement from one atom to another. It is used to separate conductors and conductive materials, which should not be connected to one another.

Common types of cable insulation and their properties are as follows:

- **PVC (polyvinyl chloride)** – tough, cheap and flexible but no good below 0°C or above 60°C. When burnt the fumes are toxic.
- **Synthetic rubbers** – including vulcanised butyl rubber. They can withstand higher temperatures and are used for immersion heaters, boilers, etc.
- **Silicon rubber** – can withstand high temperatures (up to 200°C) and is used on FP200 cable (see below).
- **Magnesium oxide** – a white powder used in MICC cables (see below), which can withstand temperatures approaching 2800°C. It is hygroscopic (i.e. absorbs water), so needs to be sealed.
- **Phenol-formaldehyde** – a thermosetting polymer, which is hard and used for making sockets, light switches, consumer units, etc.

Cable insulation is identified by colour codes. These changed with effect 1 April 2004. Table 4.03 shows the current colours in accordance with BS 7671.

Function	Colour
Protective conductors	Green and yellow
Functional earthing conductor	Cream
a.c. power circuit[1]	
Phase of single-phase circuit	Brown
Neutral of single- or three-phase circuit	Blue
Phase 1 of three-phase a.c. circuit	Brown
Phase 2 of three-phase a.c. circuit	Black
Phase 3 of three-phase a.c. circuit	Grey

Two-wire unearthed d.c. power circuit	
Positive of two-wire circuit	Brown
Negative of two-wire circuit	Grey

Two-wire earthed d.c. power circuit	
Positive (of negative earthed) circuit	Brown
Negative (of negative earthed) circuit	Blue
Positive (of positive earthed) circuit	Blue
Negative (of positive earthed) circuit	Grey

Three-wire d.c. power circuit	
Outer positive of two-wire circuit derived from three-wire system	Brown
Outer negative of two-wire circuit derived from three-wire system	Grey
Positive of three-wire circuit	Brown
Mid-wire of three-wire circuit[2]	Blue
Negative of three-wire circuit	Grey

Control circuits, extra low voltage (ELV) and other applications	Brown, black, red, orange, yellow, violet, grey, white, pink or turquoise
Phase conductor	

Neutral or mid-wire[3]	Blue

NOTES

[1] Power circuits include lighting circuits.

[2] Only the middle wire of three-wire circuits may be earthed.

[3] An earthed Protected extra low voltage (PELV) conductor is blue.

Table 4.03 Identification of conductors in accordance with BS 7671

Table 4.04 shows the old colours, which may still be found in existing installations.

Conductor	Old colour
Phase	Red
Neutral	Black
Protective conductor	Green and yellow
Phase one	Red

Phase two	Yellow
Phase three	Blue
Neutral	Black
Protective conductor	Green and yellow

Table 4.04 Old conductor insulation colours

Cable types

Cable is available to meet a range of conditions. These include:

- ambient temperature (i.e. surrounding temperature, whether high or low)
- surrounding moisture (water and electricity do not mix!)
- electrolytic action
- presence of corrosive substances (e.g. lime in cement, plaster undercoats, magnesium chloride, acidic woods like oak)
- possibility of damage by animals, especially on farms
- exposure to direct sunlight, which causes PVC cable to dry out and crack
- mechanical stresses when suspended between buildings (use a supporting catenary wire).

Table 4.05 gives the maximum loads that flexible cables can carry.

Table 4F3A Flexible cords weight support			
Conductor (cross-sectional area mm²)	**Current carrying capacity**		**Maximum mass**
	1-phase a.c.	**3-phase a.c.**	
0.5	3 A	3 A	2 kg
0.75	6 A	6 A	3 kg
1	10 A	10 A	5 kg
1.25	13 A	10 A	5 kg
1.5	16 A	16 A	5 kg
2.5	25 A	20 A	5 kg
4	32 A	25 A	5 kg

Table 4.05 Maximum loads on flexible cables

Mechanical damage can be protected against by an outer sheath, conduit, trunking, etc.

1. Road crossing accessible to vehicles

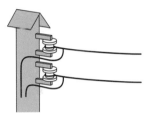

All methods of suspension 5.8 m minimum above ground

2. Accessible to vehicles but not a road crossing

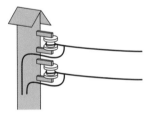

All methods of suspension 5.2 m minimum above ground

3. Inaccessible to vehicles

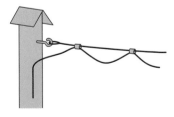

PVC cables supported by a catenary wire. 3.5 m minimum above ground

Figure 4.06 Suspension heights for cables

PVC insulated

This is the most popular cabling as it is tough, cheap and easy to work with, though has limitations in conditions of excessive heat or cold and may need mechanical protection in some situations. Main PVC variants available are:

- **Single core PVC insulated unsheathed cable** – Designed for drawing into trunking and conduit installations, often in industrial or commercial premises. Either solid or stranded copper conductors are available in all required insulation colours.
- **Single core PVC insulated and sheathed cable** – Used for surface wiring where there is little risk of mechanical damage. It has an extra layer (sheath) of PVC insulation. Commonly used for connecting an electricity meter to the consumer unit in domestic environments.
- **Single core PVC insulated and sheathed cable with a cpc** – Similar to the above but with a bare copper cpc included. It is used for domestic and general wiring where a cpc is required for all circuits.
- **PVC insulated and sheathed flat cable** – Used for domestic and industrial wiring where there is little risk of mechanical damage, usually 2- or 3-core cables plus an uninsulated cpc, and either solid or stranded main conductors, outer sheath coloured either grey or white.
- **PVC insulated and sheathed flexible cords** – Suitable for use up to 85°C ambient temperature but not in heat appliances. It comprises stranded copper conductors insulated with heat resistant PVC; available as: 2-core (brown and blue); 3-core (brown, blue and green/yellow); 4-core (black, grey, brown and green/yellow); and 5-core (as 4-core plus blue).
- **PVC insulated and sheathed flat twin flexible cord** – It has stranded copper conductors with brown and blue PVC; used for light duty, supplying appliances that do not require an earth conductor such as a radio or TV.
- **PVC insulated bell wire** – Used for wiring doorbells, alarms and other indicators; with either one or two core insulated copper conductors, one of the cores identified by a coloured stripe on the outside.
- **PVC/SWA/PVC cable** – This has a PVC insulated outer sheath with a layer of galvanised steel wire armouring underneath and below that another PVC sheath covering PVC insulated conductors. It can be installed underground in cable ducts, on to cable tray or attached via clips to various surfaces. It is used mainly for mains and sub-mains distribution systems.
- **PVC/GSWB/PVC cable** – This has an outer sheath of PVC, with a layer of galvanised braided steel wire underneath and below that an inner sheath and aluminium screen covering PVC insulated conductors. This type of cable is more flexible than PVC/SWA/PVC cable. It is used in instrumentation applications or where shielding is required for signal applications.

Definition

cpc – Stands for 'circuit protective conductor', commonly known as an earth conductor.

Cables with thermosetting insulation

Also known as XLPE (cross laced polyethylene), these can sustain higher operating temperatures up to 90°C, as opposed to 70°C for PVC. They are used for mains distribution, allowing a smaller csa to be used.

LSF cables

These are cables that give off low smoke and fumes, if they burn.

PILCSWA cable

Paper Insulated Lead Covered Single Wire Armoured cable is used for mains distribution systems of 3.3 kV and above.

Trailing cables

Cables may have to be used where they may be driven over or have to withstand severe weather conditions, such as in mines or on construction sites. They, typically, have stranded conductors sheathed in an outer steel braiding for mechanical protection, which in turn is covered in heavy duty rubber sheathing; and are terminated using specialist conductors. Cables feeding lighter equipment may only have the rubber sheath without the steel braiding.

Mineral insulated copper cable (MICC)

The mineral insulation is magnesium oxide. Copper can withstand temperatures of 1000°C and the magnesium oxide powder can withstand 2800°C, so are ideal for high temperature environments and for use in fire alarm systems. The cables offer several other advantages including robustness, long life, no toxic fumes if burnt and a high current carrying capacity for a given csa. They are used in locations like boiler houses where there are high temperatures and moisture; though the powder can absorb this if not sealed correctly.

FP200 cable

FP200 cable is insulated with a fire resistant material (Insudite). This is covered with a laminated aluminium sheath, which in turn is covered by a low smoke/zero halogen sheath. The cable is normally used for fire alarms and fire detection systems. FP200 Gold has solid conductors and FP200 Flex has stranded conductors.

FP200 gold is available with 2-, 3- or 4-cores as standard with 7-, 12- and 19-cores available. Cross sectional areas range from 1 mm^2 to 4 mm^2. It can be fixed almost anywhere and does not need special tools to terminate it. However, it is not mechanically strong and the bending radius should not be less than six times the cable diameter.

Definition

csa – Stands for 'cross sectional area' and is how cable is sized. The formula used to calculate it is πr^2, where r is the radius of the conductor.

Definition

kV – Stands for kilovolt and means one thousand volts.

Fibre optic data cable

Each fibre comprises a thin core of glass, or more usually now, optical quality plastic, and with a PVC sheath. Laser light passes from one end to the other carrying multiple digital pulses. The core is essentially a large mirror formed into a thin tube, no thicker than a human hair. It can carry 10 billion digital bits of information per second along its length, enough for tens of thousands of simultaneous phone calls; and many fibres can be bundled together within a single outer sheath. It is widely used for telecommunications tasks, including undersea cables.

Cat (Category) 5 cable

This consists of four pairs of copper conductors, insulated from each other and housed in an outer-screened sheath and an overall PVC sheath. It is used for high frequency transmission of data, typically 350 MHz, in computer installations.

Installation techniques

These vary with the type of installation and cable and are tightly controlled by Regulations, especially BS 7671.

Rewiring an existing building

Most rewiring of houses involves buildings at least 25 years old. Houses wired before 1956 were wired in either vulcanised rubber insulated (VRI) cable or in conduit using single core versions of the same cable. Both are due for rewiring. Modern installations use PVC cables with a far longer lifespan.

Modern domestic wiring is normally installed under flooring or, for sockets or other wall mounted equipment, recessed into walls. The Regulations covering wiring are in BS 7671.

Floorboards

These need to be removed where necessary to install new cables and equipment.

- Cut the tongues using a chisel, saw or power saw.
- Apply leverage using a hammer or such like.
- Cut the floorboard near to a joist and remove.

Figure 4.07 Tongue and groove floorboards

Refitting requires a fillet to be fastened to the joist where the board was cut to give more support and then the floorboard either nailed or screwed back down.

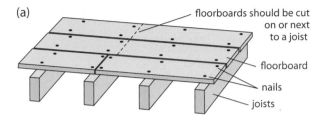 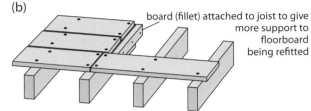

Figure 4.08 (a) and **(b)** Cutting and refitting floorboards

Cables run into walls

Cables in walls must be at least 50 mm below the surface or, if not, must be protected against mechanical damage by screws or nails using earthed metallic conduit, armoured cables, etc. Cables that are not mechanically protected must be run within 150 mm of the top of the wall (to ceiling) or within 150 mm of the corner of the wall, or run horizontally or vertically to the item of equipment or accessory and not at an angle. If cables are not mechanically protected and the installation is not under the supervision of a skilled or instructed person then they must be afforded additional protection by a 30 mA RCD (Regulation 522.6.7). This requirement is applicable no matter how deep the cables are from the surface in metallic partition walls (Regulation 522.6.8).

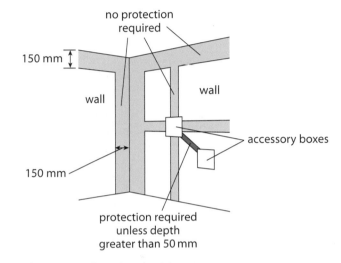

Figure 4.09 Permitted cable routes

Creating a slot in a masonry wall to house cable and or sockets, etc. is called chasing. It is done with a chisel and hammer, or electrical attachment on a drilling machine.

Wiring in partitions

Wiring is installed prior to the plasterboard being fitted to the framework. It must be at least 50 mm from the finished surface. Back boxes for electrical components must also be fitted to noggins, or dry-lining boxes used if the partition lining has sufficient strength and thickness.

Ceiling fittings

Ceiling fittings must be securely fitted to joists or a noggin set between them.

Safety tip

Wear safety goggles and gloves whilst cutting into walls.

Definition

Noggins – Short pieces of wood attached to a timber frame or joist as a brace or to fasten items like back boxes for electrical equipment.

Figure 4.10 Cables through joists

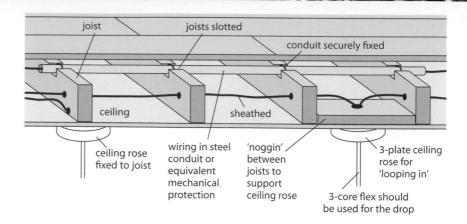

Protection of cables

Some of the requirements have been mentioned above but are included here:

- When installed under floors, above ceilings or in walls, cables must be at least 50 mm below the finished surface or, if not, then protected against mechanical damage (Regulations 522.6.5, 522.6.6, 522.6.7).
- Where cables pass through any metalwork (back boxes included) then a grommet must be fitted to prevent the cable being damaged (Regulation 522.6.1).
- Cable insulation used inside a fitting or appliance must be able to withstand the heat produced. If not, it should be relocated or have additional protection provided.
- Where a wiring system passes through the floor of a building then the material it passes through must be resealed around the cable to prevent the spread of fire (Regulation 527.2.1).
- Where a wiring enclosure penetrates a specific fire resistance part of the structure then it must be sealed internally as well as externally (Regulation 527.2.4).

Cable support and bends

The requirements for bends and supports are to be found in Tables 4A to 4E in the *IEE On-Site Guide* (16th Edition).

Remember

Minimise the amount of damage to building structures, as this has to be made good after the job is completed.

Safety tip

Wear the correct PPE, and use the correct tools and materials.

Installing PVC/PVC cables

PVC/PVC cables are installed with the use of cable clips, which incorporate a masonry-type of nail. The cable must not be bent to a radius that would cause damage (defined in Table 4E of the *IEE On-Site Guide*).

Cables should not cross over each other, nor should they come into contact with water or gas pipes or other non-earthed metalwork. Also installing in polystyrene insulation should be avoided, as it can cause a chemical reaction that attacks the PVC insulation.

Terminating and joining cables

Terminating cables and flexible cords

Where the cable enters the equipment or plug, the outer sheath should protrude at least 10 mm and be anchored securely on its outer sheath. Stranded conductors should have the strands twisted together to provide a better connection and care should be taken not to damage them. No bare copper should be shown or loose strands protrude out of the terminal.

Pillar terminals 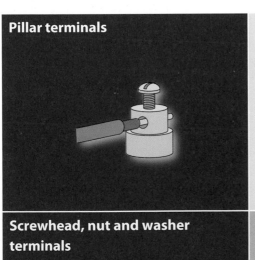	A pillar terminal is a brass pillar with a hole through its side into which the conductor is inserted and secured with a setscrew. If the conductor is small in relation to the hole it should be doubled back. When two or more conductors are to go into the same terminal they should be twisted together. Care should be taken not to damage the conductor by excessive tightening.
Screwhead, nut and washer terminals 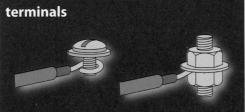	Using round-nosed pliers form conductor end into an eye, slightly larger than the screw shank but smaller than the outside diameter of the screwhead, nut or washer. The eye should be placed in such a way that rotation of the screwhead or nut tends to close the joint in the eye.
Claw washers 	Claw washers are used to get a better connection. Lay the looped conductor in the pressing. Place a plain washer on top of the loop and squeeze the metal points flat using the correct tool.

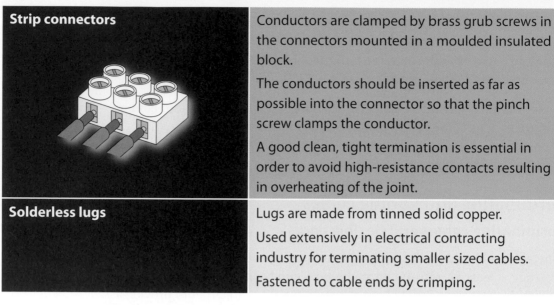

Strip connectors	Conductors are clamped by brass grub screws in the connectors mounted in a moulded insulated block.
	The conductors should be inserted as far as possible into the connector so that the pinch screw clamps the conductor.
	A good clean, tight termination is essential in order to avoid high-resistance contacts resulting in overheating of the joint.
Solderless lugs	Lugs are made from tinned solid copper.
	Used extensively in electrical contracting industry for terminating smaller sized cables.
	Fastened to cable ends by crimping.

Figure 4.11 Types of terminal

Effective termination of conductors sometimes requires a special terminal that can be mechanically crimped (compressed) on to the conductor using a crimping tool.

Cable joints and connections

These should be avoided wherever possible. If unavoidable then suitable connections, which are mechanically and electrically robust, must be used.

Every joint must be accessible for inspection, testing and maintenance unless exempt by Regulation 526.3. Exemptions include compound filled or encapsulated joints, joints made by soldering, brazing, welding or a compression tool or proprietary joints.

Joints must be made within suitable accessories and enclosures in accordance with Regulation 526.5.

Some common connectors include:

- **Plastic connector** – These come in blocks of up to 12 connections, which can be separated if needed, often known as 'chocolate block' connectors. Ratings range from 5 amps to 50 amps.
- **Porcelain connectors** – Similar to the above but made of porcelain and can withstand high temperatures.
- **Screwits** – Cone shaped porcelain connectors that are threaded internally and are twisted on to the conductors to join them together.
- **Compression joints** – These can be mechanically crimped on to the conductor using a special tool.
- **Uninsulated connectors** – Used in consumer units and wiring panels for connecting together cpcs and other protective conductors.
- **Junction boxes** – Used extensively, especially in domestic situations. They come in a variety of current sizes and terminal configurations.

- **Soldered joints** – Rarely used now, except in electronics or large feeder cables.

Terminating PVC/SWA/PVC cable

This is a skilled task. The basic method is as follows:

- Remove enough outer sheath for the length of conductors needed to terminate.
- Measure approximately 1½ times the length of the armoured gland cone and remove armouring by cutting part way through and snapping off.
- Slide on the PVC shroud and then the back nut of the gland, open the armouring strands into a cone shape and attach the main body of the gland.
- Screw both parts together, making sure the armouring is secured between the two parts.
- Remove the second outer sheath and leave at least 10 mm protruding past the end of the gland.
- Attach to the electrical equipment using a lock nut. The conductors are then ready for termination.

The steel wire armouring is the cpc, so it must be securely gripped by the gland. The gland must also be securely fitted to the accessory and supplementary bonding used from the gland's earth tag to the main equipment earth connection.

Termination of MICC cables

This is also a skilled task and only an outline of the methodology is described here:

- Remove the outer PVC sheath (if fitted).
- Slide the PVC shroud, gland nut, compression ring and gland body over the cable.
- Remove the outer copper sheath until the correct length of conductors is obtained.
- Screw on the pot using a pot wrench tool.
- Fit the sealing ring and fill the pot with insulating compound.
- Crimp together using a crimping pot tool.
- Apply coloured sleeving to the copper conductors.

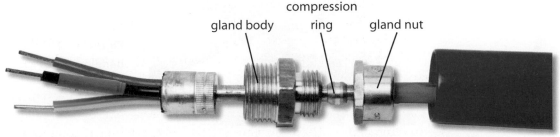

MICC gland and seal

- Test the insulation of the cable for short circuits between conductors and earth (outer copper sheath).
- Test again 24 hours later in case moisture has contaminated the magnesium oxide. The reading should be at least 200 MΩ and higher than that recorded previously.

Terminating FP200 gold

Because of the lack of mechanical strength it is important to follow manufacturer's instructions for terminating the cable. A recognised method is as follows:

- Score around the outer sheath with a knife.
- Bend the cable until the outer sheath breaks and then pull it off.
- Use the appropriate gland to anchor into equipment.
- Connect the aluminium sheath to the cpc for effective earthing.

Conduit

Steel conduit is widely used for commercial and industrial wiring systems. It is either seam welded or solid drawn, usually made of mild steel and painted with black enamel paint. In damp or corrosive environments, galvanised conduit is used.

Single core PVC cables are installed in the conduit, with the conduit providing mechanical protection and, in certain conditions, can be used as earth continuity. Conduit can be bent easily using the correct tools and the ends are screwed to provide secure entry into various items of electrical equipment. A wide range of accessories enables the installer to complete whole installations without terminating the conduit.

Bending steel conduit

This is best done using a bending machine. In the bending machine illustrated: **A** is the swivel arm, **B** the conduit guide, **C** is the adjusting arm for the conduit, **D** the locking pin and **E** is the rear leg.

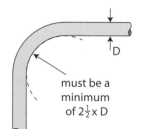

Figure 4.12 Minimum bending radius allowed

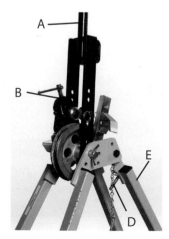

Bending machine

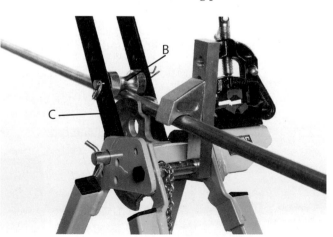

Bending machine with conduit inserted, which prevents the swivel arm from hanging down

Bending conduit is a skill which takes practice. Only the main bends are illustrated here.

Right-angled bend	This is used to go around a corner or change direction by 90 degrees. When bending, measurements may be taken from the back, centre or front of the bend. Allowance should be made for the depth of the fixing saddle bases.	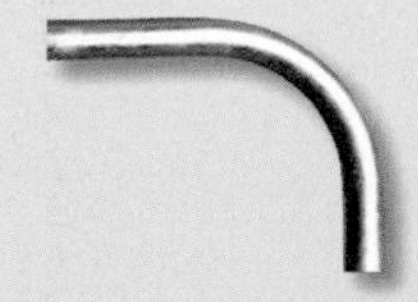
Set	The set is used when surface levels change or when terminating into a box entry. Sets should be parallel and square, not too long and not too short so that the end cannot be threaded. Where there are numerous sets together all sets must be of the same length. The double set is used when passing girders or obstacles, as shown.	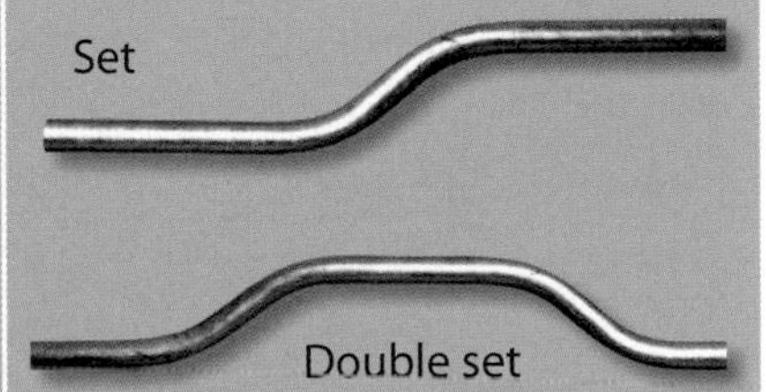 Set Double set
Kick	The kick is used when a conduit run changes direction by less than 90 degrees.	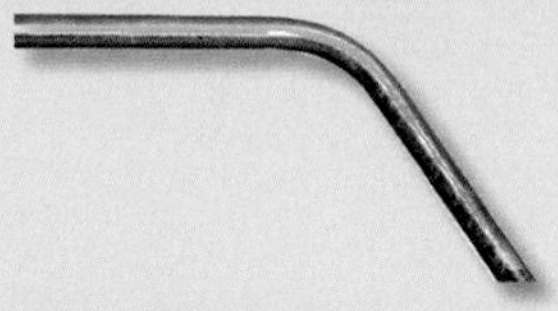
Bubble set or saddle set	The bubble set or saddle set is used when passing obstructions, especially pipes or roof trusses, etc. The centre of the obstruction should be central to the set.	

Figure 4.13 Types of bend

Steel conduit fixings

The *IEE On-Site Guide* lays down how conduit should be fixed. The parameters are included in Table 4.06.

Nominal size of conduit	Maximum distance between supports					
	Rigid metal		Rigid insulating		Pliable	
	Horizontal 2 m	Vertical 3 m	Horizontal 4 m	Vertical 5 m	Horizontal 6 m	Vertical 7 m
1 m						
Not exceeding 16 metres	0.75	1.00	0.75	1.00	0.30	0.50
Exceeding 16 but not exceeding 25 metres	1.75	2.00	1.50	1.75	0.40	0.60
Exceeding 25 but not exceeding 40 metres	2.00	2.25	1.75	2.00	0.60	0.80
Exceeding 40 metres	2.25	2.50	2.00	2.00	0.80	1.00

Table 4.06 Conduit fixing parameters (Table 4C, *On-Site Guide*)

distance saddle — hospital saddle

crampet pipe hook —

— strap saddle

Conduit fixings

Some of the fixings available are:

- **Half or strap saddle** – Used to fix conduit to cable tray.
- **Spacer bar saddle (not shown)** – Used on an even surface (2 mm clearance).
- **Distance saddle** – Used on uneven surfaces or where there is a lot of condensation on the surface.
- **Hospital saddle** – Used where it is necessary to clean behind the conduit.
- **Multiple saddle strip (not shown)** – Used to fasten multiple conduit runs together.
- **Girder clamp saddle (not shown)** – Used to fasten to girders without the need to drill the girder.
- **Crampet pipe hook** – Used to fasten to walls or when cast in concrete.

Coupling and terminating steel conduit

Screw threads are cut into the ends of conduit for either inserting into a running coupling or for termination. The thread is cut using stocks and dies and a suitable cutting paste. The length of thread is usually half the length of a conduit coupling. The rough edges should be cleaned off inside, as this can damage the insulation of the cables when installing them.

> **Did you know?**
>
> It is best to turn stocks and dies clockwise ½ turn and then anti-clockwise ¼ turn to clean the thread.

Running couplings are required when two pieces of conduit must be joined but both are fixed. A long thread is cut on one of the conduits to the length of the coupling plus locking ring thickness. A normal thread is cut on the other. A locking ring and coupling is screwed on to the long thread and then slowly screwed on to the other threaded conduit and finally locked into position with the locking ring.

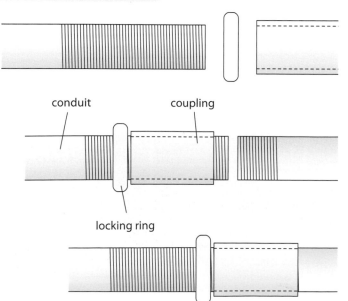

conduit

coupling

locking ring

Figure 4.14 The running coupling

Three methods of terminating conduit are illustrated.

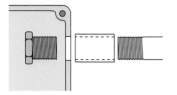

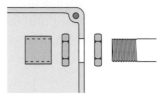

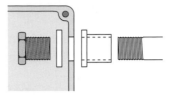

Figure 4.15 Terminating conduit at a box using a conduit coupling and brass male bush

Figure 4.16 Terminating conduit at a box using locknuts and a brass female bush

Figure 4.17 Flanged coupling washer and brass male bush method for use with PVC box

Fitting the bush

Tightening the bush

Use of non-inspection elbows and tees

Non-inspection elbows and tees are installed adjacent to an outlet box or inspection type of fitting, as illustrated.

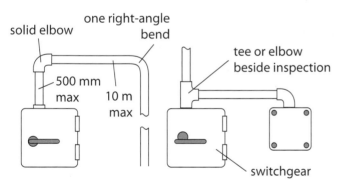

Figure 4.18 Non-inspection elbows and tees

Wiring steel conduit

Conduit installations must be complete before any cable is installed in it. The process is then as follows:

- Insert a steel wire or tape (fish tape) into the conduit.
- Attach a single core PVC cable and pull it through to act as a draw wire.
- Attach cables to the draw wire and pull these through.

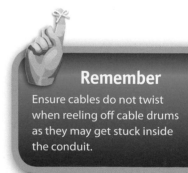

Remember

Ensure cables do not twist when reeling off cable drums as they may get stuck inside the conduit.

There are limits on the number of conductors that can be installed in different sizes of conduit, which are given in tables in the *IEE On-Site Guide*. The overall limiting factor is that the combined csa of the cables must not exceed 45 per cent of the internal csa of the conduit; but it is also affected by, for example, the number of bends there are in the installation.

Plastic (PVC) conduit

This comes in two types, flexible and rigid, and withstands acids, alkalis, oil, soils, fungus, salt water corrosion and atmospheric conditions. It is used on farms where animals are kept and can be buried in plaster or lime without any harmful effects.

It needs more supports than metal conduit, because it expands and contracts more and will distort if enough supports are not fitted. Expansion joints must be installed to allow for expansion.

It can be cut to size with a junior hacksaw. It can be bent by inserting a coiled spring, heat applied to the bending area and then bent over the knee or thigh. It needs to be bent more than is needed, as conduit will spring back towards its original position. PVC adhesive can then be used to join conduit and accessories together.

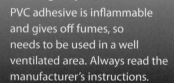

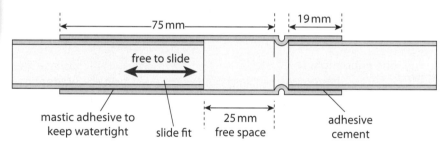

Figure 4.19 Expansion provision in conduits

Trunking

Trunking is a steel or PVC fabricated enclosure, used when many cables follow the same route, to avoid using lots of conduits or for runs of MICC. It is also used when there are likely to be frequent changes to installations to support new equipment.

It normally has a rectangular cross section with one side hinged to provide access and comes in 3 m lengths. Sizes range up to 225 mm × 100 mm cross-section. Many prefabricated bends and sets are available to allow for the different contours and obstacles within a building.

Main types of trunking

- **Floor trunking** – Trunking recessed into the floor.
- **Multi compartment trunking** – Segregated trunking for separating different circuits (alarm circuits from mains, etc.).
- **Flush cable trunking** – Recessed into building structures with the cover overlapping.
- **Skirting trunking** – Used in offices and schools, surface mounted on to the wall and incorporating mains supplies and data, computer and phone cables.
- **Busbar trunking (overhead)** – Used in factories and commercial buildings to provide multiple options for accessing the supply.
- **Busbar trunking (rising main)** – Used in multi-storey developments to distribute electricity throughout a building and installed in a vertical position.

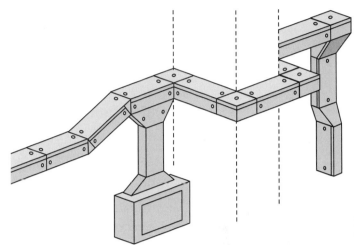

Figure 4.20 Steel trunking

Feed units are fitted to the trunking, which can have pre-wired conduit or PVC/SWA cable connected to them ready for installation. HBC fuses should be used for these units to give better protection against short circuits.

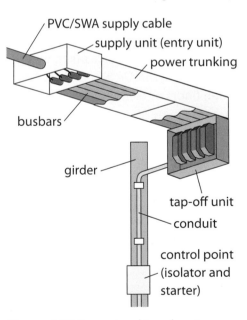

Figure 4.21 Power trunking showing tap-off unit

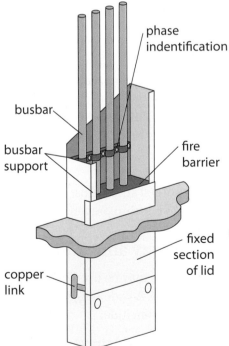

Figure 4.22 Rising mains busbar trunking

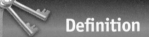

Definition

Short circuit – A fault producing negligible impedance between two or more conductors, which could result in a fault current of many thousands of amps.

Did you know?

Busbars are mounted on a substantial insulated support rack within the busbar enclosure to allow them to expand upwards without distorting.

Site built trunking accessories

Trunking systems always use prefabricated bends and sets to save the time it would take to hand make them. However, they can be made on site with practice.

PVC trunking

Essentially the same accessories are available as for steel trunking. PVC trunking is lighter and more pleasing to the eye but expands and requires more support.

Regulations covering trunking

Regulation 521.5.2 states that all conductors in an alternating current circuit, including the neutral, must be installed in the same trunking to prevent eddy currents.

Regulation 521.5.1 states that all conductors within the trunking must be able to withstand any electromagnetic forces that may occur when a fault current flows.

Regulation 521.6 states that, where applicable, all trunking shall comply with the appropriate part of BS EN 50085.

Some dos and don'ts:

- Trunking must be securely fixed and protected from mechanical damage.
- Trunking must not have more than 45 per cent of the space taken up by cables (tables are available in Appendix 5 of the *IEE On-Site Guide*).
- Where trunking/conduit passes through floors or ceilings then the area around them must be sealed with fire proof material.
- Copper links for earth continuity must be fitted across each joint in a trunking installation.
- Cable entry holes must be protected with grommets to prevent damage to cables.
- Grommet strips must be used where slots are cut into the trunking for cable entry, to prevent damage.

> **Definition**
>
> **Eddy currents** – Induced currents caused by the magnetic effect of current carrying conductors passing through openings of ferromagnetic enclosures.

Cable tray and ladders

Cable trays may be used in large installations where several cables take the same route. A wide range of sizes and strengths is available for different tasks. They include:

- **Standard cable tray** – For light duty and available in widths up to 915 mm, with a flange of either 13 mm or 19 mm.
- **Heavy duty tray** – Available in widths up to 610 mm and with a larger flange for added strength usually 38 mm deep.
- **Return-flange tray** – Available in the same widths as other trays but stronger because of the returned flange stopping it deflecting. The flange is usually 25 mm deep with a 6 mm return flange.

- **Heavy duty return flange tray** – a larger version of the return flange tray.
- **Basket tray** – a lightweight basket style tray usually hung from special brackets.

Cable ladders can be used to span large gaps with little support. They are made from 2 mm thick steel, reinforced in the ladder side channels with the ladder rungs slotted to take a variety of cable fasteners. They are used mostly for large PVC/SWA cables.

Trays and ladders come in a range of finishes and are manufactured to BSEN 61537. Hot dipped galvanised is the most common and suitable for most environments. Plastic coating by either a polyethylene or PVC coating is used against chemical contamination, or in areas where hygiene is a requisite. Stainless steel is used for special applications, such as food or marine applications.

A variety of prefabricated bends and sets are available.

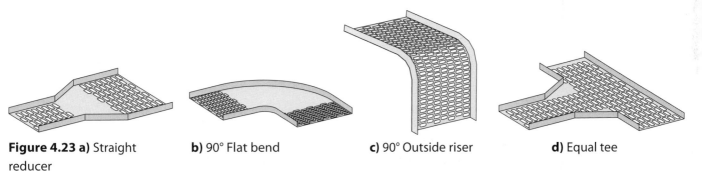

Figure 4.23 a) Straight reducer   **b)** 90° Flat bend   **c)** 90° Outside riser   **d)** Equal tee

Special fittings are available to join the various lengths of tray together or they can be welded. However, if welded then the weld must be coated with zinc paint to prevent corrosion on hot dip galvanised finishes, suitable plastic for plastic coated or paint for stainless steel finishes.

Fittings can be fabricated on site.

Three basic methods for fixing a tray are illustrated.

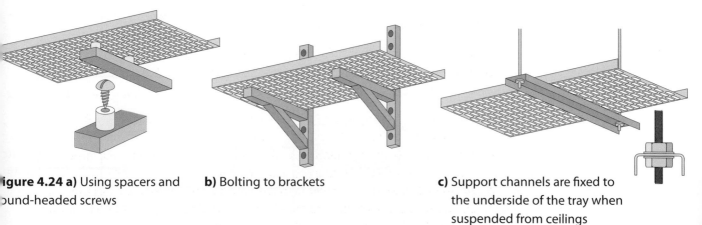

Figure 4.24 a) Using spacers and round-headed screws   **b)** Bolting to brackets   **c)** Support channels are fixed to the underside of the tray when suspended from ceilings

Switching of lighting circuits

Many different switching circuits are used. Some of the commonest are covered here.

Wiring with single core cable

Single core cable is carried in conduit and trunking.

One-way switching

This is the most basic circuit, only switching a light on from one place. The line (brown) wire is fed to terminal A. When the switch is operated it connects the line wire through to the light until switched off again.

Additional lights can be wired in parallel.

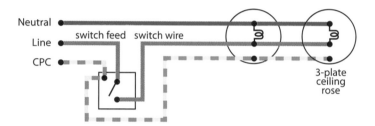

Figure 4.26 Extra lighting fed from the same switch, wired in parallel (new cable colours)

Two-way switching

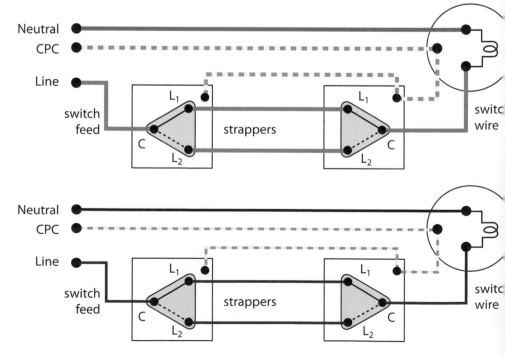

Figure 4.27 Full circuit wired with single-core cable

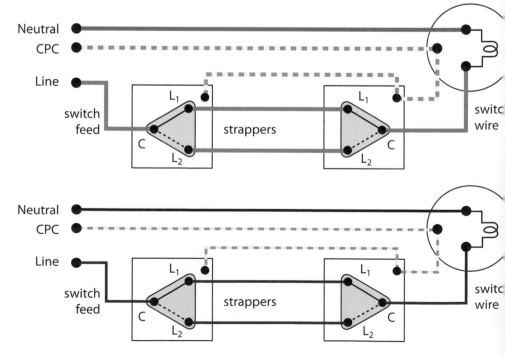

Figure 4.25 Simple one-way switching

This enables a light to be switched on from two places independently. The live feed (line wire) is taken to a common terminal (C) in the first switch. Strappers are then connected between the L1 terminals and the L2 terminals in each switch. The common terminals act as a pivot point. Activating either switch causes the light to go on or off. In Figure 4.27 the light would be illuminated with the switches in their current positions.

Intermediate switching

An intermediate switch is required when more than two switches are used to operate a light. An unlimited number of intermediate switches can be connected. These have four terminals, two marked L1 and two L2, which are strapped to the two end switches or to another intermediate switch. Operating an intermediate switch either connects L1 to L1 and L2 to L2, or crosses them so that each L1 connects to a different L2.

Figure 4.28 shows the intermediate switch in the cross over position and, with the end switches as set, the light is off. Switching the intermediate switch, so that L1 was connected to L1, would turn the light on. (L2 is also then connected to L2 but this is irrelevant until either of the end switches is operated, when it would become part of the new circuit.)

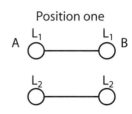

Position one

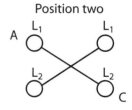

Position two

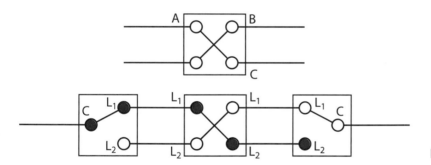

Figure 4.28 Intermediate switch

Wiring with multicore cable

These cables have three or more cores within a single sheath. There is less flexibility in planning cable runs than using single core wiring. For domestic lighting circuits the size is normally 1.5 mm² csa.

One-way switching

Figure 4.29 shows a single switch arrangement using 3-core cable. Note that the *blue* conductor is sleeved with a *brown colour* to show it becomes live (i.e. the line wire) when the switch is operated.

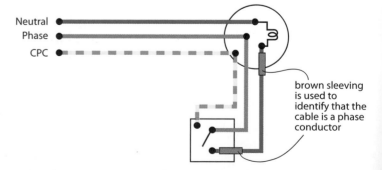

brown sleeving is used to identify that the cable is a phase conductor

Figure 4.29 Single switch using multicore cable

Two-way switching circuit

This uses 4-core cable (three conductors plus cpc). A two-way switch replaces a one-way switch. This is then connected to a *second switch*, as shown in Figure 4.30. Note that brown sleeving is fitted to both the non-brown conductors (the line wires), as all three can be live. The light, with connections as shown, is off.

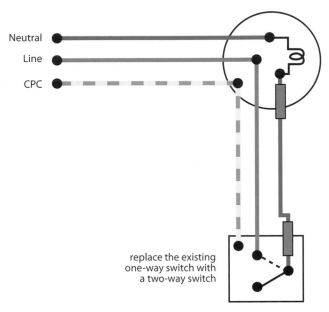

replace the existing one-way switch with a two-way switch

Figure 4.30 Two-way switching with multicore cable

Intermediate switching

An arrangement for including intermediate switching is shown in Figure 4.31.

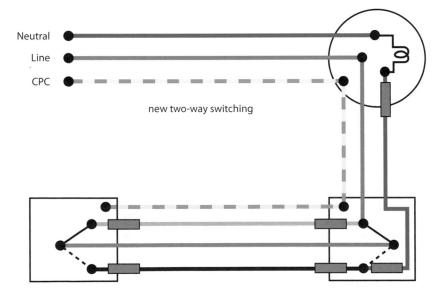

new two-way switching

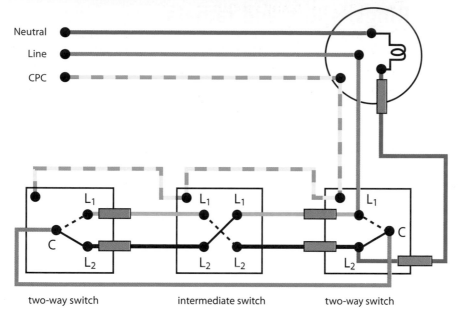

two-way switch   intermediate switch   two-way switch

Figure 4.31 Intermediate switching with multicore cable

Wiring using a joint/junction box

This is not very common nowadays. A one-way switch with a junction box is illustrated.

The following precautions should be noted:

- The outer sheath should protrude inside the box by at least 10 mm.
- No bare conductor should protrude outside the terminal.
- Slack should be left to allow for retermination.
- Cables should not cross over each other inside the box.
- The box should be fastened to a solid surface.
- Correct sized boxes should be used.

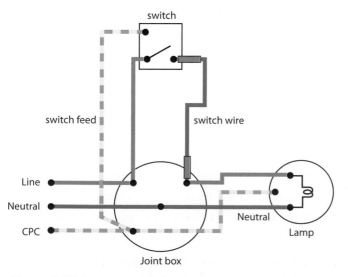

Figure 4.32 One-way switch using a joint/junction box

Rings, spurs and radials

These are the common power circuits found in domestic premises.

Ring circuits

These start at the consumer unit (line, neutral and cpc), connect into each socket in turn and return from the last socket to their respective terminals in the consumer unit.

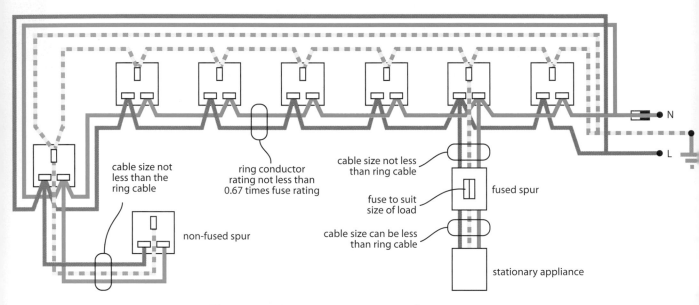

Figure 4.33 Domestic ring circuit with spurs

An unlimited number of sockets can be installed provided the Regulations are adhered to. The following are the main points to be observed:

- The floor area served by a ring main must not exceed 100 m².
- Twin or multiple sockets are classed as one outlet.
- The fuse size is either 30 amp or 32 amp.
- The cable size is 2.5 mm² csa.
- Consideration must be given to the loading on the circuit. Kitchens and utility rooms may require separate circuits.
- Where more than one circuit is installed, the number of sockets should be shared to equalise the assessed loading.
- Some items like immersion heaters and space heating may need to be connected to separate circuits.
- Cookers, ovens and hobs with a rating exceeding 2 kW may need to be connected to separate circuits.
- Socket outlets provided for general use by ordinary persons must have additional protection by means of a 30 mA (or less) RCD (see Regulation 411.3.3).

Permanently connected equipment should be locally protected by a fuse not exceeding 13 A and controlled by a switch complying with BS 7671, or a circuit breaker not exceeding 16 A rating.

Spurs

Spurs go to single sockets or permanently installed items of equipment. They may come directly from the consumer unit, a junction box or from the ring circuit (as shown in Figure 4.33). They may be fused or non-fused.

Non-fused spurs:

- may supply one single or one double socket outlet, or a single item of permanently connected equipment
- must use cable of the same size as the ring circuit
- are limited in total to the number of sockets or items of fixed equipment on the ring.

Fused spurs are connected via a fuse related to the current carrying capacity of the cable but not exceeding 13 A. For sockets the minimum cable size is 1.5 mm² csa for PVC/copper or 1 mm² for MICC. The total number of fused spurs is unlimited (subject to loading).

Radial circuits

Radial circuits do not form a loop back to the consumer unit but end at the last socket.

A2 radial circuit

- The floor area is a maximum of 75 m².
- The protective device must be 30 A or 32 A cartridge fuse or MCB.
- Cable size must be at least 4 mm² csa for PVC or 2.5 mm² for MICC.

A3 radial circuit

- The floor area is a maximum of 50 m².
- The protective device must be 20 A.
- It uses PVC/copper cable, size 2.5 mm² csa.

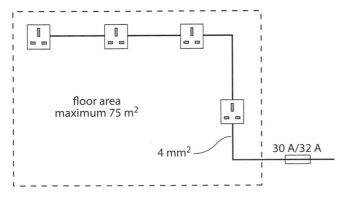

Figure 4.34 A2 radial circuit

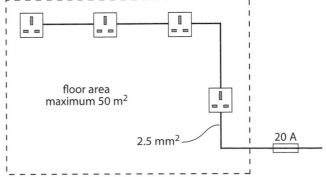

Figure 4.35 A3 radial circuit

Short answer questions

1. Name five different types of screw.
2. Describe how a Simmonds locknut fastener works.
3. Describe how to terminate a PVC/SWA cable.
4. Describe how to terminate a MICC cable.
5. Describe how to make a 90 degree bend in a length of conduit (use drawings to help).
6. Name the different materials used for conduit.
7. What are the three main types of cable tray coverings/materials?
8. How many light switch terminals are there in an intermediate circuit?
9. Describe where to terminate the ends of a ring main circuit in the consumer unit.
10. How many terminals are used in a junction box when connecting a socket as a spur? What are they used for?

Multiple-choice test

1. What is the reduced voltage used for power tools?
   a. 230 volts
   b. 110 volts
   c. 24 volts
   d. 12 volts

2. What are the three most common wood screw sizes used in electrical work?
   a. 6, 8, 10
   b. 2, 4, 6
   c. 10, 12, 14
   d. none of these

3. How long is the thread on a machine screw?
   a. ½ length
   b. ¼ length
   c. full length
   d. ¾ length

4. What colour rawl plug is used with No. 14 screws?
   a. red
   b. white
   c. brown
   d. blue

5. Which of the following is NOT a conductive material?
   a. carbon
   b. copper
   c. XLPE
   d. aluminium

6. Maximum volt drop allowed for lighting is?
   a. 10% of supply
   b. 4% of supply
   c. 3% of supply
   d. none of these

7. The colours of conductors in a 3-phase supply are?
   a. brown, black, grey, blue
   b. black, black, black, blue
   c. black, grey, black, black
   d. brown, brown, brown, black

8. How far down should a cable be installed under the floorboards?
   a. 100 mm
   b. 60 mm
   c. 25 mm
   d. none of these

9. Within what distance can cables be installed on a wall where it joins the ceiling?
   a. 50 mm
   b. 100 mm
   c. 150 mm
   d. any distance

10. What does SWB stand for in a PVC/SWB/PVC cable?
    a. steel wire banded
    b. silicon wound basket
    c. steel wire braided
    d. soft wired braiding

11. What frequency does CAT 5 cable use to transmit data?
    a. 230 Hz
    b. 350 MHz
    c. 3000 MHz
    d. 350 Hz

12. How many bits of data can be transmitted in one second in a fibre optic cable?
    a. 10 million
    b. 100 billion
    c. 10 billion
    d. 100 million

13. What temperature can copper withstand?
    a. 100 degrees Kelvin
    b. 1000 degrees Celsius
    c. 2800 degrees Celsius
    d. 70 degrees Celsius

14. What is the insulant used in MICC cable?
    a. magnesium dioxide
    b. magnesia
    c. magnesia oxide
    d. magnesium oxide

15. What csa conductor is used in a 2L1 MICC cable?
    a. 1 mm^2
    b. 2.1 mm^2
    c. 2 mm^2
    d. 1.1 mm^2

16. What is the maximum number of conductors in an FP200 gold cable?
    a. 7
    b. 19
    c. 3
    d. 12

17. What is the clearance provided by a spacer saddle?
    a. 4 mm
    b. 1 mm
    c. 2 mm
    d. 6 mm

18. What is the percentage space factor for cables installed in conduit?
    a. 25%
    b. 50%
    c. 10%
    d. 45%

19. What type of fuses must be used for feed units used on busbar systems?
    a. rewirable
    b. cartridge
    c. HBC
    d. any type

20. What type of currents must be avoided when installing cable in trunking?
    a. fault currents
    b. eddy currents
    c. magnetic currents
    d. flux currents

21. What are the three terminals labelled as on a 2-way lighting switch?
   a. *L1, L2, L3*
   b. *C, L1, L2*
   c. *1, 2, 3*
   d. *a, b, c*

22. How many conductors are there between two 2-way switches?
   a. *4*
   b. *3*
   c. *6*
   d. *5*

23. What is the minimum size for a ring main cable?
   a. *4 mm²*
   b. *2.5 mm²*
   c. *1.5 mm²*
   d. *6 mm²*

24. What is the maximum floor area served by a ring circuit?
   a. *50 m²*
   b. *75 m²*
   c. *unlimited*
   d. *100 m²*

25. An A3 radial circuit is protected by what size device?
   a. *30 amp*
   b. *16 amp*
   c. *20 amp*
   d. *10 amp*

The answer section is at the back of the book.

05 Statutory regulations and codes of practice

Electricity, when properly installed, used and maintained is a very safe and useful commodity. However, if you 'break the rules' it can deliver death and destruction with lightning speed. This chapter summarises the Regulations and codes of practice covering electrical installations, which help to ensure that they are safe.

This guide will cover the following:
- BS 7671 Requirements for Electrical Installation (IEE Wiring Regulations 17th Edition)
  - The role of the Regulations
  - Plan and style of the Regulations
  - Parts of the Regulations
  - Locations containing a bath or shower
  - Construction site installations
- Electricity at Work (EAW) Regulations 1989
- Hazardous installations
  - Zoning
  - Selection of equipment
  - Installations in potentially explosive areas
  - Ignition sources – identification and control
  - Petrol filling stations

BS 7671 Requirements for Electrical Installation (IEE Wiring Regulations 17th Edition)

The *IEE Wiring Regulations* are written by the Institute of Electrical Engineers (IEE). They became a British Standard in 1992 and the 17th Edition was published in January 2008. Their full title is BS 7671 Requirements for Electrical Installation (IEE Wiring Regulations 17th Edition) but are generally referred to as the Regulations or BS 7671.

The role of the Regulations

The Regulations have developed to take account of new types of electrical equipment and its usage, covering all aspects of the installation process. They are designed to protect persons, property and livestock from electric shock, fire and burns, and injury from mechanical movement of electrically operated equipment. They are not designed to instruct untrained persons, nor take the place of a detailed specification, nor to provide information for every circumstance.

These Regulations are not a statutory document. However, compliance with the Regulations will allow compliance with such legislation as Electricity at Work Regulations 1989 and the Health and Safety at Work Act 1974, which are statutory documents and enforceable by law.

Many other British Standards are referred to throughout the Regulations, such as BS 6551 which deals with protection of structures against lightning. In some cases these have a BS EN number, which refers to European harmonisation standards. These harmonised standards are co-ordinated by representatives from all the countries in the European Union via an organisation known as CENELEC.

The IEE has published eight 'Guidance Notes' that simplify BS 7671 requirements:

1: *Selection and Erection of Equipment*
2: *Isolation and Switching*
3: *Inspection and Testing*
4: *Protection against Fire*
5: *Protection against Electric Shock*
6: *Protection against Overcurrent*
7: *Special Locations*
8: *Earthing and Bonding*

Plan and style of the Regulations

The Regulations are divided into seven parts with 15 appendices, and each of the Regulations is numbered in a unique way to identify which part of the Regulations it refers to.

For example, for Regulation 433.1.1:

- The 1st digit, 4, refers to the part of the Regulations, in this case Part 4.
- The 2nd digit, 3, when attached to the 1st digit, refers to the chapter within that part of the Regulations, which in this case is Chapter 43.
- The 3rd digit, 3, when attached to the previous two digits, refers to the section within the chapter, which in this case is Section 433.
- The 4th digit, when attached to the previous ones, refers to the sub-section within the section, which in this case is sub-section 433.1.
- The last digit, 1, when attached to the previous ones, refers to the actual Regulation number, which in this case is Regulation 1.

Remember

A useful book is the *IEE On-Site Guide*, an abbreviated version of BS 7671 which also gives practical explanations, and in some cases drawings, of the more commonly used Regulations as well as useful cable tables, etc. Another useful reference is produced by the trade union Amicus.

Parts of the Regulations

Part 1 Scope, object and fundamental principles

This has three chapters and numerous sections within each chapter, the first chapter dealing with what the Regulations actually cover and what they do not.

The Regulations apply to the design, selection, erection, inspection and testing of electrical installations such as:

- residential premises
- commercial premises
- public premises
- industrial premises
- agricultural and horticultural premises
- prefabricated buildings
- caravans, caravan parks and similar sites
- construction sites, exhibitions, fairs and other installations for temporary purposes, including professional stage and broadcast applications
- marinas
- external lighting and similar installations
- mobile or transportable units
- photovoltaic systems
- low voltage generating sets
- highway equipment and street furniture

They do not cover:

- distributors' equipment
- railway traction equipment
- equipment of motor vehicles

- equipment on board ships covered by BS 8450
- equipment of mobile and fixed offshore installations
- equipment of aircraft
- mines and quarries
- radio interference equipment (unless it affects safety of electrical installations)
- lightning protection of buildings covered by BS EN 62305 (previously BS 6651 and BS EN 81-1)
- lift installations covered by BS 5655 and BS EN 81-1
- electrical equipment of machines covered by BS EN 60204

Voltages covered are up to and including 1000 volts a.c. or 1500 volts d.c. between conductors, or 600 volts a.c. or 900 volts d.c. between conductors and earth.

'Objects and effects' (Chapter 12) deals with what the Regulations are designed to protect: 'The regulations are designed to protect persons, property and livestock from electric shock, fire and burns and injury from mechanical movement of electrically operated equipment.'

'Fundamental principles' (Chapter 13) deals with how installations are to be made safe by stating means of protection, types of wiring, types of supply, etc. Compliance with the fundamental principles are likely to satisfy the statutory requirements of the Electricity at Work Regulations 1989.

Other statutory regulations include:

- Cinematograph Regulations 1955 made under the Cinematograph Act 1909, and/or Cinematograph Act 1952
- Electricity Supply Quality and Continuity Regulations 2002
- Agriculture (Stationary Machinery) Regulations 1959
- Building Standards (Scotland) Regulations 1990.

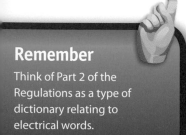

Remember

Think of Part 2 of the Regulations as a type of dictionary relating to electrical words.

Part 2 Definitions

Here the terms used in the Regulations are given specific meaning, so that when one person talks about a circuit breaker, for example, everyone else knows what they mean.

Part 3 Assessment of general characteristics

This part is about assessing the general characteristics of the supply and type of installation proposed, and takes into account (in conjunction with Parts 4 and 5 of the Regulations) the following:

- what the installation is to be used for, the supply used (single phase or three phase), type of earthing (TNS, TNC-S, TT, etc.); these are in Chapter 31
- the external influences to which the installation will be exposed, such as temperature, water, corrosion, etc.; these external influences are listed in Appendix 5 of the Regulations

- the compatibility of the equipment to be used, with reference to such things as other electrical equipment or services and the supply; the effects include fluctuating loads, starting currents, etc.; details of other effects are in Chapter 33
- the maintainability of the installation, how often it will need maintenance, how easily periodic inspections can be carried out, and reliability of the equipment.

Part 4 Protection for safety

This deals with the protective measures to be taken to prevent electric shock risk (basic protection and fault protection) and other dangers arising from the use of electricity. If the risk of electric shock is increased because of the location (e.g. bathroom or construction site) then the requirements of Part 6 should be used as well.

Chapters 41–44 deal with what the requirements are for protection, such as protection against electric shock (41), protection against thermal effects (42), protection against overcurrent (43), as well as Chapter 44 dealing with the requirements for protection against voltage and electromagnetic disturbances.

Part 5 Selection and erection of equipment

This part deals with the selection of equipment and its erection to provide compliance with the following:

- measures of protection for safety (e.g. correct voltage and current rating)
- proper functioning for the intended use of the installation (e.g. isolators and switches)
- appropriate requirements for the likely (and foreseen) external influences (e.g. presence of water or corrosive substances).

Generally speaking, any item of equipment used must have a relevant British or European Standard, which confirms that it complies with the use for which it is intended. Any item that does not have either of these standards can be specified by a designer provided that the equipment provides the same level of conformance with the Regulations.

Part 6 Inspection and testing

Every installation during erection, on completion and before being put into use must be inspected and tested to verify that the requirements of the Regulations have been met. While this process is being carried out precautions must be taken to prevent danger to persons, property and the installed equipment.

Any alteration or addition to an existing installation requires the relevant inspections and tests to be carried out to ensure compliance with the Regulations and also to ensure that the existing installation has not been made less safe.

Installations should also be tested on a regular basis. This is known as Periodic Inspection and Testing and the time interval varies depending on the type of installation. Initial verification (visual inspection) covers such things as identification of conductors, routing of cables, connection of conductors and so on.

Part 6 covers certification and reporting of work. Details of the tests, along with topics such as periodic test intervals, are expanded in *Guidance Note 3*, the *Amicus guide or IEE On-Site Guide (Section 9)*. Reference must be made to the relevant Regulations to ensure that results obtained are within the limits set.

Part 7 Special installations or locations

Certain locations are deemed more hazardous to persons and livestock because of the environment in which the equipment is used. Additional (or in some cases replacement) regulations are needed to provide greater safety.

The special locations identified by the Regulations are those agreed internationally:

- locations containing a bath or shower (covered in more detail below)
- swimming pools and other basins
- rooms and cabins containing sauna heaters
- construction and demolition site installations (covered in more detail below)
- agricultural and horticultural premises
- conducting locations with restricted movement
- electrical installations in caravan/camping parks and similar locations
- marinas and similar locations
- exhibitions, shows and stands
- solar photovoltaic (PV) power supply systems
- mobile or transportable units
- electrical installations in caravans and motor caravans
- temporary electrical installation for structures, amusement devices and booths at fairgrounds, amusement parks and circuses
- floor and ceiling heating systems.

Guidance Note 7 – Special Locations gives guidance to some of the above and in addition covers medical locations, which are not yet part of the international agreements. Other areas that were previously covered as 'special locations' have been incorporated into the redrafted sections.

Appendices

Appendix 1 British Standards to which reference is made in the Regulations

Appendix 2 Statutory regulations and associated memoranda

Appendix 3 Time/current characteristics of overcurrent protective devices and RCDs

Did you know?

BS 7671 does not consider a kitchen to be a special location. However electrical installation work in a kitchen needs to be notified under Part P of the Building Regulations.

Appendix 4 Current carrying capacity and voltage drop for cables and flexible cords

Appendix 5 Classification of external influences

Appendix 6 Model forms for certification reporting

Appendix 7 Harmonised cable core colours

Appendix 8 Current carrying capacity and voltage drop for busbar trunking and powertrack systems

Appendix 9 Definitions – multiple source, d.c. and other systems

Appendix 10 Protection of conductors in parallel against overcurrent

Appendix 11 Effect of harmonic currents in balanced three-phase systems

Appendix 12 Voltage drop in consumers' installations

Appendix 13 Methods for measuring the insulation resistance/impedance of floors and walls to earth or to the protective conductor system

Appendix 14 Measurement of earth-fault loop impedance: consideration of the increase of the resistance of conductors with increase of temperature

Appendix 15 Ring and radial final circuit arrangements, Regulation 433.1.

Did you know?

The **Index** lists where the various topics can be found alphabetically and is very good as a quick reference guide to finding the Regulation you need.

Locations containing a bath or shower

Certain locations are deemed to be more hazardous to persons and livestock because of the environment in which the equipment is used. Additional (or in some cases replacement) Regulations are, therefore, needed to provide greater safety. In particular, locations containing baths, showers and cabinets containing a shower and/or bath and the surrounding zones, present a greater risk of electric shock than dry locations.

Classification by zones

The areas are divided into zones (Zones 0, 1 and 2) taking into account walls, doors, fixed partitions, ceilings and floors. The Regulations dictate the type of electrical equipment, etc. that may be installed (or not) within each.

Zone 0 is the interior of the bath tub or shower basin. In a location containing a shower without a basin, it is limited by the floor and by the plane 0.10 mm above the floor and for the same horizontal distance as Zone 1.

Zone 1 is limited by:

- the finished floor level and the horizontal plane 2.25 m above the floor, or the highest fixed shower head, whichever is the greatest

- by the vertical plane circumscribing the bath tub or shower basin, including the space below the bath tub or shower basin if accessible without the use of a tool
- for a shower without a basin, and with a demountable showerhead able to be moved around in use, the vertical plane 1.2 m from the water outlet at the wall
- for a shower without a basin and with a showerhead which is not demountable, the vertical plane 600 mm from the showerhead.

Zone 2 is limited by:

- the vertical plane external to Zone 1 and the parallel vertical plane 600 mm external to Zone 1
- the floor and horizontal plane 2.25 m above the floor, or the highest fixed shower head, whichever is the greater.

Protection for safety

The following protective measures are not permitted:

- obstacles
- placing out of reach
- non-conducting location
- earth-fire local equipotential bonding.

Additional protection shall be provided for all circuits of the location by one or more 30 mA RCDs (Regulation 701.411.3.3).

Supplementary equipotential bonding

Local supplementary equipotential bonding, complying with Regulation 415.2, shall be provided connecting together the terminals of the protective conductors associated with Class I and Class II equipment in Zones 1 and 2 and extraneous conductive parts in these zones, including the following:

- metallic pipes supplying services and metallic waste pipes
- metallic central heating pipes and air conditioning systems
- accessible metallic structural parts of the building (not metallic doorframes or windows, unless connected to the metallic structure of the building)
- metallic baths and metallic shower basins
- connections to pipes to be made with BS 951 clamps (complete with 'Safety Electrical Connection' – Do Not Remove label).

Where the bath or shower is in a building with a protective earthing and bonding system, the supplementary bonding may be omitted if the electrical equipment in the location is protected by an RCD not exceeding 30 mA.

External influences

Any external equipment should have the following degrees of protection:

- **Zone 0:** IPX7
- **Zones 1 and 2:** IPX4 or, where water jets are likely to be used for cleaning purposes in communal baths or communal showers, protection required to be at least IPX5

Switch gear and control gear

The following requirements do not apply to switches and controls incorporated in fixed current using equipment suitable for use in that zone.

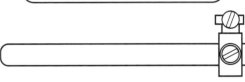

Safety label

- **Zone 0:** switchgear or accessories shall not be installed.
- **Zone 1:** only switches of SELV circuits supplied at a nominal voltage not exceeding 12 volts r.m.s.a.c. or 30 volts ripple free d.c., the safety source being installed outside Zones 0, 1 and 2.
- **Zone 2:** switchgear, accessories incorporating switches or socket outlets shall not be installed with the exception of switches and socket outlets of SELV circuits, the safety source being outside Zones 0, 1 and 2, and shaver supply units complying with BS EN 61558-2-5.

Socket outlets complying with section 414 may be installed in a location at a distance of more than 3 m horizontally from the edge of Zone 1.

Fixed current using equipment

In Zone 0 only fixed current using equipment, can be installed but should be suitable for the conditions of this zone. It must be protected by SELV, operating at a voltage of less than 12 V a.c. or 30 V d.c. It can include water heaters, shower pump, SELV current using equipment, other fixed current equipment provided it is protected by a RCD with an operating current not greater than 30 mA and provided the equipment is suitable for that zone.

Zone 2 can include towel rail, electric showers, luminaire, ventilation equipment and appliance units for whirlpools.

Electric heating units in the floor may be installed below any zone provided they are covered by an earthed metallic grid or an earthed metallic sheath connected to the protective conductor of the supply circuit.

Construction site installations

Construction sites also present a greater risk of electric shock because of the conditions that may occur. The Regulations cover:

- new building construction
- repair, alteration, extension or demolition of existing buildings or parts of existing buildings
- engineering construction
- earthworks
- work of similar nature.

They **do** apply to main switch gear and protective devices and everything on the load side of these including mobile and transportable electrical equipment. They **do not** apply to construction site offices, cloakrooms, meeting rooms, canteens, restaurants, dormitories and toilets, nor to installations covered by IEC 6062 series 2 (mines and quarries).

Supplies

Equipment must be identifiable, colour coded and keyway interlocked in the case of plugs and socket outlets, and compatible with the particular supply from which it is energised.

The following nominal voltages must not be exceeded:

- **SELV** – use of portable hand held lamps only in confined or damp places
- **110 V 1-phase, centre point earthed** – reduced low voltage system, portable hand lamps for general use, portable hand tools and local lighting up to 2 kW.
- **110 V 3-phase, star-point earthed** – reduced low voltage system, portable hand held tools and local lighting up to 2 kW, and small mobile plant to 3.75 kW
- **230 V, 1-phase** – fixed floodlighting. Socket outlets with a rating up to 32 A and any other circuit supplying hand held equipment up to 32 A must be protected by automatic disconnection and additional protection by 30 mA RCD.
- **400 V, 3-phase** – fixed and moveable equipment above 3.75 kW.

The colour codes for plugs and socket outlets for the various voltages are:

400 V red	240 V blue	110 V yellow
50 V white	25 V violet	

Protection for safety

An IT supply system must not be used if there is an alternative type, such as TNS, TT, etc. as permitted by the Electicity Safety Quality and Continuity Regulations 2002. However, the distribution network operator (DNO) may not allow connection to a protective multtiple earthed (PME) network because of the difficulty of installing and maintaining the main equipotential bonding.

Supplementary equipotential bonding

In a location intended for livestock, supplementary bonding must connect all exposed and extraneous conductive parts which can be touched. Concrete reinforcement and other extraneous conductive parts in or on the floor shall be supplememtary bonded.

Application of protective measures

Each socket outlet and any permanently connected hand held equipment up to and including 32 A must be protected by a RCD, unless it is individually fed from, and protected by, an isolating transformer.

Selection and erection of equipment

Every assembly used for the distribution of electricity on construction and demolition sites must comply with BS EN 60439-04. Other equipment must have a degree of protection appropriate to the external influences, e.g. IP rating.

Wiring systems

Cables must not be installed across a site road or walkway unless they are adequately protected against mechanical damage. For reduced low voltage systems the type of cable must be low temperature, 300/500 V, thermoplastic (PVC) flexible cable or equivalent. For higher voltages the flexible cable should be HO7 RN-F type or equivalent, having a rating of 400/750 V, and be resistant to abrasion and water.

Isolation and switching devices

Every assembly for construction must include devices for switching and isolating the incoming supply.

Every circuit supplying current using equipment must be fed from an ACS that incorporates:

- overcurrent protection devices (fuses, MCBs)
- devices that protect against indirect contact (RCDs)
- socket outlets (if required).

Safety and standby supplies must be connected by devices (inter-locking) that are arranged to prevent interconnection of different supplies.

Plugs and socket outlets

Every socket outlet must be incorporated as part of an assembly that complies with BS 4363 and BSEN 60439-4. Every plug and socket outlet must comply with BSEN 60309-2. Luminaire supporting couplers must not be used.

Cable couplers

Every cable coupler must comply with BSEN 60309-2.

Electricity at Work (EAW) Regulations 1989

The Electricity at Work Regulations require precautions to be taken against the risk of death or personal injury from electricity in work activities. They were made under the Health and Safety at Work Act 1974, which imposes duties on employers, employees and the self-employed, but are more specific. They concentrate on work activities at or near electrical equipment and make one person primarily responsible to ensure compliance in respect of systems, electrical equipment and conductors. This person is referred to as the 'duty holder'.

They also include systems, etc. not covered by BS 7671, such as voltages above 1000 volts a.c.

There are 33 Regulations and three appendices but not all apply to all situations. This chapter contains an overview but, for detailed information, read *The memorandum of guidance on the Electricity at Work Regulations 1989.*

EAW Regulation 1 only states that these Regulations came into force on 1 April 1990.

EAW Regulation 2 defines what is meant by certain words or phrases.

EAW Regulation 3 deals with **duty holders** and the requirements imposed on them. There are three categories: employers, employees and self-employed persons.

The duty holder is the person who has a duty to comply with these Regulations because they are relevant to circumstances within their control. Such a person must be competent. Whenever a Regulation uses the phrase **'as far as is reasonably practicable'** this means that the duty holder must assess the magnitude of the risks against the costs in terms of physical difficulty, time, trouble and expense involved in minimising that risk(s). The duty holder may have to prove in a court of law that he or she took all steps 'as far as is reasonably practicable'.

EAW Regulation 4 has four parts. The first deals with the construction of electrical systems to ensure that the equipment is suitable for its intended use and does not give rise to danger as far as is reasonably practicable.

The second deals with the maintenance of systems, whereby all systems should be maintained to prevent danger (this includes portable appliances) as far as is reasonably practicable. Records of maintenance, including test results, should be kept.

The third part deals with ensuring safe work activities near a system, including operation, use and maintenance 'as far as is reasonably practicable'. This could include non-electrical activities such as excavation

Remember

Whenever a Regulation does not use the phrase 'so far as is reasonably practicable' this means it is an absolute duty; **it must be done regardless of cost or any other consideration.**

near underground cables, and erecting scaffolding near overhead lines. Safe work activities include:

- company health and safety policy
- Permit to Work systems
- clear communication
- use of competent people
- personnel attitudes.

The fourth part deals with provision of protective equipment such as insulated tools, test probes, insulating gloves, rubber mats, etc. which must be suitable for use, maintained in that condition and properly used. **This is an absolute duty.**

EAW Regulation 5 has four parts. It requires that 'no electrical equipment must be used where its strength and capability may be exceeded and give rise to danger'. For example, switch gear should be capable of handling fault currents as well as normal load currents, have correct size cable, etc.

EAW Regulation 6 deals with siting and/or selection of electrical equipment and whether it would be exposed to, or could foreseeably be exposed to, adverse or hazardous environments. This could include:

- protection against mechanical damage
- effects of weather, natural hazards, temperature or pressure
- effects of wet, dirty, dusty or corrosive conditions
- any flammable or explosive substances, including dusts, vapours or gases.

EAW Regulation 7 is concerned with conductors in a system and whether they present a danger to persons. All conductors must be suitably covered with insulating material and protected or, if not insulated (such as overhead power lines), placed out of reach as far as is reasonably practicable.

Remember

The definition of 'placed out of reach' is in Part 2 of BS 7671.

EAW Regulation 8 deals with the requirements for earthing, or other precautions, to reduce the risk of electric shock when a conductor (other than a circuit conductor) becomes live under fault conditions. This includes earthing the outer conductive parts of electrical equipment, which could be touched, and other conductive metalwork in the vicinity, such as water and gas pipes. Other methods could be reduced voltage systems, double insulated equipment and RCDs. **This is an absolute duty.**

EAW Regulation 9 is about maintaining the integrity of referenced conductors, which in simple terms means that the neutral conductor must not have a fuse or switch placed in it. The only exception is that a switch may be placed in the neutral conductor, if that switch is interlocked to break the line conductor(s) at the same time. **This is an absolute duty.**

EAW Regulation 10 requires that all joints and connections in a system must be mechanically and electrically suitable for its use. For example, things like taped joints on extension leads are not allowed. **This is an absolute duty.**

EAW Regulation 11 states that every part of a system must be protected from excess current that may give rise to danger. This means that suitably rated fuses, circuit breakers, etc. must be installed so that, in a fault situation, they will interrupt the supply and prevent a dangerous situation happening. **This is an absolute duty.**

EAW Regulation 12 deals with the need for switching off and isolating electrical equipment and, where appropriate, identifying circuits. Isolation means cutting off from every source of electrical energy in such a way that it cannot be switched back on accidentally, in other words a means of 'locking off' the switch securely. **This is an absolute duty.**

EAW Regulation 13 covers precautions required when work is taking place at or near electrical equipment that is to be worked on, whether it be electrical or non-electrical work that is taking place. The electrical equipment must be isolated, locked off and tested for absence of live parts before the work takes place and must remain so until all persons have completed their work. A safe isolation procedure or written Permit to Work scheme should be used. **This is an absolute duty.**

EAW Regulation 14 refers to the precautions needed when working on or near live conductors. An absolute duty is imposed that conductors must be isolated unless certain conditions are met. Precautions considered appropriate are:

- properly trained and competent staff
- provision of adequate information regarding the nature of the work and system
- use of appropriate insulated tools, equipment, instruments, test probes and protective clothing
- use of insulated barriers
- accompaniment of another person
- effective control of the work area.

This is an absolute duty.

EAW Regulation 15 covers work at or near electrical equipment to prevent danger and provide adequate working space, access and lighting. **This is an absolute duty.**

EAW Regulation 16 deals with the competency of persons working on electrical equipment to prevent danger or injury. To comply with this regulation a person should conform to the following, or be under such a degree of supervision as appropriate, given the type of work to be carried out:

- adequate understanding and practical experience of the system to be worked on

- an understanding of the hazards that may arise
- the ability to recognise at all times whether it is safe to continue.

The Regulation tries to ensure that no one places themselves or anyone else at risk due to their lack of technical knowledge or practical experience. This is an **absolute** Regulation.

EAW Regulations 17 to 28 apply to mines and quarries only.

EAW Regulation 29 is what is known as the 'Defence' Regulation. If an offence is committed by the duty holder under these Regulations (the absolute ones) and criminal proceedings are brought by the HSE (Health and Safety Executive) then, if the duty holder can prove that they took all reasonable steps and exercised due diligence to avoid committing that offence, they will not be found guilty.

EAW Regulation 30. A duty holder can apply to the HSE for exemption from these Regulations for:

- any person
- any premises
- any electrical equipment
- any electrical system
- any electrical process
- any activity.

Exemptions will only be granted by the HSE provided they do not prejudice the health and safety of any persons.

EAW Regulation 31 deals with work activities and premises outside Great Britain. If the activity or premises is covered by Sections 1 to 59 and Sections 80 to 82 of the Health and Safety at Work Act 1974 then these regulations apply.

EAW Regulation 32 details what these regulations do not apply to:

- sea going ships
- aircraft or hovercraft moving under their own power.

EAW Regulation 33 deals with changes and modifications to these regulations since they were brought in.

EAW Appendix 1 lists the HSE guidance publications available for help in understanding and applying the regulations.

EAW Appendix 2 lists various other codes of practice and British Standards that could help in the understanding and application of these regulations.

EAW Appendix 3 deals with the legislation concerning working space and access regulations.

Hazardous installations

A hazardous area can be defined as: 'an area in which explosive gas/air mixtures are, or may be expected to be, present in quantities such as to require special precautions for the construction and use of electrical apparatus'.

Zoning

Hazardous areas are defined in the Dangerous Substances and Explosive Atmospheres Regulations 2002 (DSEAR) as 'any place in which an explosive atmosphere may occur in quantities such as to require special precautions to protect the safety of workers'. In this context, 'special precautions' is best taken as relating to the construction, installation and use of apparatus, as given in BS EN 60079-10.

Area classification is a method of analysing and classifying the environment where explosive gas atmospheres may occur. The main purpose is to facilitate proper selection and installation of apparatus to be used safely in that environment, taking into account the properties of the flammable materials that will be present. DSEAR specifically extends the original scope of this analysis, to take into account non-electrical sources of ignition, and mobile equipment that creates an ignition risk.

Hazardous areas are classified in zones based on the assessed frequency of the occurrence and duration of an explosive gas atmosphere, as follows:

- **Zone 0:** An explosive gas atmosphere is present continuously or for long periods.
- **Zone 1:** An explosive gas atmosphere is likely to occur in normal operation.
- **Zone 2:** An explosive gas atmosphere is not likely to occur in normal operation and, if it occurs, will only exist for a short time.

There are no official time limits for explosive atmosphere in each zone, and for the majority of situations a qualitative approach is adequate, but the most common values used are:

- **Zone 0:** more than 1000 hours per year
- **Zone 1:** more than 10, but less than 1000 hours per year
- **Zone 2:** less than 10, but still sufficiently likely as to require controls over ignition sources.

When the hazardous areas have been classified, the remainder will be defined as non-hazardous, sometimes referred to as 'safe areas'.

Term	Definition
Explosive limits	The upper and lower percentages of a gas in a given volume of gas/air mixture at normal atmospheric temperature and pressure that will burn if ignited.
Lower explosive limit (LEL)	The concentration below which the gas atmosphere is not explosive.
Upper explosive limit (UEL)	The concentration of gas above which the gas atmosphere is not explosive.
Ignition energy	The spark energy that will ignite the most easily ignited gas/air mixture of the test gas at atmospheric pressure; hydrogen ignites very easily, whereas butane or methane require about 10 times the energy.
Flash point	The minimum temperature at which a material gives off sufficient vapour to form an explosive atmosphere.
Ignition temperature or auto ignition temperature of a material	The minimum temperature at which the material will ignite and sustain combustion when mixed with air at normal pressure, without the ignition being caused by any spark or flame.

Table 5.01 Definitions of key terms

Selection of equipment

DSEAR sets out the link between a zone and the equipment that may be installed there. This applies to new or newly modified installations. The equipment categories are defined by the ATEX equipment directive, set out in UK law as the Equipment and Protective Systems for Use in Potentially Explosive Atmospheres Regulations 1996.

Standards set out different protection concepts, with further subdivisions for some types of equipment according to gas group and temperature classification. Most of the electrical standards have been developed over many years and are now set at international level, while standards for non-electrical equipment are only just becoming available from CEN.

The DSEAR ACOP describes the provisions concerning existing equipment. There are different technical means (protection concepts) of building equipment to the different categories. The current standards are listed below.

Remember
Ignition temperature is not the same as flash point, so don't confuse them!

Installations in potentially explosive areas

Within hazardous areas there exists the risk of explosions and/or fires due to electrical equipment 'igniting' the gas, dust or flammable liquid. These areas are not included in BS 7671 but are covered by IEC Standard BS EN 60079 as follows:

- **BS EN 60079 Part 10** – Classification of hazardous areas
- **BS EN 60079 Part 14** – Electrical apparatus for explosive gas atmospheres
- **BS EN 60079 Part 17** – Inspection/maintenance of electrical installations in hazardous areas.

BS EN 60079 has been in place since 1988, replacing the old BS 5345. However, many installations still exist that were completed in accordance with BS 5345 and new European Directives (ATEX) address safety where there is a danger from potentially explosive atmospheres. Other statutory regulations, such as the Petroleum Regulation Acts 1928 and 1936 and local licensing laws, govern storage of petroleum.

Ignition sources – identification and control

There are many possible ignition sources, including naked flames, hot surfaces, sparks, lightning strikes and electromagnetic radiation. Sources of ignition should be controlled in all hazardous areas by design measures and systems of work, including:

- using electrical equipment and instrumentation classified for the zone in which it is located
- earthing all plant and equipment
- eliminating surfaces above ignition temperatures of flammable materials being handled or stored
- lightning protection
- selection of vehicles and internal combustion engines to work in zoned areas
- selection of equipment to avoid high intensity electromagnetic radiation sources, e.g. limiting power input to fibre optic systems, avoidance of high intensity lasers or sources of infrared radiation
- prohibition of smoking, and any use of matches or lighters
- controlling the use of normal vehicles
- controlling activities that create intermittent hazardous areas, e.g. tanker loading or unloading
- controlling maintenance activities that may cause sparks, hot surfaces or naked flames through a Permit to Work system.

Petrol filling stations

The primary legislation controlling storage and use of petrol is the Petroleum (Consolidation) Act 1928 (PCA). This requires anyone who keeps petrol to obtain a licence from the local Petroleum Licensing Authority (PLA). It is usually issued subject to conditions set by the PLA, but they must be related to the safe keeping of petrol. The Local Authority Co-ordinating Body on Food and Trading Standards (LACOTS) has issued a set of standard licence conditions which most PLAs apply to their sites.

Installations within petrol filling stations are effectively also covered by BS EN 60079 Parts 10, 14 and 17. Additionally there is industry developed guidance for this sector in IP/APEA's *Guidance for the Design, Construction, Modification and Maintenance of Petrol Filling Stations (Institute of Petroleum and the Association for Petroleum and Explosives Administration)*. This guidance replaced most of HS(G)41 and was published in 1999 by IP/APEA with input from HSE.

Short answer questions

1. What is BS 7671 designed to do?
2. List six of the special locations identified by BS 7671.
3. List six special areas that are included in IEE Guidance Note 7.
4. What is the difference between 'absolute' and the term 'as far as is reasonably practicable' when used in statutory regulations?
5. What is the difference between statutory and non-statutory regulations?

Multiple-choice test

1. Which of the following is NOT statutory?
   a. EAW 1989
   b. HASW 1974
   c. BS 7671
   d. Electricity Supply Regulations 1988

2. Which digits of a Regulation number identify the chapter?
   a. 1st
   b. 2nd and 3rd
   c. 5th and 6th
   d. 1st and 2nd

3. Which of the following is not covered by BS 7671?
   a. commercial premises
   b. distributors' equipment
   c. caravans, caravan parks
   d. highway power supplies

4. What is the voltage range between conductors that are covered by BS 7671?
   a. up to 1000 V a.c. or 1500 V d.c.
   b. up to 1000 V d.c. or 1500 V a.c.
   c. up to 415 V a.c. or 600 V d.c.
   d. between 110 V a.c. and 415 V a.c.

5. How many parts are there in BS 7671?
   a. 5
   b. 7
   c. 9
   d. 3

6. Which of the following is not a category of duty holder?
   a. employer
   b. member of the public
   c. self-employed person
   d. employee

7. Which of the following is not covered by EAW 1989?
   a. sea going ships
   b. power lines
   c. hospitals
   d. factories

8. How many zones are there in a bathroom?
   a. 2
   b. 4
   c. 3
   d. 5

9. What is the nominal r.m.s.a.c. voltage for SELV supplies?
   a. 12
   b. 1104
   c. 24
   d. 30

10. What is the IP rating for equipment in zone 0?
    a. IPX4
    b. IPX7
    c. IPX5
    d. IPX9

11. Which of the following is NOT covered by Part 7 Special installations or locations?
    a. construction site offices
    b. engineering construction
    c. earthworks
    d. new building construction

12. What is the colour coding of a 230 volt plug/socket on a construction site?
    a. red
    b. blue
    c. yellow
    d. white

13. What is the minimum distance that radiant heaters must be from livestock?
    a. 1 metre
    b. 5 metres
    c. 0.25 metres
    d. 0.5 metres

14. What is the minimum current rating for a caravan supply?
    a. 32 amp
    b. 6 amp
    c. 16 amp
    d. 20 amp

15. What is the maximum disconnection time for highway power supplies?
    a. 0.4 seconds
    b. 5 seconds
    c. 200 milliseconds
    d. 40 milliseconds

16. What is the voltage range covered by Part 7 for caravans?
    a. 230/400 V
    b. 250/440 V
    c. 110/1000 V
    d. up to 600 V

06 Earthing and protection

By the end of this chapter you should be able to demonstrate your knowledge and understanding of earthing and protection systems in the following areas, relative to the electrical construction environment:

- Purpose of earthing
  - Results of an unearthed appliance
  - Results of a bad earth
  - Results of a good earth
  - Earth-fault loop path
- Earthing systems
  - TN systems
  - Protective multiple earthing (PME)
  - Lightning protection
- Electric shock
  - Prevention of direct contact
  - Prevention of indirect contact
- Overcurrent protection
  - Residual current device (RCD)
  - Residual current circuit breaker with overload protection (RCBO)
  - Fuses and circuit breakers
  - Fusing factor
  - Prospective short circuit current (PSCC)

- Electrical faults
  - Discrimination
- Cable selection
  - External influences
  - Design current (I_b)
  - Rating of the protective device (I_n)
  - Reference methods
  - Correction factors
  - Application of correction factors
  - Voltage drop
  - Shock protection
  - Thermal constraints
  - Diversity

Purpose of earthing

The purpose of earthing is to connect together all metal work (other than that which is intended to carry current) so that dangerous potential differences cannot exist between different metal parts or between metal parts and earth.

By adhering to the correct earthing procedures including correct lightning protection, the danger to life and the risk of fire to property can be greatly reduced.

Figure 6.01 illustrates the return path from the consumer's earth to supply earth. Connection at the consumer's earth is made by either an earth electrode at the building or by means of a cable run back to the generator or transformer and connected to an earth point.

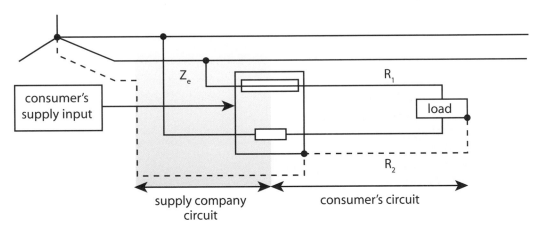

Figure 6.01 The earth-fault loop path

At the point of supply the transformer or generator always has an earth point. Therefore a circuit is formed when earth fault currents flow. If these currents are large enough, they will operate the relevant protective device, thus isolating the circuit.

The star point of the secondary winding of a three-phase four-wire distribution transformer is connected to the earth to maintain the neutral at earth potential.

Results of an unearthed appliance

The case of the appliance shown is live due to a fault. A person touching this appliance will complete the earth circuit and receive an electric shock.

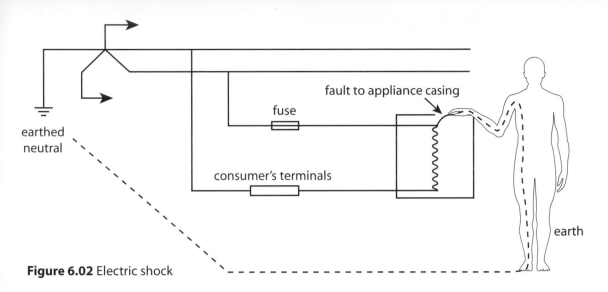

Figure 6.02 Electric shock

Results of a bad earth

A circuit with too much resistance can sometimes have a more disastrous effect than having no earth at all. The illustration shows where the earth fault circuit has a high resistance due to a bad contact at point A. The severity of the shock will depend upon three things:

- the surroundings
- the condition of the person receiving the shock
- the type of supply.

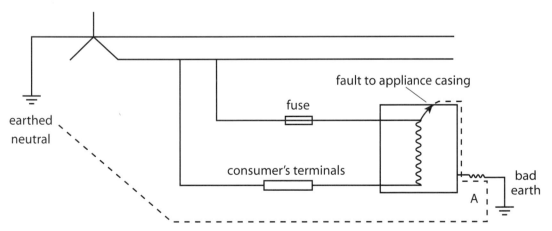

Figure 6.03 Bad earth path

When current starts to flow, the high resistance connection will heat up. This could be a fire hazard, because the current flow may not be high enough to operate the protective device. The appliance casing, therefore, remains live.

Results of a good earth

A good earth path is a low resistance one allowing a high current to flow. This causes the protective device to operate quickly, thereby isolating the circuit and giving protection against electric shock.

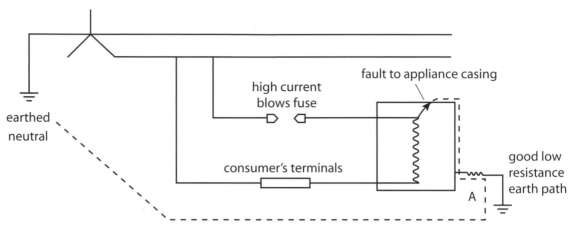

Figure 6.04 Good earth path

Earth-fault loop path

The path the earth fault current takes is called the earth-fault loop or line-earth loop. It has impedance because the transformer or generator windings are part of the circuit and are inductive. This inductance, and the resistance of the cables to and from the fault, make up the impedance.

The earth fault leakage, in ohms (Ω), is obtained from the formula:

$$Z_s = Z_e + (R_1 + R_2)$$

Where Z_e = loop impedance external to the installation

R_1 = the resistance of the installation line conductor to the fault point

R_2 = the resistance of the installation return conductor to the fault point

Z_s = total fault loop impedance.

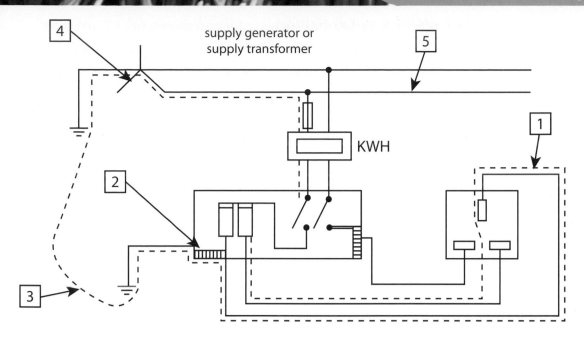

1. The circuit protective conductor (cpc) within the installation.
2. The consumer's earthing terminal and earthing conductor.
3. The earth return path, which can be either by means of an electrode or via the cable armouring.
4. The path through the earthed neutral point of the transformer and the transformer winding (or generator winding).
5. The phase conductor.

Figure 6.05 Earth-fault loop impedance

Earthing systems

An efficient and effective earthing system is essential to allow protective devices to operate. The limitation values of earth-fault loop impedance are found in Tables 41, 604 and 605 of BS 7671 IEE Regulations. Section 542 has details of the earthing arrangements to be incorporated in the supply system to meet the requirements of the Regulations.

A system comprises an electrical installation connected to a supply and systems are classified by a capital letter designation. There are six systems, but only TT, TN-S, and TN-C-S are suitable for public supplies:

- TT
- TN-S
- TN-C
- TN-C-S
- Protective multiple earthing (PME)
- IT

The first letter indicates the supply earthing arrangements. ('T' indicates one or more points of the supply directly connected to earth.)

The second letter indicates the relationship of the exposed conductive parts to earth. 'T' indicates exposed conductive parts directly connected to earth, which is independent of the supply. 'N' indicates that exposed conductive parts are connected directly to the earth point of the source of the supply.

TN systems

Arrangement of the neutral and protective conductors in TN systems is indicated by a third letter.

- S means separate neutral and protective conductors.
- C means neutral and protective conductors combined in a single conductor.

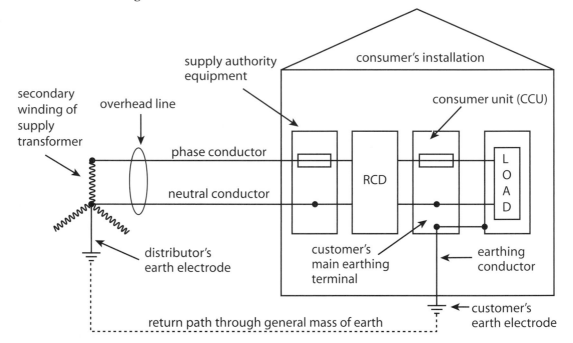

Figure 6.06 Earthing with customer's earth electrode and ground earth return path

TN-C has the neutral and protective functions combined in the same conductor. There must be no metallic connection between this system and the supply company system. It is relatively uncommon and restricted to specific situations.

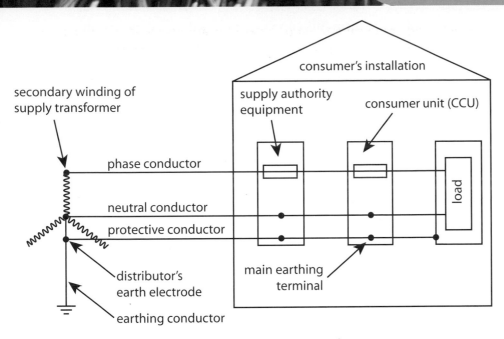

Figure 6.07 TN-S earthing system with metallic return path

Protective multiple earthing (PME)

PME is an earthing arrangement found in a TN-C-S system where the supply neutral conductor is used to connect the earthing conductor of an installation with earth. It is extremely reliable, and is the most commonly used distribution system in the UK today.

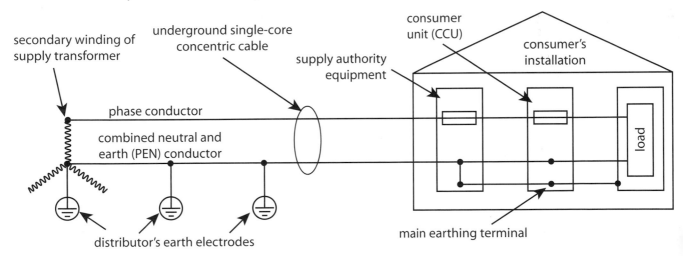

Figure 6.08 TN-C-S, protective multiple earthing (PME) system

The neutral of the incoming supply is used as the earth point, where all circuit protective conductors (cpc) connect all the metalwork to be protected to the main earth terminal.

All line to earth faults are converted into line to neutral faults, ensuring that under fault conditions a heavier current will flow operating protective devices rapidly.

However, the increase in fault current may produce two hazards:

- Increased fault current leads to an increased fire risk.
- If the neutral conductor rises to a dangerous potential relative to earth, the resultant shock risk would be extended to all the protected metalwork on every installation connected to this distribution network.

Because of these hazards, certain conditions are required before a PME system can be used. These include:

- PME can only be installed by the supply company.
- The neutral conductor must be earthed at a number of points along its length.
- There must be no link or fuse in the neutral conductor breaking the neutral path.
- Where PME conditions apply, the main equipotential bonding conductor must be selected in accordance with the neutral conductor of the supply and Table 54.8 of BS 7671.

Lightning protection

The protection of buildings and structures against lightning involves connecting various conducting parts to earth. A lightning protection system consists of a network of conductors (copper or aluminium) fixed at specified distances along the roof and walls of a structure, and bonded to other parts of a structure, such as radio and TV masts. These are then connected to a common point discharging to earth. The maximum resistance of this network of conductors should not exceed 10 ohms.

Lightning conductor connection

Electric shock

Electrical shock is a dangerous physiological effect, which results from the passage of an electric current through either a human body or livestock. BS 7671 deals with protection against electrical shock resulting from direct and indirect contact (now called 'basic protection' and 'fault protection') with a live source.

Basic protection

Measures to give basic protection include:

- **Insulating live parts** – Insulation should be of a minimum standard only to be removable by destruction.
- **Barriers and enclosures** – Used when live parts are contained within an enclosure or situated behind a barrier.
- **Obstacles** – Used to ensure any unintentional bodily contact with any live parts when equipment is being operated. Access is restricted to either skilled or instructed persons working under supervision.
- **Placing out of reach** – As in overhead lines or any parts that, when in normal use, cannot be protected by any other means.

Fault protection

This is the contact of either persons or livestock with exposed conductive parts that have become live under fault conditions. Measures to give fault protection include the following:

- protective equipotential bonding and automatic disconnection of the supply (PEBAD, previously known as EEBAD)
- use of Class II equipment and/or equivalent insulation
- non-conducting location based on physical separation from exposed conductive parts and no earth connection
- earth free local equipotential bonding, so that every part is bonded and there is no voltage difference
- electrical separation using a transformer or isolated generator supply.

PEBAD requires all exposed conductive parts within an installation to be connected or bonded together to prevent a difference in potential between these various parts under fault conditions. This includes metal casings of appliances as well as metal conduit, tray or trunking. Extraneous conductive parts within a building, such as the copper water and gas pipes and fittings, should also be bonded to earth.

Overcurrent protection

An overload is a current that exceeds its rated value in what is normally referred to as a healthy circuit. Overload currents usually occur due to abuse by the consumer or by bad design or wrong modification by the installer. Overcurrent and earth-fault protection is provided by means of a circuit breaker or fuse. These devices operate within specific limits, disconnecting the supply automatically in the event of a fault current flowing (overload, short circuit or earth faults).

Residual current device (RCD)

An RCD is a type of circuit breaker that compares the current in the line and neutral conductors on a continuous basis. In a healthy circuit both currents will be equal. If a fault occurs, some current will flow to earth and the currents in the line and neutral will become unbalanced. The RCD detects the imbalance and disconnects the circuit.

Functional testing of an RCD should be carried out by operating the test button at regular intervals. Additional tests should be conducted as part of periodic inspection and test procedures.

Residual current circuit breaker with overload protection (RCBO)

This is a combination of a miniature circuit breaker (MCB) and an RCD. It offers protection against the effects of earth leakage, overload, and short circuit currents. A standard range of devices include 10 A/30m A, 16 A/30m A, 20 A/30m A and 40 A/30m A.

Fuses and circuit breakers

A fuse is a device that, when inserted in a circuit, is designed to break the circuit if the current exceeds a rated value for a given time. It comprises a fuse element that melts and a fuse carrier, which allows the fuse to be removed and replaced.

Rewirable fuses (BS 3036)

The rewirable fuse consists of a fuse holder, a fuse element and fuse carrier. The holder and carrier are made of either bakelite or porcelain. The fuse has a colour code, marked on the fuse holder, to indicate the circuit it is designed for:

- 5 amp white
- 15 amp blue
- 20 amp yellow
- 30 amp red
- 45 amp green.

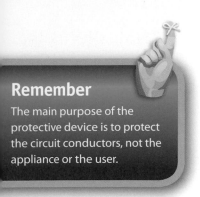

Remember

The main purpose of the protective device is to protect the circuit conductors, not the appliance or the user.

Definition

Short circuit – An overcurrent resulting from a fault of negligible impedance between live conductors that would have a difference in potential under normal operating conditions. Short circuits normally occur as a result of accidents, which cannot be predicted.

This type of fuse was very popular in domestic installations but has been replaced in a lot of installations by the circuit breaker.

Disadvantages of rewirable fuses	Advantages of rewirable fuses
• Easily abused when the wrong size of fuse wire is fitted. • Fusing factor of around 1.8–2.0 means they aren't guaranteed to operate until up to twice the rated current is flowing; as a result cables protected by them must have a larger current carrying capacity. • Precise conditions for operation cannot be easily predicted. • Do not cope well with high short-circuit currents. • Fuse wire can deteriorate over time. • Danger from hot scattering metal if the fuse carrier is inserted into the base when the circuit is faulty.	• Low initial cost. • Can easily see when the fuse has blown. • Low element replacement cost. • No mechanical moving parts. • Easy storage of spare fuse wire.

Table 6.01 Advantages and disadvantages of rewireable fuses

Nominal current of fuse wire (A)	Nominal diameter of wire (mm)
3	0.15
5	0.20
10	0.35
15	0.50
20	0.60
25	0.75
30	0.85
45	1.25
60	1.53
80	1.80
100	2.00

Table 6.02 Size of tinned copper wire for use in semi-enclosed fuses

Cartridge fuses (BS 1361/1362)

The cartridge fuse consists of a porcelain tube with metal end caps to which the fuse element is attached. The tube is filled with granulated silica. The BS 1362 fuse is used mainly in 13 amp plug tops, for which there are two common fuse ratings available, 3 amp and 13 amp.

Disadvantages of cartridge fuses	Advantages of cartridge fuses
• More expensive to replace than rewireable fuses. • Can be replaced with an incorrect size fuse (plug top type only). • The cartridge can be shorted out with wire or silver foil in extreme cases of bad practice. • Not possible to see if the fuse has blown. • Require a stock of spare fuses to be kept.	• No mechanical moving parts. • Declared rating is accurate. • The element does not weaken with age. • Small physical size and no external arcing, which permits their use in plug tops and small fuse carriers. • Low fusing factor; around 1.6–1.8. • Easy to replace.

Table 6.03 Advantages and disadvantages of cartridge fuses

High breaking capacity (HBC) fuses (BS 88)

The HBC fuse is normally found protecting motor circuits and industrial installations. It consists of a porcelain body filled with silica, a silver element and lug-type end caps. Another feature is the indicating bead, which shows when the fuse element has blown. It is a very fast acting fuse and can discriminate between a starting surge and an overload current.

These types of fuses would be used when high prospective fault current exists.

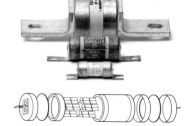

Figure 6.09 A sectional view of a typical BS 88 HBC fuse

Disadvantages of BS 88 fuses	Advantages of BS 88 fuses
• Very expensive to replace. • Stocks of these spares are costly and take up space. • Care must be taken when replacing them, to ensure that the replacement fuse has the same rating and also the same characteristics as the fuse being replaced.	• No mechanical moving parts. • The element does not weaken with age. • Operation is very rapid under fault conditions. • It is difficult to interchange the cartridge, since different ratings are made to different physical sizes.

Table 6.04 Advantages and disadvantages of BS 88 fuses

Miniature circuit breakers (MCB)

An MCB provides an automatic switch that opens in the event of excessive current flow in a circuit. It can be closed when the circuit returns to normal operation.

The contacts of a circuit breaker are closed against spring pressure and held closed by a latch arrangement. A small movement of the latch will release the contacts, which then open quickly against the spring pressure and break the circuit.

The breaker is so arranged that normal currents will not affect the latch. However, excessive currents will move it to operate the breaker. The two basic methods by which overcurrent can trip the latch are:

- **Thermal tripping** – Here the load current passes through a small heater coil wrapped around a bi-metallic strip situated inside the MCB housing. The amount of heat created depends upon the current. Excess current warms up the bi-metallic strip, causing it to bend and trip the latch to open the contacts.
- **Magnetic tripping** – The principal applied here is the force of attraction set up by the magnetic field of a coil carrying a load current. The magnetic field is set up by a current in the flexible strip that attracts the strip to the iron. Overload currents will operate the latch and cause main contacts to trip.

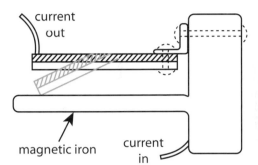

Figure 6.10 A simple attraction type of magnetic trip

Combined tripping

With thermal tripping, there is always a delay in the operation of the thermal strip, as the heat produced by the load currents has to be transferred to the bi-metal strip. Thermal tripping is therefore best suited to small overloads of comparatively long duration.

Magnetic trips are fast acting for large overloads or short circuits. The two methods are often combined to take advantage of the best characteristics of each.

Disadvantages of MCBs	Advantages of MCBs
<ul><li>They have mechanical moving parts.</li><li>They are expensive.</li><li>They must be regularly tested.</li><li>Ambient temperature can change performance.</li></ul>	<ul><li>They have factory-set operating characteristics which cannot be altered.</li><li>They will maintain transient overloads and trip on sustained overloads.</li><li>Easily identified when they have tripped.</li><li>The supply can be quickly restored.</li></ul>

Table 6.05 Advantages and disadvantages of MCBs

Fusing factor

In order to classify protective devices, we require to know their circuit breaking and 'fusing' performance. This is achieved for fuses by using the fusing factor:

$$\text{Fusing factor} = \frac{\text{Fusing current}}{\text{Current rating}}$$

Where 'fusing current' is the minimum current that will cause the fuse to blow; and 'current rating' is the maximum current that the fuse will allow before blowing.

Thus a 20 amp fuse that operates when 25 amps flows will have a fusing factor of $25/20 = 1.25$. Because the protective device must always carry the rated current it follows that the fusing factor must always be greater than 1. The closer the fusing factor is to 1 the better the protection.

Fusing currents can be found in Appendix 3 of BS 7671. These tables are in logarithmic form and the scales increase by factors of ten. The interpretation of these scales requires practice.

Fusing factors for the above devices are usually grouped as follows.

- BS 3036 Rewireable fuses 1.8–2.0
- BS 1361 Cartridge fuses 1.6–1.9
- BS 88 HBC fuses 1.25–1.27
- MCBs up to 1.5.

The higher the fusing factor the less accurate and the less reliable the protective device will be. The protective device must be able to make or break a current without damage to its surroundings.

Prospective short circuit current (PSCC)

The effects of a short circuit are:

- **Thermal effect** – This can cause melting of conductors, insulation or fire.
- **Mechanical effect** – The result of large magnetic fields, causing mechanical damage.

Rapid disconnection of the supply is essential to prevent such damage, especially where a short circuit occurs, which will cause maximum damage.

Possible causes of a short circuit are:

- contact between two poles of the supply
- failure of equipment
- ingress of moisture
- accidental damage.

Electrical faults

A fault is any circuit condition in which current flows through an abnormal or unintended path. There are numerous causes.

If a fault has negligible impedance then the main restriction to the amount of current that will flow in the circuit is that of all the conductors. Because conductors have a low resistance then this total would be low and the current flowing could be very high.

If a phase to neutral short circuit fault occurs within a final circuit then the final protective device should operate first.

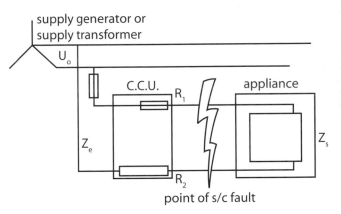

Figure 6.11 Short circuit loop impedance

Discrimination

When a fault occurs, only that device nearest the fault should operate, ensuring minimum disruption to other circuits not associated with the fault.

Discrimination is said to have taken place when the smaller rated local device operates before the larger device. Because protective devices have different characteristics we cannot work on the assumption that discrimination will be achieved, for example a 32 A mcb in use with a 13 A cartridge fuse. This is especially the case where a mixture of devices is being used purely on the grounds of their current rating (I_n).

However when protective devices are used in series with an installation, a 2:1 ratio with the lower rated devices will be satisfactory.

Cable selection

Cable selection is defined as the rules you should follow when deciding which cable to choose for any installation. There are 10 key ones described in this section.

External influences

These include any influence external to an installation that affects the safe operation and design of that installation.

Appendix 5 of BS 7671 provides a 'Classification of external influences', where each condition of external influence is designated with a code that comprises a group of two capital letters and a number.

Design current (I_b)

This is the normal resistive load current. It is calculated by the following formula:

For single phase supplies: $U_o = 230\,V$ and $I_b = \dfrac{Power}{U_o}$

For three phase supplies: $U_o = 400\,V$ and $I_b = \dfrac{Power}{\sqrt{3} \times U_o}$

In an a.c. circuit, the effects of a high inductive or high capacitive load can produce a poor power factor (PF). Allowances must be made for this, giving the following equations for the design current.

For single phase circuits: $Ib = \dfrac{Power}{U_o \times PF}$

For three phase circuits: $Ib = \dfrac{Power}{\sqrt{3}U_o \times PF}$

Where PF is the power factor of the circuit concerned (explained in Chapter 3).

Rating of the protective device (I_n)

Having calculated the design current (I_b), it is possible to work out the current rating or setting (I_n) of the protective device.

IEE Regulation 433.1.1 states that a current rating (I_n) must be no less than the design current (I_b) of a circuit. This is because the protective device must be able to pass enough current for the circuit to operate at full load but without the protective device operating and disconnecting the circuit.

Reference methods

Table 4A2 of the IEE Regulations lists all the methods that can be used to install a cable.

Correction factors

There are five correction factors that need to be applied to the nominal rating of the protection. These are listed in tables within BS 7671.

Correction factor	Tables for correction factor values	Symbol
Ambient temperature	Tables 4B1, 4B2 and 4B3	Ca
Grouping factors	Tables (4C1, 4C2, 4C3, 4C4, 4C5)	Cg
Thermal insulation	Table 52.2 reg 523.7	Ci
BS 3036 fuse	0.725	Cr
Mineral-insulated cable	0.9	N/A

Table 6.06 Tables for correction values

Ambient temperature

This is the temperature of the air or other medium where the equipment is to be used. The tables are corrections from an ambient temperature of 30 °C. When a cable runs through areas having different ambient temperatures, correction factors should be applied to the highest temperature only.

Grouping

If a group of cables run together and touch each other, they will produce heat when they are carrying current. The effect of this is that they are less able to cool down. So, when installing cables, they should be kept separate in order to reduce overheating.

If each cable is separated by a clearance to the next surface by at least one cable diameter (De) they are classified as spaced. Care must be taking when choosing the correction factor. When the horizontal clearance to the next cable is more than 2 × De then no correction factor is needed.

Thermal insulation

There are two ways thermal insulation is relevant in electrical installations:

- Where the cable is in contact with thermal insulation on one side of the cable only, Methods 4 or 6 are used for selecting a cable type from Table 4D5A of BS 7671.
- Where the cable is totally enclosed in thermal insulation for any length from 50 mm up to 400 mm, a cable must have a correction factor applied as stated in Regulation 523.7 Table 52.2. If more than 500 mm of cable is to be totally enclosed then the correction factor to be applied must be 0.5. The cable rating is then effectively halved.

Length in insulation (mm)	De-rating factor
50	0.89
100	0.81
200	0.68
400	0.55

Table 6.07 Cable rating

BS 3036 fuse

The BS 3036 semi-enclosed rewireable fuse is the only protective device that does not disconnect in sufficient time. In this case we must always use a factor of 0.725 when calculating current carrying capacity.

Mineral insulated cable

Table 4G1A states that, for bare cables (no PVC outer covering) exposed to touch, the tabulated values should be multiplied by 0.9.

Table 4G2A states that no correction factor for grouping need be applied.

Application of correction factors

Correction factors are applied to make sure that the cable is large enough to carry the current without too much heat being generated.

If the cable's ability to give off heat is reduced by external conditions, the cable size will need to be increased. This is because the use of correction factors will require an increase in the physical cross section area of the cable, which in turn increases the cable capacity to carry current and give off heat.

When the right correction factors have been applied, we know the effective current capacity of the conductor (I_z). We then need to apply the result obtained from the formula to the correct cable table to find the correct cable size. This value of current, tabulated in Appendix 4 of BS 7671, is given the symbol I_t, which must be greater than I_z.

Hence:

$$I_t \geq I_z \geq \frac{I_n}{C_a \times C_g \times C_i \times C_c}$$

(Where C_a, etc. are correction factors, where they apply.)

You can then use the value of I_z, together with the correct table from BS 7671 (Tables 4D1A to 4J4B) to find the size of cable to use, given these correction factors.

Voltage drop

Regulation 525.3 states that the voltage drop between the origin of the installation and a socket outlet should not exceed 5 per cent of the supply voltage. For lighting circuits the maximum permissible volt-drop should not exceed 3 per cent.

The voltage drops because the resistance of the conductor becomes greater as the length of the cable increases or a cross section area (csa) of the cable is reduced. This means that, on long cable runs, the cable csa may have to be increased to allow the current to flow more easily and reduce the voltage drop across the circuit.

Hence the maximum permissible voltage drop for circuits other than lighting (5%) allowed is:

For single phase 230 volts systems $= \dfrac{230 \times 5}{100} = 11.5$ volts

For three phase 400 volts systems $= \dfrac{400 \times 5}{100} = 20$ volts

The values for cable voltage drop are given in the accompanying tables of current carrying capacity in Appendix 4 of BS 7671. The values are giving in millivolts per ampere per metre (mV/A/m).

$$\text{Voltage drop (Vd)} = \frac{mV/A/m \times I_b \times L}{1000}$$

Where mV/A/m is the value given in the Regulation tables.

I_b is the circuit's design current.

L   is the length of the cable used in the circuit measured in metres.

Shock protection

The speed of operation of the protective device is very important. It would depend on the size of the fault current. This, in turn, depends on the impedance of the earth-fault loop path.

The value of the earth-fault impedance (Z_s) should not be larger than the values given in Tables 41.2, 41.3 and 41.4 of BS 7671 or otherwise protected as described in Part 7 for special locations.

Situation	Table	Max disconnection time (seconds)
Construction sites	41.5	0.2
Agricultural and horticultural premises	41.5	0.2
Socket outlets	41.2	0.4
	41.3	0.4
Fixed equipment	41.2/41.3	0.4

Table 6.08 Maximum allowed value of earth loop impedance (T.N. System)

Note

Fixed equipment = final circuits not exceeding 32 A (otherwise 5 seconds, 41.3/41.4)

Thermal constraints

This is a check to make sure that the size of the circuit protective conductor (cpc) complies with BS 7671. It must be large enough to carry the earth fault current without causing any heat or fire damage.

The formulae used to check this situation is the **adiabatic equation**. The cpc will only need to carry the fault current until the protective device operates.

$$S = \frac{\sqrt{I^2 \times t}}{k}$$

Where:

    S   the cross-sectional area of the cpc in mm^2

    I   the value of the fault current I for earth fault current (this is sometimes referred to as I_a)

    t   the operating time of the disconnecting device in seconds

    k   a factor depending on the conductor and its insulating material.

To apply the adiabatic equation, we first need to calculate the value of fault current from the following equation:

$$I = \frac{U_o}{Z_s}$$

Where:

    U_o is the nominal supply voltage

    Z_s is the earth fault loop impedance.

If using Method (i) from Regulation 543.1.2 and applying the adiabatic equation, we must find out the time/current characteristics of the protective device. A selection of time/current characteristics for the standard overcurrent protective devices is given in Appendix 3 of *IEE Wiring Regulations*. We can get the time (t) for disconnection to the corresponding earth fault current from these graphs.

Both the calculation and the graphical method can be used. However, the calculation method can be advantageous, because it may lead to savings in the size of the cable.

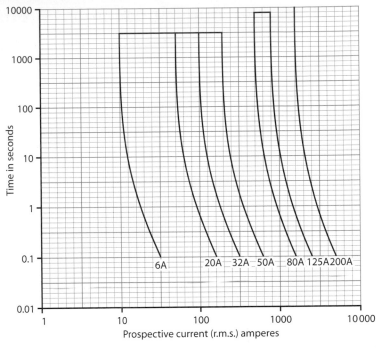

Figure 6.12 Time/current characteristics graph

Diversity

The current demand for a final circuit is determined by adding up the current demands of all points of utilisation and equipment in the circuit and, where appropriate, making allowance for diversity. See Appendix 1 Table 1A of the *IEE On-Site Guide* (or page 40 of the AMICUS Guide to BS 7671).

Main or sub-main cables will supply a number of final circuits. The various loads they carry must be considered. If they are simply totalled, a larger cable than necessary will be selected at considerable extra cost.

A method of assessing the load must be used where it will take into consideration that every appliance will not be requiring its maximum current at the same time.

Appendix 1 Table 1B of the *IEE On-Site-Guide* gives one method of achieving this. This allows diversity to be applied depending upon the type of load and installation premises.

By adding the individual circuit loads we determine the total 'assumed current' demand for the installation. This value is then used to determine the rating of suitable protective devices and cable size, taking into consideration any influencing factors.

Short answer questions

1. Overcurrent can be subdivided into what categories?
2. State two advantages of the BS 3036 rewiring fuse.
3. You are designing an installation. How many correction factors are required to be applied to the nominal voltage rating of the protection (I_n)?
4. State two advantages and two disadvantages of a BS 88 HBC fuse.
5. How is earth fault protection provided?
6. How does an RCD operate?
7. What is an exposed conductive part?
8. What formula would you use to calculate the fusing factor?
9. Explain the formula for calculating voltage drop.
10. Define Z_e and Z_s.

Multiple choice test

1. Why is an electrical installation earthed?
   a. *To enable insulation resistance tests to be carried out.*
   b. *To protect against short circuit faults.*
   c. *To prevent exposed metalwork from becoming live.*
   d. *To prevent a voltage appearing on the neutral conductor.*

2. When testing the continuity of a protective conductor using a.c. the test voltage must not exceed what value?
   a. *230 V*
   b. *110 V*
   c. *50 V*
   d. *40 V*

3. The exposed non-conducting metalwork of an electrical installation should be earthed for what reason?
   a. *prevent short circuit faults*
   b. *protect against electric shock*
   c. *reduce the risk of corrosion*
   d. *avoid the flow of earth leakage currents*

4. Supplementary bonding is required in what situations?
   a. *domestic kitchen*
   b. *water pipes*
   c. *washrooms that don't have a bath or shower*
   d. *toilets that don't have a bath or shower*

5. A protective conductor is 1.5 mm². The size of bonding required (mechanically protected) between extraneous conductive part is what size?
   a. *4 mm²*
   b. *2.5 mm²*
   c. *1.5 mm²*
   d. *6 mm²*

6. What is one advantage of an MCB over other forms of excess-current protection?
   a. *Its on-off position can be easily identified.*
   b. *Its operation is silent over a wide range of fault levels.*
   c. *It operates on both earth fault and short-circuit fault.*
   d. *It is easily installed and reset quickly.*

7. Under the 'conditions of supply', who is responsible for the earthing of a consumer's installation?
   a. Area Electricity Board
   b. Central Electricity Generating Board
   c. Local authority
   d. Owner of the premises

8. Which of the following protective devices has a relatively high fusing factor?
   a. BS 88 Part 2 fuse
   b. BS 3871 Part I MCB
   c. BS 1361 fuse
   d. BS 3036 fuse

9. The use of a residual device should only be considered when the product of its operating current and earth loop impedance does not exceed what value?
   a. 25 V
   b. 30 V
   c. 40 V
   d. 50 V

10. TT system is a system that relies on earth leakage current travelling back to the supply source via a protective conductor. What statement applies here?
   a. It is true.
   b. It is false.
   c. It is only true if an MCB is installed.
   d. It is only true if the system is PME.

11. Where bonding is made on a gas meter, the connection should be made within what distance?
   a. 0.6 m
   b. 0.5 m
   c. 0.4 m
   d. 0.3 m

12. Good earth continuity implies which of the following?
   a. open circuit
   b. high resistance
   c. low resistance
   d. low conductivity

13. A PEN conductor is used throughout in what system?
   a. TN-S
   b. TT
   c. TN-C-S
   d. TN-C

14. Which of the following is not a method of protection against direct contact?
   a. placing out of reach
   b. provision of barriers
   c. insulation of live parts
   d. equipotential bonding

15. Which of the following is not an acceptable method of protection for a TT system?
   a. overcurrent protective device
   b. semi-conductor device
   c. RCD
   d. fault voltage operated device

16. Bonding is defined in what part of BS 7671?
   a. Part 2
   b. Part 3
   c. Part 6
   d. Part 7

17. The smallest size of main bonding conductor permitted is …?
   a. 16 mm
   b. 10 mm
   c. 6 mm
   d. 4 mm

18. Which of the following is an example of an extraneous conductive part?
   a. conduit (metal)
   b. trunking (metal)
   c. gas pipes
   d. metal light switch face plate

19. The formula: length of run (m) × load current (I) × millivolt/A/m (mV) is used in cable selection procedures to find which volt drop?
   a. permissible volt drop
   b. actual volt drop
   c. assumed volt drop
   d. rated volt drop

20. What is the letter designation classifying a PME system?
a. TN-C
b. TN-C-S
c. TN-S
d. TT

21. The over current protective device, which protects socket outlet circuits and any other fixed equipment, must operate within what time delay?
a. 0.02 s
b. 0.4 s
c. 5 s
d. 45 s

22. Which formula should be used to calculate the value of Z_s?
a. $Z_s = Z_e - (R_1 + R_2)$
b. $Z_s = Z_e + (R_1 - R_2)$
c. $Z_s = Z_e + (R_1 + R_2)$
d. $Z_s = Z_e - (R_1 - R_2)$

23. Protective device Z_s values within the on-site-guide are corrected to what percentage?
a. 65%
b. 75%
c. 80%
d. 85%

24. A 5 A BS 3026 fuse has a fusing factor of 2. What current will blow the fuse?
a. 6 A
b. 10 A
c. 15 A
d. 25 A

25. Under fault conditions the protective device nearest to the fault should operate, leaving other healthy circuits unaffected. This is one definition of which of the following?
a. fusing factor
b. effective discrimination
c. miniature circuit breaker
d. circuit protective conductor

26. A cable has a design current of 8 amps and a volt drop of 15 mV/A/m. If it is allowed maximum voltage drop, what is the longest length of cable that can be used on a 240 V supply?
a. 100 m
b. 75 m
c. 50 m
d. 25 m

27. An impedance test of the final circuit revealed the value 0.6 ohms. If the value of Z_e was given as 0.3 Ω, the circuit phase and protective conductor resistances would be limited to what value?
a. 2.4 Ω
b. 1.66 Ω
c. 0.98 Ω
d. 0.38 Ω

28. If the earth fault loop impedance of a ring circuit was 0.5 Ω, and the fault current was 480 amps. What range would the supply voltage fall in?
a. extra low voltage
b. low voltage
c. medium voltage
d. high voltage

29. The assumed *external* impedance Z_e for a TN-C-S system is what value?
a. 1.8 Ω
b. 0.8 Ω
c. 0.35 Ω
d. 0.02 Ω

The answer section is at the back of the book.

07 Lighting

By the end of this chapter you should be able to demonstrate your knowledge and understanding of the following topics:

- Incandescent lighting
  - Tungsten filament lamp (GLS)
  - Tungsten halogen lamp
  - Types of lamp fitting or cap
- Discharge lighting
  - Low pressure mercury vapour lamp (fluorescent lamp)
  - Starter circuits
  - Stroboscopic effect
  - High frequency operation
  - Other discharge lamps
  - Lighting types compared
- Regulations concerning lighting circuits
- Illumination measurement and calculations
  - Units and quantities used in illumination
  - Inverse square law
  - Cosine rule

Incandescent lighting

This uses a fine filament of wire that is heated by an electric current until it is white hot, when it will give off light. It is not an efficient light source as much of the energy is given off as heat.

Tungsten filament lamp (GLS)

The general lighting service (GLS) lamp is commonly referred to as the light bulb and has at its core a very thin tungsten wire, which is formed into a small coil and then coiled again. All the air is removed from the glass bulb and replaced by gases such as nitrogen and argon, except in low power lamps (e.g. 15 and 25 watts), which may remain a vacuum. Nitrogen minimises the risk of arcing and argon reduces evaporation from the filament, so extending its life.

In operation, current passing through the tungsten filament causes it to reach 2500–2900°C, so that it glows brightly. However, the output is only 10–18 lumens per watt, so the efficacy is low compared to other lamps. It also has an average life of only 1000 hours after which the filament will rupture, causing a high current to flow for a fraction of a second; often sufficient to operate a 5 A or 6 A miniature circuit breaker protecting the lighting circuit. High wattage lamps are provided with a tiny integral fuse within the body of the lamp to prevent damage occurring when the filament fails.

If the lamp is run at a lower voltage than its rating, this reduces the light output but at a greater rate than the electricity consumption, thus reducing the lamp's efficacy. It does increase the life and can be useful where lamps are difficult to replace or where light output is not the main consideration.

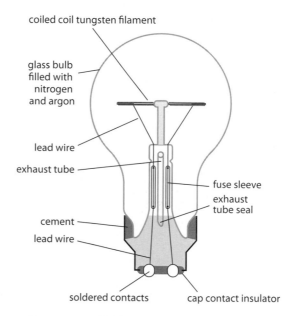

Figure 7.01 GLS lamp

Running the lamp at higher than its design voltage results in shorter lamp life. An increase in 5 per cent of the supply voltage can reduce the lamp life by half. Increasing it by just 1 per cent will increase lamp output by 3.5 per cent.

The main advantages over other lamps are comparatively low initial costs, immediate light when switched on and no control gear. It can also be easily dimmed with a dimmer switch.

Tungsten halogen lamp

A tungsten filament is enclosed in a gas filled quartz tube containing a halogen gas, such as iodine or argon. There are two basic designs: the double-ended linear and the single-ended.

Did you know?

The first lamp developed for indoor use was the carbon filament lamp. Although dim by modern standards, it was cleaner and far less dangerous than the exposed arc lamp.

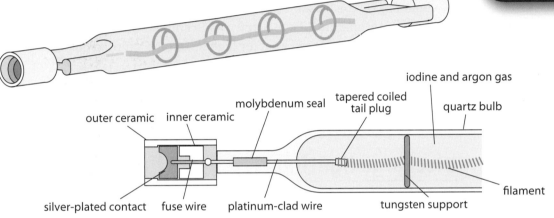

Figure 7.02 Double-ended linear tungsten halogen lamp

Halogen allows the filament to burn at a higher temperature than incandescent lamps and also produces a regeneration effect, which prolongs the life of the lamp. However, the linear version must be installed within 4° of the horizontal to prevent the halogen from migrating to one end of the tube and causing early failure.

The single-ended lamp has both contacts embedded in the seal at one end. It has been produced to work on extra low voltages (12 V) and is used extensively in the automotive industry for vehicle headlamps. It can also be used in display spotlights where extra low voltages are required. These lamps may be supplied from an in-built 230 V / 12 V transformer.

In addition to being able to work at low voltages these lamps last longer (up to 2000 hours), have increased efficacy (up to 23 lumens per watt) and are smaller compared to GLS lamps.

However, it is important not to touch the glass envelope with bare fingers, as the grease from fingers will cause the lamp to fail. They should be cleaned with methylated spirits before use.

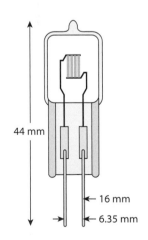

Figure 7.03 Single-ended tungsten halogen lamp

Types of lamp fitting or cap

There are various methods of connecting lamps to the supply. They divide into three groups, based on the design of the cap (or fitting).

- **Bayonet cap** – Most widely used on GLS lamps in the UK, they have contacts on the base and lugs on the side. The lamp is pushed into the lamp holder against sprung electrical contacts and then twisted, locking the lugs into slots and keeping the lamp connected to the supply. They come in two forms: the standard bayonet cap (BC) and the small bayonet cap (SBC).
- **Screw fitting** – Widely used in much of the world and available in the UK, the locking lugs are replaced by screw threads, so that the bulb is screwed into the lamp holder to make contact with the supply. Most are variations on the Edison Screw (ES), including the Small Edison Screw (SES), the Miniature Edison Screw (MES) and the Goliath Edison Screw (GES). The Goliath is reserved for higher wattage lamps of 300–500 W used in floodlighting.
- **Plug fitting** – These have contacts protruding from the base, which plug into connectors in the lamp holder. They are either push fit or bayonet fit, the latter being twisted to lock into slots in the lamp holder.

Discharge lighting

Discharge lighting refers to illumination derived from ionisation of a gas.

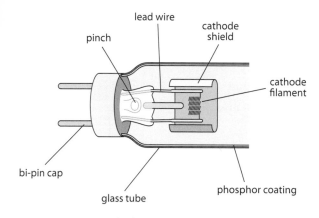

Figure 7.04 Detail of one end of a fluorescent tube

Low pressure mercury vapour lamp (fluorescent lamp)

The lamp consists of a glass tube filled with mercury vapour at low pressure, and a small quantity of argon gas to assist starting. The inside of the tube is coated with a fluorescent phosphor. At each end there is a sealed set of oxide-coated electrodes or cathodes that emit electrons when heated. The circuit includes a highly inductive coil, called a choke or ballast, which assists in starting and also controlling the current through the lamp.

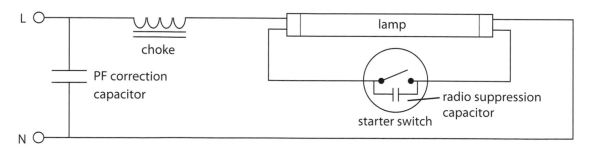

Figure 7.05 Basic starter circuit

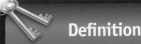

Sequence of operations

- When the supply is switched on, the starter contacts are closed so the current passes through the choke, the starter and both cathodes.
- The starter contacts (usually of the bi-metallic type) separate when current passing through them heats them up.
- This creates an open circuit in the choke, which being highly inductive causes a high voltage to appear across the tube.
- This causes the main discharge across the lamp, switching it on and ionising the gas.
- When the gas is fully ionised, the choke limits the current to a predetermined value. The light emitted, which is mainly ultraviolet, is converted to white light when it strikes the phosphor coating.

> **Definition**
>
> **Bi-metallic strip** – This has two different metals bonded together, which when heated expand at different rates. This causes them to bend to open or close a set of contacts.

The capacitor connected across the supply terminals is to correct the poor power factor for this type of light. Without this, the circuit, being highly inductive, would cause the current to lag behind the voltage and reduce the effective power of the circuit.

Efficacy

The efficacy of a fluorescent lamp is 40–90 lumens per watt. It is more efficient and longer lasting than all incandescent types. The most economic tube life is limited to around 5000–6000 hours. In industry, tubes are changed at set time intervals, well before they fail. This saves money on maintenance, stoppage of machinery, scaffold erection, etc.

Colour

The type of phosphor used on the lamp inner surface governs the quantity and quality of light output from the lamp, including its colour.

Colour rendering describes a lamp's ability to render colours as they truly are. This can affect people's attitude to work, etc. and true colour may be essential for some tasks. By restoring or providing a full colour range the light may also appear to be better or brighter than it really is.

Colour appearance describes the actual look of the lamp. The two ends of the scale are referred to as 'warm' and 'cold'. Generally, 'warm' lamps are used to give a relaxed atmosphere whilst 'cold' lamps are used where efficiency and businesslike attitudes are the priorities.

Starter circuits

There are different starter circuits in use, including glow-type, semi-resonant, quick and thermal.

Glow-type starter

This has a set of normally open contacts mounted on bi-metallic strips and enclosed in an atmosphere of helium gas. It is shown in the circuit in Figure 7.05.

When the supply is switched on, the helium gas ionises and heats up, causing the contacts to close, which energises the cathodes. With the contacts closed the discharge in the helium ceases. Thus the contacts cool and open once again, causing the highly inductive choke in the circuit to initiate a high voltage across the tube and the main discharge to take place.

The assembly is housed in a metal or plastic canister with two pins. Its main disadvantage is that it may not succeed first time and can result in the characteristic flashing on and off when first switching on a fluorescent light.

Semi-resonant starting

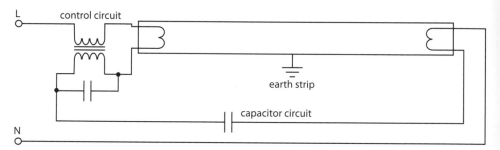

Figure 7.06 Semi-resonant starter circuit

The primary winding of a specially wound transformer takes the place of the choke. The current flows through one cathode of the lamp and back through the secondary winding. A large capacitor is connected between the secondary winding and the second cathode of the lamp.

As the primary and secondary coils are wound in opposition, the 180° out of phase voltages increase the voltage across the tube, causing the arc to strike. The primary winding then behaves like a choke, stabilising the current.

The advantages are high power factor and easy starting at low temperatures.

Quick start

The cathodes are rapidly preheated by the end windings of an autotransformer. The difference in potential between the cathodes and an earthed metal strip in close proximity to the tube causes ionisation.

This results in quicker starting. However, difficulties may occur in starting if the voltage is low.

Thermal starter circuit

The normally closed contacts are mounted on a bi-metallic strip. A small heater coil heats one of these when the supply is switched on. The contacts open, creating a momentary high voltage and starting the discharge.

This starter is easily recognised by having four pins instead of two, the extra pins being the heater connections. It is not now much used but many are still in service.

Stroboscopic effect

Standard fluorescent circuits operate at mains frequency of 50 Hz. Hence, the discharge across the cathodes is extinguished 100 times a second, which produces a flicker. Rotating machinery, illuminated from a single source, may appear to slow down, stop, or even change direction.

Although this can be used to advantage when measuring the speed of CDs or in automotive applications, it is potentially dangerous to the operators of rotating machinery, such as lathes and mills in engineering workshops. The operator may think that the machinery is stationary whereas it is still operating at full speed.

Stroboscopic effects can be overcome or reduced by:

- fitting tungsten lamps locally to lathes, etc. to lessen the effect
- connecting adjacent fluorescent fittings to a different phase, which reduces the effect, as each phase flickers at a different time
- wiring pairs of lamps to a lead-lag circuit (see below) to counteract each other
- using high frequency fluorescent lighting (see below), which can reduce the stroboscopic effects by 60 per cent.

A lead-lag circuit contains one lamp with a leading power factor, provided by a series capacitor, and one lamp with a lagging power factor, naturally produced by the inductive circuit. The stroboscopic effect of the two circuits combined cancel each other out, as there is always one lamp on at any moment of time.

High frequency operation

High frequencies at 30 kHz (30,000 Hz) can be used to operate fluorescent lamps.

The advantages are:

- higher lamp efficacy
- first time starting
- noise free
- the ballast shuts down automatically on lamp failure
- no stroboscopic effect.

Did you know?

Certain frequencies of stroboscopic flash can induce headaches, eye fatigue, disorientation and, in extreme cases, epileptic fits.

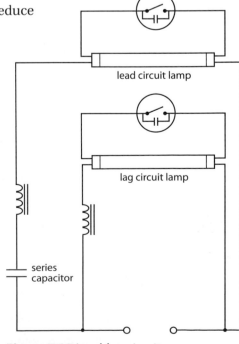

lead circuit lamp

lag circuit lamp

series capacitor

Figure 7.07 Lead-lag circuit

The disadvantages are:

- interference occurs if the supply cables within the fitting run next to the leads connected to the ballast output terminals
- initial cost is greater than glow-type starter switching.

Other discharge lamps

Some other discharge lamps include:

- **High-pressure mercury vapour lamp** – A quartz tube filled with high pressure mercury vapour and a little argon. Efficacy is 50 lm/W. It has a blue-green light output and is used for street lighting.
- **Low-pressure sodium lamp** – A U-shaped thick glass tube with some solid sodium and a small amount of neon gas inside, with the whole contained within an outer glass tube. The tube has to be installed horizontally to avoid the sodium collecting at one end. Efficacy is high with a light output at 140 lm/W but the light is yellow-orange and, therefore, only used as street lighting.
- **High-pressure sodium lamp** – Efficacy is high with a light output at 100 lm/W. Its golden-white light output makes it suitable for lighting shops, car parks and sports centres.
- **Neon lamp** – This has a neon filled tube operating from a transformer that provides up to 5 kV. The characteristic red colour is useful for decorative signs. Other gases such as nitrogen, carbon dioxide and helium will produce other colours.

Lighting types compared

Table 7.01 provides a comparison of lighting systems.

Lamp	Efficacy (lumens/watt)	Life in hours	Comment
Tungsten (GLS)	10 – 18	1000	Cheap
Tungsten halogen	23	2000	Small
Fluorescent	40 – 90	5000 – 6000	Different colour tubes
Low pressure sodium	140	6000	Orange light
High pressure sodium	100	16,000 – 24,000	Golden white light
High pressure mercury	25 – 60	16,000 – 24,000	Blue green light
Neon			Red light

Table 7.01 Comparison of lighting systems

Regulations concerning lighting circuits

Although a number of Regulations have been covered in this book, there are several others that specifically apply to the installation of lighting circuits:

Regulations concerning lighting circuits

(i)   Where flexible conductors enter a luminaire as, for example, when a bulkhead fitting or batten lampholder is used, the conductors should be able to withstand any heat likely to be encountered or sleeved with heat resistant sleeving: see Regulation 522.2.2.

(ii)   A ceiling rose, unless specially designed for the purpose, should have only one flexible cord: see Regulation 559.6.1.3.

(iii)   A ceiling rose shall not be installed in any circuit operating at a voltage normally exceeding 250 volts: see Regulation 559.6.1.2.

(iv)   Where a flexible cord supports or partly supports a luminaire, the maximum mass supported shall not exceed the values stated in Appendix 4 Table 4F3A of BS 7671.

(v)   For circuits on a TN or a TT system, the outer contact of every Edison screw or single-centre bayonet cap-type lamp holder shall be connected to the neutral conductor: see Regulation 559.6.1.8.

(vi)   Semi-conductors used in dimmer controls may be used for functional switching (not isolators) provided that they comply with Sections 512 and 537.5.2.2 of BS 7671.

(vii)   When installing lighting circuits, the current assumed is equivalent to the connected load, with a minimum of 100 watts per lampholder: see Table 1A of the *IEE On-Site Guide*. However, it should be noted that diversity could be applied to lighting circuits in accordance with Table 1B of the *IEE On-Site Guide*.

(viii)   Final circuits for discharge lighting (this includes fluorescent luminaires) shall be capable of carrying the total steady current. Where this information is not available the demand in volt-amperes can be worked out by multiplying the rated watts by 1.8: see Table 1B of the *IEE On-Site Guide*.

Figure 7.08 Lighting circuit regulations

Illumination measurement and calculations

A summary is given below of some of the terms, units of measurement and calculations relating to illumination.

Units and quantities used in illumination

Illumination is the quantity of light (luminous flux) falling on a surface of a given area. Table 7.02 summarises the quantities associated with illumination.

Quantity	Symbol	Unit	Abbreviation	Definition
Luminous intensity	I	candela	cd	Brightness of light source
Luminous flux	F	lumen	lm	Amount of light emitted
Illuminance or illumination	E	lux or lumen/m²	lm/m²	Amount of light falling on a surface
Luminous efficacy	K	lumen per watt	lm/W	Light per watt or efficiency
Power	P	watt	W	Power consumed

Table 7.02 Units and quantities used in illumination

Inverse square law

The illumination on a surface is inversely proportional to the square of the distance of the surface from the source of light.

This is given by:

$$E = \frac{I}{d^2}$$

Where E is the illuminance (luminous flux per square metre), I is the luminous intensity in candelas and d is the perpendicular distance from the light source to the surface on which the light falls.

This means that, if the source is moved twice as far from a surface, the illumination will be 2^2 or 4 times less. If it is moved three times further away, the illumination will be 3^2 or 9 times less.

Cosine rule

The illumination on a surface is proportional to the cosine of the angle made by a line perpendicular to the surface with the direction of the light.

This is given by:

$$E = \frac{I\,(\cos\theta)^3}{d^2}$$

Where E is the illuminance (luminous flux per square metre), I is the luminous intensity in candelas, $(\cos)\theta$ is the angle of incidence (from the perpendicular) and d is the perpendicular distance from the light source to the surface on which the light falls.

Remember the trigonometrical relationships for a right angle triangle:

$$\sin\theta = \frac{\text{opposite}}{\text{hypotenuse}} \qquad \cos\theta = \frac{\text{adjacent}}{\text{hypotenuse}} \qquad \tan\theta = \frac{\text{opposite}}{\text{adjacent}}$$

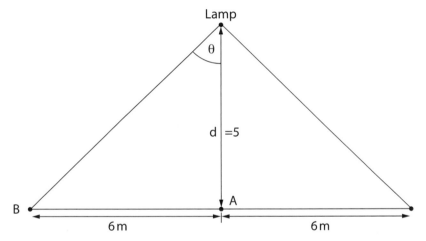

Figure 7.09 Cosine rule

Short answer questions

1. What does the phosphor coating do on the inside of the fluorescent tube?
2. What are the three factors to consider when choosing different fluorescent tubes?
3. What does lamp efficacy mean?
4. What are the two functions of the choke (inductor or ballast) in the glow-starter fluorescent lamp circuit?
5. List the five advantages that high frequency fluorescent circuits have over the standard circuits.
6. How can the stroboscopic effect be dangerous around moving machinery and how can it be minimised?
7. List four advantages and one disadvantage of a GLS lamp.
8. When installing tungsten halogen lamps what precautions must be taken?
9. What four advantages do tungsten halogen lamps have over GLS lamps?
10. Name three types of discharge lamp.
11. A lamp producing 2500 candela is placed 5 metres above the centre of a work bench 2 metres wide. Calculate the illuminance on the bench surface directly under the lamp and at the edge of the bench.

Multiple-choice test

1. What are the electrodes at each end of a fluorescent tube known as?
   a. anodes
   b. cathodes
   c. bi-pin cap
   d. filaments

2. Within what range will the efficacy of a fluorescent tube vary?
   a. 30–90 lumens
   b. 30–100 lumens
   c. 40–80 lumens
   d. 40–90 lumens

3. What is the expected life span of a fluorescent tube?
   a. 4000–5000 hours
   b. 4000–6000 hours
   c. 5000–6000 hours
   d. 6000–7000 hours

4. In the glow starter type circuit what is the primary function of the choke?
   a. To reduce current flow.
   b. To improve power factor.
   c. To provide the high voltage spike.
   d. To help the bi-metallic strip make contact.

5. In the semi-resonant circuit, the voltages across each end of the tube are out of phase with each other. By how many degrees are they out of phase?
   a. 120°
   b. 160°
   c. 180°
   d. 220°

6. High frequency lamps operate on a frequency of?
   a. 10,000 Hz
   b. 20,000 Hz
   c. 30,000 Hz
   d. 40,000 Hz

7. In a 50 Hz fluorescent tube, how many times per second will the electrodes be extinguished?
   a. 50 times
   b. 100 times
   c. 200 times
   d. 500 times

8. Which of the following methods is *not* suitable for reducing the stroboscopic effect?
   a. Tungsten filament lamps fitted near the machinery.
   b. The use of high frequency lighting.
   c. Fluorescent tubes fitted on the same phases.
   d. Install lead-lag circuits.

9. Which type of lamp is recognised by having four pins instead of the usual two?
   a. quick start
   b. thermal starter
   c. semi-resonant
   d. glow starter

10. What is *not* affected by the type of phosphor coating on the inside of a fluorescent tube?
    a. colour appearance
    b. colour rendering
    c. lamp life
    d. lamp efficacy

11. What temperature will the filament wire reach in an incandescent lamp?
    a. 2500°C – 2900°C
    b. 2500°C – 3900°C
    c. 2900°C – 3500°C
    d. 2900°C – 3900°C

12. Which of the following statements is not an advantage of a GLS lamp?
    a. can be easily dimmed
    b. low cost
    c. immediate light when switched on
    d. gives off heat

13. What is the efficacy range of a GLS lamp?
    a. 10–18 lumens per watt
    b. 10–20 lumens per watt
    c. 18–20 lumens per watt
    d. 18–30 lumens per watt

14. What is the average life span of a GLS lamp?
    a. 600 hours
    b. 700 hours
    c. 900 hours
    d. 1000 hours

15. By how much does the voltage need to increase in order to half the life span of a GLS lamp?
    a. 1%
    b. 5%
    c. 10%
    d. 50%

16. The tungsten halogen lamp needs to be installed within how many degrees of the horizontal to prevent halogen vapour migration?
    a. 2°
    b. 3°
    c. 4°
    d. 5°

17. What is the expected lumen output of a tungsten halogen lamp?
    a. 13 lumens per watt
    b. 23 lumens per watt
    c. 33 lumens per watt
    d. 43 lumens per watt

18. What is the maximum operating voltage that a ceiling rose should not exceed?
    a. 110 volts
    b. 230 volts
    c. 250 volts
    d. 400 volts

19. How many flexible cords would you normally expect to find installed in a ceiling rose?
    a. 1
    b. 2
    c. 3
    d. 4

20. The centre cap of an Edison screw lamp should be connected to which conductor?
    a. Phase
    b. Neutral
    c. Earth
    d. Switch wire

21. What power range in watts was the GES lamp
cap developed for?
  a. *60–100 W*
  b. *100–150 W*
  c. *150–250 W*
  d. *300–500 W*

22. What is the effect when a bulb filament fails in a
GLS lamp?
  a. *The current ceases to flow immediately and
     the light goes out.*
  b. *A very high current flows which may trip the
     circuit breaker.*
  c. *The lamp glows red for a short time before
     going out.*
  d. *It causes a voltage surge and the light flashes.*

The answer section is at the back of the book.

08 Circuits and systems

By the end of this chapter you should be able to demonstrate your knowledge and understanding of the following circuits and systems:

- Timers and programmers
  - Simple timers
  - Complex timers
- Emergency lighting, fire alarms and standby power supplies
  - Emergency lighting
  - Fire-alarm systems
  - Standby power supplies
- Water heating
  - Immersion heaters
  - Cistern-type water system
  - Non-pressure water system
  - Instantaneous water system
- Space heating
  - Direct acting heaters
  - Thermal storage devices
- Cooker thermostats and controllers
  - Simmerstat (energy regulator)
  - Oven thermostats

- Closed circuit television and camera systems
  - Wireless systems
  - Wired systems
  - PC-based systems
  - Cameras
  - Monitoring and recording
- Intruder alarm systems
  - Proximity switches (perimeter protection)
  - Inertia switches (perimeter protection)
  - Passive infrared (space detection)
  - Ultrasonic devices (space detection)
  - Control panels
  - Audible (sounder) and visible warning devices

Timers and programmers

Timers and programmers can control simple and/or complex switching operations in all aspects of modern living and come in a range of sizes and shapes.

Simple timers

These include:

- timers that switch lights on and off rapidly or in a pattern
- timers that delay the operation of contactors in motor control circuits
- plug-in clock timers that switch lights or heaters on and off.

Complex timers

Complex timers can be programmed to carry out multiple functions when external inputs are received or a certain time is reached.

Heating and hot water programmer

This is the type of complex timer you are most likely to see in domestic premises. The programmer can be set to switch on/off either the heating or hot water, or both, several times a day for varying lengths of time.

The programmer is usually supplied via a fused spur fitted with a 3 or 5 A fuse and, as a backup, there is an internal rechargeable battery to maintain programme details for up to 48 hours.

Inputs to the programmer include some or all of the components listed in Table 8.01.

Room thermostat	Interrupts the supply to the boiler when the selected temperature has been reached in the room.
Hot water thermostat	Interrupts the supply to the boiler when the selected water temperature in the hot water cylinder has been reached.
Diverter valve	An electrically operated (via a small motor) two-way valve that opens or shuts off either the hot water or central heating flow when the selected temperatures have been reached.
Zone valve	An electrically operated valve that shuts off the water flow to part of the central heating system.
Outside temperature sensor	Detects the outside temperature and compares it with the selected temperature and maintains a differential between them by switching the boiler on/off.

Frost override	A thermostat housed on the water pipes near the boiler. If the ambient temperature drops below a set temperature (typically 5˚C), it will override all the controls and switch on the boiler to stop the pipes from freezing.
Circulating pump	Circulates hot water through the system, including the radiators, usually to and from the hot water tank and boiler.

Table 8.01 Programmer inputs

Outputs go to the boiler and the circulating pump.

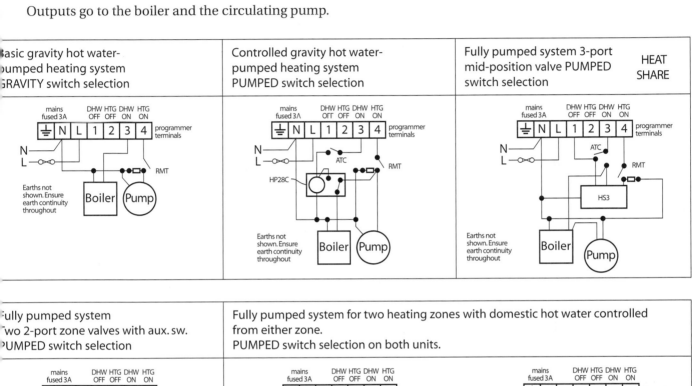

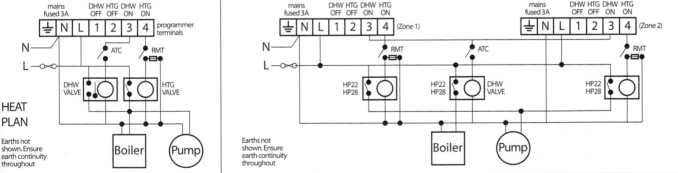

Figure 8.01 Wiring diagram for timer and programming domestic system

Emergency lighting, fire alarms and standby power supplies

This section covers emergency lighting systems (maintained, non-maintained and sustained), fire alarms and standby power supplies.

Emergency lighting

Effective emergency lighting is required in public buildings to help people, who may be unfamiliar with their surroundings, to easily identify an escape route in an emergency situation.

Terminology

There are two main types of emergency lighting, as shown below.

- **Standby lighting** – This allows normal activities to continue in the event of a power failure.
- **Emergency escape lighting** – This enables safe exit if the normal supply fails:
  - **escape route lighting** – provides sufficient lighting and direction on escape routes and ensures that fire fighting and safety equipment can be seen and used.
  - **open area (anti-panic) lighting** – provides adequate levels of lighting and direction to reduce the risk of panic and enable people to move safely towards escape routes.
  - **high risk/task area lighting** – ensures the safety of people responsible for completing vital shut-down operations in order to protect other occupants of the premises.

Formats and types

There are two emergency lighting formats:

- individual, self-contained systems with their own emergency battery power source
- centralised battery backup systems.

Both formats use one or more of the following types of emergency lighting:

- **Maintained** – The same lamp is permanently illuminated, either by the mains or an emergency battery backup system. It is easy to see if the lamp is working or needs replacing. However, it is impossible to tell if the lamp is lit by the mains or the battery unless an indicator light or buzzer is fitted.

- **Non-maintained** – This type of emergency lighting only illuminates when the mains supply fails and the battery takes over. It is cheaper to operate than a maintained system because it is not on all the time. However, an emergency lighting test switch is required so that the mains supply can be temporarily disconnected to test that the emergency system and lamps are operating properly.
- **Sustained** – This is an additional lamp, housed inside the normal light fitting, which only comes on when the mains fails.

Siting of luminaires

Luminaires should be sited so that architectural features involving changes of level or direction, such as landings and staircases; fire-alarm points and fire fighting equipment; and obstructions are visible in reduced levels of lighting.

Additional emergency lighting should also be sited in lifts and on escalators, in toilet facilities, in open tiled areas over 8 m^2, in motor generator, control or plant rooms and in covered car parks on normal pedestrian routes.

Standby lighting must be provided where a process (for example, in industry or a hospital operating theatre) must continue even if the mains lighting fails.

Minimum illuminance levels

- On escape routes, the horizontal illuminance at floor level must be:
  - not less than 0.2 lux along the centre line of a defined route
  - and, in addition, at least 0.1 lux on at least 50 per cent of the width of a route up to 2 m wide.
- In open areas (excluding a 0.5 m perimeter), minimum illuminance levels must be:
  - 1 lux average at floor level in areas larger than 60 m^2
  - 0.5 lux anywhere at floor level, excluding the shadows thrown by contents.
- In areas where high-risk tasks take place, emergency illuminance levels at the reference plane (not necessarily at floor level) must be as high as the task demands, subject to a minimum of 10 per cent of the normal lighting or 15 lux, whichever is greater. This is usually achieved with permanently illuminated fluorescent or tungsten lamps.

Remember

A maintained emergency lighting system must be used in areas such as cinemas or theatres where lighting can be dimmed.

Definition

Luminaires – BS 7671 Part 2 defines luminaires as all the parts of a lighting system except the lamp bulb and include the covers, switches, lamp holders, ceiling roses, etc.

Remember

BS 5266, EN 1838 and IS 3217 provide detailed guidance on where luminaries should be installed, the minimum levels of illumination on escape routes and in open areas, and minimum periods of duration.

Did you know?

0.2 lux is similar to the brightness of a full moon.

Break glass detector

Fire-alarm systems

'Fire detection and alarm system' is probably a more accurate term than 'fire-alarm system'. They are designed and installed to protect either property or life.

BS 5839 Part 1 classifies fire-alarm systems into three basic types:

- **type M** – **manual** break-glass detectors operating sounders for protection of life
- **type L** – automatic detection for protection of **life**
- **type P** – automatic protection of **property**.

Property protection

An effective fire-alarm system for protecting property automatically detects fire and indicates its location at an early stage, and sounds an alarm in time to alert any resident fire fighting staff and summon the fire service. An automatic direct link to the fire service is usually standard to ensure that the fire service arrives in less than 10 minutes.

Property protection is classed as:

- **P1** – All areas of the building (except lavatories, water closets and small voids less than 800 mm high) must be covered by detectors.
- **P2** – Only defined areas of high risk are covered by detectors and other areas are protected by fire-resistant materials.

Life protection

An effective fire-alarm system for protecting life must sound an alarm in the event of fire in sufficient time and with sufficient volume to enable occupants to escape.

Life protection is classed as:

- **M** – Minimum protection is provided by manual break-glass detectors, operated by the people it is designed to protect.
- **L1** – All areas of the building (except lavatories, water closets and small voids less than 800 mm high) must be covered by detectors.
- **L2** – Automatic detection is provided in high-risk areas such as kitchens, sleeping areas, areas for old or disabled people, or where there are people unfamiliar with the layout.
- **L3** – Includes all the following escape routes, as well as L2 areas:
  - corridors, passageways and circulation areas
  - all rooms opening on to escape routes
  - stairwells
  - landing ceilings
  - top of vertical risers (e.g. lift shafts, building services risers)
  - within 1.5 m of access to lift shafts or other vertical risers.

Types of fire-alarm system

Most fire-alarm systems belong to one of the following types:

- **Conventional** – This type is a simple radial circuit using detectors and/or break-glass detectors. Usually, there is one circuit per zone per floor. A control panel indicates which zone the alarm has operated in, but not which detector.
- **Addressable** – This is the same as the conventional system, but the control panel can identify exactly which detector has been activated. Each circuit is wired as a loop, which can have several detectors with programmable addresses connected to it.
- **Radio addressable** – This is the same as the addressable system, but with the benefit of wireless technology.
- **Analogue** – These are intelligent systems with more sophisticated features. Some have detectors with built-in microprocessors that can identify different situations, such as whether there is a fire or a change in circumstance likely to lead to one, if there is a fault or if a detector head needs cleaning.
- **Fire prevention systems** – Still in development, these systems reduce the level of oxygen if the risk of fire is detected. Although there are potential drawbacks, such systems could be useful in historic buildings, archive facilities or dangerous unmanned environments, such as chemical storage/process areas.

Zones

Dividing a building into separate fire detection zones helps to identify the source of a fire quickly.

Zone guidelines include:

- floor areas of less than 300 m² only need to have one zone regardless of the number of floors in the building
- the total floor area of one zone should not exceed 2000 m²
- the search distance to locate a fire visually within a zone should not exceed 30 m
- stairwells that extend beyond one floor should be a separate zone
- zones should not cover more than one fire compartment or cover more than one occupancy.

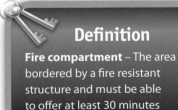

Definition

Fire compartment – The area bordered by a fire resistant structure and must be able to offer at least 30 minutes resistance to a fire.

System devices

The control panel

This panel monitors the detection devices, checking for faults or operational problems. If a device operates, the panel sounds the alarm and identifies the appropriate zone. The panel must be located where fire services can easily find it, such as the entrance to a building.

Break-glass contacts (manual call points)

These units have a fragile glass cover (protected by thin plastic to prevent injury), which can easily be broken to activate the alarm. They should be sited according to the following guidance.

- They should be located on exit routes and especially on staircase landings and all exits to the outside.
- There should be no more than 30 m between each detector.
- Ideally they should be sited about 1.4 m above floor level, easily accessible and well illuminated.

Automatic detectors

A detector needs to be able to differentiate between fire and acceptable situations such as people smoking, steam in kitchens and bathrooms, etc.

A fixed-temperature type of detector operates when a predetermined temperature, usually 60 or 90°C is exceeded. It is used in boiler rooms or kitchens where fluctuations in temperature are normal.

A rate-of-rise type of detector samples the temperature between two heat-resistant thermocouples in the same housing and operates if there is a sudden rise in temperature. It can be used in areas where there is normally a constant temperature.

Smoke detectors

There are two types:

- ionisation detectors detect fine smoke particles, such as those produced by burning paper
- optical detectors detect large smoke particles, such as those produced by burning plastics.

There are strict rules about the location of smoke detectors. These are stated in BS 5839 Part 6 and specify exactly where to site them, e.g. within 3 m of the bedroom door and between the sleeper and the likely site of a fire; not over heaters or cookers, etc.

Alarm sounders

All sounders, whether a bell or electronic, must be audible throughout the building to alert the occupants. There must be a minimum of one sounder per zone and all sounders on the same system must sound the same.

A minimum level of 65 dbA, or 5 dbA above any background noise, must sound in all parts of the building that are occupied. In hotels and guesthouses, where people are sleeping, the sounder must be 75 dbA at the bedhead. No sounder should be loud enough to damage the hearing.

> **Remember**
>
> Using the correct type of detector reduces the chances of false alarms.

Always select the correct type of smoke detector to avoid a false alarm or no alarm at all

Alarm sounder

Wiring systems for fire alarms

Only two types of cable may be used when prolonged operation during a fire is needed – MICC or Fire-tuf/FP200.

MICC is mineral-insulated copper-covered cable, commonly known as Pyro. It withstands extremes of temperature (from well below zero to hundreds of degrees Celsius) and other environmental conditions. The insulant is magnesium oxide and the outer sheath is copper, which is sometimes covered with PVC for identification by colour.

Fire-tuf/FP200 also withstands extremes of temperature, although the upper limit is usually 200°C. The copper conductors are insulated with silicon and housed inside an aluminium sheath, which is usually covered in PVC for identification by colour.

Did you know?

If the alarm at a nightclub is activated, the control panel must also shut off the electricity supply to the music system, otherwise nobody will hear the fire alarm.

Standby backup for fire-alarm systems

Battery backup is required for a fire-alarm system and must be able to power the system in full normal operation for a minimum of 24 hours and, at the end of that period, still be able to sound the alarm sounders for a minimum of 30 minutes in all zones.

Remember

All wiring from fire alarms must be installed in accordance with BS 7671.

Typical maintenance checks for a fire alarm system

Daily inspection	Annual test
• Check that the control panel indicates normal operation. Report any fault indicators or sounders not operating to the designated responsible person.	• Repeat the quarterly test. • Check all call points and detectors for correct operation. • Enter details of test in logbook.
Weekly test	**Every two to three years**
• Check panel key operation and reset button. • Test fire alarm from a call point (different one each week) and check sounders. • Reset fire-alarm panel. • Check all call points and detectors for obstruction. • Enter details of test in logbook.	• Clean smoke detectors using specialist equipment. • Enter details of maintenance in logbook.

Quarterly test	Every five years
• Check all logbook entries and make sure any remedial actions have been carried out. • Examine battery and battery connections. • Operate a call point and detector in each zone. • Check that all sounders are operating. • Check that all functions of the control panel are operating by simulating a fault. • Check sounders operate on battery only. • Enter details of test in logbook.	• Replace battery (see manufacturer's information).

Table 8.02 BS 5839 recommendations

Standby power supplies

A standby system must be available to critical operations, such as hospitals, airports and chemical plants, where an interruption to power supply would be dangerous. Such systems need a petrol/diesel engine-powered generator to provide essential electrical services if the mains power fails.

Smaller places, such as offices and shops, need a more affordable type of backup. A self-contained battery within an Uninterruptible Power Supply (UPS) will automatically cut in if the mains power fails and will supply power for essential computer communication and data storage.

Water heating

There are two main methods of heating water electrically and three different types of water system, as shown below.

Water heating

- heating a large quantity of water with an immersion heater and storing it in a storage tank

- heating just the amount of water needed on demand

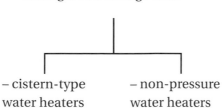

– cistern-type water heaters   – non-pressure water heaters

– instantaneous water heaters

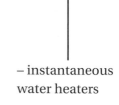

Remember

Water and electricity do not mix! Ensure that any exposed and extraneous conductive parts are correctly earthed.

Immersion heaters

An immersion heater, fitted in a water tank, will heat a large quantity of water. As hot water is drained from the tank, a tap opens to allow cold water to fill the tank at mains pressure, ready for heating.

- In domestic premises, the immersion heater must be supplied via its own (typically 16 A) MCB or fuse in the consumer unit.
- It can be switched on or off manually or via a timer/ programmer.
- There must be a double pole isolation switch near the water tank.
- Flexible heatproof cable must be used for the final connection to the heater, because of the high ambient temperature in the cupboard where a hot water tank is normally housed.
- Immersion heaters usually have a 3 kW rating.
- The temperature of the water is controlled by a stem-type thermostat. This type uses the principle of dissimilar metals expanding at different rates and is also used in oven thermostats. The copper tube expands at a greater rate than the Invar rod it houses and operates a plunger mechanism, opening or closing the contacts.

Cistern-type water system

This works in the same way as an immersion heater, but heats a larger volume of water and has a storage cistern of cold water above it. It is often used in large guesthouses where there is high demand for hot water. The heater typically has a 9 kW rating.

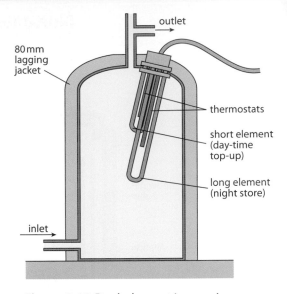

Figure 8.02 Dual-element immersion heater for hot water

Remember

All cables for water heaters must be the correct size for full load current.

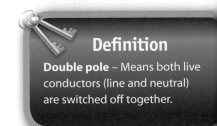

Definition

Double pole – Means both live conductors (line and neutral) are switched off together.

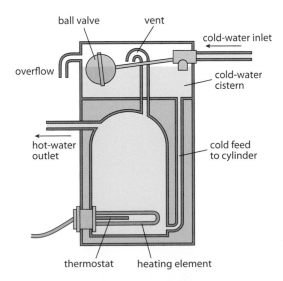

Figure 8.03 Cistern-type water heater

Non-pressure water system

This also works on the same principle, but heats a smaller volume of water for local use and is usually positioned above a sink. This type of heater typically has a rating of less than 3 kW.

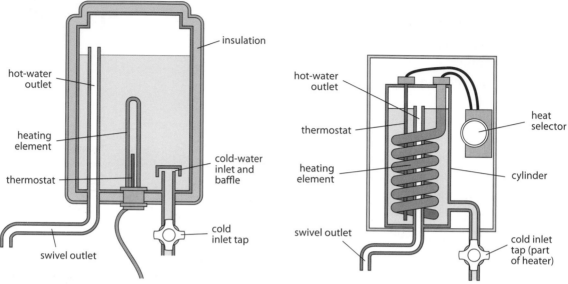

Figure 8.04 Non-pressure water heater

Figure 8.05 Instantaneous water heater

Instantaneous water system

This only heats water on demand, by controlling the flow of water through a small internal tank that houses the heating elements. The heater is supplied by its own MCB or fuse via a double pole switch and is typically rated between 7 and 10 kW. It is commonly used for electric showers.

Space heating

There are two types of electrical heating, either direct or storage, as shown below.

Space heating

- Direct acting heaters

  - – Radiant heaters
  - – Convection heaters

- Thermal storage devices

Direct acting heaters

Direct acting heaters are simply switched on or off and can be thermostatically controlled. There are two types, radiant and convection heaters.

Radiant heaters

These radiate heat, often assisted by a reflecting surface. Various types are available:

- **Bar electric fire** – The heating element is supported on insulated blocks and heat is reflected by the polished reflector behind the element. Sizes range from 750 W to 3 kW.
- **Infrared heater** – A nickel-chrome element is housed in a glass silica tube and mounted in front of a polished reflector. Sizes range from 500 W to 3 kW and the smaller types can be incorporated into a light fitting to provide both light and heat in bathrooms.
- **Oil-filled radiator** – This is a sealed unit filled with oil. The heating elements, typically ranging from 500 W to 2 kW, heat up quickly to give a surface temperature of 70°C.
- **Tubular heater** – This low-temperature unit consists of a mild steel or aluminium tube which houses a low-wattage element, rated from 200 W to 260 W per metre length and ranging from 300 mm to 4.5 m in length. It gives a typical surface temperature of 88°C.
- **Under-floor heating** – Heating elements made of various conductive materials, such as chromium, aluminium, copper, silicon or manganese alloys, are embedded under the floor tiles, which heat up to a surface temperature of about 24°C. The room temperature is controlled by a thermostat.

Did you know?

Oil heats up or cools down more quickly than water because it has a lower specific gravity.

Convection heaters

These consist of a metal cabinet in which a heating element heats up the air. Cold air enters the bottom of the unit and forces the hot air out. The heaters can be fan-assisted and thermostatically controlled.

Thermal storage devices

The heating elements in thermal storage heaters are mounted inside firebricks made of clay, olivine, chrome or magnesite. They are heated up during off-peak hours and store the heat until released when needed during peak times to heat the surrounding air.

Cooker thermostats and controllers

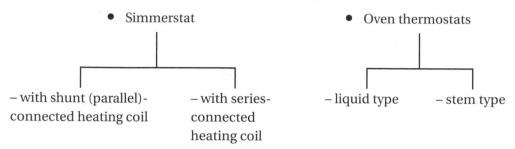

Cooker thermostats and controllers

- Simmerstat
  - with shunt (parallel)-connected heating coil
  - with series-connected heating coil
- Oven thermostats
  - liquid type
  - stem type

Simmerstat (energy regulator)

Simmerstats are used to control the electric hotplates on a cooker to maintain a constant temperature. When the current is switched on with the control knob, the heater coil heats the bi-metal strip around which it is wrapped. This causes the strip to bend and open a set of contacts. The contacts open for different lengths of time depending on the knob setting, but at the appropriate setting will keep a liquid at simmering point. When the current is switched off, the coil cools, and the strip bends back and switches the hotplate element back on.

There are two types of simmerstat, one with a shunt (parallel)-connected heating coil and the other with a series-connected heater coil, which both work on the same principle.

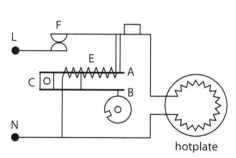

Figure 8.06 Shunt-wired regulator

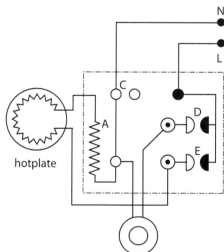

Figure 8.07 Series-wired regulator

Oven thermostats

There are two types, which both work on the same principle:

- **Capillary type** – In this type of thermostat, liquid in the capillary tube expands as the heat-sensitive phial at the end of the tube heats up. The expanded liquid operates a set of contacts to switch the heating element on or off. The amount of expansion needed to operate the contacts is governed by the setting (tension) on the plunger mechanism.

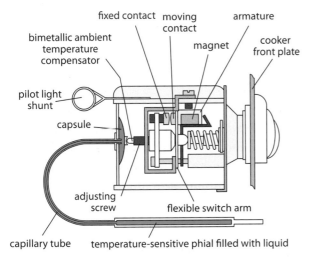

Figure 8.08 Capillary type oven thermostat

- **Stem type** – This type uses the principle of dissimilar metals expanding at different rates and is also used in water-heating systems. The copper tube expands at a greater rate than the Invar rod it houses and operates a plunger mechanism, opening or closing the contacts.

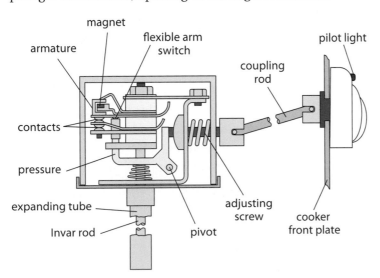

Figure 8.09 Stem type oven thermostat

Closed circuit television and camera systems

There are many different types of CCTV and camera systems, but the following systems and components are typical.

Wireless systems

- The cameras have built-in transmitters, which relay images back to a central monitor or recorder.
- They require a power supply (usually 9–12 volts d.c.).
- The maximum transmission range is typically 100 m outdoors and 30 m indoors.
- They are prone to radio interference, but are useful where it is difficult to install cables.

Wired systems

- Cabling is needed from the camera to the central monitor or recorder.
- The same cabling can be used to power the cameras and transmit images.
- The maximum transmission range is hundreds of metres.
- They are not normally prone to interference.

PC-based systems

A cheap reliable digital system can be created by loading appropriate software on a PC. This type of system has many advantages:

- The system is easy to expand.
- It is easy to record images.
- It is easy to change the monitoring configurations.
- Remote viewing via another computer is possible.
- The images can be emailed or sent to a mobile phone.

Cameras

There are two main types of camera, CMOS and CCD. CCD is more expensive but produces very clear images for easily identifying people and vehicles. Both types can produce colour or black and white images. High ambient light levels are needed for colour images. However, an infrared light source will give clear black and white images in poor light condition.

The ability of a camera to produce clear images depends on the light levels available. Typical light levels in different environments are shown in Table 8.03. When choosing a camera for a particular environment, it should be specified at 10 times the minimum light level for that environment.

Environment	Typical light level
Summer sunlight	50,000 lux
Dull daylight	10,000 lux
Shop/office	500 lux
Main street lighting	30 lux
Dawn/dusk	1–10 lux
Side street lighting	3 lux

Table 8.03 Typical light levels

Monitoring and recording

Most systems use multiple cameras, which send images back to a central control to be viewed or recorded. There are several ways to view and record the images, as listed below:

- **Switcher** – This switches from one image to another, to view or record one image at a time.
- **Quad processor** – Four images can be viewed on one screen at the same time. One image, or four at poorer quality, can be recorded at the same time.
- **Multiplexer** – This displays and records multiple full-size images without loss of quality.

Standard recording tapes can be set to record over periods of 24, 240 or 960 hours (40 days!). They last even longer if the cameras only switch on when there is something to view. This can be achieved using a motion detector, typically activated by passive infrared sensors.

Did you know?

Images can be recorded for longer periods of time by using slower tapes.

Intruder alarm systems

There are two methods of protecting a property. Perimeter protection sounds the alarm before the intruder gets into the property and space detection sounds the alarm after the intruder is in. Sometimes both methods are used together for extra security.

Many different systems are available, but typical types and components are given below.

Proximity switches (perimeter protection)

These are also known as a magnet and reed switches. The magnet and reed parts are fixed side by side on a window or door, usually less than 6 mm apart. When the window or door opens, the circuit opens and operates the alarm. They can be surface or flush-mounted.

Inertia switches (perimeter protection)

These type of switches detect the vibration when a window or door is being forced open and activate the alarm. The switch usually needs its own supply (12 volts d.c.) and the sensitivity can be adjusted.

Passive infrared (space detection)

These devices activate the alarm when they detect the movement of body heat within the viewing range. They are capable of protecting large areas. The range can be adjusted, as can the viewing angle with the use of different lenses. They need a 12 volt d.c. supply.

Ultrasonic devices (space detection)

These devices send out sound waves and are tuned to receive the same frequency back. If the sound wave is disturbed by an intruder, the alarm sounds. They also need a 12 volt d.c. supply.

Control panels

All parts of an alarm system are connected to a control panel. Most are operated by a digital keypad, which is either on the panel or mounted elsewhere in the building. They can easily be reprogrammed to change entry and exit delays, zone omission or phone diallers. They require mains supply to an integral transformer/rectifier, reducing down to 12 volts d.c. for operation, with a battery backup.

Audible (sounder) and visible warning devices

The most common type of system has a loud, electronic sounder to attract attention. There will also usually be a xenon light (strobe light) fitted to the sounder box, which identifies which sounder is activated. The light will continue flashing after the sounder has stopped so that the owner can see that there has been an alarm condition, which will only switch off when the panel is reset.

Did you know?

An alarm must only sound for a maximum of 20 minutes by law. After it has switched off, it can either re-arm itself or, if there is a fault on the system, stay off.

Short answer questions

1. Name three electrical components on a typical central heating circuit?
2. Describe the main differences between maintained and non-maintained emergency lights?
3. What are the three general types of fire alarm system as stated in BS 5839?
4. What three parts form the fire triangle?
5. Describe what qualifies as a weekly inspection of a fire system.
6. Why is it important to ensure that the exposed and extraneous conductive parts are bonded to earth on a water heating system?
7. Referring to Figures 8.06 and 8.07, describe briefly how the simmerstat operates and controls the hotplate.
8. What is the main difference between a quad processor and a multiplexer as used in a CCTV system?
9. Describe the difference between perimeter and space protection provided by an intruder alarm system?
10. Why does the xenon light continue flashing after the sounder has stopped?

Multiple-choice test

1. Which of the following is not used in a gravity hot water-pumped system?
   a. programmer
   b. pump
   c. diverter valve
   d. thermostat

2. What is the BS for emergency lighting?
   a. BS 7671
   b. BS 5839
   c. BS 5200
   d. BS 5266

3. What is the minimum illuminance level on an escape route?
   a. 10 lux
   b. 0.2 lux
   c. 0.1 lux
   d. 5 lux

4. Which of the following is not a type of emergency light?
   a. maintained
   b. sustained
   c. temporary
   d. non-maintained

5. What is the BS for fire alarm systems?
   a. BS 5839
   b. BS 5829
   c. BS 4839
   d. BS 2391

6. In P1 protection for property, which of the following need not have a detector?
   a. stairwell
   b. landing
   c. toilet
   d. vertical riser

7. How many categories of life protection systems are there?
   a. 6
   b. 3
   c. 5
   d. 4

8. How many floors can be covered by one zone?
   a. 2
   b. 1
   c. 3
   d. 0

9. Which of the following is not needed for a fire?
   a. oxygen
   b. heat
   c. carbon dioxide
   d. fuel

10. What happens to thermistor resistance when the temperature rises?
    a. decreases
    b. stays the same
    c. increases
    d. short circuits

11. What is the minimum dba level for a sounder?
    a. 70
    b. 65
    c. 90
    d. 40

12. How often should the battery be changed in a fire alarm system?
    a. 1 year
    b. 3 years
    c. 2 years
    d. 5 years

13. What is the tube made from in an infrared heater?
    a. quartz
    b. stainless steel
    c. ceramic
    d. glass silica

14. What is used as the rod inside the copper tube on an oven thermostat?
    a. brass
    b. Invar
    c. cast iron
    d. manganese steel

15. What is the maximum time that a sounder can operate for?
    a. until it is switched off
    b. 60 minutes
    c. 20 minutes
    d. 24 hours

The answer section is at the back of the book.

CHAPTER 09

Inspection, testing and commissioning

To comply with the Electricity at Work Regulations and to ensure that the installation continues to be safe to use, all electrical installations initially and at regular intervals should be inspected and tested.

At the end of this chapter, you will be confident in answering questions about inspection, testing and commissioning. The chapter gives particular attention to the following:

- Statutory and non-statutory documentation
  - BS 7671
  - Electricity at Work Regulations 1989
  - Electricity Safety, Quality and Continuity Regulations 2002
- Initial inspection and commissioning
  - Compliance with BS 7671
  - Compliance with the project specification
  - Competence and responsibilities of the inspector
- Periodic inspection and testing
  - The purpose
  - Intervals between tests
  - Routine checks
- The inspection process
  - Items to be covered
  - Preparing for inspection
  - Damage and safety issues
  - Detailed inspection requirements
  - The sequence of tests
  - Periodic testing
  - Detailed test procedures
  - Inspection checklists

- Instruments and their use
  - Types of instrument
  - Calibration and instrument accuracy
  - Testing procedures
- Certification and reporting
  - Periodic inspection report
  - Electrical Installation Certificate (Type 1)
  - Electrical Installation Certificate (Type 2)
  - Guidance notes for those receiving a certificate
  - Inspection schedule
  - Schedule of test results
  - Electrical Installation Minor Works Certificate
- Procedures for dealing with the client and reports
  - The customer
  - Handover to the client

Statutory and non-statutory documentation

Statutory and non-statutory documentation, relating to inspection and testing, include:

- BS 7671
- Electricity at Work Regulations 1989
- Electricity Safety, Quality and Continuity Regulations 2002
- BS 5266 Pt.1 Code of Practice for emergency lighting systems (other than cinemas); other Regulations and intervals cover testing of batteries and generators
- BS 5839 Pt.1 Code of Practice for the design, installation and servicing of fire alarm systems
- local authority conditions of licence
- SI 1995 No 1129 (clause 27) The Cinematography (Safety) Regulations.

BS 7671

BS 7671 is the main document supported by the *IEE On-Site Guide* and the *IEE Guidance Note 3 on Inspection and Testing*. These contain tables and charts with maximum values and check lists, against which comparisons have to be made. Further information is included in contract specifications and drawings and manufacturers' instructions.

BS 7671 states that, as far as is reasonably practicable, an inspection shall be carried out to verify that:

- all equipment and materials used in the installation are of the correct type and comply with the appropriate British Standards or acceptable equivalent
- all parts of the installation have been correctly selected and installed
- no part of the installation is visibly damaged or otherwise defective.

Electricity at Work Regulations 1989

In addition to BS 7671, testing and inspection of installations also confirms compliance with EAWR. For inspection purposes, EAWR requires that:

- only competent persons should be engaged in the testing procedure (Regulation 16)
- suitable precautions for safe isolation need to be taken (Regulation 14)
- padlocks and isolock systems should be used so that control of isolation remains under the control of the inspector (Regulation 13).

Remember

It is not possible for anyone to remember all the information relating to BS 7671. Therefore an essential part of the toolbox for someone involved in the inspection and testing of installations is a copy of these documents.

Electricity Safety, Quality and Continuity Regulations 2002

These Regulations include reference to streetlights, traffic signals and bollards, etc. and could, therefore, become part of the requirements for someone involved in the test and inspection of these installations.

Regulation 29 gives area supply boards the power to refuse to connect their supply to an installation that, in their opinion, is not constructed, installed and protected to an appropriately high standard. This regulation would only be enforced if the installation failed to meet the requirements of BS 7671.

Initial inspection and commissioning

The initial inspection and test procedure must be carefully planned and carried out and the results correctly documented. Inspection and testing is required to check for compliance with BS 7671, to confirm that the installation is as the original job specification required and that it is safe to use.

Compliance with BS 7671

BS 7671 Part 6 states that every electrical installation shall, either during construction, on completion or both, be inspected and tested to verify, so far as is reasonably practicable, that the requirements of the Regulations have been met. In carrying out such inspection and test procedures, precautions must be taken to ensure that no danger is caused to any person or livestock and to avoid damage to property and installed equipment.

Remember

All electrical items *must* be tested before finally being put into service.

Compliance with the project specification

Once the installation is complete, it must be tested against the original specification to check that the finished installation matches the requirements laid out by the customer and is fit for use in the environment where it will be used. This includes:

- **Pre-commissioning** – A full inspection of the installation and the carrying out of all tests before the installation is energised (continuity, insulation resistance and polarity).
- **Commissioning** – Functional testing of all equipment, isolation, switching, protective devices and circuit arrangements, the measurement of the earth-fault loop impedance and functional testing of RCDs.

As commissioning involves the initial energising of an installation, this has to be carried out with the knowledge of everyone involved in a controlled situation. This includes all persons working on site, who must be informed that power will be applied to the installation, so that all precautions can be taken to prevent danger.

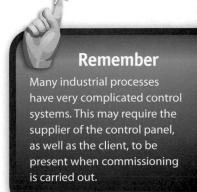

Remember

Many industrial processes have very complicated control systems. This may require the supplier of the control panel, as well as the client, to be present when commissioning is carried out.

The final act of the commissioning process is to ensure the safe and correct operation of all circuits and equipment that have been installed, and that the customer's requirements have been met. This will also confirm that the installation works and, more importantly, will work under fault conditions.

Competence and responsibilities of the inspector

The testing of electrical installations can be dangerous. It is the responsibility of the person carrying out the tests to ensure the safety of themselves and others. *Health and Safety Executive Guidance Note GS38* (*Electrical test equipment for use by electricians*) details relevant safety procedures and should be observed in full.

Any person undertaking these duties must be skilled and experienced and have sufficient knowledge of the type of installation. They must:

- have a thorough understanding of the equipment use and rating
- ensure that all safety procedures are being followed
- ensure that all instruments conform to the appropriate British Standard (i.e. BS EN 61010 or older instruments manufactured to BS 5458), are in good condition and recently calibrated
- check that test leads, including probes and clips, are in good condition, are clean and have no cracked or broken insulation. Where appropriate the requirements of GS38 should be observed, including the use of fused test leads.

It is the responsibility of the inspector to:

- ensure no danger occurs to people, property and livestock
- confirm the test and inspection results comply with BS 7671 and the designer's requirements
- express an opinion as to the condition of the installation and recommend remedial works
- make immediate recommendations, in the event of a dangerous situation, to isolate the defective part.

Periodic inspection and testing

All electrical installations deteriorate due to factors such as damage, wear and tear, corrosion, excessive electrical loading, aging and environmental influences. Hence, periodic inspection and testing must be carried out at regular intervals. Most of the factors relating to the initial verification process also apply to periodic inspection and testing.

The purpose

The purpose of periodic inspection and testing is to:

- confirm the safety of persons and livestock against the effects of electric shock or burns
- ensure protection against damage to property by fire or heat arising from an installation defect
- confirm that the installation has not been damaged and has not deteriorated to the extent that it may impair safety
- identify any defects in the installation or non-conformity with the current edition of the Regulations that may cause danger.

> **Remember**
>
> With periodic inspection and testing, inspection is the vital initial operation and testing is subsequently carried out in support of that inspection.

Intervals between tests

The intervals between tests is determined by:

- the requirement for installations to be maintained in a safe condition Table 9.01 details the maximum period between inspections of various types of installation
- licensing authorities, public bodies, insurance companies and other authorities may require public inspection and testing of electrical installations
- compliance with BS 7671
- change of use of the premises, any alterations or additions to the original installation, any significant change in the electrical loading of the installation, and where there is the possibilty that damage may have been caused to the installation.

Location	Interval	Location	Interval
Domestic Or if change of occupancy	10 years	Theatres	3 years
Commercial Or if change of occupancy	5 years	Public houses	5 years
Educational premises	5 years	Village halls/community centres	5 years
Industrial	3 years	Agricultural/horticultural	3 years
Hospitals	5 years	Caravans	3 years

Residential accommodation Or if change of occupancy	10 years	Caravan parks	1 year
Offices	5 years	Highway power supplies	6 years
Shops	5 years	Marinas	1 year
Laboratories	5 years	Fish farms	1 year
Cinemas	3 years	Swimming pools	1 year
Churches	5 years	Emergency lighting	3 years
Leisure complexes	3 years	Fire alarms	1 year
Places of public entertainment	3 years	Launderettes	1 year
Restaurants	5 years	Petrol filling stations	1 year
Hotels	5 years	Construction sites	3 months

Table 9.01 Frequency of inspection

In an installation that is under constant supervision while in normal use, such as a factory or other industrial premises, periodic inspection and testing can be replaced by a system of continuous monitoring and maintenance of the installation. However adequate records of such maintenance must be kept.

When designing and specifying equipment for an electrical installation the designer should take into account the likely quality of the maintenance programme and the periods between periodic inspection and testing to be specified on the Electrical Installation Certificate.

Both Section 6 of the Health and Safety at Work Act and the Construction (Design and Management) Regulations require information on routine checks and periodic inspections to be provided.

Routine checks

The occupier will soon notice any damage to electrical equipment. In commercial or industrial installations a suitable reporting system should be available to report any potential danger from deteriorating or damaged equipment.

A system of routine checks should also be set up between formal periodic inspections. The frequency of these depends on the nature of the installation. Routine checks are likely to include activities such as those listed in Table 9.02.

Activity	Check
Defect reports	Check that all reported defects have been rectified and that the installation is safe.
Inspection	Look for: • breakages • wear or deterioration • signs of overheating • missing parts (covers/screws) • switchgear still accessible • enclosure doors secure • labels still adequate (readable) • loose fittings.
Operation	Check operation of: • switchgear (where reasonable) • equipment (switch off and on) • RCD (using test button).

Table 9.02 Routine checks

In summary, the inspection should ensure that:

- the installation is safe and has not been damaged
- the condition of the installation has not deteriorated
- any items that no longer comply with the Regulations, or may cause danger, are identified.

The inspector is carrying out a general inspection to ensure that the installation is safe, but also records, and make recommendations on, any items that do not comply with the current edition of the Regulations.

The inspection process

In new installations, inspection should be carried out as the installation is installed and must be completed before it is energised. As far as is reasonably practicable, an initial inspection should be carried out to verify that:

- all equipment and material is of the correct type and complies with applicable British Standards or acceptable equivalents
- all parts of the fixed installation are correctly selected and erected
- no part of the fixed installation is visibly damaged or otherwise defective.

Items to be covered

- **Connection of conductors** – These must provide durable electrical continuity and adequate mechanical strength.
- **Identification of each conductor** – Table 51 of BS 7671 provides colour identification of each core of a cable and its conductors.
- **Routing of cables** – Cable routes shall be selected with regard to the cable's suitability for the environment and be routed out safely and protected against mechanical damage where necessary.
- **Current-carrying capacity** – Cable size should be assessed against the protective device with reference to Appendix 4 of BS 7671.
- **Verification of polarity** – No single pole switch or protective device should be installed in a neutral conductor. All protective devices and switches must be connected in the line conductor only. No switches are permitted in the cpc.
- **Accessories and equipment** – Correct connection is to be checked.
- **Selection and erection to minimise the spread of fire**
- **Basic protection** – Protection is provided using the following methods:
  - **Insulation** – Is the insulation damaged or has too much been removed?
  - **Barriers** – Have all covers, lids and plates been securely fitted?
  - **Obstacles** – If this method is used, the area should be accessible only to skilled or instructed persons under supervision.
  - **Out of reach** – The requirements for this method are given more fully in Appendix 3 of the *Memorandum of Guidance to the Electricity at Work Act*.
- **Fault protection** – Earthing provides protection against this type of fault. Extraneous conductive parts must be correctly bonded with protective conductors. An extraneous conductive part is a conductive part with a potential, generally earth potential, but does not form part of an electrical installation (e.g. metal sink tops, metal water pipes, etc.) Bonding ensures that all extraneous conductive parts are at the same potential.
- **Protective devices** – Have they been set correctly for the load?
- **Documentation** – Diagrams, schedules, charts, instructions and any other information must be available if inspection and testing is to be carried out.

Did you know?

Typical earthing arrangements for domestic installations are shown diagrammatically in the *IEE On-Site Guide*. For other types of installation the appropriate size of earthing and bonding conductors should be determined in accordance with BS 7671 Chapter 54.

- **Marking and labelling** – These should show the origin of every installation and indicate differences in voltages, earthing and bonding connections and RCDs.
- **Warning notices** – These should be fixed to equipment operating in excess of 250 volts where this voltage would not normally be expected.

Preparing for inspection

Before carrying out the inspection and test of an installation BS 7671 requires the person carrying out the work to be provided with the following information:

- the maximum demand of the installation expressed in amperes per phase after diversity has been applied
- the number and type of live conductors, at the point of supply and for each circuit to be used within the installation (e.g. single-phase two-wire a.c. or three-phase four-wire a.c. etc.)
- details of the method selected to prevent danger from shock in the event of an earth fault including the type of earthing arrangements, equipotential bonding arrangements and automatic disconnection of supply
- the type and composition of circuits, including points of utilisation, number and size of conductors and types of cable installed.
- the location and description of protective devices (fuses, circuit breakers, etc.), isolation and switching and its location

- the presence of any sensitive electronic devices and any circuit or equipment that may be vulnerable to test
- the nominal voltage (U_o)
- the prospective short circuit current at the origin of the installation (kA)
- the earth-fault loop impedance (Z_e) of that part of the system external to the installation
- the type and rating of the overcurrent device acting at the origin of the installation.

The Health and Safety at Work Act 1974 and the Construction (Design and Management) Regulations 1994 both state the requirements for the provision of such information to be included in the operation and maintenance manual prepared for the project. This should also contain a description of how the installation is to operate and include copies of distribution board details, identifying the circuits, the protective devices, the wiring system and the installation methods as well as the technical data for all items installed, such as switchgear, luminaires and any special control systems that may have been incorporated.

Precise details of all equipment installed should also be obtained from the manufacturers or suppliers to check that the required standards have been met, to ensure satisfactory methods of installation have been used and provide the information necessary to confirm correct operation.

Where a diagram, chart or tables are not available, a degree of exploratory work may be necessary so that inspection and testing can be carried out safely and effectively. Note should be made of any known changes in environmental conditions, building structure and alterations, which may have affected the suitability of the wiring for its present load and method of installation.

Damage and safety issues

A careful check should be made of the type of equipment on site so that the necessary precautions can be taken, where conditions permit, to disconnect or short out electronic and other equipment which may be damaged by subsequent testing. Special care must be taken where control and protective devices contain electronic components. It is essential to determine the degree of these disconnections before planning detailed inspection and testing.

If disruption to others is to be kept to a minimum they will need to be advised of when, and in what areas, the activity will be taking place. They will also need to know the amount of time that the supply may be disrupted. For other contractors it may be necessary to provide them with temporary supplies, derived from other sources, to enable them to continue their work activities.

Inspection

An inspection of the installation should be completed before beginning any tests or opening enclosures removing covers, etc. So far as is reasonably practicable, the inspection must verify that the safety of persons, livestock and property is not endangered. A thorough inspection should be made of all electrical equipment that is not concealed and should include the accessible internal condition of a sample of the equipment. External conditions should be noted and damage identified or, if the degree of protection has been impaired, the matter should be recorded on the schedule of the report. This inspection should be carried out without power supplies to the installation, wherever possible, in accordance with the Electricity at Work Regulations 1989.

Isolation

It is not adequate to simply isolate a circuit electrically before commencing work on it. **It is vital to ensure that once a circuit or item of electrical equipment has been isolated, it cannot be inadvertently switched back on.** A good method for full electrical and mechanical isolation is to lock off the device (or distribution board containing the device) with a padlock, with the person working on the isolated equipment holding the key. A skilled person should be the only one allowed to carry out this or similar responsible tasks.

Did you know?

If inspection and testing cannot be carried out safely without diagrams or equivalent information, they must be prepared for compliance with Section 6 of the Health and Safety at Work Act 1974.

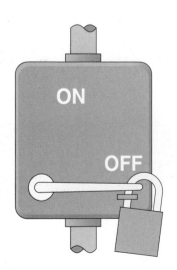

Figure 9.01 Device locked off with padlock

Detailed inspection requirements

The inspection should include a check on the condition of all electrical equipment and materials, taking into account any available manufacturer's information with regard to the following:

- safety
- wear and tear
- corrosion
- damage
- excessive loading (overloading)
- age
- external influences
- suitability.

The assessment of condition should take account of any known changes in conditions influencing and affecting electrical safety, e.g. extraneous conductive parts, plumbing, structural changes, etc. It is not always practical to conduct a complete installation, so a random sample is selected. This should include:

- checking joints and connections are secure and there are no signs of overheating
- checking electrical and mechanical conditions of switches
- checking rating and type of protective devices
- checking conductors have not suffered mechanical damage and are not overheating
- checking enclosures remain satisfactory for the type of protection required.

Joints and connections

It might be impossible to inspect every joint and termination in an electrical installation. Again a sample inspection can be made. All switchgear and distribution boards should be accessible and a full inspection of all conductor terminations should be carried out with overheating or loose connections investigated and reported. For lighting points and socket outlets a suitable sample should be inspected in the same way.

Conductors

Check the means of identification of every conductor including protective conductors and any damage or deterioration. Every distribution board within the installation should be inspected and a suitable sample of lighting points, switching points and socket outlets.

Remember

Although the major part of any inspection will be visual, other human senses may be employed, e.g. a piece of equipment with moving parts may generate an unusual noise if it is not working correctly, or an electrical device which overheats will be hot to touch as well as giving off a distinctive smell.

Flexible cables and cords

Where flexible cables or cords form part of the fixed installation the inspection and examination should include:

- cable or cord for damage or deterioration
- terminations and anchor points for any defects
- additional mechanical protection or the application of heat resistant sleeving

Switches

The *IEE Guidance Notes 3* (*Inspection and Testing*), recommends that a random sample of at least 10 per cent of all switching devices be given a thorough internal inspection to assess their electrical and mechanical condition. If the inspection reveals excessive wear and tear or signs of damage due to arcing or overheating then the inspection should be extended to include all remaining switches within the installation.

Protection against thermal effects

This can be difficult due to the structure of the building, but the presence of fire barriers and seals should be checked.

Basic and fault protection

Separated Extra Low Voltage (SELV) is commonly used as a means of providing both basic and fault protection. When inspecting this type of system, the points to be checked include the use of a safety isolating transformer, the need to keep the primary and secondary circuits separate and the segregation of exposed conductive parts of the SELV system from any connection with the earthing of the primary circuit or from any other connection with earth.

Inspection of the installation should confirm that all the requirements of the Regulations have been met with regard to basic protection against contact with live conductors. This means checking to ensure there has been no damage or deterioration of any of the insulation within the installation, no removal of barriers or obstacles and no alterations to enclosures that may allow access to live conductors.

The method used for fault protection must be established and recorded on the Inspection Schedule. Where protective equipotential bonding and automatic disconnection of the supply is used, a check on the condition of the main equipotential bonding conductor and the satisfactory connection of all other protective conductors with earth are essential.

Protective devices

Each circuit must be adequately protected with the correct type, size and rating of fuse or circuit breaker. Each protective device must be suitable for the type of circuit it is protecting and the earthing system used.

Remember

An RCD must not be used as the sole means of basic protection against contact with live parts.

Did you know?

For certain installations where there are increased risks or occupation by members of the public, such as cinemas, public houses, restaurants and hotels, etc. the local licensing authority may impose additional requirements, especially in the area of regular inspection and testing.

Enclosures and mechanical protection

The enclosures of all electrical equipment and accessories should be inspected to ensure that they provide protection not less than IP2X or IPXXB, and where horizontal top surfaces are readily accessible they should have a degree of protection of at least IP4X. IP2X represents the average finger of 12.5 mm diameter and 80 mm in length and can be tested by a metal finger of these dimensions. IP4X provides protection against entry by strips greater than 1.0 mm or solid objects exceeding 1.0 mm in diameter.

The sequence of tests

Initial tests should be carried out in the following sequence where applicable, before the supply is connected or with the supply disconnected as appropriate:

- continuity of protective conductors (cpc) including circuit protective conductors, main and supplementary equipotential bonding circuits
- continuity of ring final circuit conductors
- insulation resistance
- protection by separation of circuits
- insulation resistance of floors and walls
- protection by automatic disconnection of supply
- polarity
- earth electrode resistance.

With the electrical supply connected, testing of the following (where relevant) should be carried out:

- earth-fault loop impedance
- operation of residual current devices
- additional protection
- prospective fault current
- check of phase sequence
- functional testing (operation of RCDs, switchgear, controls etc.)
- verification of voltage drop.

The list indicates the order in which the tests should be conducted to ensure that the results obtained are reliable. Tests 1–8 are dead tests, to ensure that it is safe to put the supply on. It is therefore important to prove the continuity of protective conductors before beginning insulation resistance tests.

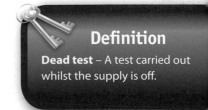

Definition

Dead test – A test carried out whilst the supply is off.

Periodic testing

Periodic testing is supplementary to periodic inspection and the same level of testing as for a new installation is not necessarily required.

When a building is unoccupied, isolation of the supply for testing purposes is not a problem. However when the building is occupied, then as little inconvenience as possible should be caused. Disconnection should be for as short a time as possible. Tests may need to be outside of normal working hours in order to keep disruption to a minimum.

The recommended sequence of carrying out periodic tests is different from the sequence of tests for a new installation:

- continuity of all protective conductors (including equipotential bonding conductors and continuity of ring circuit conductors where required)
- polarity
- earth-fault loop impedance
- insulation resistance
- operation of devices for isolation and switching
- operation of residual current devices
- operation of circuit breakers.

Detailed test procedures

Continuity of protective conductors and equipotential bonding conductors

Cpcs and equipotential bonding conductors should be disconnected from the main earthing terminal to verify their continuity.

Where the installation cannot be isolated inspection, continuity and earth loop impedance testing should be carried out.

When testing the effectiveness of the main bonding conductors or supplementary bonds, the resistance value between any service pipe or extraneous metalwork and the main earthing terminal should not exceed 0.05 ohms.

Polarity

Polarity tests should be carried out to check that:

- it is correct at the intake position and the consumer unit or distribution board; and that single pole switches or control devices are connected in the live conductor only
- socket outlets and other accessories are connected correctly
- centre contact bayonet and Edison screw type lamp holders have their outer or screwed contact connected to the neutral conductor
- all multi-pole devices are correctly installed.

Polarity tests must confirm that all single pole switches and protective devices are fitted in the line conductor. Switches fitted in the neutral conductor would result in the supply to the electrical equipment being broken and effectively being able to be turned on and off and when the switch was in the off position the supply would still be live up to the terminals of the equipment.

Reverse polarity would put the protective devices in the neutral conductor. In the event of an earth fault, the fault current would not pass through the protective device. Automatic disconnection of the supply would not occur and this could lead to fatal electric shock.

Earth-fault loop impedance

Earth-fault loop impedance tests should be carried out at the origin of each installation and at each distribution board, all socket outlets and at the furthest point of each radial circuit. Results obtained should be compared against previous tests, with increases investigated.

Insulation resistance

These can only be carried out where it is possible to safely isolate the supply. All electronic equipment susceptible to damage should be disconnected or the insulation resistance test should be made between line and neutral conductors connected together and earth. Where practicable the tests should be carried out on the whole of the installation with all switches closed and all fuse links in place. Alternatively the installation may be subdivided by testing each separate distribution board one at a time.

BS 7671 Table 61 states a minimum acceptable resistance value of 1 MΩ. However, if the measured value is less than 2 MΩ then further investigation is required to determine the cause of the low reading.

Operation of main switches and isolators

All main switches and isolators should be inspected for correct operation and clear labelling and to check that access to them has not been obstructed. Test lamps between each line and the neutral on the load side of the device may need to be connected when these are not visible, to ensure that all supply conductors have been broken.

Operation of Residual Current Devices

RCDs should be tested for correct operation with a RCD tester to ensure they trip out in the time required by BS 7671 as well as by use of the integral test button. A check should also be made that the tripping current for the protection of a socket outlet to be used for equipment outdoors does not exceed 30 mA.

Operation of circuit breakers

All circuit breakers should be inspected for visible signs of damage or damage caused by overheating. Where isolation of the supply to individual subcircuits will not cause inconvenience, each circuit breaker should be manually operated to ensure that the device opens and closes correctly.

Basic and fault protection

Separated extra low voltage (SELV) is the most common method of providing both basic and fault protection. Requirements for this type of system include:

- an isolated source of supply, e.g. a safety-isolating transformer to BS 3535 (also numbered BS EN 60742 1996)
- electrical separation, which means no electrical connection between the SELV circuit and higher voltage systems
- no connection with earth or the exposed conductive parts or protective conductors of other systems.

The following factors should also be tested and inspected:

- Prevention of mutual detrimental influence – means avoiding cables in close proximity from damaging each other
- Isolating and switching devices – to ensure that all installations can be isolated
- Under voltage protection – to avoid sudden drop in voltage causing damage, such as a motor starter designed to prevent automatic restarting
- Selection of appropriate equipment for enviroment
- Access to switchgear
- Presence of diagrams and charts
- Safe erection and fitting of cables, conduits, switchgear etc.

Inspection checklists

To ensure that all the requirements of the Regulations have been met, inspection checklists should be drawn up and used as appropriate to the type of installation being inspected. Examples of suitable checklists are given below. When produced for use they should be spaced out and tick boxes provided against each.

Switchgear (tick if satisfactory)

- All switchgear is suitable for the purpose intended.
- Meets requirements of the appropriate BS EN standards.
- Securely fixed and suitably labelled.
- Suitable glands and gland plates used (526).
- Correctly earthed.
- Conditions likely to be encountered taken account of, i.e. suitable for the scene environment.
- Correct IP rating.
- Suitable as means of isolation.
- Complies with the requirements for locations containing a bath or shower.
- Need for isolation, mechanical maintenance, emergency and functional switching met.
- Fireman switch provided, where required.
- Switchgear suitably coloured, where necessary.

- All connections secure.
- Cables correctly terminated and identified.
- No sharp edges on cable entries, screw heads, etc. which could cause damage to cables.
- All covers and equipment in place.
- Adequate access and working space.

Wiring accessories (general requirements) (tick if satisfactory)

- All accessories comply with the appropriate British Standard.
- Boxes and other enclosures securely fastened.
- Metal boxes and enclosures correctly earthed.
- Flush boxes not projecting above surface of wall.
- No sharp edges which could cause damage to cable insulation.
- Non-sheathed cables not exposed outside box or enclosure.
- Conductors correctly identified.
- Bare protective conductors sleeved green and yellow.
- All terminals tight and contain all strands of stranded conductor.
- Cord grips correctly used to prevent strain on terminals.
- All accessories of adequate current rating.
- Accessories suitable for all conditions likely to be encountered.
- Complies with the requirements for locations containing a bath or shower.
- Cooker control unit sited to one side and low enough for accessibility and to prevent trailing flexes across the radiant plates.
- Cable to cooker fixed to prevent strain on connections.

Socket outlet (tick if satisfactory)

- Complies with appropriate British Standard and is shuttered for household and similar installations.
- Mounting height above floor or working surface is suitable.
- All sockets have correct polarity.
- Sockets not installed in bathroom or shower room unless they are shaver-type socket or SELV.
- Sockets not within 3 m horizontally from boundary of zone 1 in a bathroom.
- Sockets controlled by a switch if the supply is direct current.
- Sockets protected where floor mounted.
- Circuit protective conductor connected directly to the earthing terminal of the socket outlet on a sheathed wiring installation.
- Earthing tail provided from the earthed metal box to the earthing terminal of the socket outlet.
- Socket outlets not used to supply a water heater with un-insulated elements.

Lighting controls (tick if satisfactory)

- Light switches comply with appropriate British Standard.
- Switches suitably located.
- Single-pole switches connected in line conductor only.

- Correct colour-coding of conductors.
- Correct earthing of metal switch plates.
- Switches out of reach of a person using bath or shower.
- Switches for inductive circuits (discharge lamps) de-rated as necessary.
- Switches labelled to indicate purpose where this is not obvious.
- All switches of adequate current rating.
- All controls suitable for their associated luminaire.

Lighting points (tick if satisfactory)

- All lighting points correctly terminated in suitable accessory or fitting.
- Ceiling roses comply with appropriate British Standard.
- No more than one flexible cord unless designed for multiple pendants.
- Devices provided for supporting flex used correctly.
- All switch wires identified.
- Holes in ceiling above ceiling rose made good to prevent spread of fire.
- Ceiling roses not connected to supply exceeding 250 V.
- Flexible cords suitable for the mass suspended.
- Lamp holders comply with appropriate British Standard.
- Luminaire couplers comply with appropriate British Standard.

Conduits (general) (tick if satisfactory)

- All inspection fittings accessible.
- Maximum number of cables not exceeded.
- Solid elbows used only as permitted.
- Conduit ends reamed and bushed.
- Adequate number of boxes.
- All unused entries blanked off.
- Lowest point provided with drainage holes where required.
- Correct radius of bends to prevent damage to cables.
- Joints and scratches in metal conduit protected by painting.
- Securely fixed covers in place; adequate protection against mechanical damage.

Rigid metal conduits (tick if satisfactory)

- Complies to the appropriate British standard.
- Connected to the main earth terminal.
- Line and neutral cables contained within the same conduit.
- Conduits suitable for damp and corrosive situations.
- Maximum span between buildings without intermediate support.

Rigid non-metallic conduits (tick if satisfactory)

- Complies with the appropriate British Standard.
- Ambient and working temperature within permitted limits.
- Provision for expansion and contraction.
- Boxes and fixings suitable for mass of luminaire suspended at expected temperatures.

Flexible metal conduit (tick if satisfactory)

- Complies with the appropriate British Standard.
- Separate protective conductor provided.
- Adequately supported and terminated.

Trunking (tick if satisfactory)

- Complies to the appropriate British Standard.
- Securely fixed and adequately protected against mechanical damage.
- Selected, erected and rooted so that no damage is caused by ingress of water.
- Proximity to non-electrical services.
- Internal sealing provided where necessary.
- Hole surrounding trunking made good.
- Band 1 circuits partitioned from band 2 circuits, or insulated for the highest voltage present.
- Circuits partitioned from band 1 circuits, or wired in mineral-insulated and sheathed cable.
- Common outlets for band 1 and band 2 circuits provided with screens, barriers or partitions.
- Cables supported for vertical runs.

Metal trunking (tick if satisfactory)

- Line and neutral cables contained in the same metal trunking.
- Protected against damp corrosion.
- Earthed.
- Joints mechanically sound, and of adequate earth continuity with links fitted.

Circuit protective conductors (enter circuit details from specifications)

1. ....
2. ....
3. ....
4. ....
5. ....
6. ....
7. ....

Instruments and their use

This section covers instruments suitable for testing and commissioning. All test equipment must be regularly checked to make sure it is in good and safe working order. Calibration indicates that the instrument is working properly and providing accurate readings, otherwise test results could be void. If in doubt about an instrument or its accuracy ask for assistance, as test instruments are very expensive.

Types of instrument

Voltage detection

Instruments used solely for detecting a voltage fall into two categories:

- an illuminated lamp (test lamp) or meter scale (test meter)
- detectors using two or more independent indicating systems of which one may be audible (e.g. a two-pole voltage detector with integral test probe, interconnecting lead and second test probe).

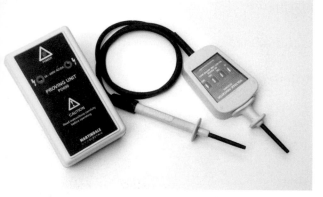

Voltage-indicating device

All limit the current and energy that can flow into the detector, usually by a combination of circuit design and current-limiting resistors in the test probes. Detectors are also provided with in-built test features to check the functioning of the detector before and after use. The interconnecting lead and second test probes are not detachable. They do not require additional current-limiting resistors or fuses to be fitted, provided they are made to an acceptable standard and the contact electrodes are shrouded.

Test lamps and voltage indicators should be clearly marked with the maximum voltage which may be tested, and any short time rating if applicable (the recommended maximum current that should pass through the device for a few seconds).

Low-reading ohmmeters

Low-reading ohmmeters are used when testing earth continuity, ring-circuit continuity and polarity. It is recommended that the test current should be from a supply of not less than 4 V and no greater than 24 V with a short circuit current not less than 200 mA (instruments manufactured to BS EN 61557 will meet the above requirements).

Errors can be introduced by contact or by lead resistance. Contact resistance errors cannot be eliminated entirely and may introduce errors of 0.01 ohm or greater. Lead resistance can be prevented by clipping the leads together and zeroing the instrument before use or measuring the resistance of the leads and subtracting this from the reading.

Insulation-resistance ohmmeters

Insulation resistance meters must have the ability to measure the high resistance readings from the high value of insulation resistance. The test voltage required for measuring insulation resistance is given in BS 7671 Table 61, as shown in Table 9.03.

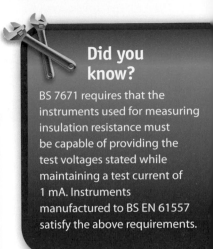

Circuit nominal voltage (volts)	Test voltage d.c. (volts)	Minimum insulation resistance (megaohms)
SELV and PELV	250	>0.5
Up to and including 500 V with the exception of the above	500	>1.0
Above 500 V	1000	>1.0

Table 9.03 Test voltage required for measuring insulation resistance (from BS 7671)

Instruments for high and low resistance values are usually kept in a fully insulated case for safety reasons and have a range of switches to set the instrument correctly for the type of test being carried out. The instrument can also be set to the voltage range required, e.g. 250 V, 500 V, 1000 V.

Earth-fault loop impedance testers

Earth-fault loop impedance testers can measure both earth loop impedance and also potential short circuit current, depending on which function is selected. The instrument also has a series of LED warning lights which indicate when circuit polarity is incorrect. The instrument gives a direct digital readout of the value of the measurement being taken at an accuracy of plus or minus 2 per cent.

Modern insulation and continuity tester

Earth electrode resistance testers

These have four or three terminals and are best used with long leads and temporary test spikes that are placed in the ground.

Earth-fault loop impedance tester

RCD testers

These test instruments have to be capable of delivering the full range of test currents required for a maximum period of two seconds and will give a readout calibrated in seconds. One selection switch should be set to the rated tripping current of the RCD (e.g. 30 mA, 100 mA, etc.); the other switch to the test current required, i.e. 50 per cent or 100 per cent of the rated tripping current.

RCD tester

All in one tester

All in one tester

A recent entry onto the market is the 'all in one' instrument with the ability to carry out the most common tests required by the Regulations:

- continuity tests (including polarity tests)
- insulation resistance tests
- earth loop impedance tests
- RCD tests
- measurement of prospective short circuit current.

Tong testers

Tong testers, or clamp meters, work by magnetic induction to measure the value of current flowing in an a.c. circuit. They do not require the supply to be interrupted. The magnetic field around the conductor induces an e.m.f. When the jaws of the tester are closed over the conductors the circuit is complete and the instrument measures the current. If both live and neutral conductors are held, the equal magnetic fields would prevent a reading

Applied voltage testers

These should be able to provide an output current that does not exceed 5 mA and a required test voltage of 3750 V a.c. The instruments should be capable of maintaining a test voltage continuously for at least one minute, and should have a means of indicating when a failure of the insulation has occurred.

Calibration and instrument accuracy

British Standards

The basic standard covering the performance and accuracy of electrical test instruments is BS EN 61557. BS EN 61010 covers basic safety requirements for electrical test instruments.. Older instruments may have been manufactured in accordance with BS 5458 but, if they are in good condition and have been calibrated correctly they may be used.

Displays

Instruments may be analogue or digital. Insulation and continuity testers can be either while earth-fault loop impedance testers and RCD testers are digital.

Accuracy

To ensure that the reading being taken is reasonably accurate, all instruments should have a measurement accuracy of at least 5 per cent. In the case of analogue instruments an accuracy of 2 per cent of full-scale deflection should ensure the required accuracy of measured values over most of the scale.

Remember

Older instruments often generated their own operating voltage by use of an in-built hand-cranked generator. Modern instruments have internal batteries which must be checked regularly; including absence of corrosion at the terminals.

Calibration

All electrical test instruments should be calibrated at least once every twelve months in laboratory conditions against national standards.

On being calibrated the instrument will have a calibration certificate and label attached to it stating the date the calibration took place and the date the next calibration is due. The instrument should always be checked to ensure it is within calibration before use.

An adhesive label is often placed over the joint in the instrument casing, stating that the calibration is void should this seal be broken. This will indicate that the instrument has been opened and possibly tampered with.

Instruments subject to any electrical or mechanical misuse (e.g. if the instrument undergoes an electrical short circuit or is dropped) should be returned for recalibration before being used again.

Storage and handling

When not in use electrical test equipment should be stored in clean, dry conditions at normal room temperature. Care should also be taken to prevent damage to insulation of leads and probes and to maintain them in a good, safe working condition.

Testing procedures

This section lists some of the main testing procedures that are used during inspection and testing.

Testing resistors

Remove resistors to prevent false readings from a circuit before testing. The leads of a suitable ohmmeter should be connected to each resistor connection lead and the reading should be close to the preferred value and within the stated tolerance.

Resistors often have to carry large values of current but must not overheat or be damaged. The power rating states the maximum temperature at which the resistor is designed to operate. The more power a resistor is designed to desolve the larger it's size; the resulting larger surface area aiding the dissipation of heat. Typical power ratings for resistors are shown in Table 9.04. Manufacturers quote a maximum voltage rating, which indicates the insulation properties of parts of the resistor. When this is exceeded, it can damage the resistor both internally and externally.

Remember

When using an instrument on site, the accuracy of the instrument will probably not be as good as the accuracy obtained under laboratory conditions. Operating accuracy is always worse than basic accuracy and can be affected by battery condition, generator cranking speed, ambient temperature, instrument alignment or loss of calibration.

| Instrument serial no.: |
| Date tested: |
| Date next due: |

Figure 9.02 Adhesive calibration label

Calibration void if seal is broken

Figure 9.03 Calibration seal

Remember

Records of calibrations carried out and copies of all calibration certificates issued should be retained in a safe place in case it is necessary to validate test results carried out at a later date.

Carbon resistors	0 to 0.5 watts
Ceramic resistors	0 to 6 watts
Wire wound resistors	0 to 25 watts

Table 9.04 Typical power ratings for resistors

Continuity testing of circuit protective conductors (cpc)

Every protective conductor, including each bonding conductor, should be tested to verify that it is electrically sound and correctly connected. The two tests are described below and will check the continuity of the protective conductor and measure $R_1 + R_2$ which, when corrected for temperature, can be used to obtain the calculated earth-fault loop impedance (Z_S).

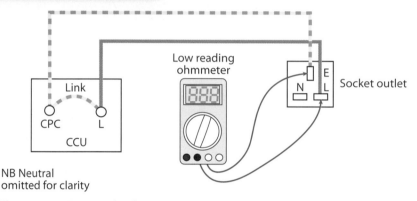

NB Neutral omitted for clarity

Figure 9.04 Test method 1

Test method 1. The line conductor and the protective conductor are linked together at the consumer unit or distribution board. The ohmmeter is used to test between the line and earth terminals at each outlet in the circuit. The measurement at the circuit's extremity is the value of $R_1 + R_2$. This should be carried out before any supplementary bonds are made.

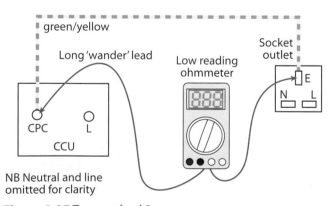

NB Neutral and line omitted for clarity

Figure 9.05 Test method 2

Test method 2. One lead of the continuity tester is connected to the consumer's main earth terminals. The other lead is connected to a trailing lead, to make contact with protective conductors at light fittings, switches, spur outlets, etc. In this method the protective conductor only is tested and this reading (R_2) is recorded on the installation schedule. This method is used for testing main and supplementary bonding conductors.

Continuity of bonding conductors

Test method 2 above is used for this purpose. The ohmmeter leads are connected between the point being tested and between simultaneously accessible extraneous conductive parts, or between simultaneously accessible extraneous conductive parts.

Continuity of ring final circuit conductors

The continuity of each conductor including the circuit protective conductor (cpc) of every ring final circuit must be verified. The test results should conclude that the ring is complete and has no interconnections and is not broken. Figure 9.06 shows a ring circuit illustrating these faults.

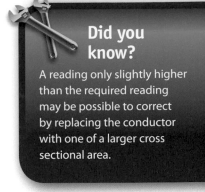

Did you know?

A reading only slightly higher than the required reading may be possible to correct by replacing the conductor with one of a larger cross sectional area.

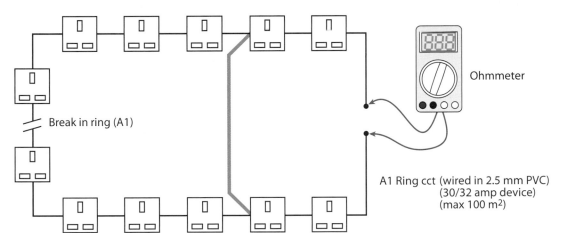

Break in ring (A1)

Ohmmeter

A1 Ring cct (wired in 2.5 mm PVC)
(30/32 amp device)
(max 100 m²)

Figure 9.06 Test of continuity of ring final circuit conductors

The line, neutral and protective conductors have their end-to-end resistances measured separately. These are known as R_1, R_n and R_2. A finite reading confirms that there is no open circuit on the ring conductors under test.

The resistance values should be within 0.05 ohms, if the conductors are the same size. If the protective conductor has a reduced csa, the resistance of the protective loop will be proportionally higher than that of the line or neutral loop.

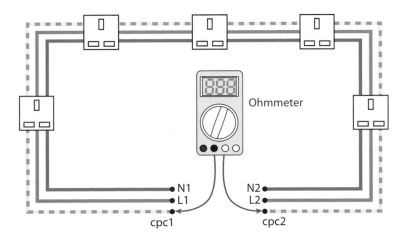

Ohmmeter

N1
L1
cpc1

N2
L2
cpc2

Figure 9.07 Measurement of line, neutral and protective conductors

The line and neutral conductors are then joined so that the outgoing line conductor is connected to the returning neutral conductor and *vice versa*. The resistance between line and neutral conductors is then measured at each socket outlet. The readings obtained from those outlets wired into the ring should be mostly the same and the value will be approximately half the resistance of the line or the neutral loop resistance or $(R_1 + R_n)$.

This is repeated with the line and cpc cross-connected. The resistance between line and earth is then measured again at each outlet. The highest value recorded represents the maximum $R_1 + R_2$ of the circuit and can be used to determine the earth loop impedance (Z_s) of the circuit. This test also verifies the polarity at each outlet.

Testing insulation resistance

Insulation resistance tests verify that insulation of conductors, electrical accessories and equipment is correct and that conductors are not short-circuited, or show a low insulation resistance. Before testing ensure that:

- pilot or indicator lamps and capacitors are disconnected from circuits
- voltage sensitive electronic equipment such as dimmer switches, delay timers, etc. are disconnected
- there is no electrical connection between any line and neutral conductor (e.g. lamps left in).

An insulation resistance tester is used, with tests carried out using the appropriate d.c. test voltage as specified in Table 61 of BS 7671. The main switchboard and each distribution circuit with its final circuits only connected must have an insulation resistance not less than that specified in Table 61.

The tests should be carried out with the main switch off if the tails have been energised, all fuses in place, switches and circuit breakers closed, lamps removed, and fluorescent and discharge luminaires and other equipment disconnected.

Simple installations containing no distribution circuits can be tested as a whole. Complex installations can be subdivided. An insulation resistance value of not less than 1 MΩ complies with the Regulations. A value less than 2 MΩ makes it possible a latent fault exists. So, each circuit should be separately tested.

Test 1 – Insulation resistance between live conductors

For single-phase circuits the test is between the line and neutral conductors at the appropriate switchboard. On a two-way circuit the two-way switch must be operated and retested to make sure all of the strappers have been tested.

For three-phase circuits first disconnect the incoming neutral so there is no connection with earth. Then tests are made between live conductors in turn at the appropriate switchboard:

- between brown line and to the black line, grey line and neutral (blue) grouped together
- between black line and to the grey line and neutral (blue) grouped together
- between grey line and neutral (blue).

Test 2 – Insulation resistance from earth to line and neutral connected together

For single-phase circuits the test is between the line and neutral conductors and earth at the appropriate distribution board. Repeat this for any two-way switches operated.

Three-phase circuits are measured between all line conductors and neutral bunched together, and earth. Where a low reading is obtained (less than 2 MΩ) it may be necessary to test each conductor to earth separately. Figure 9.08 shows the test of insulation resistance between earth to line and neutral connected together on a socket outlet circuit.

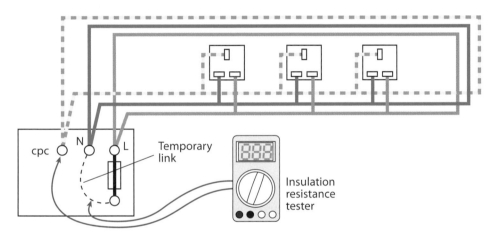

Figure 9.08 Insulation resistance test between earth to line and neutral connected together on socket outlets

A zero value of insulation resistance could be a short circuit between live conductors or an earth fault. Both must be immediately investigated.

A low value reading of below 2 MΩ indicates a latent weakness in the insulation. This could be due to the ingress of damp or dirt in such items as distribution boards, joint boxes or lighting fittings, etc. Other causes of low insulation resistance can be rats, mice or insects.

Polarity testing

A test needs to be performed to check the polarity of all circuits before connection to the supply, using either an ohmmeter or the continuity range of an insulation and continuity tester. This confirms that all protective devices and single-pole switches are connected to the line conductor, and that the line terminal in socket outlets and the centre contact of screw-type lamp holders are also connected to the line conductor. (In addition, when the installation is energised a live polarity test should be made to ensure

Did you know?

Although PVC-insulated cables are not generally subject to a deterioration of insulation due to dampness, mineral-insulated cables can be affected if dampness has entered the end of a cable before the seal has been applied properly.

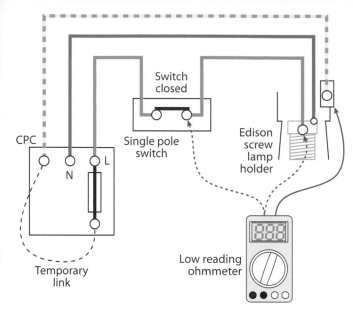

Figure 9.09 Polarity test of lighting circuit using continuity tester

that the polarity of the incoming supply is correct, otherwise the whole installation could have the wrong polarity.) Lighting switches must be closed before carrying out the test.

If the tests required by Regulation 612.2.2 for ring circuit continuity have been carried out, the correct connections of line conductors and cpcs will have been verified and no further dead testing is required.

Earth electrode resistance testing

Where the earthing system incorporates an earth electrode, the resistance to earth needs to be measured. Metal pipes of water mains were used but the change to more plastic pipe work means this practice can no longer be relied upon. Some accepted earth electrodes are:

- earth rods or pipes
- earth tapes or wires
- earth plates
- underground structural metalwork embedded in foundations
- lead sheaths or other metallic coverings of cables
- metal pipes.

The resistance to earth depends upon the size and type of electrode used. Connection to the electrode is above ground level. Tests should be carried out during bad conditions (such as dry weather) as this produces higher resistance.

After first switching off the supply the earthing conductor to the earth electrode must be disconnected, either at the electrode or at the main earthing terminal, so all the test current passes through the earth electrode alone.

The test uses two temporary test electrodes (spikes) as shown in Figure 9.10. The distance between the test spikes is important. If they are too close together their resistance areas will overlap.

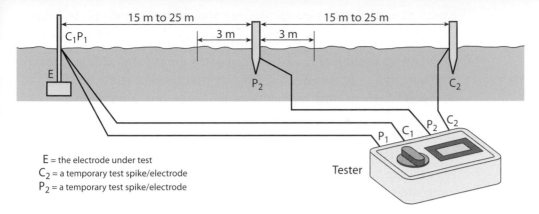

E = the electrode under test
C_2 = a temporary test spike/electrode
P_2 = a temporary test spike/electrode

Tester

Figure 9.10 Earth electrode test

Three readings are taken:

- with the potential spike initially midway between the electrode and current spike;
- at a position 10 per cent of the electrode-to-current spike distance back towards the electrode;
- and at a position 10 per cent of the distance towards the current spike.

A percentage deviation can be determined from the average of the three readings.

The accuracy approximately 1.2 times the percentage deviation of the readings. To improve accuracy the test is repeated with larger separation between the electrode and the current spike.

Earth-fault loop impedance

The earth-fault loop path is made up of the parts of the supply system external to the premises being tested (Z_e) and the line conductor and circuit protective conductor within the installation ($R_1 + R_2$), the total earth-fault loop impedance being $Z_s = Z_e + (R_1 + R_2)$. After determining the earth-fault loop impedance (Z_s) at the furthest point in each circuit compare the readings obtained with the values in BS 7671 or the *IEE On-Site Guide*.

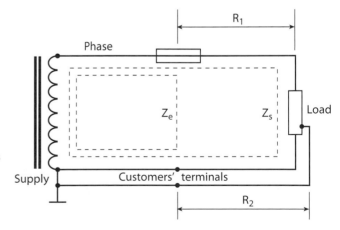

Figure 9.11 Earth-fault loop

The value of earth-fault loop impedance may be determined by:

- direct measurement of Z_s – use a earth-fault loop impedance tester
- direct measurement of Z_e at the origin of the circuit and adding to this the value of $R_1 + R_2$ measured during continuity tests – this can also be gained from an earth loop impedance tester, but requires great care due to the exposure of live parts. The means of earthing must be disconnected for the test to prevent parallel paths.
- obtaining the value of Z_e from the electricity supplier and adding to this the value of $R_1 + R_2$, but then testing that the main earthing terminal is connected to earth, using an earth loop impedance tester or an approved test lamp.

The values of earth loop impedance obtained (Z_s) should be compared with one of the following:

- values given in the *IEE On-Site Guide* after correction for ambient temperature (this applies for PVC insulated cables)
- earth-fault loop impedance values determined by the designer
- values given in Tables 41.2, 41.3 and 41.4 of BS 7671 IEE Wiring Regulations (after the difference between normal conductor operating temperature and the ambient temperature has been accounted for)

If the value of impedance measured is higher than that required by the tables in Chapter 41 of BS 7671, then this means of disconnection of the protective device during earth fault may not happen.

Options available would be to:

- check the effectiveness of the terminations
- increase the size of the cpc
- change the type of the protective device used
- add a RCD to protect the circuit providing it is electrically sound.

Operation of residual current devices (RCDs)

All RCDs are electromechanical devices that must be checked regularly. Regulation 514.12.2 requires a notice stating the presence of an RCD to be prominently displayed. The integral test button checks the mechanical parts. An RCD tester measures the operating time of the device at various currents.

The test is made on the line conductor of the protected circuit and the associated circuit protective conductor with the load disconnected. The test instrument simulates a fault current through the RCD and measures the time taken for the device to trip. Test criteria are generally as follows:

- The device should not open with an earth leakage current at 50 per cent of its rated tripping.
- It should trip in 200 milliseconds when reacting to its tripping current, if designed to BS 4293.

- For general purpose RCDs to BS EN 61008 or RCBOs to BS EN 61009, an earth leakage current equivalent to 100 per cent of the rated tripping current of the RCD should cause the device to open in less than 300 milliseconds (only Type 5, with a purpose built delay, should not.
- Where an RCD with an operating current not exceeding 30 mA is used, a test current of five times the rated trip current should cause the RCD to open in less than 40 milliseconds.

A final mechanical function check should be carried out to ensure that the operating switch of the residual current device is functioning correctly. Results of all the above tests should be recorded on the appropriate test results schedule.

Under certain circumstances these tests can result in potentially dangerous voltages appearing on exposed and extraneous conductive parts within the installation, therefore suitable precautions must be taken to prevent contact by persons or livestock. Other building users should be made aware of the tests being carried out and warning notices posted as necessary.

Certification and reporting

Following the inspection and testing of all new installations, or alterations and additions to existing installations, an Electrical Installation Certificate together with a schedule of test results should be given to the client. Included on the test certificate is a recommendation as to when the installation should be retested; to which the client's attention must be drawn. Other forms are also used to record and report.

Examples of forms appear in Appendix 6 of the Regulations and are also referred to in the *IEE On-Site Guide* and *IEE Guidance Note 3*. The different types of forms available are as follows.

- Periodic inspection report
- Electrical Installation Certificate (Type 1)
- Electrical Installation Certificate (Type 2)
- Inspection schedule
- Schedule of test results
- Electrical Installation – Minor Works Certificate.

The general requirements for the content and completion of all the above documents are stated in the introduction to Appendix 6 of BS 7671 and are summarised below:

- Electrical Installation Certificates and Electrical Installation Minor Works Certificates must be completed and signed by a competent person or persons in respect of the design, the construction, and the inspection and test of the installation.
- Periodic inspection reports must be completed and signed by a competent person in respect of just the inspection and test of the installation and state who is responsible for this test.

Safety tip

Prior to RCD tests being carried out, it is essential for safety reasons that the earth loop impedance of the installation has been tested to check that the earth-return path is sound and that all the necessary requirements have been met. BS 7671 stipulates the order in which tests should be carried out.

Remember

A competent person must have relevant knowledge and experience of the work and BS 7671, as well as test procedures in the Regulations..

- Electrical Installation Certificates must identify who is responsible for the design, construction, and inspection and testing, whether this is new work or an alteration or addition to an existing installation.
- Minor Works Certificates must also identify who is responsible for the design, construction, and inspection and testing of the work carried out.
- A schedule of test results must be issued with all Electrical Installation Certificates and periodic inspection reports.

Periodic inspection report

The periodic inspection report is completed when carrying out a routine periodic inspection and testing of an existing installation, not when alterations and additions are made. An inspection schedule and a schedule of test results should accompany the periodic inspection report. If possible, causes must be reported and repaired immediately.

For design
I/We being the person(s) responsible for the design of the Electrical Installation (as indicated by my/our signatures) particulars of which are described above, having exercised reasonable skill and care when carrying out the design hereby CERTIFY that the design work for which I/we have been responsible is to the best of my/our knowledge and belief in accordance with BS 7671 amended to .... except for the departures (if any) detailed below.

Details of departures from BS 7671 (if any)
....
....

The extent of liability of the signatory is limited to the work described above.
For the DESIGN of the installation.

Signature : .... Date .... Name : .... Designer No. 1

Signature : .... Date :................. Name : .... Designer No. 2

For construction
I/We being the person(s) responsible for the construction of the Electrical Installation (as indicated by my/our signatures) particulars of which are described above, having exercised reasonable skill and care when carrying out the construction hereby CERTIFY that the construction work for which I/we have been responsible is to the best of my/our knowledge and belief in accordance with BS 7671 amended to .... Except for the departures (if any) detailed below.

Details of departures from BS 7671 (if any)
....
....

The extent of liability of the signatory is limited to the work described above.
For the CONSTRUCTION of the installation.

Signature : .... Date :.................. Name : .... Constructor

For inspection and testing
I/we being the person(s) responsible for the inspection and testing of the Electrical Installation (as indicated by my/our signatures) particulars of which are described above, having exercised reasonable skill and care when carrying out the inspection and testing hereby CERTIFY that the work for which I/we have been responsible is to the best of my/our knowledge and belief in accordance with BS 7671 amended to .... except for the departures detailed below.

Details of departures from BS7671 (if any)
....
....

The extent of liability of the signatory is limited to the work described above.
For the INSPECTION and TEST of the installation

Signature : .... Date :................... Name : .... Inspector

Figure 9.12 Electrical Installation Certificate (Type 1)

Electrical Installation Certificate (Type 1)

These are used when inspecting and testing a new installation, a major alteration or addition to an existing installation where the design, construction, and inspection and testing of the installation are the responsibility of different organisations. It requires the signatures of those responsible for these duties.

Electrical Installation Certificate (Type 2)

This is a shortened version of the Type 1 form and is used when one person is responsible for the design, construction, and inspection and testing of the installation.

The original certificate is given to the client and a copy retained by the contractor. This certificate is not valid unless accompanied by a Schedule of Test Results. It should be kept safe.

The recommended time to the next inspection should be stated. This should take into account the frequency and quality of maintenance that the installation is likely to receive.

Inspection schedule

The inspection schedule confirms that an inspection has been carried out as required by Part 6 of BS 7671 and lists all the inspection requirements of Regulation 611.3. The completed inspection schedule is attached to, and forms part of, the Electrical Installation Certificate.

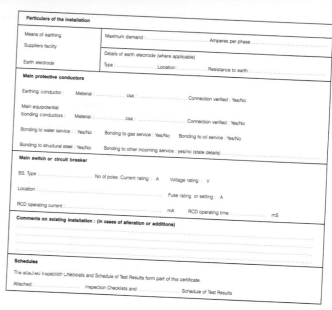

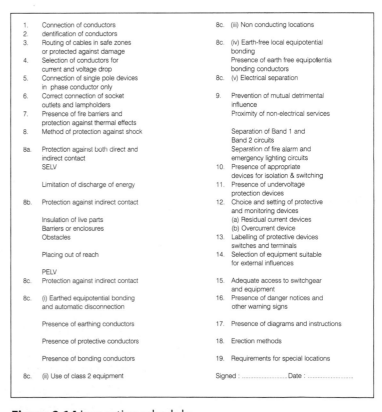

Figure 9.13 Electrical Installation Certificate (Type 2)

Each item on the inspection schedule should be checked and either ticked as satisfactory or ruled out if not applicable. In almost all cases, basic protection will be by the presence of insulation and the enclosure of live parts. Fault protection will be by earthed equipotential bonding and automatic disconnection of the supply (together with the presence of earthing and bonding conductors). On completion it should be signed by the person responsible for inspection.

1. Connection of conductors
2. Identification of conductors
3. Routing of cables in safe zones or protected against damage
4. Selection of conductors for current and voltage drop
5. Connection of single pole devices in phase conductor only
6. Correct connection of socket outlets and lampholders
7. Presence of fire barriers and protection against thermal effects
8. Method of protection against shock

8a. Protection against both direct and indirect contact
    SELV

    Limitation of discharge of energy

8b. Protection against indirect contact

    Insulation of live parts
    Barriers or enclosures
    Obstacles

    Placing out of reach

    PELV
8c. Protection against indirect contact

8c. (i) Earthed equipotential bonding and automatic disconnection

    Presence of earthing conductors

    Presence of protective conductors

    Presence of bonding conductors

8c. (ii) Use of class 2 equipment

8c. (iii) Non conducting locations

8c. (iv) Earth-free local equipotential bonding
    Presence of earth free equipotential bonding conductors
8c. (v) Electrical separation

9. Prevention of mutual detrimental influence
    Proximity of non-electrical services

    Separation of Band 1 and Band 2 circuits
    Separation of fire alarm and emergency lighting circuits
10. Presence of appropriate devices for isolation & switching
11. Presence of undervoltage protection devices
12. Choice and setting of protective and monitoring devices
    (a) Residual current devices
    (b) Overcurrent device
13. Labelling of protective devices switches and terminals
14. Selection of equipment suitable for external influences
15. Adequate access to switchgear and equipment
16. Presence of danger notices and other warning signs
17. Presence of diagrams and instructions
18. Erection methods
19. Requirements for special locations

Signed : ....Date : ....

Figure 9.14 Inspection schedule

Contractor : .... Address /Location of distribution board .... Type of supply TN-S /TN-C-S/TT....... Instruments : ....
Date of test : .... Ze at origin : .... Continuity : ....

Signature : .... PFC: .... Insulation : ....
Method of protection against indirect contact : .... Loop impedance: .... RCD tester : ....

Description of work :

Circuit description	Overcurrent device		Wiring			Test Results									
	Short circuit capacity KA		Ref method	Conductors		Continuity			Insulation Resistance		P	Zs	Functional Testing		Remarks
	Type	Rating		Live	cpc	R_1+R_2	R_2	Ring	Live-live	Live-earth			RCD (time)	Other	
1															
2															
3															
4															
5															
6															
7															
8															
9															
10															
11															
12															

Note 1 Any equipment vulnerable to testing : ....

Note 2 Any deviations from BS7671 : ....

Figure 9.15 Schedule of test results

Schedule of test results

The schedule of test results is a written record of the results obtained when carrying out the electrical tests required by Part 6 of BS 7671. The following notes give guidance on the compilation of the schedule, which should be attached to the Electrical Installation Certificate. The schedule should:

- determine the type of supply
- measure Z_e with the main bonding disconnected
- show the value of the prospective fault current is higher than that between live conductors or line and earth
- record details of protective device
- record method used to install cables
- check polarity of fuses, lamp holders with outer contact connected to neutral, socket outlets and accessories
- check continuity of protective conductors and ring circuit conductors
- record sum of the resistances of the live conductor and protective conductor and used to determine earth-loop impedance (Z_s).
- check insulation resistance
- recheck polarity before further testing
- carry out functional testing and RCDs and RCBOs.

Electrical Installation Minor Works Certificate

Minor works are defined as an addition to an electrical installation that does not extend to the installation of a new circuit, e.g. either the addition of a new socket outlet or of a lighting point to an existing circuit. The certificate is designed to confirm the work confirms to BS 7671.

Part 1 – Description

- Full and accurate description of the minor works
- Location/address of the property
- Date of completion.
- Departures from BS 7671 (if any) – these will not be common!

Part 2 – Installation details

- Earthing arrangements
- Method of fault protection
- Type and rating of protective device
- Any comments on existing installation

Part 3 – Essential tests

- Earth continuity
- Insulation resistance
- Earth-fault loop impedance
- Polarity
- RCD operation.

Part 4 – Declaration

- The certificate must be completed and signed by a competent person in respect of the design, construction, and inspection and testing of the work carried out (in the case of minor works this will probably be the responsibility of one person). The company the person represents must be clearly stated.

PART 1 – Description

1. Description of the Minor Works : . . . .
   . . . .
2. Location/Address : . . . .
   . . . .
3. Date of completion : . . . .
4. Departures from BS 7671 (if any) : . . . .
   . . . .

PART 2 – Installation details

1. Earthing arrangements (where known) :   TN-C-S   TN-S   TT
2. Method of protection against indirect contact : . . . .
3. Protective device for the modified circuit :   Type : . . . .   Rating : . . . .
4. Comments on existing installation (including adequacy of earthing and bonding arrangements)
   . . . .

PART 3 – Essential tests

1. Earth continuity satisfactory : Yes/No
2. Insulation resistance :   Phase /Neutral : . . . .   Megohms . . . .

   Phase/Earth : . . . .   Megohms . . . .

   Neutral/Earth : . . . .   Megohms . . . .

3. Earth fault loop impedance : . . . . ohms
4. Polarity correct : Yes/No
5. RCD operation (if applicable) :   Operating current : . . . . mA   Operating time : . . . . ms

---

PART 4 – Declaration

I/We CERTIFY that the said works do not impair the safety of the existing installation, that the said works have been designed, constructed and inspected and tested in accordance with BS 7671 amended to . . . . and that the said works have to the best of my/our knowledge and belief, at the the time of my/our inspection complied with all the requirements of BS 7671 except as detailed in Part 2.

2.   Name : . . . .   3. Signature : . . . .

   For and on behalf of : . . . .   Position : . . . .

   Address : . . . .   Date : . . . .

Figure 9.16 Minor Works Certificate

Procedures for dealing with the client and reports

This section describes the procedures for dealing with the customer and the reports.

The customer

Following initial verification, BS 7671 requires that an Electrical Installation Certificate, together with a schedule of test results and an inspection schedule, should be given to the person ordering the work. Until this has been done, the Regulations have not been met.

Sometimes the person ordering the work is not the end user; e.g. the builder of a new housing estate sells the individual houses to various occupiers. In these cases it is recommended that copies of the inspection and test certificates, together with a test results schedule, are passed on to the new owners.

Handover to the client

Handover of the installation to the client is the final task. This should include a tour of the installation, an explanation of any specific controls or settings and, where necessary, a demonstration of any particularly complicated control systems. The operation and maintenance manuals produced for the project should be formally handed to the client at this stage, including copies of the Electrical Installation Certificate, the schedule of test results and the inspection schedule.

Short answer questions

1. Give the sequence of testing for a small business installation.
2. Provide a list of instruments required for the test procedures.
3. List the general characteristics of the supply that are required before testing begins.
4. Provide the principle means of protection against direct contact.
5. Give examples of the use of both types of Electrical Installation Certificate.
6. Describe the test method used to confirm continuity of supplementary bonding, assuming safe isolation.
7. State the three steps involved in confirmation of ring final circuit conductors, and state the two items that are confirmed at the same time (assuming safe isolation).
8. If a reading of 1.25 MΩ is recorded when carrying out an insulation resistance test:
   a. Is this acceptable? Give reasons.
   b. What action should be taken?
9. Give four reasons for the necessity of a Periodic Inspection Report.
10. Define indirect contact and give the principle of protection.

Multiple-choice test

1. Which of the following is the statutory document?
   a. BS 7671
   b. GS38
   c. Electricity at Work Regulations
   d. On-Site Guide

2. Which is an exposed conductive part?
   a. plastic casing of a computer
   b. steel framework of the building
   c. metal switch enclosure
   d. metal gas pipe

3. Which of these methods provides both basic and fault protection?
   a. SELV
   b. PELV
   c. FELV
   d. RCD

4. Which document carries the test results?
   a. Test Result Schedule
   b. Inspection Schedule
   c. Minor Works Certificate
   d. Sunday Times

5. Which instrument would you use to test continuity of ring final circuits?
   a. loop tester
   b. PSCC tester
   c. low ohms meter
   d. insulation resistance tester

6. What is the maximum period between testing for a domestic installation?
   a. 5 years
   b. 10 years
   c. 15 years
   d. 20 years

7. Which does not form part of the earth-fault loop path in a TN-CS installation?
   a. earth electrode
   b. Z_s
   c. Z_e
   d. R_2

8. When should an Initial Verification be carried out?
    a. with the addition of a new lamp
    b. on a new installation
    c. when there is a change of ownership
    d. when Licensing requirements apply

9. In the formula $Z_s = Z_e + (R_1 + R_2)$, what does R_2 signify?
    a. external impedance
    b. system impedance
    c. resistance of the line conductor
    d. resistance of the cpc

10. What is not a basic requirement in the periodic checking procedure?
    a. wear and tear
    b. competency
    c. external influences
    d. damage

11. What is not a requirement during testing?
    a. costs are kept down
    b. no danger is caused to persons
    c. no danger is caused to livestock
    d. avoiding damage to property

12. An installation has been in use for 10 years. Which test procedure is most appropriate?
    a. minor works
    b. initial verification
    c. periodic inspection and test
    d. portable appliance testing

13. During an inspection and test a dangerous condition is noticed, what is the correct procedure?
    a. Stop work and make safe if possible.
    b. Carry on and tell someone later.
    c. Ignore it and hope it will go away.
    d. Put some line tape on it.

14. What does not form part of test documentation?
    a. electrical installation certificate
    b. test result schedule
    c. inspection schedule
    d. designer's specifications

15. What is the BS EN number for test instruments?
    a. BS EN 7671
    b. BS EN 3535
    c. BS EN 61010
    d. BS EN 1066

16. Which information is not required by the inspector of an installation?
    a. maximum demand
    b. name of the caretaker
    c. number and type of live conductors
    d. presence of any sensitive devices

17. What is not acceptable for an earth electrode?
    a. rods and tapes
    b. earth plates
    c. underground water pipes
    d. lead sheath of supplier's cable

18. What should be given to the customer when testing is completed?
    a. original test documentation
    b. copy of the drawings
    c. technical advice on the use of equipment
    d. designer's specifications

19. Compliance with what document will satisfy the requirements of the relevant statutory regulations?
    a. BS 5900
    b. GN3
    c. On-Site Guide
    d. BS 7671

20. What is not a requirement of the Construction (Design and Management) Regulations 1994?
    a. measurement of the earth loop impedance
    b. handover to the client
    c. energising individual circuits in the installation
    d. energising the site huts first

21. What is not required in the actual handover?
    a. explanation of the controls
    b. demonstration of some systems
    c. operations manuals
    d. inspector's qualifications

22. Which is not an acceptable method of verifying the measured value of Z_s?
 a. *Table 54.7 (BS 7671)*
 b. *Tables 2A–2 D (On-Site Guide)*
 c. *rule of thumb (GN3)*
 d. *design values*

23. Who must sign the completed certificate?
 a. *competent person*
 b. *client*
 c. *designer*
 d. *installer*

24. Which is not a requirement of functional testing?
 a. *all switch gear*
 b. *control gear assemblies*
 c. *earth-fault loop testing*
 d. *RCD testing*

25. The use of a Minor Works Certificate is used for what of the following?
 a. *replacing accessories on a 'like for like' basis*
 b. *radial circuit for fixed equipment*
 c. *major modification for the whole installation*
 d. *PAT testing*

26. Which is not a requirement for the inspection procedure?
 a. *connection of conductors*
 b. *loop impedance test*
 c. *verification of polarity*
 d. *basic protection*

27. Which area does 'removing the means of supply to prevent danger' cover?
 a. *isolation*
 b. *emergency switching*
 c. *functional switching*
 d. *switching for mechanical maintenance*

28. Which is not an external influence?
 a. *corrosion*
 b. *cable carrying capacity*
 c. *impact*
 d. *presence of water or foreign bodies*

29. What information must be included in diagrams, charts, etc.?
 a. *location of the first aid kit*
 b. *diagram of the canteen*
 c. *chart of the dry risers*
 d. *nature of protective devices*

30. Who can carry out the routine checks?
 a. *caretaker*
 b. *maintenance electrician*
 c. *user in a domestic installation*
 d. *all of the above*

The answer section is at the back of the book.

10 Fault diagnosis and rectification

Electricians must be able to recognise when a piece of equipment is not working correctly, or up to standard. If, on inspection, an installation is not working properly, an electrician must be able to find the fault and rectify it, so that the equipment measures up to the manufacturer's specification. Fault diagnosis and rectification is one of the most difficult of all the electrician's skills. This chapter covers:

- Safe working practices for fault diagnosis
  - Safe isolation
  - Test instruments
  - Operating devices
  - On-load and off-load devices
  - Restoration of supply
- Diagnosis and rectification of faults
  - Principles of fault diagnosis
  - Operation of protective devices
  - Transient voltages
  - Insulation failure
  - Plant, equipment or component failure
  - Faults caused by abuse, misuse or negligence
  - Prevention of faults by regular maintenance
- Specific types of fault
  - Cable interconnections
  - Cable terminations seals and glands
  - Accessories including switches, control equipment, contactors and solid state devices
  - Control equipment
  - Contactors
  - Electronic and solid state devices
  - Instrumentation

- Protective devices
- Luminaires
- Flexible cables and cords
- Portable appliances and equipment
- Knowledge and understanding of electrical systems and equipment
  - Understanding the electrical system, installation and equipment
  - Optimum use of personal and other persons' experience of systems and equipment
- Stages of diagnosis and rectification
  - A logical approach
  - Interpretation of test results
  - Functional testing including RCD testing
- Factors affecting the fault repair process
  - Cost of replacement
  - Availability of replacement
  - Downtime under fault conditions
  - Legal responsibility
  - Other factors affecting the fault repair process
  - Special requirements
  - Special precautions

Safe working practices for fault diagnosis

The Electricity at Work Regulations 1989, forbids live working in almost all situations. Cost and convenience are not reasons to undertake live work. Safe working on an installation for fault diagnosis requires understanding of how an installation works and the correct electrical testing and safe isolation procedures. Furthermore, an understanding of the latest edition of BS 7671 is essential.

Safety tip

If extraordinary circumstances require live working then special training must be given and special equipment used.

Safe isolation

The Joint Industry Board (JIB) has set out a standard for the safe isolation of electrical installations, to be used before all work is carried out on or near live parts.

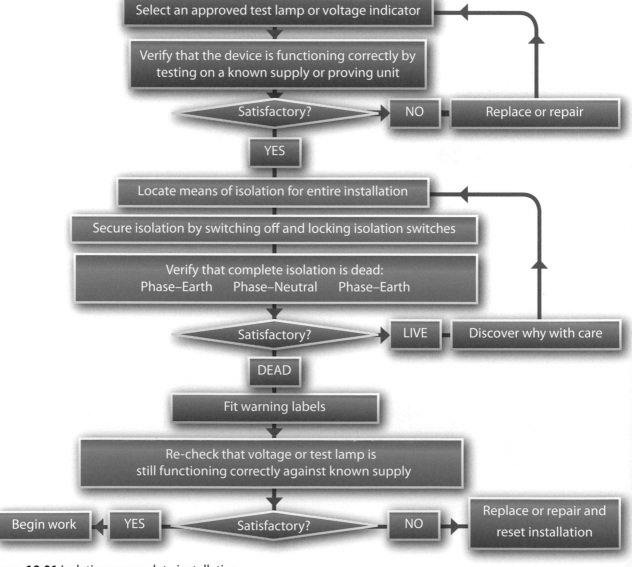

Figure 10.01 Isolating a complete installation

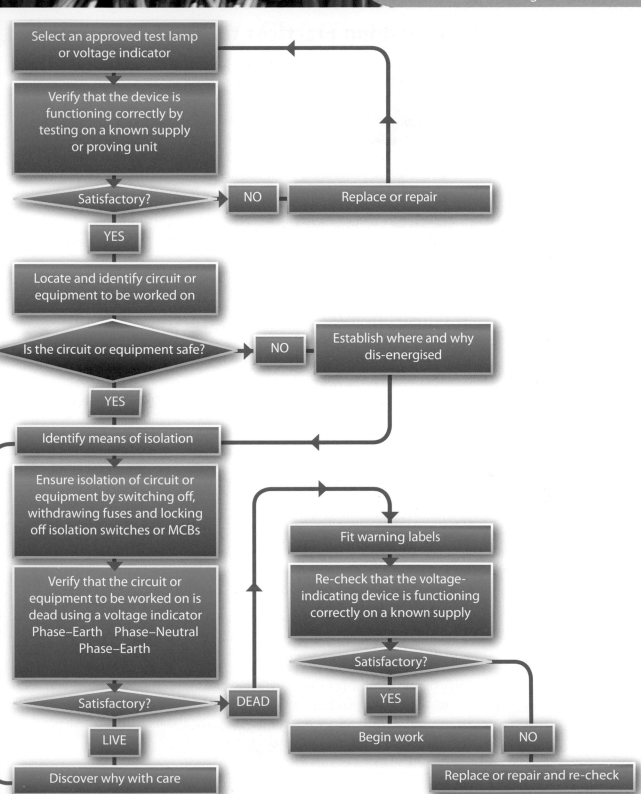

Figure 10.02 Isolating an individual circuit or item of equipment

This is a basis for safe isolation and should be adapted each time it is used. For example, on a single phase circuit protected by a miniature circuit breaker, an MCB locking device can be used and authority maintained over the key to the device, which should be unique. On a three phase installation, protected by fuses, the fuses should be withdrawn and authority maintained over them. The enclosure should be locked and a sign placed to prevent other fuses being used.

MCB locked off

Remember

All test equipment must comply with GS 38, the Health and Safety Executive (HSE) guidelines for test equipment. A so called 'electrical test screwdriver' that requires the user to become part of the circuit DOES NOT comply with GS 38.

Remember

In a light circuit, operate the switches to ensure all switch lines and strappers are tested.

Safety tip

Be aware of timers, thermostats, etc. that may re-energise the system without warning.

Safety tip

Instruments must be tested before and after use. Otherwise something might be labelled NO VOLTAGE when a lethal voltage was present.

Test instruments

Test equipment must be in good working order and approved for the task. They must be regularly checked by the user and calibrated.

Guidance note GS 38

All test equipment must comply with Guidance note GS 38. This is published by the HSE and gives guidance in the use of test instruments, including leads and probes, by electrically competent people. They are people with training and experience in the equipment and systems under test.

Voltage indicating devices

Voltage indicators are used solely to indicate the presence or absence of a voltage. They fall into two categories:

- A test lamp, which is a detector that relies on a 15 watt lamp to illuminate. It does not indicate the value of the voltage.
- A meter, which has a scale indicating the size of voltage.

They should be clearly marked with the maximum voltage to be tested, and the maximum time current can flow through it, as they are not designed to be used for more than a few seconds. They must also be used with a proving unit or tested against a safe known source.

Operating devices

There is only one way to work safely on a circuit. That is to ensure it cannot be either inadvertently or intentionally energised. There are several ways to do this:

- Lock off the local isolating device.
- Lock the distribution board or consumer unit closed.
- Lock the intake room door.

The closer to the point of work the isolating device is situated the less disruption will be caused.

As well as isolating devices, installations usually have operating devices that can carry out more than one function, such as:

- control
- isolation
- protection.

This can be seen in most installations with:

- a main switch for isolation
- MCBs or fuses for protection
- switches for control.

On-load and off-load devices

Not all devices are designed to be used on-load, as the arc generated by switching may cause damage to the device itself.

An off-load device is not usually operated when the system is in use, only after it has been switched off from the source. After switching off, the installation in question can then be worked on, either for fault diagnosis or general maintenance.

An on-load device is used to break the circuit under load.

Restoration of supply

When the rectification process has been completed, the installation must be tested before the supply is restored. The amount of testing depends on the type of work carried out. If a simple replacement, then a continuity test may be sufficient. A more substantial repair may require the full test procedure required in BS 7671 Part 6, which includes functional testing.

Remember

The key used must be unique and the person carrying out the work must retain authority over the key at all times.

Safety tip

Light switches, etc. must not be used for isolation.

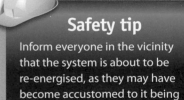

Safety tip

Inform everyone in the vicinity that the system is about to be re-energised, as they may have become accustomed to it being shut down.

Diagnosis and rectification of faults

There are many types of fault to consider and each has its own peculiarities. Both the location of the fault and how it was caused have a bearing on the approach to diagnosis and rectification.

Principles of fault diagnosis

In order to diagnose and rectify most types of common fault effectively, there are two basic requirements:

- a sound knowledge of the system involved
- a logical diagnostic technique, which can be used on most systems.

However, installation techniques change and are becoming more complex, so an increasing level of expertise may be required for some faults. Equipment may need specific knowledge, which only the installer will have. Even on the most basic level of fault diagnosis the electrician must remain flexible, as no two faults are ever the same.

Adherence to BS 7671 in the design and erection stages should avoid many problems.

- Installations should be divided into circuits to avoid danger in the event of a fault.
- Safe operation, inspection, testing and maintenance procedures should be facilitated.
- The correct cable and protective devices must be selected, thus limiting the effects of the fault.
- There should be good planning, maintenance and record keeping. This will reduce the likelihood of a fault occurring in the first place, and increase the maintenance staff's ability to detect faults early, thus reducing the effects of the fault if it does occur.

Increasing the number of circuits makes it easier for a fault to be detected by the simple method of observing which protective device has operated.

Remember

Good record keeping can detect a fault before it happens. For example, a gradually worsening insulation resistance reading over time indicates a latent fault.

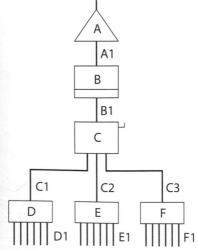

A	Supply company's service with incoming supply cable and fuses	C3	Sub-final circuit conductors grey phase
A1	Supply company's cables feeding KWh meter	D	Consumer's unit with DP main switch and protective devices
B	Supply company's metering equipment (KWh meter)	E	Consumer's unit with DP main switch and protective devices
B1	Consumer's meter tails	F	Consumer's unit with DP main switch and protective devices
C	Consumer's main switch – typical TP&N 100 amp	D1	Consumer's final circuits, i.e. sockets and lighting
C1	Sub-final circuit conductors brown phase	E1	Consumer's final circuits, i.e. sockets and lighting
C2	Sub-final circuit conductors black phase	F1	Consumer's final circuits, i.e. sockets and lighting

Figure 10.03 Typical three-phase supply for a small installation

The circuit can then be broken down into gradually smaller parts until the faulty part(s) become apparent. The diagram shows how an installation can be divided up.

Complete loss of supply at the origin of the installation

As can be seen from Figure 10.03 the installation is divided into areas of responsibility. The section A–B1 is the responsibility of the Regional Supply Company (RSC) and a fault there, which is usually caused outside the premises (a mechanical digger breaking a supply cable for instance), is referred to them.

The RSC protective devices could still trip due to a fault in the installation, resulting in overall power loss, but is likely to be the result of poor design or management of the installed load.

Localised loss of supply

Figure 10.03 shows that the closer to the origin the more the installation will be affected by a fault. A fault at C2 for instance would affect the whole of consumer unit E. Careful planning and design will minimise danger, damage and inconvenience in the event of a fault. It still requires the electrician to be familiar with the system.

Did you know?

If more capacity is required, consult the RSC and arrange to upgrade the supply. Not a project to be embarked upon lightly but preferable to installation downtime and constantly replacing fuses.

Operation of protective devices

A basic principle of cable selection is that the rating of the protective device has to be equal to or greater than the design current of the circuit it is protecting, and the rating of the cable selected has to be equal to or greater than them both. Therefore, if a fault develops in a lighting final circuit with 10×100 watt lamps (4.34 amperes), the 5 or 6 amp fuse or miniature circuit breaker (MCB) selected will open before any damage can occur.

In a circuit designed to facilitate portable or hand held equipment, each piece of equipment must be provided with a fuse consistent with its current rating. For example, an appliance with a rating of 2.5 kW has a total current of 10.9 amperes. The nearest standard fuse is 13 amperes, which should then be fitted in the plug top.

Protective devices are designed to operate when an excess of current passes through a designed weak link in the circuit (i.e. the protective device) and causes it to open. This excess of current is termed overcurrent. Three definitions of overcurrent are:

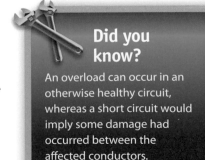

Did you know?

An overload can occur in an otherwise healthy circuit, whereas a short circuit would imply some damage had occurred between the affected conductors.

- **Overload** – a current that exceeds the design value of the protective device.
- **Earth fault current** – a fault current that flows to earth.
- **Short circuit current** – a fault of negligible impedance between live conductors.

The protective device must be selected with great care, as an uncontrolled rise in temperature will cause damage to the conductors and/or equipment. This underlines the importance of correct cable selection.

If incorrectly selected, a protective device can be 'fooled' into operating in its overload mode by a large inrush of current from a highly inductive load, such as a motor or a large transformer. This could cause the device to open.

Meltdown of insulation due to overcurrent

Overload faults can include:

- multi-adaptors used in socket outlets, causing the rated load of the socket to be exceeded
- unauthorised extending of existing circuits, increasing the load
- incorrect selection of the protective device by not taking into account high inrush currents on a motor circuit.

Short circuit faults can include:

- insulation breakdown due to a variety of causes, such as age and mechanical damage
- severing of one or more live conductors in an enclosure
- bad workmanship during installation, such as incorrect polarity, and not discovered during testing or energised before testing.

Poorly wired 13 A plug resulting in dangerous working conditions

Earth faults can include:

- insulation breakdown due to a variety of causes, such as age and mechanical damage
- incorrect polarity not tested, or not discovered due to incorrect test methods
- bad workmanship during installation, such as allowing copper strands to be exposed and in contact with earth.

Transient voltages

A transient voltage is almost any temporary change to the nominal declared voltage. This could be an increase in voltage, a surge, or an unaccounted voltage drop. Normal volt drop is accounted for at the design stage.

It is now standard practice to install surge protection in circuits likely to suffer from this problem, such as circuits supplying Information Technology equipment, in industry, commercial and domestic installations.

Common causes are:

- supply company faults
- electronic equipment
- bringing heavy current using equipment on line
- earth fault voltages
- lightning strikes.

Some are more common than others. Supply company faults are rare.

Insulation failure

As insulation is one of the principle means of basic protection, the failure of the insulation of conductors can lead to danger from:

- contact with live parts
- contact with exposed/extraneous conductive parts made live by a fault
- fire
- explosion.

Insulation failure can be caused by:

- poor workmanship during installation
- poor maintenance and record keeping
- excessive ambient temperatures, following a change of use of the installation for example
- high fault current levels
- damage or abuse by a third party.

Plant, equipment or component failure

In the design and erection stage and diligent maintenance, almost all problems in the installation can be avoided. Unfortunately, none of the above can hold back time, and the accompanying wear and tear on plant, equipment components and the actual installation itself. Good design and maintenance will prolong the life of the installation, but eventually, all things wear out.

Examples are:

- switches not operating correctly, or at all, due to age
- motors not running due to worn brushes
- lamps blown in lighting circuits
- starter or lamp expired in fluorescent luminaires
- outside equipment not working due to ingress of moisture or vermin.

Remember

Many of these problems can be solved, or avoided altogether, by proper procedures at the design stage and by a rigorous maintenance programme.

Faults caused by abuse, misuse or negligence

All items used in an installation, or connected for the user, must comply with the relevant BS or BSEN requirements. These are tested and proven to be safe and should give good service under normal usage.

If an item of equipment, or the installation itself, is routinely abused, misused and neglected, BS/BSEN safeguards may become null and void, and the affected parts fail and/or become dangerous. Also warranties or guarantees would also be void.

Installation of the proper equipment at the design and installation, such as tamper proof switches, heavy duty equipment, and careful planning of cable routes, etc, will, if not solve these problems, certainly lessen the effects. Good workmanship and materials, including inspection and testing, must be used as required by BS 7671. This will also help prevent faults caused by negligence during the erection stage.

User misuse can include:

- using an MCB as functional switching
- damage caused to terminals due to arcing when unplugging on-load appliances
- using incorrect equipment in inappropriate areas, such as when a change of use has occurred and the equipment has not been upgraded (e.g. changing a storage facility to a car wash)
- MCBs nuisance tripping, caused by connecting inductive loads to a standard circuit.

Installer misuse can include:

- incorrect termination of conductors causing arcing or overheating
- loose bushes, couplers and earth tags providing no earth continuity and, thus, the risk of electric shock
- incorrect cable selection, which could lead to overload of the conductors, causing insulation breakdown, exposed cables and the risk of shock, fire or explosion.
- incorrect installation methods when drawing in cables, thus damaging insulation
- exceeding the capacity of conduit or trunking, causing overheating and insulation breakdown.

If, for example, the circuit is protected by a 32 amp MCB, and the conductors are only rated at 14 amps then the MCB will simply not open when the cable is overloaded. Together with the loose bush and coupler scenario, the MCB will not even open for a short circuit and there is a recipe for disaster.

These are fairly typical examples of misuse by a non-qualified person, though not exclusively, as there are incompetent practitioners in every

Did you know?

Damage caused by arcing can go on for years, as it is sometimes a slow process causing extensive damage to conductors and, if poorly installed, even fire.

trade. Correct training, experience and adequate supervision should avoid installer problems.

Prevention of faults by regular maintenance

As required by the Electricity at Work Regulations 1989, any 'reasonably practicable means' must be used to ensure the safe erection and use of an electrical installation including:

- correct design
- correct installation methods
- inspection and testing before use
- after commissioning, a frequent maintenance schedule including periodic inspections and planned maintenance.

Correct maintenance provides the user with continued good service from the installation. It also deters people from attempting repairs that are beyond their competence to avoid down time or a call out fee.

If machinery needs to be switched off, this can be planned for expected periods of quiet trading. Uncomplicated jobs, such as lamp changes and cleaning, can be done at night. Staff holidays can be used to carry out major projects. These periods are predictable, so jobs can be planned well in advance, to avoid unnecessary complications or down time.

Specific types of fault

Any equipment installed in an installation must comply with the latest BS or BSEN requirements, as should the materials used in the installation. The installer sometimes takes it for granted that the designer has made the correct selection. Chapter 52 of BS 7671 covers the selection and erection requirements, in particular:

- selection of type of wiring system
- external influences
- current carrying capacity of conductors
- voltage drop
- electrical connections
- minimising the spread of fire
- proximity to other services
- maintainability.

It is important to be aware of the use the installation is going to be put to, in order to know if the equipment is acceptable.

Everyone involved in the design, erection and testing of the installation has a responsibility to ensure, not only that their own work is compliant but also that of others. If any departure from the standards is recognised, it is the person's responsibility to bring this to notice.

Cable interconnections

Generally, during an initial installation the use of a joint box or connector blocks is considered poor planning. However, if good working practices are followed, then they are acceptable during an extension, alteration or repairing damage. This may include:

- lighting circuit joint boxes for line, neutral, switch line and strappers
- additional power circuits, ring final socket outlet wiring and spurs, etc.
- street lighting and underground cables, where longer runs are required
- alterations and additions to a circuit
- rectification to faults or damage to wiring.

The work carried out must be mechanically and electrically sound and accessible for inspection. Connector strip or screw connectors must not be left bare. The connector strip should be in an enclosure and secured.

The following are exceptions to this requirement:

- a compound filled or encapsulated joint
- connection between a cold tail and heating element
- joints made by welding, soldering or compression
- a proprietary joint

The connection made should not detract from the mechanical or electrical integrity of the cable. This includes the size of the cable and the temperature requirements. The connector should be suitable for the higher requirement, if two differing cables are used.

Some common types of terminating devices used are:

- plastic connectors
- soldered joints
- compression joints
- junction boxes.

The following terminating devices are not used so often, as the Screwit, for example, is lacking in mechanical strength although it does have the required electrical continuity:

- porcelain connectors
- Screwits
- uninsulated connectors.

In order to stay within the requirements of the cable calculations, any connectors must be of the same criteria as the cables, i.e.:

- be the correct size as the cable it is joining
- be equal to, or greater than, the current rating of the conductor it is joining
- have the same cable operating temperature as the cable it is joining
- must comply with the same requirements as the cable with reference to BS 7671 Chapter 5, i.e. external influences, etc.

Remember
High resistance joints, caused by bad workmanship, can cause a significant rise in temperature and possibly fire.

One of the greatest problems with connections is stress on the cable where it is joined. If a proper enclosure with either 'stuffing glands' or cable supports is used and is properly secured, then this problem can be avoided.

Cable terminations seals and glands

Terminations

The same requirements for terminations apply as for interconnections, i.e. good mechanical strength and good electrical continuity. It is of no use having one without the other, as simply twisting two conductors together will give continuity but the slightest tug will leave the conductors open circuit or with a high resistance joint, which in some ways is a worst case as it can lead to fires.

These are some requirements when terminating conductors:

- Damage to the cable must be avoided, as a 'ringed cable' is weakened and has a higher resistance.
- Care must be taken to secure all the wires of the conductor, so as not to impose any stress on the terminal.
- Terminations must not be over tightened, but heat produced by current flow will cause expansion and contraction on a termination and, if not sufficiently tight, it will come loose under stress.
- Power factor capacitors are designed to reduce the current in light fittings. If this becomes loosened or disconnected current will increase.
- A loose or dirty terminal will cause a high resistance joint, with subsequent high temperature at that joint.
- Removing strands, or leaving strands from a cable out of the connector, reduces the cross sectional area (csa) of the cable, which again causes a higher resistance than the designer intended, causing a rise in temperature.

Some examples of terminals are:

- pillar terminal found in metallic back-boxes and earth terminations, etc.
- screwhead, nut and washer terminals, used where larger cables are used and a greater pressure needs applying
- strip connectors used in various ways for interconnections and in connecting appliances; not designed to connect two loose flexible cables together
- terminals incorporated in the accessory.

Did you know?

A loose, dirty or reduced termination in a protective conductor could result in the failure of the protective device to open in the required time.

Definition

Dirty terminal – A termination that has some insulation inside the terminal, resulting in a high resistance joint or even open circuit on that conductor.

Remember

Terminals must be tight but not over tight. A light tug should suffice to check for a good connection.

Figure 10.04 Pillar terminal

Figure 10.05 Screwhead nut and washer terminals

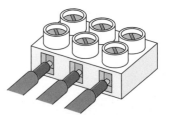

Figure 10.06 Strip connectors

Seals and entries

Where both the accessory and cable have their own integrity, they both must be maintained.

- PVC/PVC twin and cpc has a layer of PVC for insulation and a layer of PVC as mechanical protection. The latter is not intended to serve as insulation.
- PVC/steel wire armoured has PVC insulation, with the steel wire and other layers as mechanical protection.
- PVC covered mineral insulated copper cable (MICC or MIMS for metal sheathed) is a strong, durable and long lasting cable.
- FP200 is gradually replacing MICC.

When installing conductors, good workmanship and materials should be used as required by Regulation 134.1.1, which means that the cables should:

- not be damaged
- be correctly connected
- be correctly identified
- be correctly routed
- be correctly selected
- have correct entry into accessories
- have the correct cable gland or seal used.

To comply with Regulation 611.2, an inspection shall be made to verify that the installed electrical equipment is not visibly damaged or defective so as to impair safety. This includes checking that seals, fire barriers and cable routes have been correctly sealed.

Accessories including switches, control equipment, contactors and solid state devices

Nothing lasts forever but, with proper servicing, the maximum life can be obtained from electrical equipment. Wear and tear accounts for most problems and correct selection and regular inspection can reduce down time due to unexpected breakdowns.

Items in constant use are the most likely suffer from wear and tear, so it makes sense to inspect these most often. These include:

- entrance hall switches
- socket outlets in kitchen used routinely, i.e. kettles
- cleaner's sockets or a lone socket that would be used most often
- any item that is used on a regular basis.

Although 10 per cent is an allowable initial percentage to inspect, it must not be the same 10 per cent every inspection and must be increased if problems are found. A rolling programme is the most effective means of including all of the installation over a period of time.

Control equipment

Control equipment is more commonly known as switchgear and normally found between the RSC metering equipment and the installation proper. It can be large or small, depending on the size of the load it is required to switch. Here are a few examples:

- domestic installation, double pole switch in a consumer unit
- industrial installation, single-phase double pole switch fuse, or three-phase triple pole and neutral switch fuse
- large industrial installation, moulded case circuit breakers, polyphase
- switch rooms industrial/commercial as above, also oil and air blast arc suppressor types.

All this switch gear opens the neutral as well as the line conductors. It must be able to handle not only the load of the installation but also the prospective fault current expected.

The magnitude of a fault developing in an installation has an inverse relationship to the impedance of the cable. Therefore, the longer the cable the more impedance, the more impedance the less current. A fault may not necessarily open the switch gear automatically and manual operation may be required.

The protective devices usually found in switch gear are:

- high breaking (or rupturing) capacity fuses, HBC or HRC
- moulded case circuit breaker (when used as a main switch).

In older installations, switch gear and other parts of the installation may be prone to fault due to lack of maintenance. In cases such as low levels of arc quenching oil (a special oil designed to quench arcing at high fault levels) the problem may not be discovered until a fault develops. This further underlines the need for routine checks.

Contactors

A contactor is a switch with the contacting parts held apart by springs. They can usually be found in:

- motor control panels
- control panels
- electronic controllers
- remote switching.

When a current is applied to a coil this operates a magnet, which draws the contacting parts together. Remove the current and the springs will open the contacts.

Did you know?

Polyphase means more than one phase – usually three phase.

Remember

Permission from the client must be obtained before any closures on installations for maintenance purposes.

The advantage of this type of switch is that a small operating current can switch a large load. An example would be using a 6 amp light switch to operate the lighting for a whole car park or sports arena. A typical cause of failure is burnt out coils caused by connection to the wrong voltage, a 230 V coil to a 400 V supply for instance. In most cases, contactors are repairable but, generally, it is just as cost effective to replace the whole unit.

Electronic and solid state devices

Most installations have some kind of electronic or solid state controlling device. Electronic ballasts on fluorescent luminaires and power factor capacitors, for instance, operate on a very small voltage and current band and are very susceptible to mains voltage and heat. Most circuit boards have a means of maintaining temperature as an increase in heat causes an increase in resistance, which causes more heat and so on, until the resistor breaks down. Special knowledge is required in many cases to check these levels of resistance. Great care must be taken during the inspection and testing of all installations, as high current and voltage levels used during testing would damage this sensitive electronic equipment. In some cases specialist advice and skilled operatives may be required to install such equipment.

Instrumentation

Many large users of electricity have metering equipment installed to allow the consumer to keep a check on, and budget energy usage, thus conserving energy.

Transformers, known as current transformers (CTs) and potential (voltage) transformers (PTs), reduce current and voltage to values suitable for the monitoring equipment. Burnt out transformers and faulty equipment are the most common types of remedial work required. Due to the large voltages and currents sometimes involved, care must be taken and strict isolation procedures followed.

Protective devices

Protective devices are designed to open in the event of a fault occurring in an installation or piece of equipment. Typical faults are:

- short circuit between line conductors
- earth fault between any line conductor and earth
- overload, exceeding the design specification of the conductor(s) in the circuit.

If a conductor has a rating of 14 amps and the protective device has a rating of 32 amps then the conductor will overheat before the protective device operates. Therefore, if a protective device fails to operate, it is important to:

- find out why it did not operate
- find the cause of the original problem.

Did you know?

The neutral conductor is defined as a live conductor in BS 7671.

Operating any equipment with uncorrected faults will only result in damage. If the protective device has been incorrectly selected, then damage to the conductors, equipment and even more serious consequences may occur.

Luminaires

The most common cause of failure of luminaries is that the lamp has blown. For incandescent lamps, replacement is the only action needed. Discharge lighting is more complex and therefore more prone to go wrong:

- If the capacitor for power factor correction is broken, it would not stop the lamp operating but make it less efficient.
- If the choke or ballast, used to assist starting, is broken it must be replaced.
- If the lamp does not start then the fluorescent tube and/or starter switch may need replacement.

Flexible cables and cords

A flexible cable is defined as 'a cable whose structure and material make it suitable to be flexed' while in service. A flexible cord is a flexible cable with cross sectional area not exceeding 4 mm^2. Typical applications are:

- pendant ceiling lamp holders
- flex outlet spur units
- fused plugs to portable appliances
- immersion heaters
- flexible connections to fans and motors.

All cables and cords shall comply with the latest amendments to BS 7671. In installations where old and harmonised colours are used, appropriate signage must be displayed.

As well as colour code requirements, all other requirements of Regulation 134.1.1 regarding good workmanship and materials, must also be adhered to. Typical faults with flexible cables and cords are:

- Poor termination into accessory. All the mechanical outer cover of the flex should go into the accessory and no unprotected conductors should be visible.
- Wrong type of flex installed. Ambient temperature must be taken into consideration, just as in cable selection for the installation wiring.
- Incorrect size of conductor. Cable carrying capacity must be considered, just as in cable selection for the installation wiring.
- Incorrectly installed. The support lugs built into pendant fittings must be used, where the flex supports the weight of the fitting.

Most of these problems should be identified at the inspection stage of the installation.

Remember

Select the correct type and rating of starter switch, as excess power demand will damage it.

Did you know?

Flexible cords were amongst the first cables to comply with European Harmonisation requirements, having core colours of brown and blue as far back as 1975.

Remember

The manufacturer will recommend the total weight that can be suspended from the fitting. If the luminaries are too heavy, chains or other supports should be used.

Portable appliances and equipment

The most common use for flexible cables and cords are with portable appliances. Fixed equipment such as computers and televisions, in business and domestic installations, are also supplied with flexible cables and cords.

They must comply with BS 7671, which will ensure that:

- the correct size conductor is used for the load
- the correct type of cord or cable is used for the environment, considering all external influences such as temperature, moisture and corrosion
- the correct termination methods are used
- the correct type and rating of protective device are used to protect the cable and appliance.

Extension leads must meet the same requirements as the rest of the installed equipment. They are classed as portable equipment and should be included on the Portable Appliance Register, and tested as such.

Knowledge and understanding of electrical systems and equipment

When investigating a fault in an installation the electrician needs all the information available. This can be obtained through:

- **Enquiry** – asking the user what the problems are is an obvious first step. Also, if technical specifications are needed then enquiries can be made to the relevant person.
- **Investigation** – if required, some investigation can be carried out, using great care and ensuring safe isolation procedures have been carried out.
- **Measurement** – a low range ohmmeter, or insulation resistance tester, can give valuable indicators as to the type and position of the fault.

Knowledge is also built up through experience.

Understanding the electrical system, installation and equipment

When faults arise during installation, the process of fault diagnosis is more straightforward as all information should be to hand. If not, the sort of information required before starting work will include:

- nominal voltage (230 or 400 volts for low voltage and 0–50 for ELV)
- installation type (domestic, industrial, commercial or agricultural)
- system type (lighting, power, heating, emergency lighting, fire alarms, etc.)
- earthing system (TT, TN-S, TN-C-S, or in extraordinary cases TN-C or IT)
- earthing arrangement
- location of incoming services (gas, water, air conditioning, etc.)
- location of incoming electrical supplies

- distribution board schedules, containing the location, type and rating of protective devices and type and composition of circuits
- drawings indicating the location of plant and machinery
- diagrams, manufacturers' technical information and design criteria.

This information should be kept in or near the supply intake but in some installations some investigation is required. In older installations, where additions and alterations have been made, it is unwise to rely too much on distribution board schedules, as the information may be false. Care must be taken to check that the schedule is correct before starting.

Optimum use of personal and other persons' experience of systems and equipment

It is common sense to listen to the person who operates the equipment on a daily basis. Other people, who may have access to relevant information to help diagnose and rectify the fault, include:

- electricians who previously worked on the system
- design engineer
- works engineer
- maintenance electrician
- plant operator
- home owner
- site foreman
- shop manager
- school caretaker.

Stages of diagnosis and rectification

Whilst knowledge of the installation and equipment is required, a logical and systematic approach to the investigation is a necessity. Some faults are obvious and can be rectified immediately. Others are more complex requiring thought and planning. In an emergency, there may not be much time for reflection.

Where supplies must be shut down, liaison with the client is necessary to keep disruption to a minimum. If any rewiring is required then an inspection and test may be required before re-energisation. Competency in the use of test instruments and the testing procedures is needed.

A logical approach

Unless the fault is obvious a logical and progressive process will be needed to find it.

- Identify the symptom.
- Gather information.
- Analyse the evidence.

Remember
If you are not familiar with the plant or equipment call a specialist.

Remember
If further damage is suspected then a periodic test report may be required.

- Check the supply.
- Check protective devices.
- Isolate and test.
- Interpret information and test results.
- Rectify the fault.
- Carry out tests.
- Restore the supply.

Information required may include:

- operating manuals
- wiring and connection diagrams
- manufacturers' product information
- maintenance records
- inspection and test results
- installation specifications
- drawings
- design data
- site diary.

Interpretation of test results

Non-live tests

BS 7671 requires that certain tests are carried out before any energisation takes place. These ensure the installation is safe to energise to carry on testing:

- continuity of protective and bonding conductors
- continuity of ring final circuit conductors
- insulation resistance
- polarity.

Continuity of protective and bonding conductors

Each circuit needs a conductor to carry fault currents to earth. Each point of utilisation requires a connection to the protective conductor. In the event of a fault, the protective conductor transfers the fault current round the earth-fault loop path and causes the protective device to open. The speed at which it opens depends on how quickly the fault current travels around the earth-fault loop path. This depends to a great degree on the continuity and the low resistance value of the protective conductor. It must be tested to ensure this value is achieved.

Using a typical test current of 200 mA minimum, the earth continuity reading for equipotential bonding would be between 0.01 to 0.05 Ω. A reading of over 0.5 Ω would need investigating.

Continuity of ring final circuit conductors

This test is to ensure all ring final circuits are actually in the form of a ring and do not have any breaks and interconnections.

A correctly performed test has three steps. If readings gradually increase during the second or third test then an interconnection or break are indicated. The exception to this is any spurred connections, which should comply with the requirements of BS 7671. The information required before testing begins would indicate the presence of spurs in the circuit. Typical readings will be 0.01 to 0.1 Ω.

Did you know?

A 'ring main' is used by the distributor to supply the sub-station with. In an installation all such ring circuits are known as 'ring final circuits'.

Insulation resistance

Insulation resistance testing is intended to ensure that the resistance of the insulation between conductors, and between conductors and earth, is sufficiently high. A test reading of a healthy circuit would be greater than 200 MΩ, but Table 61, BS 7671 indicates that a measurement of 1 MΩ may be accepted. Any measurement between 1 and 2 MΩ must be investigated.

In the case of larger installations being tested as a whole, lower values may be obtained, due to the effect of the parallel paths of other circuits. Providing the insulation resistance value remains above 0.5 MΩ for the whole installation, and no individual circuit is below 2 MΩ, then the installation may be acceptable.

Polarity

Polarity is checked to ensure that:

- all single pole switches are in the line conductor
- all protective devices are in the line conductor
- all equipment has been correctly connected.

Most of this requirement is carried out at the inspection stage and either a low ohmmeter or a continuity tester may be used.

Functional testing including RCD testing

If an RCD is being used then it should be tested, using an RCD tester, as follows:

- half rated value of RCD (should **not** trip within 2 seconds)
- rated value of RCD (**should** trip within 200 ms)
- rated value of RCD × 5 (**must** trip within 40 ms)
- functional facility is tested by pushing the integral test button.

All functional tests should include:

- lighting controller and switches
- motor fixings, drives, pulleys, etc.
- motor controls
- controls and interlocks
- main switches
- isolators.

This includes physical operation to ensure a positive switching action, enclosure doors cannot be opened when the interlock is operating, etc.

Remember

Test instruments should only be used by competent persons.

Earth-fault loop impedance testing

This test is carried out at the end of the circuit where the remedial work has been carried out to ensure that the earth-fault loop path has not been compromised by any work carried out. Where 'flying leads' are used then great care should be taken. The test is carried out with all bonding in place and after polarity has been confirmed. The leads are then attached to the line, neutral and earth. A reading is obtained and compared with the requirements of BS 7671.

The limitation and range of test instruments

Table 10.01 gives guidance on the limitation and range settings of test instruments.

Test	Instrument	Range
Continuity of protective conductors	Low resistance ohmmeter	0.005 to 2 ohms or less
Continuity of ring final circuit conductors	Low resistance ohmmeter	0.05 to 0.8 ohms
Insulation resistance	High reading ohmmeter	1 megohm to greater than 200 megohms
Polarity	Ohmmeter	Low resistance
	Bell/Buzzer	None

Table 10.01 Limitation and range of test equipment

Inspectors should be aware of the range and limitation of their instruments, be adept in their use and understand the readings obtained from the tests conducted. A suitable checklist for use before testing begins is as follows:

- Check the instrument leads for damage.
- Zero the instrument.
- Check battery condition.
- Check the correct scale for testing (if not sure, select highest range available).

- Check calibration date and record serial number.
- Ensure operation of instrument by checking open and closed circuit on test leads. If required record resistance of test leads.
- Record test results.
- Switch off after use.
- Store in case in a suitable location.

Factors affecting the fault repair process

Some faults can be diagnosed and repaired in a straightforward manner. Some, however, pose a problem which, for a number of reasons to do with cost, convenience, down time, legal concerns, etc., will involve other people and not be left to the responsibility of the electrician. Some of these problems are covered here.

Cost of replacement

If a contractor carries out work at a set rate and the work required falls outside the terms of any contract, then before going ahead with any repairs or replacement an agreement must be made as to how much it will cost and who will pay for the work. It may require:

- full replacement
- partial replacement
- full repair.

In some cases a partial repair may be carried out but the time taken may make this uneconomic, as the cost of a replacement may be less. All this must be agreed before the work can start.

Availability of replacement

Replacements may not always be on the shelf and if a piece of equipment has reached the end of its useful life then a replacement must be found.

Most manufacturers have a system in place either to rebuild or to redesign a replacement part or to deal with a supplier who in turn will be able to find a replacement.

Remember

In-house maintenance often avoids major problems by carrying out a planned service schedule.

Down time under fault conditions

Manufacturers bear the expense of maintenance staff as it is usually more expensive to have production halted due to breakdowns. This could be because of:

- lost production due to plant and machinery not working
- lost business due to production schedules not being met and repeat business lost
- data loss due to unexpected power failure and interruptions during repair.

Not all faults are the consumer's responsibility, and disruption may be outside the consumer's control. Where continuity of supply is essential an alternate means of supply may be required, such as a reserve generator or battery back-up.

Availability of resources and staff

In-house maintenance may deal with routine and most minor problems but, in the event of a major breakdown, a different strategy may be required as it may not be practical to commit the whole of the company maintenance staff to one project that may last for weeks or even months and leave the rest of the installation understaffed.

In this case the best solution may be to contract in outside help. The following should be considered:

- **Availability of staff** – Has the company enough staff available to carry out the work?
- **Competency** – Does the company have staff with relevant experience?
- **Cost implications** – Can the company pay for the contract?
- **Special plant and machinery** – Has the company the resources available?

In some extreme cases, companies have used major repairs and renovations as a reason to relocate to more up-to-date premises.

Legal responsibility

As not all eventualities can be foreseen, it is important to decide who is going to be responsible for what. This generally means who will pay for unexpected repairs or replacements. A contract is usually drawn up and signed by both parties to decide areas of responsibility. This would include:

- costs
- time taken
- period of guarantee or warranty
- areas of omission as issues to be negotiated (such as discovering a problem after removing large plant or machinery).

Contracts must be adhered to and any work claimed for must be carried out. Breach of contract can be the subject of legal action.

Costing is an important part of the process, and an accurate analysis is required to be able to give an estimate or fixed price for the job. A guarantee is usual both for the work done and materials used. In the case of an older installation, old or renovated items may be used to cut costs. If this is the case, they should be written out of the contract and a clause entered to the effect that they might compromise other work and be prone to failure.

Remember
A temporary generator may be hired if a substantial shut-down is planned.

Remember
Skill updates and enhancing qualifications are a means of maintaining competence.

Other factors affecting the fault repair process

Whilst in-house maintenance can reduce downtime due to breakdowns, faults do happen and maintenance staff can only minimise the disruption caused, but good planning can also reduce down time and lost production.

In-house staff, whilst having the skills to deal with most every day problems, may find that some problems are beyond their competence. An outside contractor may be required. The electrician must have a generic contingency plan to deal with fault finding on other people's premises. These procedures may include:

- signing in
- wearing identification badges
- identifying and locating supervisory and key personnel
- locating kcy data and drawings
- liaison with customer before commencing work
- insisting on following safe isolation procedures.

Special requirements

Other issues may have to be taken into consideration besides the job in hand:

- **Access to premises** – This may need to be arranged if after normal working hours, as it may not be possible to change the normal day-to-day routine. It must include access to all parts of the installation.
- **Risk assessment** – In older buildings, asbestos and other dangerous substances may be encountered, requiring a risk assessment (work should stop immediately if a hazardous substance is discovered and it must be reported to the client).
- **Damage to the fabric** – If any part of the building fabric is disturbed then who is going to make good? If the in-house staff includes a bricklayer or plasterer then it may devolve to them. If not, it may be the inspector's responsibility.
- **Isolation section by section** – Only the part of the system being worked on should be switched off and isolated to minimise disruption.
- **Provision of emergency or stand-by supply** – A temporary supply may be necessary where the disruption to the customer cannot be tolerated. In some installations such as hospitals, merchant banks and computer installations, a permanent stand-by generator may have to be provided. Otherwise a planned maintenance period or shut down will need to be arranged.

All such issues must be resolved at the contract stage.

> **Safety tip**
>
> The work place can be a dangerous environment, so ensure that a risk assessment is carried out to ensure safety (not just electrical) at all times.

Special precautions

Risk assessments should be carried out in accordance with the Health and Safety at Work Act 1974, before any work commences. Personnel should be protected from any potential harm. This section looks at special situations and the precautions that may need to be taken.

Fibre optic cabling

Fibre optic cables carry high levels of concentrated light. Looking directly into the end of a fibre optic will irreparably damage eyesight.

Antistatic precautions

Special antistatic precautions are to be taken in locations where flammable liquids, gases or powders are present and there is a high risk of ignition or explosion, including: petrol filling stations, chemical works, offshore installations, paint stores and flour mills.

Electro-static discharge

An excess or deficiency of electrons on the surface of a material can build up an electric charge. In the proximity of another substance at a different potential, a spark will jump across the gap. If this occurs in an inflammable atmosphere, an explosion could occur. Operatives need to be 'grounded' or earthed by earthing straps and/or special antistatic clothing to avoid sparks occurring.

Static charges can be caused by:

- **Friction** – Two surfaces rubbed together, leave one surface with more electrons than the other, creating a difference in potential.
- **Separation** – Cling-film or self-adhesive tape, etc. when rapidly peeled off a reel will create the same effect.
- **Induction** – If a conducting surface, such as a printed circuit board, is placed near a charged insulator, such as a folder of paper, the electrostatic charge will be transferred to the sensitive components of the PCB by induction. All conductive items can be involved in inductive charging. Insulators are not affected, as the charge cannot redistribute itself and remains on the surface

Damage to electronic devices due to over voltage

When carrying out an insulation resistance test, the inspector must switch off or disconnect all electronic equipment, as the voltage generated by the insulation resistance tester may damage or destroy the electronic equipment. Such high voltages, which can be up to 1000 volts, will adversely

Static electricity

Remember

Some locations require special precautions against static to the extent of special footwear and clothing.

affect the sensitive components in the control circuits of such equipment as data or telecommunication systems, or the central heating controls in a domestic installation.

It may be costly to repair and will not enhance the reputation of the electrician or employer for future contracts.

Shut down of IT equipment

On no account should any circuit be isolated where computer equipment is connected without prior arrangements to avoid loss of data. The client must be given time to arrange data storage, and to download vital data to a safe location. Most large companies will have protection in the form of uninterruptible power supply (UPS) systems.

Risk of high frequency on high capacitive circuits

Capacitive circuits either have capacitors connected to them or have capacitance owing to long runs of cable, particularly mineral insulated cable. When working on such circuits, no work should commence until the capacitance has been discharged by shorting out the capacitor.

Danger from storage batteries

Batteries can be used to provide back-up for emergency lighting, fire alarms, UPS systems, etc. Special care should be taken when working on or near batteries, as they can be dangerous:

Safety tip

Only work on batteries where eye wash and clean water facilities are available.

- Lead acid cells contain sulphuric acid, which must be washed off immediately if it comes in contact with any part of the body or clothing.
- Lead acid also emits hydrogen gas when batteries are being charged. This is highly explosive so naked flames are forbidden and the area should be well ventilated.
- High voltages applied to cell terminals will damage batteries.
- When connecting batteries, a short across the cell terminals, by a spanner for instance, will cause arcing or even an explosion.
- Cells should not be disconnected as this will also cause arcing and the possibility of explosion.

Short answer questions

1. Give the correct sequences for isolating both a single and a three phase installation.
2. Define on-load and off-load devices.
3. Give five categories of fault.
4. Draw a typical installation layout, with labels, from the supply company's incoming cables to final circuits.
5. **a.** Give the reason circuits are divided into smaller circuits.
   b. Explain the technique for locating faults in Figure 10.3.
   c. Show at which point a fault would result in a complete loss of power in Figure 10.3.
6. Define:
   a. an overload, giving two examples
   b. a short circuit, giving two examples
   c. an earth fault, giving two examples
7. What are the three most usual faults on:
   a. luminaries?
   b. flexible cables and cords?
8. Give the logical sequence for fault diagnosis and rectification.
9. Explain three ways of obtaining information whilst investigating a fault.
10. Explain a typical company contingency plan when called out to an unfamiliar installation.

Multiple-choice test

1. What is the correct means of detecting voltage during safe isolation?
   a. voltage indicator and proving unit
   b. electrician's screwdriver
   c. apprentice
   d. don't bother

2. Which is the approved means of ensuring an isolating device cannot be opened by an unauthorised person?
   a. padlock and unique key
   b. close the door and hope it is not turned on
   c. piece of wire twisted in the hasp
   d. signage

3. A one-way switch can give:
   a. isolation
   b. protection
   c. control
   d. all of the above

4. Lack of maintenance or poor installation practice, can lead to:
   a. poor power factor
   b. insulation failure
   c. insufficient lighting
   d. not enough computer space

5. Fault diagnosis is complicated because:
   a. call outs occur at inconvenient times
   b. the operative will need to travel
   c. no two faults are the same
   d. all faults are similar

6. When a fault has been rectified, it is important to test for:
   a. colour co-ordination
   b. harmonics
   c. functionality
   d. EU compliance

7. 'Transient voltage' is an example of:
   a. general categories of faults
   b. normal flow of electrons
   c. poor use of cable supports
   d. transfer of voltage via the national grid

8. One of the reasons an installation is divided into circuits is to:
a. *increase the cost of installation*
b. *give more sockets*
c. *allow greater accessibility*
d. *avoid danger and minimise inconvenience in the event of a fault*

9. Normally, what is the first indication of a fault?
a. *protective device has opened*
b. *protective device has closed*
c. *circuit or equipment not working*
d. *circuit or equipment working*

10. What size fuse should be protecting a piece of mains equipment rated at 2.7 kW?
a. *3 amps*
b. *5 amps*
c. *10 amps*
d. *13 amps*

11. What size protective device would protect a standard ring final circuit?
a. *6 amps*
b. *10 amps*
c. *25 amps*
d. *32 amps*

12. An extra load added to an existing circuit can cause:
a. *overload*
b. *short circuit*
c. *earth fault*
d. *transient voltage*

13. A variation or disturbance of the normal voltage state, can be described as:
a. *overload*
b. *short circuit*
c. *earth fault*
d. *transient voltage*

14. Insulation failure can be caused by:
a. *damage by a third party*
b. *electronic equipment*
c. *reversed polarity*
d. *volt drop*

15. Using an MCB as a functional switch may cause:
a. *lights to flicker when switched on*
b. *lights to flicker when switched off*
c. *breakdown of MCB*
d. *extended life of MCB*

16. Poor termination of conductors is an example of:
a. *plant failure*
b. *insulation failure*
c. *installer misuse*
d. *localised loss of supply*

17. The most common cause of a luminaire not working is:
a. *lamp not working*
b. *starter not working*
c. *ballast not working*
d. *capacitor not working*

18. A common failure of a motor not running is:
a. *bearings worn*
b. *brushes worn*
c. *pulley worn*
d. *stator worn*

19. The most effective means of preventing problems in an installation is:
a. *replace plant and equipment annually*
b. *regular maintenance*
c. *replace equipment when it wears out*
d. *repair equipment*

20. Which is NOT an accepted method of joining cables?
a. *plastic connecters*
b. *porcelain connecters*
c. *soldered joints*
d. *twisted with pliers and taped*

21. The requirement for connections is that they be:
a. *mechanically secure*
b. *electrically secure*
c. *electrically and mechanically secure*
d. *in a correct terminal*

22. Which is a requirement in terminating cables and glands?
   a. *Care must be taken not to damage wires.*
   b. *A knife should be used.*
   c. *Dissimilar cable sizes can be used.*
   d. *External influences may not be taken into consideration.*

23. Which is not a requirement for conductor joining devices?
   a. *be the correct size for the cross sectional area of the cable*
   b. *be at least the same current rating as the conductor being joined*
   c. *have the same temperature rating as the conductor being joined*
   d. *be from the same supplier as the cable being used*

24. What is the most common fault to expect in Question 23?
   a. *loose connection*
   b. *cable size too large*
   c. *different current rating*
   d. *unsuitable for the environment*

25. Which of the following do not have mechanical protection?
   a. *PVC / PVC twin and cpc*
   b. *PVC / SWA*
   c. *FP200*
   d. *2.5 mm² single*

26. Which is not required in the inspection checklist?
   a. *connection of conductors*
   b. *routing of cables*
   c. *identification of conductors*
   d. *competency of installer*

27. Which is the percentage of accessories allowed to be inspected?
   a. *5%*
   b. *10%*
   c. *15%*
   d. *20%*

28. What is an advantage of using a contactor?
   a. *switching large loads*
   b. *switching multiple loads*
   c. *simplicity of connection*
   d. *simplicity of construction*

29. Which would not cause a protective device to operate?
   a. *short circuit*
   b. *overcurrent*
   c. *earth fault*
   d. *under voltage*

30. Which factor is not a consideration in the fault repair process?
   a. *availability of replacement*
   b. *down time under fault conditions*
   c. *inconvenience to tester*
   d. *cost of replacement*

The answer section is at the back of the book.

11

Electrical machines and motors

Chapter 3 looked at magnetism and established that a magnetic field is set up around any current carrying conductor. If this field is changing there is a force created, which can cause a conductor to move. This principle is used in all motors and generators. However, the arrangement of conductors, and how the magnetic fields are created and controlled, allows a wide variety of motors and generators to meet different requirements. This chapter covers:

- Basic a.c. and d.c. motors and generators
  - Fleming's rules
  - Construction of a simple alternator
  - Simple d.c. generator
  - Practical alternators and motors
- Types of d.c. motor
  - Series-wound universal motor
- Three-phase induction motors
  - Production of the rotating field
  - Stator construction
  - Rotor construction and principle of operation
- (Asynchronous) single-phase induction motors
  - Split-phase motor (induction start/induction run)
  - Capacitor-start motors (capacitor start/ induction run)
  - Permanent split capacitor (PSC) motors
  - Capacitor start–capacitor run motors
  - Shaded-pole motors
  - Motor speed and slip calculations

- Synchronous a.c. induction motors
  - Three-phase a.c. synchronous motors
  - Single-phase a.c. synchronous motors
- Motor windings
- Motor starters
  - Direct-on-line (DOL) starters for three-phase motors
  - Remote stop/start control
  - Star-delta starters
  - Soft starters
  - Auto-transformer starters
  - Rotor-resistance starters
- Speed control of d.c. machines
  - Armature resistance control
  - Field control
  - Pulse width modulation (PWM)
- Speed control of a.c. machines

Basic a.c. and d.c. motors and generators

Faraday's Law states that 'when a conductor cuts, or is cut, by a magnetic field, then an e.m.f. is induced in that conductor the magnitude of which is proportional to the rate at which the conductor cuts or is cut by the magnetic flux.' If the conductor is part of a circuit, a current will flow.

Also, if this field is changing there is a force created on the conductor. The direction of movement of the conductor and current is given by Fleming's rules.

Fleming's rules

In **Fleming's left hand rule (for motors)**, if the first finger, second finger and thumb of the left hand are positioned at right angles to one another then the following is true:

- The **F**irst **F**inger will show the direction of the magnetic **F**ield.
- The se**C**ond finger will show the direction of **C**urrent.
- The thu**M**b will show the direction of **M**ovement of the conductor within the magnetic field.

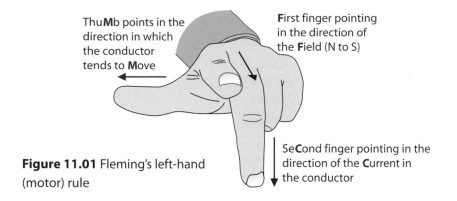

ThuMb points in the direction in which the conductor tends to Move

First finger pointing in the direction of the Field (N to S)

SeCond finger pointing in the direction of the Current in the conductor

Figure 11.01 Fleming's left-hand (motor) rule

In **Fleming's right hand rule (for generators)**, the thu**M**b indicates the direction that a conductor is being driven. The **F**irst **F**inger still shows the direction of the magnetic **F**ield and the se**C**ond finger the direction of **C**urrent.

Construction of a simple alternator

The simplest alternating current generator (alternator) is a single loop in a permanent magnetic field. If the loop is mechanically rotated, it will start to cut through the lines of flux, and induce an e.m.f.

The ends of the wire loop are brought out on to slip rings. Carbon brushes, sprung loaded to maintain contact, connect the slip rings to an external circuit. In the circuit shown this includes a lamp. If the loop is now turned in the direction shown, the conductor cuts through the lines of magnetic flux, and an e.m.f. (voltage) is induced into the conductor. This completes the circuit, and the e.m.f. causes current to flow, making the lamp illuminate.

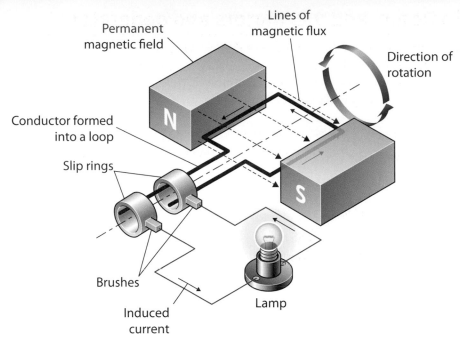

Figure 11.02 Single loop alternator attached to a simple circuit

The size of the e.m.f. (and the current, if there is a circuit) varies from zero, to a peak value when the coil is at 90° to the magnetic field, back to zero and then repeats the process with the e.m.f. generated in the opposite direction. If this is plotted as a graph, one full 360 degree revolution (cycle) of the loop would be a sine wave.

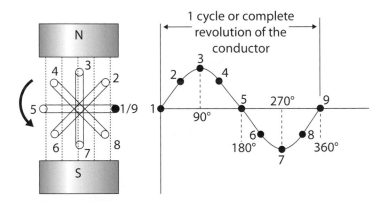

Figure 11.03 Waveform in a single loop conductor

One rotation of the conductor produces a complete sine wave. This is one cycle and the number of cycles that occur in each second is the frequency. The unit of frequency is the Hertz (Hz). In the United Kingdom, the standard frequency of supply is 50 Hz.

The strength of the induced e.m.f. is determined by:

- the strength of the magnetic flux density, between the pole faces of the magnet
- the length of the conductor in the magnetic field
- the velocity or speed of the conductor through the magnetic field.

It can be calculated using the formula: $\mathbf{e} = \mathbf{B}l\mathbf{v}$

where: e = induced e.m.f. in volts
B = magnetic flux density in tesla (T) or Wb/m^2
l = length of the conductor in metres (m)
v = velocity of the conductor in metres/sec (m/s).

> ### Definition
>
> A **commutator** is an electrical switch which periodically reverses the current in a motor or generator. This produces a steady rotating force, or **torque**.

Simple d.c. generator

If, instead of slip rings, the coils are connected to an outside circuit via a **commutator**, which reverses the contacts each time the coil goes through 180°, the current will always be in the same direction. We now have a d.c. generator, though the current is still going from zero to a peak value and back again twice every revolution, so it is a bit lumpy! However, this can be smoothed out to create a steady direct current.

The commutator is made of copper and has segments, which are insulated from each other. These are connected to each end of a coil or number of coils. Electrical contact is made by means of carbon brushes, which are spring loaded so that they maintain contact with the commutator surface.

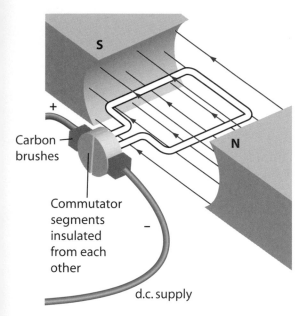

Carbon brushes

Commutator segments insulated from each other

d.c. supply

Figure 11.04 Single loop with commutator

Practical alternators and motors

The output from a single coil in a permanent magnetic field is of limited use. In practice:

> ### Definition
>
> An **armature** carries current across a field and generates an e.m.f.

- The coils are formed from many turns of wire.
- There are multiple coils set at different angles, wound on to a rotating former called the **armature**.
- There are likely to be several sets of magnetic **pole pairs**.
- The pole pairs are normally electromagnetics, created by feeding part of the armature current to their windings, called **field windings**.

A simple a.c. motor

- A commutator for d.c. connection will have multiple segments.
- The strength of the magnetic field can be varied by varying the strength of current flowing through the electromagnets. The poles of the magnet can also be reversed by reversing the supply to them, causing a motor to turn in the opposite direction. However, a more common way of reversing d.c. motor direction is to reverse the connections to the armature.
- The stationary part of the machine is called the **stator**; the rotating part is the **rotor** (usually the same as the armature).
- The construction of the armature and stator have a major impact on the performance and efficiency of motors and alternators, and are designed to give specific operating characteristics.
- A variety of sources can be used mechanically to drive an alternator, including steam, wind, waterfall or petrol/diesel driven motors.

Types of d.c. motor

There are three main types:

- series or universal motor
- shunt motor
- compound motor

The main differences are how the field windings are connected to the armature. These alter the characteristics of the motor, e.g. more torque (rotational force).

The **series motor** has the field coil in series with the armature. It is often called a series-wound universal motor, or just universal motor, because it will also operate with a.c. It has high starting torque and can have variable speed control. Speed increases as mechanical load decreases so it must always be connected to a load.

The **shunt motor** has armature and field windings connected in parallel. This gives a constant field strength and motor speed.

The **compound motor** combines the characteristics of both series and shunt motors, giving high starting torque and good speed/torque characteristics. However, speed control is complex.

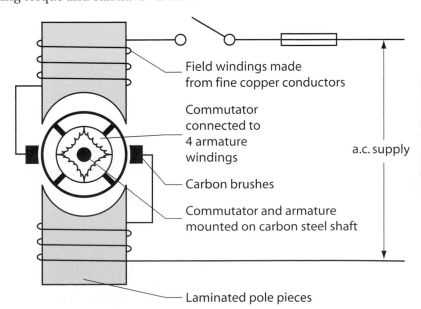

Field windings made from fine copper conductors

Commutator connected to 4 armature windings

a.c. supply

Carbon brushes

Commutator and armature mounted on carbon steel shaft

Laminated pole pieces

Figure 11.05 Series universal motor

Series-wound universal motor

For this motor to run on a.c. modifications are made both to the field windings and armature formers. These are heavily laminated to reduce eddy currents and I^2R losses, which reduces the heat generated by the normal working of the motor, making it more efficient.

The motor is generally small (less than a kilowatt) and is used to drive small hand tools such as drills, vacuum cleaners and washing machines. Friction between the brushes and the commutator causes them to wear down, increasing the gap and causing arcing. The brushes then need to be replaced, otherwise the heat generated as the gap gets larger will eventually cause the motor to fail.

The advantages of this machine are:

- more power for a given size than any other normal a.c. motor
- high starting torque
- relatively cheap to produce.

Three-phase induction motors

Induction motors operate because a moving magnetic field induces a current to flow in the rotor. This current creates a second magnetic field, which combines with the field from the stator windings to exert a force on the rotor conductors to turn the rotor.

Three-phase induction motor showing component parts

Production of the rotating field

Figure 11.06 shows the stator of a three-phase motor to which a three-phase supply is connected. The windings in the diagram are in star formation and two windings of each phase are wound in the same direction.

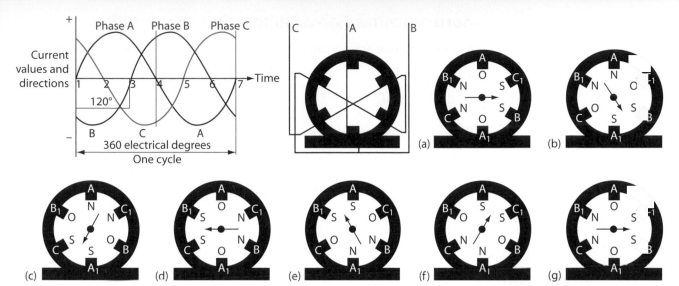

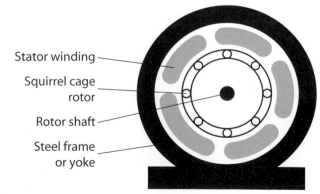

Figure 11.06 Stator of three-phase motor with three-phase supply connection showing magnetic field changes in one complete cycle

Each pair of windings produces a magnetic field, the strength depending on the current in that particular phase at any instant of time. When the current is zero, the magnetic field will be zero. Maximum current will produce the maximum magnetic field.

As the currents in the three phases are 120° out of phase the magnetic fields produced will be as well. This means the magnetic field set up by the three-phase currents will give the appearance of rotating clockwise around the stator.

The magnetic field produced by the three phases is shown by the arrow in Figure 11.06 (a to g), which show the magnetic field changes at 60° intervals through one complete cycle. The speed of rotation of the field depends on the supply frequency and the number of pole pairs, and is referred to as the **synchronous** speed.

The direction of the magnetic field rotation depends on the sequence in which the phases and windings are connected. Reversing the connection of any two incoming phases can reverse rotation of the field.

Stator construction

The stator carries the field windings, which are many turns of very fine copper wire wound on to formers. These are fixed to the inside of the stator steel frame (sometimes called the yoke).

The formers contain the conductors of the winding and concentrate the magnetic lines of flux to improve the flux linkage. They are made of laminated silicon steel sections to reduce eddy currents, thereby reducing the I^2R losses and reducing heat. The number of poles fitted will determine the speed of the motor.

Stator winding
Squirrel cage rotor
Rotor shaft
Steel frame or yoke

Figure 11.07 Stator construction

Rotor construction and principle of operation

Essentially there are two main types of rotor:

- squirrel-cage rotor
- wound rotor.

Squirrel-cage rotor

In this rotor the bars are shorted out at each end by 'end rings' to form the shape of a cage. This creates numerous circuits within it for the induced e.m.f. and resultant current to flow and produce the required magnetic field.

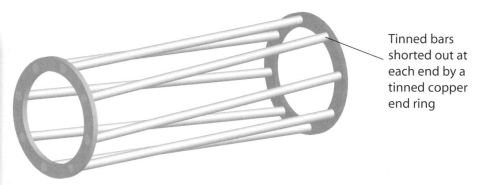

Tinned bars shorted out at each end by a tinned copper end ring

Figure 11.08 Squirrel-cage rotor

When fitted to the shaft of a motor, the rotor bars are encased within many hundreds of very thin laminated (insulated) segments of silicon steel and are skewed to increase the rotor resistance. The shaft has two low-friction bearings that enable the rotor to spin freely. The bearings and rotor are held in place within the yoke by two end caps, normally secured in place by long nuts and bolts that pass completely through the stator.

When a three-phase supply is connected to the field windings, the lines of magnetic flux produced in the stator, rotating at 50 revolutions per second, cut through the bars of the rotor and induce an e.m.f. in the bars. This produces circulatory currents within the rotor bars, producing a magnetic field around them, which distort the stator magnetic field. The interaction between these fields results in a force on the rotor bars and the rotor begins to turn. This turning force is known as a **torque**.

The construction of a complete motor is shown in Figure 11.09.

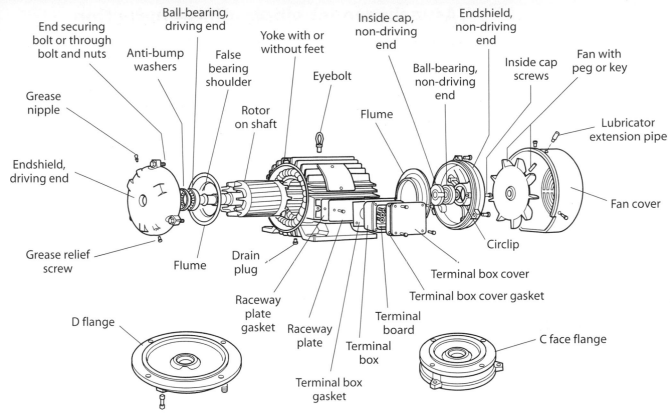

Figure 11.09 Construction of a three-phase squirrel-cage induction motor

Wound rotor

Here the rotor conductors form an internally three-phase winding. The other three ends of the windings are brought out to slip rings mounted on the shaft. The rotor bars are heavy conductors that run through the laminated steel rotor. The ends are brought out through the shaft to slip rings on the end.

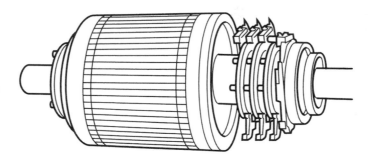

Figure 11.10 Wound-rotor motor assembly

Brush connections introduce resistance into the rotor circuit, although this is normally done on starting only to increase the starting torque. This type of motor is commonly referred to as a slip-ring motor. It is particularly effective:

- in applications where a squirrel-cage motor may result in a starting current too high for the capacity of the power system
- for high-inertia loads having a long acceleration time because of the control available of the speed, torque and resultant heating of the motor (control can be automatic or manual)
- with high-slip loads and adjustable speed installations that do not require precise speed control or regulation, such as conveyor belts, hoists and elevators.

(Asynchronous) single-phase induction motors

If an induction motor was constructed as in Figure 11.11, on connecting it to a supply it would not run. However, if we were to spin the shaft, it would start and then continue to run in whichever direction we had spun it until the supply was cut.

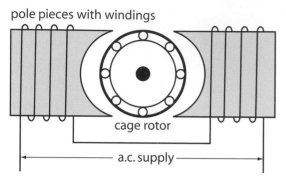

pole pieces with windings

cage rotor

a.c. supply

Figure 11.11 Simplified single-phase induction motor

This is because, when an a.c. supply is connected to the motor, the resulting current flow (and therefore the magnetic fields produced in the field windings) changes direction 100 times per second, reversing the rotational force on the rotor. When the rotor is spun the effect of the rotor bars cutting through lines of force is created, so the process starts and the motor runs up to speed.

Several means are used to create the starting conditions in single-phase machines.

Split-phase motors (induction start/induction run)

This adds another set of poles, positioned at 90° around the stator which carry start-windings.

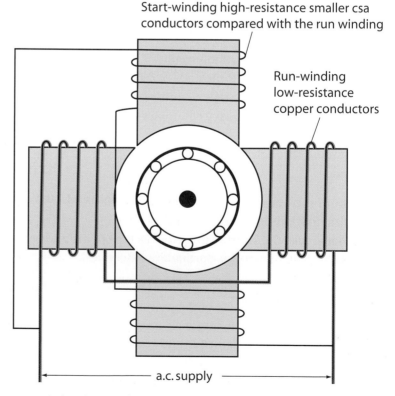

Start-winding high-resistance smaller csa conductors compared with the run winding

Run-winding low-resistance copper conductors

a.c. supply

Figure 11.12 Split-phase induction motor

When the supply is connected, both sets of windings are energised. The start-winding uses thinner wire than the main winding, so has higher resistance. This creates a small phase shift that results in the current in the start winding lagging the current in the run winding by approximately 30°, as shown in Figure 11.13. This gives the effect of a changing magnetic field and causes the motor to start turning.

Strong magnetic field in the run winding, weaker field in the start winding

Strong magnetic field in the start winding 30° later, weaker field in the run winding

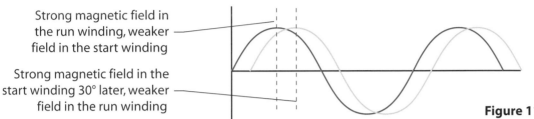

Figure 11.13 Run- and start-winding phases

The phase difference between the windings gives the motor its name. Once the motor is rotating at about 75 per cent of its full load speed, the start-winding is disconnected by a centrifugal switch attached to the shaft. This has contacts held closed by a spring. When the motor is moving sufficiently fast, a little weight is thrown away from the shaft by centrifugal force, disconnecting the start winding. Once the machine has disconnected the start winding, the machine continues to operate from the run winding.

However, it only does so because the rotor speed is always slightly lagging behind the rotating magnetic field. Therefore, these motors are known as 'asynchronous single-phase induction motors', though 'asynchronous' is normally dropped from the name.

The direction of rotation may be reversed by changing the polarity of either the start- or run-winding, but not both.

The motor is typically cheaper than other single-phase motors. However, performance is limited. Starting torque is low at about 150–175 per cent of the rated load. Also, the motor develops high starting currents of about six to nine times the full load current. A lengthy starting time can cause the start-winding to overheat and fail, so this type of motor should not be used when a high starting torque is needed. It is used on light load applications, such as small hand tools, small grinders and fans, where there are frequent stop/starts and the full load is applied after the motor has reached its operating speed.

Capacitor-start motors (capacitor start/ induction run)

This can be considered as a split-phase motor but with an enhanced start winding that includes a capacitor in the circuit to help with starting. The capacitor is mounted on the outside of the casing.

Capacitor-start split-phase motor

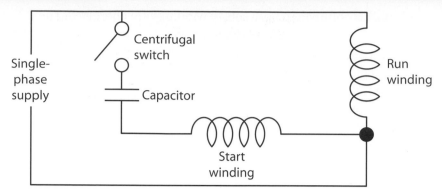

Figure 11.14 Winding connections for capacitor-start split-phase motor

In this motor the start winding has a capacitor connected in series with it. This gives a phase difference of nearly 90° between the two currents in the windings, improving the starting performance. It is also disconnected by an automatic centrifugal switch when the motor reaches about 75 per cent of its rated full-load speed.

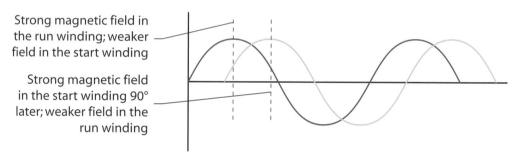

Figure 11.15 Run and start-winding phases for a capacitor-start split-phase motor

The magnetic flux set up by the two windings is much greater at starting than in the standard split-phase motor, and this produces a greater starting torque. The typical starting torque is about 300 per cent of full-load torque, and a typical starting current is about five to nine times the full-load current.

The motor is more expensive than a comparable split-phase design because of the additional cost of the capacitor but the application range is much wider because of the higher starting torque and lower starting current. It is recommended for loads that are hard to start, such as lathes, compressors and small conveyor systems. The construction of the motor is shown in Figure 11.16.

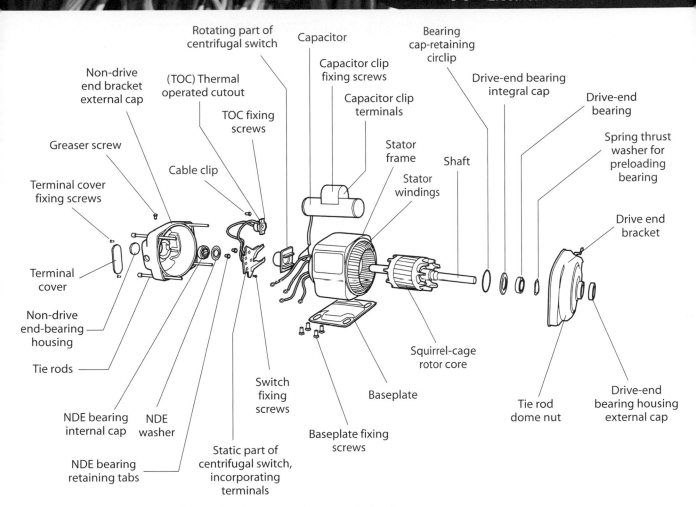

Figure 11.16 Construction of a single-phase capacitor-start induction motor

Permanent split capacitor (PSC) motors

Permanent split capacitor (PSC) motors have a capacitor permanently connected in series with the start winding. The second winding is permanently connected to the power source. This makes the start winding an auxiliary winding at running speed. Because the run capacitor must be designed for continuous use, it cannot provide the starting boost of a starting capacitor.

Starting torques for this type of motor are low, from 30 to 150 per cent of rated load, so they are not used in difficult starting applications. PSC motors have low starting currents, usually less than 200 per cent of rated load current. This makes them excellent for applications with high cycle rates.

Also, because they need no starting mechanism they can be easily reversed and designs altered for use with speed controllers. They can also be designed for optimum efficiency and high power factor at rated load. They have a wide variety of applications such as fans, blowers with low starting torque, and intermittent cycling uses such as adjusting mechanisms, gate operators and garage-door openers, many of which also need instant reversing.

Capacitor start–capacitor run motors

This motor has two capacitors mounted on the motor case.

Capacitor start–capacitor run motor

It has a start capacitor in series with the auxiliary winding (like the capacitor-start motor) and this allows for high starting torque. Like the PSC motor, it also has a run capacitor that remains in series with the auxiliary winding after the start capacitor is switched out of the circuit.

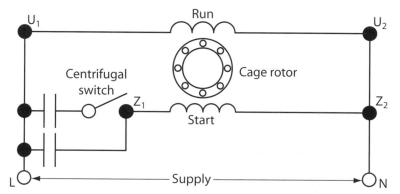

Figure 11.17 Capacitor start–capacitor run split-phase motor

This combines the best of the capacitor-start and PSC designs and can handle applications too demanding for any other kind of single-phase motor. It can be designed for lower full-load currents and higher efficiency, which means that it operates at a lower temperature than other single-phase motor types of comparable horsepower. Typical uses include woodworking machinery, air compressors, high-pressure water pumps, vacuum pumps and other high-torque applications.

Shaded-pole motors

Shaded-pole motors have only one main winding and no start winding. Starting is by means of a continuous copper loop wound around a small section of each motor pole. This 'shades' that part of the pole, causing the magnetic field in the ringed area to lag behind the field in the non-ringed section. The reaction of the two magnetic fields then starts the shaft rotating.

Because the shaded pole motor lacks a start winding, starting switch or capacitor, it is not simple and expensive. Speed can be controlled merely by varying voltage or through a multi-tap winding. Phase displacement is small so that it has a low starting torque, typically in the region of 25–75 per cent of full-load torque. It is very inefficient, usually below 20 per cent. It is suitable for light-duty applications, such as multi-speed fans for household use and record turntables.

Motor speed and slip calculations

There are two ways to express the speed of a motor:

- **Synchronous speed.** For an a.c. motor this is the speed of rotation of the stator's magnetic field. This is only a theoretical speed as the rotor will always turn at a slightly slower rate. If they were at the same speed there would be no magnetic field cut and no torque produced. (Because of this the induction motor is often called an asynchronous motor.)
- **Actual speed.** This is the speed at which the shaft rotates. The nameplate on most a.c. motors gives the actual motor speed.

Standard a.c. induction motors depend on the rotor trying to catch up with the stator's magnetic field and never succeeding. The rotor speed is slow enough to cause the proper amount of rotor current to flow. The resulting torque is large enough to overcome windage and friction losses and drive the load.

The difference between the speed of the rotor and the synchronous speed of the rotating magnetic field is called the **slip**. This is given either as a unit or percentage. The synchronous speed is calculated by the frequency of the supply and the number of pole pairs within the machine. Standard motors have two, four, six or eight poles. The rotor speed is 2–5 per cent slower, 4 per cent being common.

Determining synchronous speed and slip

Synchronous speed (n_s) in revolutions per second

$$= \frac{\text{Frequency (f) in Hz}}{\text{The number of pole pairs (p)}}$$

To convert to revolutions per minute (rpm), simply multiply n_s by 60. This new value is referred to as N_s. Percentage slip is calculated from the formula:

$$\text{Percentage slip} = \frac{\text{Synchronous speed } (n_s) - \text{Rotor speed } (n_r)}{\text{Synchronous speed } (n_s)} \times 100$$

Remember

When a conductor passes at right angles through a magnetic field, current is induced into the conductor. The direction of the induced current will depend on the direction of movement of the conductor, and the strength of the current will be determined by the speed at which the conductor moves.

Synchronous a.c. induction motors

Synchronous motors run at synchronous speed. This type of motor is not self-starting and must be brought up to almost synchronous speed by other means.

Three-phase a.c. synchronous motors

In a synchronous motor three-phase a.c. power is applied to the stator, causing a rotating magnetic field around the rotor. The rotor is then supplied via a field winding with d.c. creating north and south poles in the rotor. This attracts the rotor field activated by the d.c. The force on the rotor and rotor shaft causes it to turn and to turn a load as it rotates in step with the rotating magnetic field.

However, it cannot be started by just applying a three-phase a.c. supply to the stator. When a.c. is applied, a high-speed rotating magnetic field appears immediately. This rotating field rushes past the rotor poles so quickly that the rotor does not have a chance to start. In effect, the rotor is repelled first in one direction and then the other.

An induction winding (squirrel-cage type) is added to the rotor of a synchronous motor to cause it to start. The motor starts as an asynchronous induction motor. When the motor reaches synchronous speed, no current is induced in the squirrel-cage winding.

Synchronous motors are usually driven by transistorised variable-frequency drives (see below).

Single-phase a.c. synchronous motors

Small single-phase a.c. motors can be designed with magnetised rotors. The rotors in these motors do not require any induced current .They rotate synchronously with the mains frequency. Because of their highly accurate speed they are usually used to power mechanical clocks.

As with the three-phase version, it is difficult to accelerate the rotor instantly from stopped to synchronous speed. The motors normally require a special feature to get started. Various designs use a small induction motor (which may share the same field coils and rotor as the synchronous motor) or a very light rotor with a one-way mechanism (to ensure that the rotor starts in the 'forward' direction).

Motor windings

A motor can be manufactured with the windings internally connected. If there are three terminal connections in the terminal block labelled U, V and W, the motor windings are connected in a delta configuration.

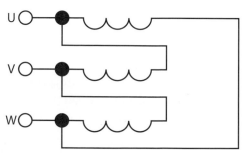

Figure 11.18 Motor windings in a delta configuration

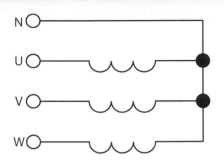

Figure 11.19 Motor windings in a star configuration

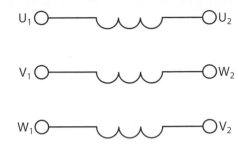

Figure 11.20 Motor windings with six connections

If there are four connections in the terminal box labelled U, V, W and N, the windings are in a star configuration.

The terminal block may contain six connections: U_1, U_2, V_1, V_2, W_1 and W_2. This is used where both star and delta configurations are required. The terminal connections can then be reconfigured for either star or delta, starting within the terminal block.

Motor starters

A motor starter must do more than just switch on the supply:

- It must automatically disconnect the motor in the event of overloads or other faults. When a condition occurs that exceeds a predetermined value, the overload device opens the motor starter control circuit, turning the motor off.
- It should prevent automatic restarting if the motor stops because of supply failure. This is called no-volts protection.
- It must provide for the efficient stopping of the motor by the user via remote stop buttons and safety interlock switches.

Direct-on-line (DOL) starters for three-phase motors

This is the easiest and cheapest way of starting squirrel-cage three-phase (induction) motors. 'Direct-on-line' means the full supply voltage is connected to the stator of the motor by a contactor-starter.

When the supply is first switched on, the initial starting current is heavy as the motor is at a standstill. This current can be six to 10 times the full load current (i.e. a motor rated at 10 A could have a starting current as high as 60 A). Initial starting torque can be 150 per cent of the full-load torque. This can cause motors to jump on starting. Direct-on-line starters are usually restricted to small motors with outputs of up to about 5 kW.

DOL starter

DOL starters should incorporate protection, operated either by magnetic or thermal overload trips. The operating principle is shown in Figure 11.21.

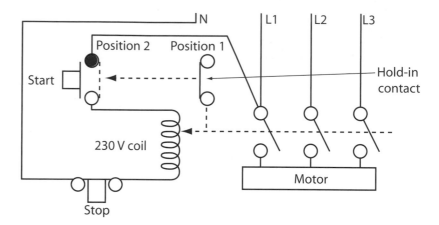

Figure 11.21 DOL starter circuit

- A three-pole switch controls the three-phase supply to the starter. This switch normally includes fuses.
- The start button is normally open. When operated, the contact is pulled on to the terminals of the start button (Position 2) and the supply continues, even when start button is released.
- The supply is broken using the stop button, normally placed in the neutral wire. The supply to the coil is broken, the coil ceases to be a magnet and the 'hold in' contact returns to its original position (Position 1). Since the start button had already returned to its original open position when released, everything is as at the start.
- Any loss of supply will immediately break the supply to the coil and also stop the motor. If a supply failure was restored, the equipment could not restart itself – someone would have to take the conscious decision to do so.

This system is often referred to as a contactor starter. They are also available with a 400 V coil, which is connected across two phases.

The motor can be reversed by interchanging any two of the incoming three-phase supply leads. If a further two leads are interchanged then the motor will rotate in the original direction.

Remote stop/start control

Control of a motor often takes place from a remote location, such as emergency stop buttons located throughout a workshop.

This is called remote stop/start station. The enclosure usually houses a start and a stop button connected in series. It is also possible to have an additional button included to give **inch control** of a motor.

Figure 11.22 shows a DOL starter with a remote stop/start station.

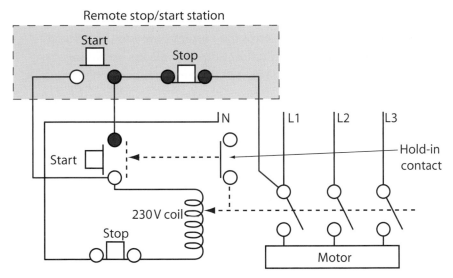

Figure 11.22 DOL starter circuit with remote stop/start control

The supply to both buttons on the main enclosure is via the remote start button at the remote station.

Star-delta starters

These can be hand operated or automatic. They provide a two-position method of starting a three-phase squirrel-cage motor. The windings first connect in star for acceleration of the rotor when starting, and then in delta for normal running.

When connected in star, the voltage to each phase winding reduces to 58 per cent of the line voltage, reducing the current in the winding to 58 per cent of the normal starting value. Applying these to the typical three-phase squirrel-cage induction motor, we would have an initial starting current of about two to three-and-a-half times full-load current and initial starting torque of about 50 per cent full-load value.

The changeover from star to delta will be made when the motor has reached a steady speed on star connection. The windings will then receive full line voltage and full-rated current.

This type of starter is relatively cheap.

Automatic versions provide the best method of starting a three-phase cage-induction motor. The starter has three triple-pole contactors, one using thermal overload protection, the second a built-in time-delay device, and the third the star points.

Soft starters

A soft starter is a type of reduced-voltage starter that reduces the starting torque for a.c. induction motors. It is in series with the supply to the motor and uses solid-state devices to control the current flow and the voltage to the motor. It can have a soft-stop function. This means the voltage is gradually reduced and also a reduction in the torque capacity of the motor.

Auto-transformer starters

These are used when star-delta starting is unsuitable. Thie could be either because the starting torque is not high enough or because there are three terminals in the motor terminal box – often found in the UK water industry.

This is a two-stage method of starting three-phase squirrel-cage induction motors. A reduced voltage is applied to the stator windings leading to a reduced current at starting. The reduced voltage is obtained from a three-phase auto-transformer with tapped windings designed to give 40 per cent, 60 per cent and 75 per cent of the line voltage.

Only one tapping is used for the initial starting, as the reduced voltage leads to reduced torque. Once the motor has reached sufficient speed, the changeover switch moves on to the run connections. This connects the motor directly to the three-phase supply.

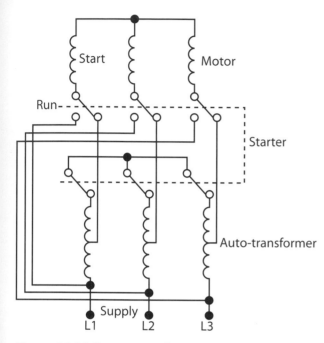

Figure 11.23 Connections for an auto-transformer starter

Rotor-resistance starters

This type of starter uses a slip-ring wound-rotor motor. These are primarily used where the motor starts against full load, because an external resistance is connected to the rotor windings through slip rings and brushes. This increases the starting torque.

When switched on, the external rotor resistance is at maximum. As the speed increases, the resistance is reduced until, at full speed, the external resistance is eliminated and the machine runs as a squirrel-cage induction motor.

The starter is provided with no-volts and protection. There is an interlock to prevent the machine being switched on with no rotor resistance connected.

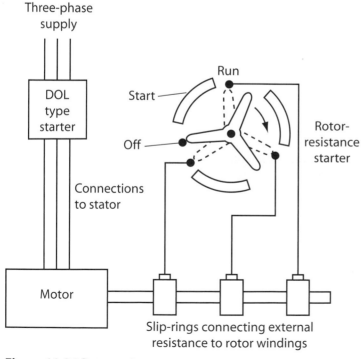

Figure 11.24 Rotor-resistance starter

Speed control of d.c. machines

One of the advantages of a d.c. machine is the ease with which the speed may be controlled. Some of the more common methods to achieve speed control on a d.c. machine are described below.

Armature resistance control

With this system, the voltage across the armature terminals is reduced by inserting a variable resistor into the armature circuit of the motor. However much of the input energy is dispersed in this variable resistor. This leads to a loss of efficiency in the motor and poor regulation of speed in shunt and compound motors.

It forms the basis of the Ward-Leonard system of speed control. This provides a variable voltage to the armature terminals by controlling the field winding of a separate generator. Although expensive, this method gives excellent speed control and, is used in passenger lifts.

Field control

This method controls the magnetic flux in the field winding by changing the field current, which controls the motor speed. As the field current is small, the power dispersed by the variable resistor is also small. In a series motor, a variable resistor is put in parallel with the series-field winding. In a shunt motor a variable resistor is put in series with the field-shunt winding.

This method is not suitable for compound machines. This is because any reduction in the flux of the shunt is offset in the motor by an increase in flux from the series field, because of the increase in armature current.

Pulse width modulation (PWM)

Although a variable resistor works well, it generates heat which wastes power. PWM control uses electronics to eliminate this problem by driving the motor with short pulses. These vary in duration to change the speed of the motor. The longer the pulse the faster the motor turns, and vice versa. The main disadvantages are added complexity and the possibility of generating radio frequency interference (RFI). This can be minimised by using short leads or additional filtering on the power supply leads.

Speed control of a.c. machines

Synchronous speed is directly proportional to the frequency of the supply and inversely proportional to the number of pole pairs. This means the speed of an induction motor changed by varying the frequency and/or the number of pole pairs. The speed can also be controlled by changing the applied voltage and armature resistance.

Variable speed drives (VSD) control the voltage and frequency supplied to the motor. This gives the user control over motor torque and reduces the current at starting. These drives control the speed of the motor during operation, allowing the user to change it at any time.

The name '**variable-frequency drives**' (VFD) is used to cover several methods. It can mean:

- a collection of mechanical and electro-mechanical components (the variable frequency inverter and motor combination) which, when connected together, will move a load.
- a variable-frequency inverter unit (the drive), with the motor as a separate component. Manufacturers of variable-frequency inverters normally refer to these as a variable-frequency drive (VFD).

VFDs have an input section – the converter – which contains diodes arranged in a bridge configuration, converting the a.c. supply to d.c. Next, the constant-voltage d.c. bus takes the d.c. voltage and filters and smoothes out the wave form. A smoother d.c. wave form means a cleaner output from the drive.

The d.c. bus then feeds the inverter, which inverts the d.c. back to a.c. using 'insulated gate bipolar transistors' (IGBT). This creates a variable a.c. voltage and frequency output.

Short answer questions

1 How is a d.c. motor reversed?
2 How are the windings connected in a series motor and what are the main characteristics of that type of motor?
3 How does the construction of a d.c generator differ from an a.c. generator?
4 What is synchronous speed and what is it dependent upon?
5 State 'Faraday's law'.
6 How is a single phase motor 'fooled' into thinking that a rotating magnetic field exists?
7 Describe briefly how a DOL starter works.
8 Describe the basic operation of an automatic star/delta starter.
9 Describe how the speed of a series and a shunt motor can be controlled by altering the field winding.
10 Describe how a VFD controls the speed of an a.c. motor.

Multiple-choice test

1. In Fleming's left hand rule what does the first finger indicate?
    a) *direction of magnetic field*
    b) *direction of current*
    c) *direction of conductor movement*
    d) *none of these*

2. What shape are the lines of force around a current carrying conductor?
    a) *oval*
    b) *square*
    c) *concentric*
    d) *straight*

3. What are the loops called that rotate in a DC machine?
    a) *commutator*
    b) *stator*
    c) *rotor*
    d) *armature*

4. Which of the following is not a DC motor?
    a) *series*
    b) *synchronous*
    c) *shunt*
    d) *compound*

5. At what point or points (in degrees) is the maximum output obtained from a generator?
    a) *45 degrees*
    b) *180 degrees and 360 degrees*
    c) *90 degrees and 270 degrees*
    d) *90 degrees*

6. Why is a universal motor so named?
    a) *it is used all over the world*
    b) *it can be used for many things*
    c) *it can be used on a.c. or d.c. supplies*
    d) *it is a shunt motor*

7. Why are armature formers laminated?
    a) *to reduce eddy current and power losses*
    b) *to make it lighter*
    c) *to reduce the strength of the magnetic field*
    d) *to increase the strength of the magnetic field*

8. What is the displacement of the three phases in a three phase supply?
   a) 180 degrees
   b) 90 degrees
   c) 120 degrees
   d) 45 degrees

9. What determines the synchronous speed of an a.c. motor?
   a) voltage and frequency
   b) pairs of poles and stator current
   c) frequency and pairs of poles
   d) strength of magnetic flux

10. In which configuration are the rotor windings connected in a wound rotor?
    a) delta
    b) series
    c) parallel
    d) star

11. How are the rotor windings connected to the external resistance bank?
    a) via a commutator
    b) slip rings
    c) armature
    d) connector block

12. In a split phase motor what is the phase displacement between the two windings?
    a) 60 degrees
    b) 45 degrees
    c) 30 degrees
    d) 90 degrees

13. At what per cent of full load speed is the start winding disconnected?
    a) 50 per cent
    b) 75 per cent
    c) 30 per cent
    d) 90 per cent

14. What disconnects the start winding?
    a) stop button
    b) tacho generator switch
    c) centrifugal switch
    d) remote sensor

15. How is a single phase motor reversed?
    a) reverse live and neutral in the 13 amp plug
    b) reverse start winding
    c) reverse start and run winding
    d) none of these

16. What is the synchronous speed of a motor with four poles and 50 Hz supply frequency?
    a) 12.5 rps
    b) 25 rpm
    c) 25 rps
    d) 200 rpm

17. If a motor has four per cent slip at a synchronous speed of 1500 rpm, what is its actual speed?
    a) 1440 rpm
    b) 750 rpm
    c) 1500 rpm
    d) none of these

18. If a motor terminal block has six terminals and three ends are connected together, how are the windings connected?
    a) delta
    b) star-delta
    c) parallel
    d) star

19. How are start buttons connected together?
    a) parallel
    b) series
    c) parallel–series
    d) delta

20. How are stop buttons connected together?
    a) parallel
    b) series
    c) parallel–series
    d) delta

21. Which contactors are energised first when the star-delta starter start button is pressed?
    a) main contactor only
    b) star and delta contactors
    c) main and delta contactors
    d) main and star contactors

22. What are the three tap windings settings on an auto transformer?

a) 20 per cent, 40 per cent, 80 per cent

b) 40 per cent, 60 per cent, 75 per cent

c) 10 per cent, 50 per cent, 100 per cent

d) 70 per cent, 0 per cent, 90 per cent

23. How much resistance is in a circuit when a rotor resistance starter is first energised?

a) all of it

b) none of it

c) half

d) one third

12 Electronics

Chapter 3 revised electron theory and the main electrical components used in simple electrical circuits. This chapter looks in more detail at these components and the main semiconductors that are used in electronics. It covers:

- Resistors
  - Fixed resistors
  - Variable resistors
  - Preferred values
  - Resistance markings
  - Thermistors
  - Light dependent resistors
- Capacitors
  - Basic principles
  - Capacitor types
  - Capacitor coding
  - Polarity
  - Capacitors in combination
  - Charging and discharging capacitors
- Inductors
- Semiconductors
  - Semiconductor basics
  - Diodes
  - Thyristors
  - Triacs and diacs
  - Photoconductive cells

- Bipolar transistors
  - Principles
  - Transistor operation
  - Current and voltage amplification
  - The transistor as a switch
  - Programmable logic control
  - Transistor codes and selection
  - Connecting and testing transistors
- Field effect transistors (FETs)
- Integrated circuits
- Rectification
  - Half-wave rectification
  - Full-wave rectification
  - Full-wave bridge rectifier
  - Smoothing

Resistors

There are two basic types of resistor: fixed and variable. The resistance of a fixed resistor cannot be changed mechanically but is affected by temperature or other external effects. Variable resistors will have some means of adjustment (usually a spindle or slider). Construction, specifications and features of both vary, depending on their use.

Fixed resistors

These are made from a material of known resistivity. Resistance is also dependent on the length of the material and reduces if the cross section increases (see Chapter 3). The dimensions of a resistor are chosen (csa and length) so that the resistance between the two points at which leads are attached matches the required value.

Fixed resistors

Many resistors still use wire, made from a metal with a relatively high resistivity (e.g. brass) and wound on to a rod of insulating material. It is usually covered with some form of enamel glazing or ceramic material to protect it from environmental and mechanical damage.

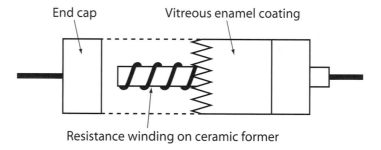

Figure 12.01 Typical wire wound resistor

Most wire-wound resistors can operate at fairly high temperatures without damage, so are very useful in applications where power may be dissipated. They are, however, expensive as they are difficult to mass produce. Other techniques have been developed for low-power applications.

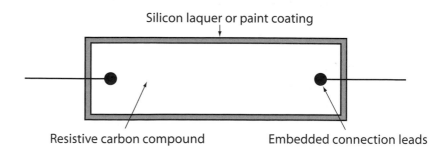

Figure 12.02 Film resistor

The resistive materials in common use now are carbon and metal oxides, coated as a thin film on to an insulating rod, usually ceramic or glass. Metal end caps, fitted with leads, are pushed over the ends of the coated rod and the whole assembly is coated with very tough varnish or similar material to protect the film from the atmosphere and during handling. They can be mass produced with great precision at very low cost.

Variable resistors

Variable resistors require a fixed resistor element and some sort of sliding contact.

Wire-wound variable resistors are made by winding resistance wire on to a flat strip of insulating material. This is then wrapped into a nearly complete circle. A sliding contact arm runs in contact with the turns of wire as they wrap over the edge of the wire strip. Straight versions are also possible.

Size, cost and other disadvantages make wire-wound variable resistors unattractive for some applications. Early alternatives had the resistive element (on which the wiper rubs) made from a carbon composition, as a track, shaped as a nearly completed circle and placed on an insulating support plate. Alternative materials for the track are carbon films or alloys of a metal oxide and a ceramic (cermet). Straight versions are possible.

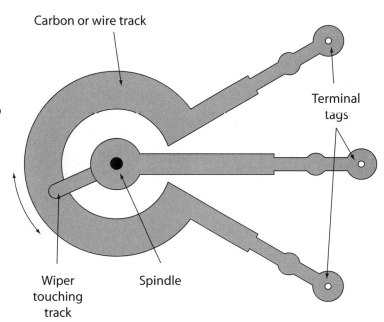

Figure 12.03 Layout of internal track of rotary variable resistor

Preferred values

Resistors can be made for any value but these would be impractical to manufacture and store. Manufacturers make a limited range of preferred resistance values and with different tolerances. Designers of electronic circuits use the value closest to the actual value needed. If the value is critical then they would use a higher tolerance component.

A resistor with a preferred value of 1000 Ω and a 10 per cent tolerance could have any value between 900 Ω and 1100 Ω. The next largest preferred value is 1200 Ω, which could be between 1080 Ω and 1320 Ω. Table 12.01 lists common preferred values at different tolerances.

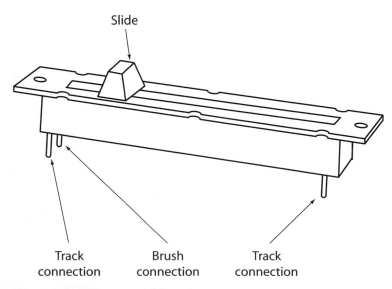

Figure 12.04 Linear variable resistor

E6 series (20% tolerance)	E12 series (10% tolerance)	E24 series (5% tolerance)
10	10	10
		11
	12	12
		13
15	15	15
		16
	18	18
		20
22	22	22
		24
	27	27
		30
33	33	33
		36
	39	39
		43
47	47	47
		51
	56	56
		62
68	68	68
		75
	82	82
		91

Table 12.01 Table of preferred values

Resistance markings

Where size allows, the resistor value can be marked directly on the component. Most are too small to be legible and standard codes are used to give nominal resistance value and tolerance. They are also commonly used to represent resistance values on circuit diagrams.

Number codes

Values are generally given in either Ω, kΩ or MΩ, using numbers from 1–999 as a prefix (e.g. 10 Ω, 567 kΩ etc.). The code system replaces these by letters:

- Ω = R
- kΩ = K
- MΩ = M.

These letters are inserted instead of the decimal point. So, for example, a resistor of 10 Ω would be shown as 10R, and 567 kΩ as 567 K. Letters are also used for tolerance values. These are added after resistor markings so that, for example, a resistor of value 2.7 MΩ with a tolerance of ±10 per cent would be shown as 2M7K.

Table 12.02 gives more examples of resistor values and Table 12.03 shows the letters commonly used for tolerance values.

> **Remember**
>
> Whole numbers could have a decimal point at the end (e.g. 10.0 or 567.0) but we normally miss them out when we write numbers down (e.g. 10 or 567).

0.1 Ω	is coded	R10
0.22 Ω	is coded	R22
1.0 Ω	is coded	1R0
3.3 Ω	is coded	3R3
15 Ω	is coded	15R
390 Ω	is coded	390R
1.8 Ω	is coded	1R8
47 Ω	is coded	47R
820 kΩ	is coded	820K
2.7 MΩ	is coded	2M7

Table 12.02 Examples of resistance value codes

F	=	± 1%
G	=	± 2%
J	=	± 5%
K	=	± 10%
M	=	± 20%
N	=	± 30%

Table 12.03 Codes for common tolerance values

Colour banding

A system of banding and colours is used when letters and numbers cannot be printed. These are located at one end of the component. Most resistors have four bands of colour, but high precision resistors often have five. The value of the colours is the same.

Figure 12.05 (a) Resistor colour code (b) Tolerance colour code (c) What this means (d) Examples of colour coding

(a) Resistor colour code

Band colour	Value
Black	0
Brown	1
Red	2
Orange	3
Yellow	4
Green	5
Blue	6
Violet	7
Grey	8
White	9
Gold	0.1
Silver	0.01

(b) Tolerance colour code

Band colour	±%
Brown	1
Red	2
Gold	5
Silver	10
None	20

(c) What this means

Band 1 First figure of value

Band 2 Second figure of value

Band 3 Number of zeros/multiplier

Band 4 Tolerance (±%) See below

Note that the bands are closer to one end than the other

> **Remember**
>
> Before you read a resistor, turn it so that the end with bands is on the left hand side. Now read the bands from left to right.

> **Remember**
>
> To help you remember the resistor colour, learn this rhyme:
>
> | | | |
> |---|---|---|
> | **Barbara** | Black | 0 |
> | **Brown** | Brown | 1 |
> | **Runs** | Red | 2 |
> | **Over** | Orange | 3 |
> | **Your** | Yellow | 4 |
> | **Garden** | Green | 5 |
> | **But** | Blue | 6 |
> | **Violet** | Violet | 7 |
> | **Grey** | Grey | 8 |
> | **Won't** | White | 9 |

(d) Examples of colour coding

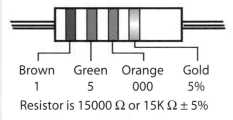

Brown	Green	Orange	Gold
1	5	000	5%

Resistor is 15000 Ω or 15K Ω ± 5%

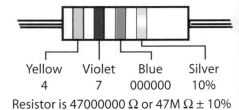

Yellow	Violet	Blue	Silver
4	7	000000	10%

Resistor is 47000000 Ω or 47M Ω ± 10%

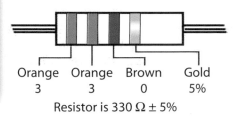

Orange	Orange	Brown	Gold
3	3	0	5%

Resistor is 330 Ω ± 5%

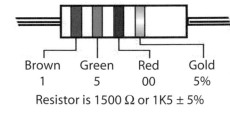

Brown	Green	Red	Gold
1	5	00	5%

Resistor is 1500 Ω or 1K5 ± 5%

Thermistors

A thermistor is a temperature sensitive resistor. They come in various shapes and sizes and are used for the measurement and control of temperature. They have a maximum useful temperature limit of about 300°C. Although being very sensitive because of their small construction, they are useful for measuring temperatures in places which are hard to access.

> **Did you know?**
>
> Thermistors are used for monitoring water temperature in a motor car.

Thermistors measure the temperature of motor windings and detect overloads. They can be wired into the control circuit so that the supply is automatically cut if the motor windings overheat. This prevents damage to the windings.

Thermistors can have a positive (PTC) temperature coefficient or negative (NTC). A PTC thermistor's resistance increases as the surrounding temperature increases. A NTC thermistor's resistance decreases.

The rated resistance of a thermistor is identified by a standard colour code or by a single body colour used only for thermistors. Typical values are shown in Table 12.04.

General appearance of a thermistor

Light dependent resistors

These resistors are sensitive to light. They have a clear window with a cadmium sulphide film under it. When light shines on the film its resistance varies. The resistance reduces as the light increases. They are commonly found in street lighting.

Light dependent resistors

Colour	Resistance
Red	3000 Ω
Orange	5000 Ω
Yellow	10,000 Ω
Green	30,000 Ω
Violet	100,000 Ω

Table 12.04 Colour coding for rated resistance of thermistors

Capacitors

A capacitor is a component that stores electric charge when a potential difference (p.d.) is applied across it.

Basic principles

A capacitor is two metallic surfaces (plates), separated by an air gap or an insulator commonly known as the dielectric. If inserted into a d.c. circuit, electrons will collect very rapidly on one plate and be removed from the other until the potential difference equals the supply voltage. The capacitor is then charged and no more current will flow. The charge will remain, unless the plates are reconnected to give a circuit through which the charge can flow around to the other plate to cancel the potential difference.

When a capacitor is connected to an a.c. supply, it is continuously storing then discharging charge as the supply moves through its positive and negative cycles. It takes time for the charge to build up in each direction and this causes the voltage to lag behind the current, but the energy that is being stored is given back to the circuit as it discharges. (See Chapter 3.)

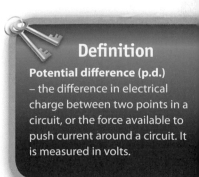

Definition

Potential difference (p.d.) – the difference in electrical charge between two points in a circuit, or the force available to push current around a circuit. It is measured in volts.

The plates are usually, though not necessarily, metal and the dielectric can be any insulating material. Air, glass, ceramic, mica, paper, oils and waxes are some of the many materials commonly used.

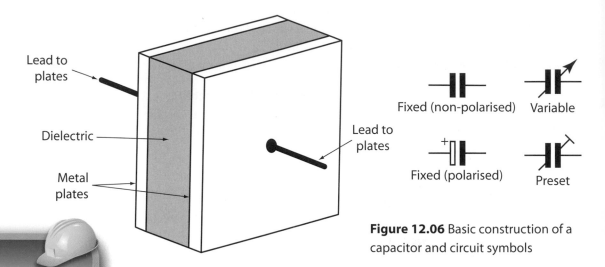

Figure 12.06 Basic construction of a capacitor and circuit symbols

The capacitance of any capacitor depends on:

- the area of the conducting surfaces (called plates) facing each other
- the separation of the plates, the closer they are the higher the charge that can be stored
- the dielectric or spacing material used.

An ideal capacitor, if isolated, would remain charged forever. In practice no dielectric insulating material is perfect and charge will slowly leak between the plates, gradually discharging the capacitor.

The dielectric will also break down if too high a voltage is applied. The working voltage of a capacitor is the maximum voltage that can be applied between the plates without causing breaking. As an example, the power factor correction capacitor found in fluorescent luminaries would be, typically, 8 µF at a working voltage of 400 V.

The capacitance value is the farad (symbol F), named after the English scientist Michael Faraday. However, for practical purposes the farad is much too large and in electrical installation work and electronics we use fractions of a farad, as follows:

- 1 microfarad = 1 µF = 1×10^{-6} F
- 1 nanofarad = 1 nF = 1×10^{-9} F
- 1 picofarad = 1 pF = 1×10^{-12} F.

One microfarad is one million times greater than one picofarad.

Capacitor types

There are two major types of capacitor, fixed and variable. Fixed capacitors are either electrolytic or non-electrolytic, and are more widely used. All capacitors possess some resistance and inductance due to their construction. This results in limitations, which often determine their applications.

Fixed electrolytic capacitors

These have a much higher capacitance, volume for volume, than any other type. This is because the plate separation is extremely small. This is caused by using a very thin dielectric. The dielectric is often created from mica or paper. They are then rolled up tight to give a very large plate area in a small volume.

An electrolytic capacitor main disadvantage is its polarisation and it must be connected the right way round in a circuit, otherwise a short circuit and destruction of the capacitor occurs. The polarity and values may be marked on the capacitor or a colour code can be used (see below). A newer type uses tantalum and tantalum oxide.

Non-electrolytic fixed capacitors

There are many types of non-electrolytic capacitor. However, only mica, ceramic and polyester are significant. Older types, using glass and vitreous enamel, are expected to disappear over the next few years. Even mica will be completely replaced by film types.

- **Mica capacitors** – Mica is a naturally occurring dielectric with very high resistance. It gives excellent stability and allows capacitors to be accurate within ±1 per cent of their marked value. They tend to be more expensive than plastic film capacitors, so are used where high stability is required, such as in tuning circuits for radio transmission.

Tantalum capacitor

Did you know?

Mica is a common mineral in rocks, including granite, some sandstones and mudstones.

Mica capacitor

Ceramic capacitor

- **Ceramic capacitors** – These are small rectangular pieces of ceramic with metal electrodes on opposite surfaces. They are mainly used for high frequency circuits subject to wide temperature variations. They have high stability and low loss.
- **Plastic film capacitors** – These include polyester, polypropylene, polycarbonate and polystyrene types. They are widely used in the electronics industry due to reliability and low cost but are not suitable for high frequency circuits. They can be as shown or in a tubular shape.

Polyester capacitor

Variable capacitors

Variable capacitors generally have air or a vacuum as the dielectric, although ceramics are sometimes used. The two main sub-groups are tuning and trimmer capacitors.

- **Tuning capacitors** – These are used in radio tuning circuits. They have two sets of parallel metal plates. One plate is isolated by ceramic supports; the other is fixed to a shaft, which allows it to be rotated in or out of the first. The plates interlock but do not touch.

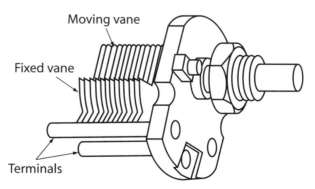

Figure 12.07 A typical variable capacitor of the turning type

- **Trimmer capacitors** – These are constructed of flat metal leaves. The leaves are separated by a plastic film and are screwed towards each other. They have less variation than tuning capacitors, so are used where small changes in value are needed.

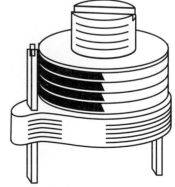

Figure 12.08 A typical capacitor used as a trimmer

Capacitor coding

Capacitors are identified by: capacitance, working voltage, type of construction and polarity (if any). Identification is not always easy because of the wide variation in shapes and sizes.

There is a colour code for marking capacitors, similar to resistors, but in most cases now the capacitance is printed on the body of the capacitor. However, the colour-coding method is still found. It is based on the standard four-band resistor colour coding. Bands are read from top to bottom.

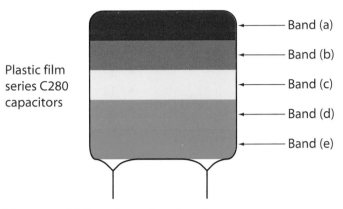

Plastic film series C280 capacitors

Figure 12.09 Capacitor colour banding

- The first three bands indicate the value in normal resistor fashion, with the value in picofarads. To convert this into nanofarads divide by 1000, or by 1,000,000 to obtain microfarads.
- The first band gives the first number of the component value.
- The second band gives the second number.
- The third band gives the number of zeros to be added after the first two numbers.
- The fourth band indicates the tolerance (different from resistors).
- The fifth band shows the maximum working voltage of the component in volts.

Colour	1st band	2nd band	3rd band	Tolerance	Max voltage
Black		0	None	20%	
Brown	1	1	1		100 V
Red	2	2	2		250 V
Orange	3	3	3		
Yellow	4	4	4		400 V
Green	5	5	5	5%	
Blue	6	6	6		630 V
Violet	7	7	7		
Grey	8	8	8		
White	9	9	9	10%	

Table 12.05 Standard capacitor colour coding

When the value of a capacitor is simply written on its body, it usually includes the tolerance and/or its maximum operating voltage. The tolerance is generally wider for capacitors than resistors, and may be omitted. Most modern resistors have tolerances of 5 per cent or better, but capacitors have a tolerance rating of generally 10 or 20 per cent.

When the value includes a decimal point, the prefix for the multiplication factor is used in place of the decimal point, as for resistors. Therefore:

- 3.5 pF capacitor would be abbreviated to 3p5
- 12 pF capacitor would be abbreviated to 12p
- 300 pF capacitor would be abbreviated to 300p or n30
- 4500 pF capacitor would be abbreviated to 4n5

Remember

1000 pF = 1 nF = 0.001 μF.

Polarity

If some capacitors are operated with the wrong polarity they will be destroyed, especially electrolytic capacitors. Polarity is indicated by + or −. Electrolytic capacitors contained within metal cans have the can casing as the negative connection. A slight indentation in the case will indicate the positive end, when there are no markings. Tantalum capacitors have a spot on one side. When this spot is facing you the right-hand lead will be the positive connection.

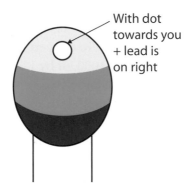

With dot towards you + lead is on right

Figure 12.10 Tantalum capacitor showing polarity marking

Capacitors in combination

Capacitors, like resistors, may be joined together in series or parallel connections. Total capacitance can be found by applying similar formulae as for resistors (see Chapter 3). However, the formulae is reversed from that used for resistors.

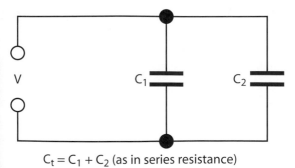

$C_t = C_1 + C_2$ (as in series resistance)

Figure 12.11 Capacitors connected in parallel

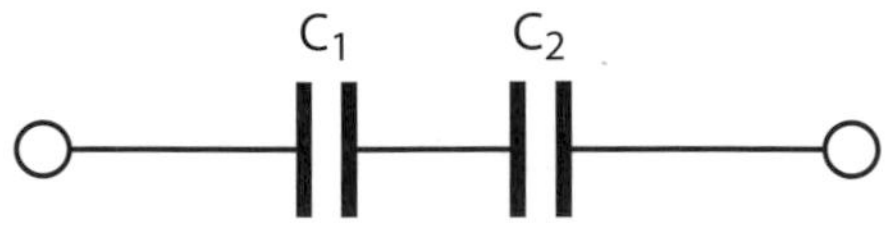

C_1 C_2

$\dfrac{1}{C_t} = \dfrac{1}{C_1} + \dfrac{1}{C_2}$ (as in parallel resistance)

or

$C_t = \dfrac{C_1 \times C_2}{C_1 + C_2}$ (when there are two capacitors in series)

Figure 12.12 Capacitors connected in series

Charging and discharging capacitors

When a capacitor is connected to a battery, the capacitor plates are charged with positive and negative charges. These charges build up fast but not instantaneously. They follow a set pattern as shown in Figure 12.13.

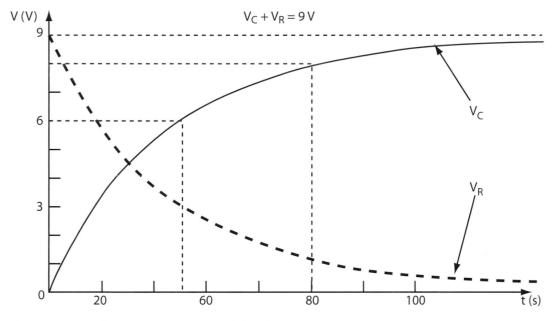

Figure 12.13 Voltage against time graph for charging the capacitor

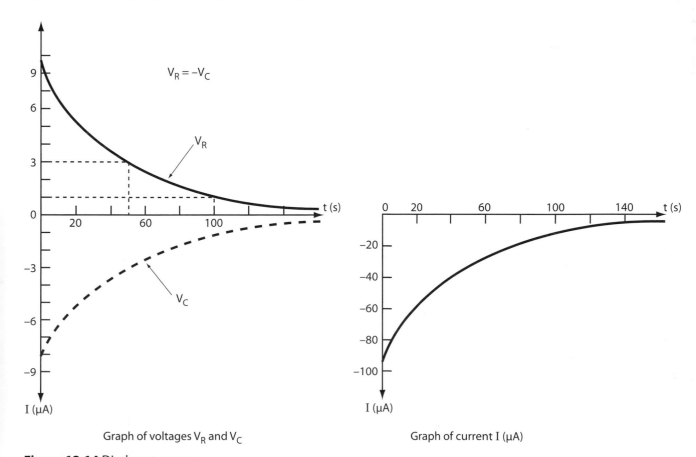

Graph of voltages V_R and V_C

Graph of current I (µA)

Figure 12.14 Discharge curves

The timescale is divided into sections called time constants. In the first time period the voltage reaches approximately two-thirds of the maximum volts. In the second to about two-thirds of what is left of the maximum. This continues until the capacitor is effectively fully charged. This usually takes five time constants. The same occurs when the capacitor is discharging through a series resistor.

Inductors

Any coil of wire can act as an inductor and nearly every component will have some inductance. The theory of inductors, and their use in simple electrical circuits, was covered in Chapter 3. Although they can be bought as electronic components, they come in many shapes and sizes and are not considered further here, except briefly as part of rectification.

Semiconductors

In Chapter 3 we defined conductors and insulators. A semiconductor is a material with electrical properties somewhere between these. It is neither a good conductor nor a good insulator. This section will cover the main semiconductor components, less transistors and integrated circuits, which are considered in separate sections that follow.

Semiconductor basics

Definition

Valence electrons – the electrons in an atom's outermost orbit.

In semiconducting materials, such as silicon or germanium, the atoms are arranged in a lattice structure. The atoms are at regular distances from each other. Each atom is linked or bonded to the four atoms surrounding it. Each atom then has four **valence electrons**.

However, with atoms of pure silicon or germanium no conduction is possible because there are no free electrons. To allow conduction to take place an impurity is added to the material via a process known as **doping**. We can add two types:

- **pentavalent** – which contains five valence electrons (e.g. arsenic)
- **trivalent** – which contains three valence electrons (e.g. aluminium).

Pentavalent (five) material introduces extra electrons to the semiconductor, providing a surplus of negative charge. Trivalent (three) material 'removes' electrons (also known as creating a 'hole'), providing a surplus of positive charge.

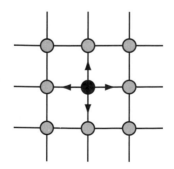

Figure 12.15 Lattice structure of semiconducting material

When there is an extra electron the material is called 'n-type'. When we have 'removed' an electron the material is called 'p-type'. It is the use of these two materials combined that produces components such as diodes and transistors.

Diodes

A semiconductor diode is created when a p-type material and n-type material are combined to form a **p–n junction**. The two materials form a barrier called the **depletion** layer. In this barrier, the coming together of unlike charges causes a small internal p.d.

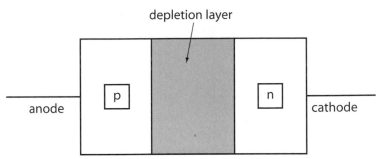

Figure 12.16 p-n junction

We call the p-junction end the anode and the n-junction end the cathode. If we now connect a battery across the ends of the two materials, with the positive connected to the anode and the negative to the cathode, and if the battery voltage is big enough, it will overcome the effect of the internal p.d. and a current will flow. This is known as **forward biased**.

Reversing the battery connections, so that the anode is now negative, causes the junction to become highly resistant and no current can flow. This is known as **reverse biased**.

When the junction is forward biased, it only takes a small voltage (0.7 V for silicon) to overcome the internal barrier p.d. When reversed biased, it takes a large voltage (1200 V for silicon) to overcome the barrier. Therefore, provided the voltage is not too high, a diode allows current to flow through it in one direction only. If this breakdown voltage is exceeded, current could now flow in either direction but it is likely to destroy the component.

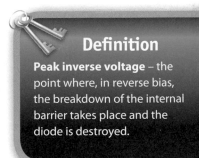

Definition

Peak inverse voltage – the point where, in reverse bias, the breakdown of the internal barrier takes place and the diode is destroyed.

We normally use the symbol in Figure 12.17 to represent a diode. In this symbol, the direction of the arrow represents the direction of conventional current flow (which is opposite to the direction that the electrons flow).

Diodes

Figure 12.17 Diode symbol

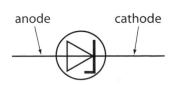

Figure 12.18 Zener diode symbol

Zener diode

If we exceed the breakdown voltage on a conventional diode, the internal barrier of the diode would break down and probably destroy the device.

Zener diodes are p–n junction devices specifically designed to operate in the reverse breakdown region without destruction. This is achieved by carefully controlling the doping level during manufacture. The breakdown voltage can be controlled quite accurately giving tolerances to within 0.05 per cent, although the most widely used tolerances are 5 per cent and 10 per cent.

When reverse biased in parallel with a variable voltage source, a zener diode acts as a short circuit when the voltage reaches the diode's reverse breakdown voltage. It therefore limits the voltage to a known value. A zener diode used in this way is known as a shunt voltage regulator ('shunt' meaning connected in parallel and 'voltage regulator' being a class of circuit that produces a fixed voltage).

They are readily available with power ratings from a few hundred milliwatts to tens of watts. Low power types are usually in glass or plastic packages, with heat transfer away from the junction occurring via the connecting wires. High power types, like power rectifiers, are packaged in metal cases designed to fit to heat sinks, so that heat can be dissipated by conduction, convection and radiation.

Light emitting diodes (LEDs)

The light emitting diode is a p–n junction made from a semiconducting material (e.g. gallium arsenide) that emits light when a current of about 10 mA flows through the junction. When the diode is reverse biased no light is emitted. If the voltage exceeds 5 volts then the diode may be damaged. If the voltage is likely to exceed 2 volts then a series connected resistor may be required for protection.

LEDs can be used for security alarms and as remote control signals for many applications by projecting a beam of infrared light (close to but not in the visible light spectrum, so invisible to the naked eye). In an alarm system, the beam is permanently directed at the receiver and the alarm is triggered if something breaks the beam. In a remote control, the beam is only present as signals are transmitted to the receiver.

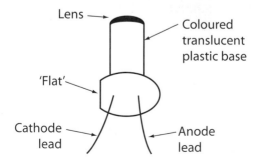
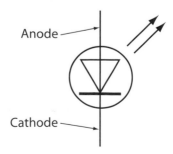

Figure 12.19 Light emitting diode and symbol

Thyristors

The thyristor is similar to a diode, but has four layers of alternating n- or p-type material. The main terminals (anode and cathode) are across the full four layers. The control terminal (the gate) is attached to one of the middle layers. It is sometimes referred to as a 'silicon controlled rectifier' (SCR).

Thyristor

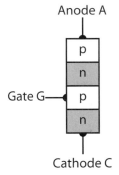

Figure 12.20 Construction of a thyristor

Figure 12.21 Thyristor symbol

In its normal or 'forward biased' state, the thyristor is an open circuit between anode and cathode, which prevents any current flow. This is known as the 'forward blocking' state. However, a small signal at the gate allows a very high current to flow until either the supply voltage is turned off or reversed, or if a minimum 'holding' current is no longer maintained between the anode and cathode.

It acts like a semiconductor version of a mechanical switch, either 'on' or 'off', and can handle megawatts of power. Therefore it is used in high voltage d.c. systems (HVDC). It can also be used on a.c. systems by controlling the time of the gate pulse in the cycle.

Triacs and diacs

These both have common features with thyristors.

Triacs

The triac is a three terminal semiconductor for controlling current in either direction. It is effectively two thyristors connected in parallel but facing opposite directions and with only one gate terminal. This is indicated by the schematic symbol for a triac, shown in Figure 12.22. We refer to this as an inverse parallel connection.

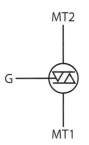

Figure 12.22 Triac symbol

It generally functions in the same way as a thyristor, but operating in both a forward and reverse direction. It is, therefore, sometimes called a bidirectional thyristor. As with the thyristor, a minimum holding current must be maintained to keep a triac conducting. One disadvantage is that triacs can require a fairly high current pulse to activate.

Did you know?

Triacs were originally developed for, and used extensively in, the consumer market. They are used in many low power control applications, such as food mixers, electric drills, lamp dimmers, etc.

Diacs

The diac is used in triac triggering circuits as it produces a pulse-style waveform. It does this without any sophisticated additional circuitry due to its electrical characteristics. It also provides protection against spurious triggering from electrical noise (voltage spikes).

Figure 12.23
Diac symbol

The device operates like two breakdown (Zener) diodes connected in series, back to back. It acts as an open switch until the applied voltage reaches about 32–35 volts, when it will conduct.

Lamp dimmer circuit

Figure 12.24 shows a typical GLS lamp dimmer circuit using a diac and triac.

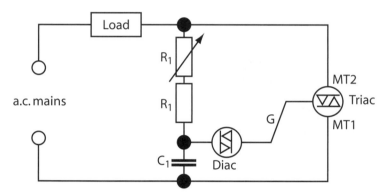

Figure 12.24 GLS lamp dimmer circuit

The GLS lamp has a tungsten filament and is wired in series with the triac. The variable resistor is part of a trigger network which provides a variable voltage into the gate circuit. This contains a diac connected in series. The time taken for the capacitor to reach its charge level to pass current into the diac circuit, increases with the value of the resistor. With reduced resistance, the triac switches on faster in each half cycle. Adjusting this allows the light output of the lamp to be controlled from zero to full brightness.

Photoconductive cells

Photoconductive cells (photocells) use semiconductors in which resistance decreases as the intensity of light increases. The effect is caused by the energy of the light freeing electrons from donor atoms in the semiconductor. This makes it more conductive.

They can change visible light, infrared and ultraviolet radiation into electrical signals and are useful in burglar and fire alarms, as well as in counting and automatic control systems. A main use is for automatic control of outside lights along streets, roads and motorways. Smaller versions are used within homes and businesses.

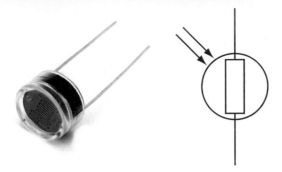

Figure 12.25 Photocell and its circuit symbol

Bipolar transistors

The name 'transistor' is usually taken to mean a bipolar transistor. This has two p–n junctions. It is capable of amplifying current and, with an added load resistor, voltage and power gain can be achieved.

Transistor

Did you know?

The term **transistor** is derived from the words 'transfer-resistor'. This is because, in a transistor, approximately the same current is transferred from a low to a high resistance region. The term **bipolar** means the flow of both electrons and holes are involved in the action of this type of transistor.

Principles

A bipolar transistor has three separate regions or areas of doped semiconductor material. It is possible to manufacture two basic types:

- If a central n-type region is sandwiched between two p-type outer regions, a **pnp transistor** is created.

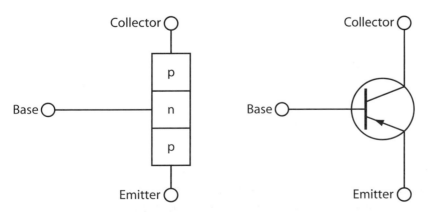

Figure 12.26 pnp transistor and its circuit symbol

- If the regions are reversed, an npn transistor is created.

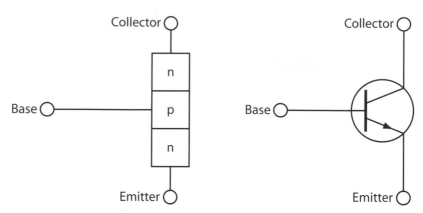

Figure 12.27 npn transistor and its circuit symbol

The outer regions are always called emitter and collector respectively; the central area is called the base. The arrow in the circuit symbol for the pnp device points towards the base. In the npn device it points away from it. This indicates the direction of conventional current in the device. (The direction of flow for 'holes'; electron flow is in the other direction.)

When constructed, the collector region is physically the largest, since it normally has to dissipate the greater power during operation. The base region is very thin, typically only a fraction of a micron (a micron is one millionth of a metre).

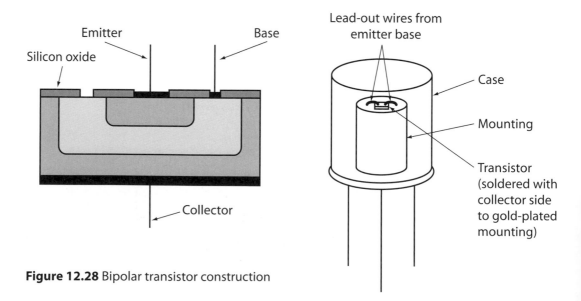

Figure 12.28 Bipolar transistor construction

Hard-wire connections are made internally. Wires are then brought out through the casing to provide an external means of connection to each region. Either silicon or germanium semiconductor materials may be used, but silicon is preferred for its temperature stability.

Transistor operation

Transistors require three conditions to operate:

- A thin base.
- Very few majority carriers in the box.
- The base–emitter junction must be forward biased and the base–collector junction must be reverse biased.

Figure 12.29 shows an npn transistor in a circuit but the principles are the same for pnp. Electrons from the emitter enter the base and diffuse through it. Due to the design base most electrons reach the base–collector junction and are swept into the collector by the strong positive potential. A few electrons stay in the base long enough to meet the holes that are present. Recombination then takes place.

'Holes' enter the base from the base bias battery (i.e. electrons are removed leaving holes) to maintain this forward bias on the base–emitter junction. This base current maintains the base–emitter forward bias and controls the size of the emitter current. The greater the forward bias on the base–emitter junction, the greater the number of emitter current carriers entering the base.

The collector current is always a fixed proportion of the emitter current. This is fixed by the thickness of the base and the amount of doping.

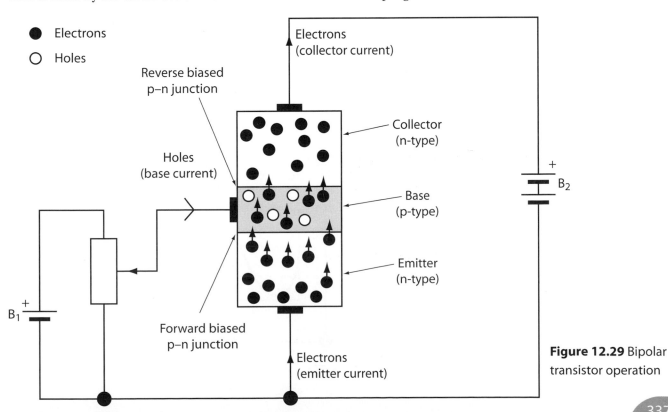

Figure 12.29 Bipolar transistor operation

Current and voltage amplification

This is simplest to describe with an example. In Figure 12.30 a base current of 0.5 mA is causing a collector current of 50 mA.

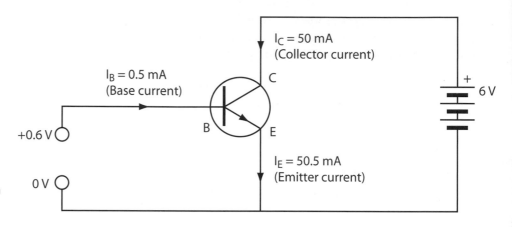

Figure 12.30 Current flow in a transistor

This relationship between I_B and I_C is termed the 'static value of the short-circuit forward current transfer', normally called the gain of the transistor. It is simply a measure of the current amplification achieved. The symbol used is h_{FE}, the ratio between the continuous output current (collector current) and the continuous input current (base current). Therefore, when I_B is 0.5 mA and I_C is 50 mA the ratio is:

$$h_{FE} = \frac{I_C}{I_B} = \frac{50 \text{ mA}}{0.5 \text{ mA}} = \text{approximately 100}$$

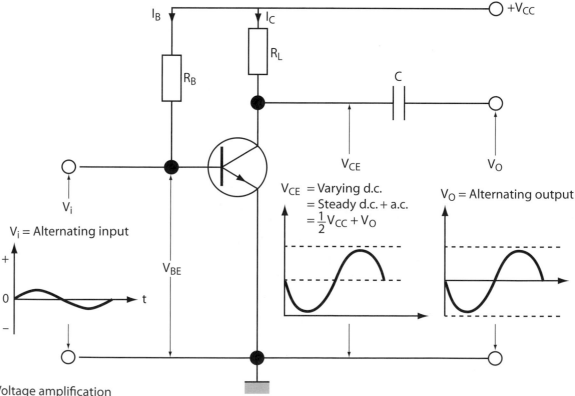

Figure 12.31 Voltage amplification

To produce a voltage output from the collector, a load resistor (R_B) is added to the collector circuit as indicated in the circuit diagram in Figure 12.31. This shows the simplest circuit for a voltage amplifier.

Initially consider that there is no input across V_i, which is called the quiescent (quiet) state. For transistor action the base–emitter junction V_{BE} must be forward biased (and has to remain so when V_i goes positive and negative due to the a.c. signal input).

By introducing resistor R_B between collector and base, a small current I_B will flow from V_{CC} through R_B into the base and down to 0 V via the emitter, thus keeping the transistor running (ticking over).

Component resistor values R_B and R_L are chosen so that the steady base current I_B makes the quiescent collector–emitter voltage V_{CE} about half the power supply voltage V_{CC}. This allows V_O to replicate the input signal V at an amplified voltage with a 180 degrees phase shift. When an a.c. signal is applied to the input V_i and goes positive it increases V_{BE} slightly to around 0.61 V. When V_i swings negative, V_{BE} drops slightly to 0.59 V. As a result a small alternating current is superimposed on the quiescent base current I_B, which in effect is a varying d.c. current.

The collector–emitter voltage (V_{CE}) is a varying d.c. voltage, in other words an alternating voltage superimposed on a normally steady d.c. voltage. The capacitor C is there to block the d.c. voltage but allow the alternating voltage to pass on to the next stage. So, in summary, a bipolar transistor will act as a voltage amplifier if:

- it has a suitable collector load R_L
- it is biased so that the quiescent value V_{CE} is around half the value of V_{CC}, which is known as the class A condition
- the transistor and load together bring about voltage amplification
- the output is 180 degrees out of phase with the input signal.

The emitter is common to the input, output and power supply circuits and is usually taken as the reference point for all voltages, i.e. 0 V. It is called 'common', 'ground', or 'earth' if connected to earth.

The transistor as a switch

If connected as in Figure 12.32, we can operate it as a switch. Transistors have many advantages, in both discrete and integrated circuit (IC) form. They are small, cheap, reliable, have no moving parts and can switch millions of times per second. The transistor has infinite resistance when 'off', no resistance when 'on' and can change from one state to another instanly but use no power.

Figure 12.32 shows the basic circuit for an npn common emitter with a load resistor R_L connected in series with the supply (V_{CC}) and the collector. R_B prevents excessive base currents, which could seriously damage the transistor when forward biased. With no input across V_i, the transistor is basically turned off. This means that there will be no current (I_C) through R_L. Therefore there will be no volt-drop across R_L, so the $+V_{CC}$ voltage (6 V) will appear across the output V_{CE}.

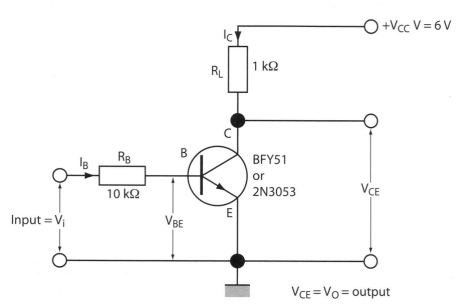

Figure 12.32 Circuit diagram for transistor used as a switch

If we now connect a supply of between 2–6 V across V_i input, the transistor will switch on, current will flow through the collector load resistor R_L and down to common, making the output V_{CE} around 0 V. From this we can state that:

- when the input $V_i = 0$ V, the output $V_{CE} = 6$ V
- when the input $V_i = 2$ V–6 V, the output $V_{CE} = 0$ V.

The transistor is either High/On (6 V) or Low/Off (0 V). This circuit can be used in alarms and switch relays for all types of processes. It is also the basic stage for programmable logic control (plc).

Programmable logic control

This uses transistors as switches to give either a one (On) or zero (Off) to represent the output from possible inputs. These are arranged in logic gate circuits. Figure 12.33 shows these with their inputs/outputs, 'truth table' and symbols identified.

Circuit NOT Gate

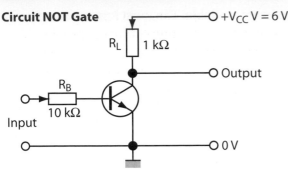

Symbol

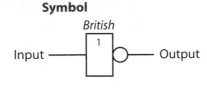

British

American

Truth table

NOT gate

Input	Output
0	1
1	0

Circuit NOR Gate

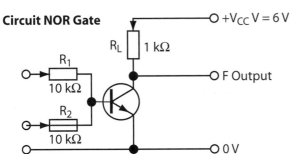

Symbol

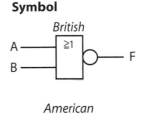

British

American

Truth table

NOR gate
(2-input)

Input		Output
A	B	
0	0	1
0	1	0
1	0	0
1	1	0

Circuit OR Gate

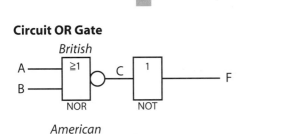

British

NOR   NOT

American

NOR   NOT

Symbol

British

American

Truth table

OR gate
(2-input)

Input		Output
A	B	
0	0	0
0	1	1
1	0	1
1	1	1

Figure 12.33 Basic logic gate circuits

Transistor codes and selection

There are three main series of transistor codes used in the UK:

- **Codes beginning with B (or A)** – The first letter (B) indicates silicon; A indicates germanium. The second letter indicates the type: C means low power audio frequency, D means high power audio frequency, F means low power high frequency. The rest of the code identifies the particular transistor and is determined by the manufacturer. Examples of this type include BC108, BC478.
- **Codes beginning with TIP** – TIP stands for Texas Instruments power transistor. The letter at the end identifies different voltage ratings. An example is TIP31A.
- **Codes beginning with 2N** – 2N identifies the part as a transistor and the rest of the code identifies the particular transistor. An example of this type is 2N3053.

There are a wide range of transistors available. The most important properties are the maximum collector current I_C and the current gain h_{FE}. The key abbreviations used are as follows:

- I_C **max** – the maximum collector current
- V_{CE} **max** – the maximum voltage across the collector–emitter junction
- h_{FE} – the d.c. current gain (100@20 mA means a gain of 100 at 20 mA)
- P_{tot} **max** – the maximum power that can be developed in the transistor.

Tables 12.06 and 12.07 show some examples.

Code	Case style	I_C max	V_{CE} max	h_{FE} min	V_{CE} max	Typical use
BC108	TO18	100 mA	20 V	110	300 mW	Low power
TIP31C	TO220	3 A	100 V	10	40 W	High power

Table 12.06 Technical data for npn transistors

Code	Case style	I_C max	V_{CE} max	h_{FE} min	V_{CE} max	Typical use
BC108	TO18	200 mA	25 V	120	600 mW	Low power
TIP32A	TO220	3 A	60 V	25	40 W	High power

Table 12.07 Technical data for pnp transistors

Connecting and testing transistors

The three leads must be connected the correct way round. A wrongly connected transistor may be damaged when power is applied.

Figure 12.34 shows the leads for some of the most common case styles. Note that this diagram shows the view from below the transistor with the leads facing towards you.

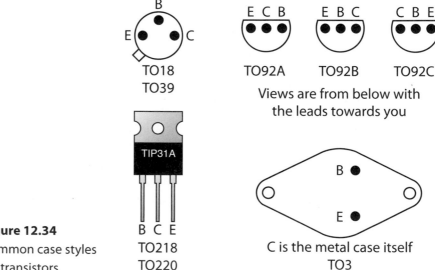

TO18
TO39

TO92A   TO92B   TO92C

Views are from below with the leads towards you

TIP31A

B C E
TO218
TO220

C is the metal case itself
TO3

Figure 12.34
Common case styles for transistors

Special meters for testing transistors are available and many testing instruments have this facility. These have three terminals. The following results should be obtained from a transistor, assuming that the red lead of an ohmmeter is positive.

A good npn transistor will give the following readings:

- Red to base and black to collector or emitter will give a low resistance reading.
- If the connections are reversed it will result in a high resistance reading.
- Connections of any polarity between the collector and emitter will also give a high reading.

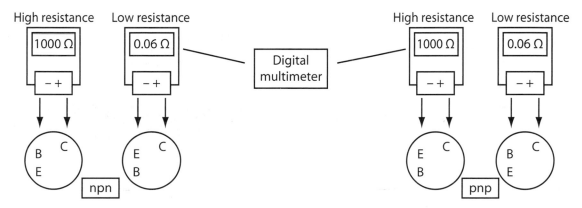

Figure 12.35 Testing transistors with a digital multimeter

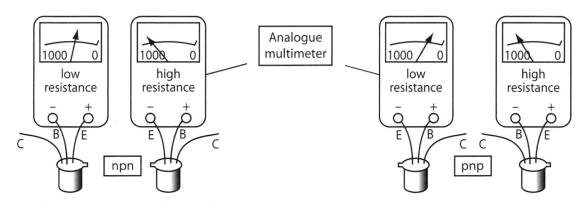

Figure 12.36 Testing transistors with an analogue multimeter

A good pnp transistor will give the following readings:

- Black to base and red to collector or emitter will give a low resistance reading.
- If the connections are reversed a high resistance reading will be observed.
- Connections of either polarity between the collector and emitter will give a high resistance reading.

Field effect transistors (FETs)

There are two types of field effect transistor: the junction gate field effect transistor, usually abbreviated to JUGFET, JFET or FET; and the metal oxide semiconductor field effect transistor known as the MOSFET. They differ significantly from the bipolar transistor in their characteristics, operation and construction.

The main advantages of an FET are:

- Its operation depends on the flow of majority current carriers only. So it is, often described as a unipolar transistor.
- It is simpler to fabricate and occupies less space in integrated form.
- Input resistance is extremely high, typically above 10 MΩ especially for MOSFET devices. This is why voltage measuring devices use FET in their input circuitry, as the voltage being measured is not altered by the instrument's connection.
- Electrical noise is generated by random minute voltages. These are caused by the movement of current carriers through the transistor structure. Since the FET does not employ minority carriers, it produces much lower noise levels than a bipolar transistor.
- It is more stable during changes of temperature as it is unipolar.

The main disadvantages of an FET over its bipolar counterpart are:

- Its very high input impedance makes it sensitive to internal damage from static electricity.
- Its voltage gain for a given bandwidth is lower, which can be a disadvantage at low frequencies (below 10 MHz).
- The FET cannot switch from its fully-on to its fully-off condition as fast as a bipolar transistor.

Figure 12.37 illustrates the basic construction of the FET, which consists of a channel of n-type semiconductor material with two connections, source (S) and drain (D). A third connection is made at the gate (G), which is made of p-type material to control the n-channel current.

The drain connection is made positive and electrons are attracted towards the D terminal. If the gate is made negative there will be reverse bias between G and S, which will limit the number of electrons passing from S to D.

The gate and source are connected to a variable voltage supply, such as a potentiometer, and increasing or lowering the voltage makes G more or less negative, which in turn reduces or increases the drain current.

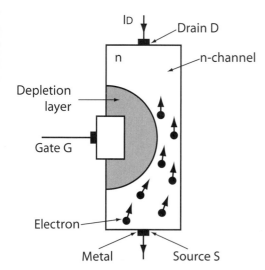

Figure 12.37 Basic construction of field effect transistor (FET)

Figure 12.38 Field effect transistor (FET) symbol

Integrated circuits

FETs first appeared as separate (or discrete) transistors, but now the field effect concept is employed in the fabrication of large-scale integration arrays, such as semiconductor memories, microprocessors, calculators and digital watches. Integrated circuits are complete electronic circuits housed within a plastic case (known as the black box). The chip contains all the components required, which may include diodes, resistors, capacitors, transistors, etc.

There are several categories. The basic layout is shown in Figure 12.39, which is an operational amplifier (dual in-line IC).

Definition

Dual in-line ICs – type of IC with the pins lined up down each side.

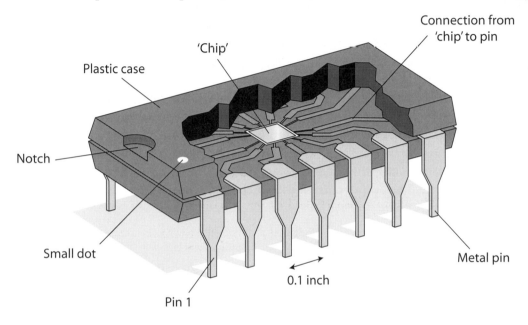

Connection from 'chip' to pin

'Chip'

Plastic case

Notch

Small dot

Metal pin

Pin 1

0.1 inch

Figure 12.39 Operational amplifier integrated circuit

The plastic case has a notch at one end when looking at this case with the notch at the top, Pin 1 is always the first one on the left-hand side. This is sometimes noted with a small dot. The other pin numbers follow down the left-hand side, 2, 3 and 4 then back up the right-hand side from the bottom right to the top, 5, 6, 7 and 8. Some chips have up to 32 pins or more.

Rectification

Rectification is the conversion of an a.c. supply to a d.c. supply. There are many applications (e.g. electronic circuits and equipment) that require a d.c. supply.

Half-wave rectification

A diode only allows current to flow in one direction. If used in an a.c. circuit, this means that only the positive half cycles are allowed through resulting in a waveform of half sine wave pulses. This is unsuitable for most applications but can be used in situations such as battery charging. A transformer is also commonly used at the supply side to ensure that the output voltage is to the required level.

Full-wave rectification

Using two diodes it is possible to give a more even supply. This is called a **biphase** circuit. The anodes of the diodes are connected to opposite ends of the secondary winding of a centre-tapped transformer. As the anode voltages will be 180 degrees out of phase with each other, one diode will effectively rectify the positive half cycle and one will rectify the negative half cycle. The output current will still be a series of pulses but much closer together.

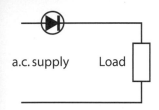

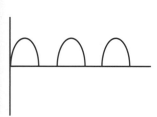

Figure 12.40 Half-wave rectification

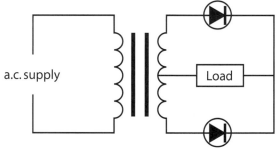

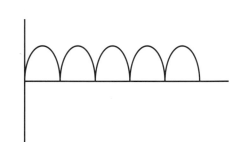

Figure 12.41 Full-wave rectification

Full-wave bridge rectifier

In this system four diodes are connected in such a way that at any instant two of the four will be conducting. Figure 12.42 shows the layout and route through the network for each half cycle.

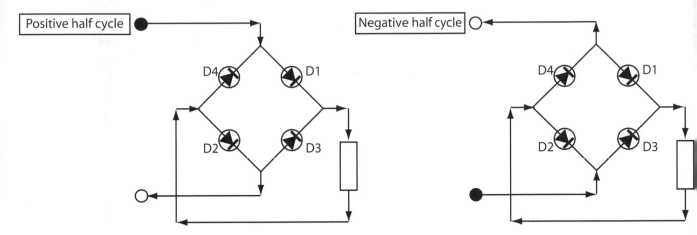

Figure 12.42 Full-wave bridge rectifier

Smoothing

The output from the above circuits is constantly changing. This is useless for electronic circuits where a smooth, **ripple-free** supply is required. There are three ways to achieve this: capacitor smoothing, choke smoothing and filter circuits.

Capacitor smoothing

A capacitor connected in parallel across the load will charge up when the rectifier allows a flow of current and discharge when the rectifier voltage is less than the capacitor. The most effective smoothing comes under no-load conditions. The heavier the load current, the worse the ripple. The capacitor is only useful as a smoothing device for small output currents.

Choke smoothing

If we connect an inductor in series with the load, then the changing current through the inductor will induce an e.m.f. in opposition to the current that produced it, which will try to maintain a steady current. Unlike the capacitor, the heavier the ripple (rate of change of current) the more the ripple will be smoothed. Therefore, the choke is more useful in heavy current circuits.

Filter circuits

These are a combination of the two previous methods. The most effective is the capacitor input filter.

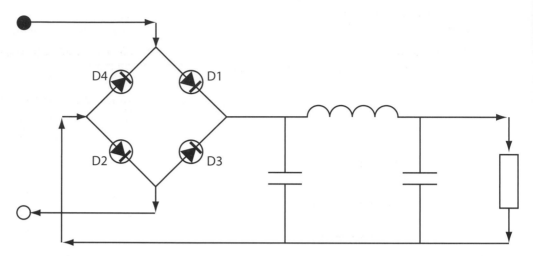

Figure 12.43 Capacitor input filter

The waveform is shown in Figure 12.44, where the dotted line indicates the waveform before smoothing.

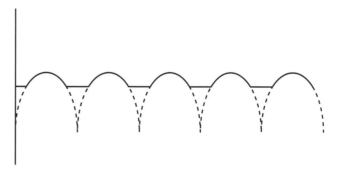

Figure 12.44 Capacitor input filter waveform

Three-phase rectifier circuits

A much smoother waveform is possible from three-phase supplies using six diodes connected as a three-phase bridge circuit. These types of rectifier are used to provide high-powered d.c. supplies.

Short answer questions

1. Sketch the BS circuit symbol for each of the following electronic components:
   a. NPN bi-polar transistor
   b. LED
   c. Zener diode
2. What are the two types of resistor and what are the differences between them.
3. What would the following colour combinations on a resistor translate as:
   a. green-black-black-gold
   b. yellow-orange-orange-silver
   c. blue-white-blue-red
4. What is the purpose of the cadmium sulphide film in a light resistor?
5. What factors does the capacitance of a capacitor rely on?
6. How are materials made suitable for conduction? Describe the methods and their results.
7. What is a zener diode designed to do?
8. What conditions must be met for a transistor to operate?
9. Describe the three main series of transistor codes used in the UK.
10. Describe the three methods used to produce a smooth supply.

Multiple choice questions

1. The main source of symbols for use in electrical drawings is:
   a. BS 7671
   b. Electricity at Work Regulations
   c. Electricity Supply Regulations
   d. BS EN 60617

2. Manufacturers only make a range of preferred value resistors because:
   a. resistors can only be made to certain values
   b. some resistor values cannot be connected into circuits
   c. it is impractical to store and manufacture every variation of resistor
   d. there is not a market demand for certain values

3. A resistor of value 0.1 Ω is connected up to a circuit. What code would this be given?
   a. R0.1
   b. R1
   c. R10
   d. R11

4. A resistor marked 3R3M would have which of the following features:
   a. 3.3 Ω and a tolerance of + 20%
   b. 330 Ω and a tolerance of + 20%
   c. 3.3 Ω and a tolerance of + 30%
   d. 390 Ω and a tolerance of + 10%

5. A thermistor is:
   a. a type of fixed resistor
   b. a light dependent resistor
   c. a temperature sensitive resistor
   d. a high tolerance resistor

6. ⊣⊦ This symbol means that a capacitor is:
   a. Fixed (non-polarised)
   b. Fixed (polarised)
   c. Variable
   d. Preset

7. Tuning capacitors are primarily used in:
   a. microwaves
   b. radios
   c. televisions
   d. DVD players

8. A capacitor has the colour coding Red, Green, Red, Green, Yellow. What does this stand for:
   a. *25 000 picofarads with a tolerance of 10% and max voltage of 250 V*
   b. *2 50 0000 picofarads with a tolerance of 10% and max voltage of 400 V*
   c. *2 500 picofarads with a tolerance of 5% and max voltage of 400 V*
   d. *5 200 picofarads with a tolerance of 5% and max voltage of 250 V*

9. On a tantalum capacitor what helps to indicate the positive connection?
   a. *A spot on one side of the capacitor*
   b. *Information from the manufacturer*
   c. *The coloured marking*
   d. *Each connection is clearly labelled*

10. Changing the battery connections to make the anode negative in a diode called:
    a. *Doping*
    b. *Forward biased*
    c. *Peak inverse voltage*
    d. *Reverse biased*

11. anode   cathode

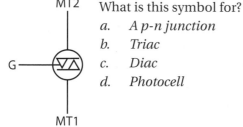

    What is this the symbol for?
    a. *Thyristor*
    b. *A p-n junction*
    c. *Zener diode*
    d. *Light emitting diode (LED)*

12.
    MT2

    G

    MT1

    What is this symbol for?
    a. *A p-n junction*
    b. *Triac*
    c. *Diac*
    d. *Photocell*

13. How many separate regions are there in a bipolar transistor?
    a. *1*
    b. *2*
    c. *3*
    d. *4*

14. Which of these conditions is not essential for the operation of a transistor?
    a. *Silicon materials must be used to construct the semi-conductor.*
    b. *The base emitter junction must be forward biased and the base collector junction reverse biased.*
    c. *It must have only a few majority carriers.*
    d. *It must have a thin base.*

15. Which of the following is not true for transistors?
    a. *They are small and cheap*
    b. *They have limited resistance*
    c. *They can switch millions of times per minute*
    d. *They have no moving parts*

16. What is signified by F in a transistor code?
    a. *Silicon*
    b. *High power frequency*
    c. *Germanium*
    d. *High power audio frequency*

17. Which of these readings will be given by a good npn transistor?
    a. *High resistance reading when the connections are reversed.*
    b. *No change in resistance when connections are reversed.*
    c. *High resistance when*
    d. *Low resistance reading when the connections are reversed.*

18. Which of the following is not an advantage of a Field Effect Transistor?
    a. *More stable during temperature changes*
    b. *Simpler to fabricate and occupies less space*
    c. *Low input impedance makes it safe from static electricity damage*
    d. *High input resistance*

19. What does the diagram opposite show?

    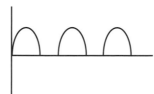

    a. *Full-wave rectification*
    b. *Smoothing*
    c. *Half-wave rectification*
    d. *Full-wave bridge rectifier*

Answers to the end-of-chapter questions

Chapter 1 – Industry and communication

Short answer questions

1. Much of the work of an electrical contractor is obtained through customer referrals. A happy, satisfied customer will be ready and willing to recommend the services of a contractor to other people if the experience they had of the contractor was a good one. Establishing and maintaining good relationships with the customer is essential in this respect. Future work and continuity of employment all depend upon the relationships created with customers.

2. A variation order is issued by the main contractor for work completed that falls outside of the scope of the original project estimate. The variation order gives permission for the contractor to start the additional works and ensures payment. For example, where additional walls are put in place that were not originally shown on the plans/tender documents, additional switch drops or socket outlets installed in these walls will not have been priced for.

3. The following laws can be described:
   a. The Clean Air Act 1993 is aimed at reducing the emissions into the atmosphere from industrial processes such as construction that would generate concrete and brick dust, smoke and other pollutants.
   b. The controlled waste regulations 1998 are also aimed at reducing the risks associated with the transport and storage of waste products, and toxic and radioactive waste will automatically be covered.
   These regulations are concerned with waste of all types removed from industrial workplaces. A duty is placed upon organisations to train all its staff in waste disposal, to register all the vehicles used for the movement of waste and to ensure that the waste is disposed of in appropriate waste sites.

4. The following laws can be described:
   a. The Disability Discrimination Act 1995 makes it unlawful to discriminate against disabled people in the selection process for employment. If a disabled person is able to do the work, then they have to be judged on merit and not the disability.
   b. The Sex Discrimination Act 1975 also makes it unlawful to discriminate against people on the basis of their gender in the selection process for employment. If two people of opposite sex are applying for the same post then selection must be on merit and not on the grounds of choosing a man over a woman or vice versa.

5. The Client is the person who ordered the work and will, at the end, pay the bill. The Architect acts on behalf of the client, interpreting the client's wishes and turning them into working plans/drawings, as well as engaging the main contractor to complete the work.

6. A circuit diagram shows the function of a circuit, it does not show how the circuit is actually wired. A wiring diagram shows the exact way the cables are routed. If you are given a circuit diagram to work from, it would be necessary to convert it to a wiring diagram before you can actually install the cable.

7. The clerk of works, employed by the architect, checks that the work installed is both to the standard required and meets the specification for the job.

8. A block diagram is one in which the sequence of control is shown, i.e. a block diagram showing the intake position of the domestic installation would show the following: Service Cut out – Meter – Consumer Unit.

9. 'As fitted' drawings are supplied to the client, by the electrical contractor, on completion of the job. These are drawings that have been marked up showing the final positioning of all installed equipment and would form part of the project file.

10. Discrimination in legal terms refers to the unfair selection/treatment of one person over another, due to that person's race, gender, disability etc.

11. The Investors in People award can benefit a company or organisation by improving its performance and competitiveness. It does this by ensuring that it keeps its staff up-to-date, encouraging them to undergo training, and by setting and achieving business goals, related to the business plan.

12. In general, there are two types of changes in demand: an increase in demand and a decrease in demand. An increasing demand results in more work being won with the requirement for a larger workforce to cope with the additional work. A decrease in demand can result in a reduction of work being won, and therefore the need to reduce the workforce. Changes in demand can be for a number of reasons, one of which can be a change in the economy of the country.

13. The nature of the electrical installation contracting sector has changed considerably over the years. It is now more customer focused, providing customers what they want when they want it. As a result, many of the contracts won have time constraints and penalties placed on them, requiring the workforce to work long unsocial hours during shutdowns, refurbishments or on emergency call-outs. If a customer is happy with performance, then they will be prepared to contract companies again, as well as recommend them to other potential customers.

14. A contract is an agreement, between two or more parties, making those affected by the contract specifically aware of what their commitments are. In most cases this means, one signatory to the contract will know exactly how much they have to pay on completion, while the other party will know exactly what they have to do, and by when, to meet the terms of the contract.

15. For a contract to be binding it must:
    • have an offer, which is clear, concise and understandable to the customer
    • be accepted by the customer without conditions
    • be an understanding of what each party is agreeing to do for the other.

16. The Electrical Contractors Association and Amicus (the trade union) sit on the Joint Industrial Board. The role of the JIB is: to reach agreement on
    • national working rules
    • conditions of employment
    • wage rates and training.

17. When a contractor is asked to provide a tender for a project, they are being asked to quote a price to do the job. The estimator will be in possession of any plans and drawings that may exist as well as the job specification, as compiled by electrical consulting engineers used by the main contractor. The estimator has to turn all this information into a price. He or she has to quantify all the materials and equipment that will be needed as well as the required amount of labour to complete the job. Added to this figure will be a percentage that will allow for the use of any plant and access equipment, plus an amount to allow for tax and profit.

18. The job specification is a document created by specialist electrical engineers at the design stage of installation. It sets the standard to which the installation is to be completed, requiring installations to comply with BS 7671. Also specifying the fixing heights, whether plastic or metallic finishes are to be used on the accessories, whether the installation is to be installed surface or as a flush installation and specifying the makes, type and sometimes the quantities of the equipment to be used.

19. Some of the things that can be done to promote good customer relationships are:
- honesty
- tidy in your personal appearance
- knowing your job and doing it well
- explaining what you're going to do and how long it will take.

20. A JIB Approved Electrician requires NVQ3, the technical certificate, C&G 2391 test and inspection and two years experience as an electrician.

Multiple-choice answers

1.	(a)	**19.**	(b)
2.	(c)	**20.**	(c)
3.	(d)	**21.**	(c)
4.	(b)	**22.**	(a)
5.	(c)	**23.**	(b)
6.	(d)	**24.**	(b)
7.	(b)	**25.**	(c)
8.	(a)	**26.**	(c)
9.	(d)	**27.**	(d)
10.	(d)	**28.**	(c)
11.	(b)	**29.**	(a)
12.	(c)	**30.**	(b)
13.	(b)	**31.**	(a)
14.	(a)	**32.**	(c)
15.	(a)	**33.**	(c)
16.	(d)	**34.**	(d)
17.	(b)	**35.**	(c)
18.	(d)		

Chapter 2 – Health and safety

Short answer questions

1. Employees must use the PPE provided and for which they have been trained to use. They must inform the employer of any defects in the PPE and they must use safety equipment as directed.

2. 'Statutory' means it is the law and as such criminal proceedings can be brought against anyone contravening the contents of the legislation.

3. 'Absolute' means that the safety or protective measure must be carried out regardless of economic cost or difficulty. 'As far as is reasonably practicable' means that the risk of danger is assessed against the cost, time, trouble and difficulty in taking steps to reduce the danger and a decision is made regarding what is needed or not depending on the circumstances.

4. A hazard is anything that can cause harm. A risk is the likelihood of that hazard causing harm.

5. The five steps are:
- Step 1: Look for the hazard
- Step 2: Describe who may be harmed and how
- Step 3: Evaluate the risks and decide whether existing measures are adequate or whether more should be done
- Step 4: Record the findings
- Step 5: Review the assessment and revise if necessary.

6. Any five from the following list:
- damaged tie rods
- cracks on stiles
- cracks on rungs
- painted ladders
- dirt on rungs
- temporary repairs
- broken rungs
- broken stiles
- warping.

7. The seven steps are:
- Step 1: Identify supply source
- Step 2: Switch off
- Step 3: Lock off
- Step 4: Test voltage indicator device
- Step 5: Test circuit or equipment
- Step 6: Test voltage indicator again
- Step 7: Fit warning notice.

8. Permit to work document should contain the following information:
- Details of work to be done.
- The persons involved.
- When the work is to be done.
- Hazards involved.
- Precautions to be taken.
- When the work should be finished.

9. The visual checks that would be carried out on a portable appliance are:
   - Check casing for signs of damage or burning.
   - Check cable for damage to its outer sheath.
   - Check cable is secure at both ends.
   - Check plug for signs of damage or burning.
   - Check conductors are mechanically sound.
   - Check fuse size is correct.

10. The following should be included in the visitors book:
    - date
    - visitors name
    - company they work for
    - who they are going to see
    - time in
    - time out
    - I.D. checked
    - badge number issued
    - H&S brief
    - visitors signature
    - some companies will also ask for car registration number.

Multiple-choice answers

1.	(c)	**11.**	(c)
2.	(b)	**12.**	(a)
3.	(d)	**13.**	(a)
4.	(b)	**14.**	(b)
5.	(c)	**15.**	(b)
6.	(c)	**16.**	(a)
7.	(b)	**17.**	(c)
8.	(c)	**18.**	(b)
9.	(d)	**19.**	(c)
10.	(b)	**20.**	(b)

Chapter 3 – Electrical science

Short answer questions

1. **Mass** is the amount of matter an object has and will stay the same throughout the universe, unless it is physically changed. **Weight** is a force, that is created by the pull gravity exerts on mass. As such, it will be different in different places, depending on the strength of the force of gravity. For example, as gravity is weaker on the moon you will weigh less, even though your mass will be the same.

2. An atom is made up of three different types of particle – protons, neutrons and electrons. Protons, which have a positive charge, cluster at the centre of an atom in the nucleus and are held in place by the neutrons, which have a neutral charge. Electrons orbit the nucleus. They have a negative charge, so cancel out the charge of the protons. The positive charge of the protons and the negative charge of the electrons attract each other, holding each in place.

3. a) A conductor is a material that has its atoms packed loosely together. This allows electrons to move through them. This means that electricity can flow very easily through these materials.
   b) An insulator is a material that has its atoms tightly packed together. This prevents free electrons from moving within it, and therefore prevents the flow of electricity.

4. The three sources of electromotive force are:
   a) chemical, such as a battery – this is created by placing two electrodes in a chemical solution, electrolyte, which causes a reaction that forces electrons to travel from one electrode to another. This creates a strong magnetic charge, which can be used to drive a circuit
   b) thermal – conductors made from different material will have a potential difference if placed in different temperatures, known as the Seebeck effect
   c) magnetic – the movement of an electrical field creates a radial magnetic field, which increases with the speed of the movement of the electrical charge. This is known as electromagnetic induction.

5. Resistance of an object is affected by:
   a) length – resistance is directly proportional to length, with two materials of equal length and cross sectional area joined together doubling resistance
   b) area – two materials of equal length and the same cross sectional area joined side by side will double the cross sectional area and halve

resistance. Resistance and area are inversely proportional

c) resistivity – this is the amount of resistance in a conductor and will change according to material, size and the distance the current has to move in the object

d) temperature – when temperature fluctuates, this affects resistivity. Most conductors have increased resistance with increased temperature. Carbon is an exception, where resistance decreases with temperature.

6. A permanent magnet is made from material that will continue to exhibit magnetic qualities after it is removed from the field that originally gave it these qualities. An electromagnet will only display magnetic qualities whilst the current that gave it this charge is flowing through it.

7. In a.c., frequency refers to the amount of cycles of the waveform that occur each second and is measured in hertz.

8. The three main types of power in an a.c. circuit are:

a) true power, which is the power consumed by the resistor and does not return to the source as it is dissipated as heat. It is measured in watts (W) and expressed with the symbol S.

b) reactive power, which is the energy stored in the magnetic field of the inductor or plates of the capacitor and returns to source. It is measured in reactive volt-amps (VAr) and expressed by the symbol Q.

c) apparent power is the sum of reactive power and true power. It is measure in volt-amps (VA) and is expressed by the symbol S.

9. A **voltmeter** measures the potential difference between two points and is connected in parallel across the load to be measured. It has a high internal resistance to get accurate readings. An **ammeter** is connected in series and measures the current passing through it. It must have a low resistance to get an accurate reading.

10. A transformer is an electronic device that transfers energy from one circuit to another via a magnetic field. It is used on a.c. circuits to transfer one voltage to another. A conductor carrying a current creates a magnetic field field which induces an e.m.f. in the secondary coil and drives a current through the coil and onto the circuit.

11. Star connections are used for an unbalanced load and are a neutral connection with an untapped earth. Delta connections are for a balanced load.

12. Magnetism causes a conductor, in the form of a loop, to rotate between two permanent poles. This makes the conductor cut through the lines of flux, inducing and e.m.f., causing current to flow if the loop is part of a circuit.

Multiple-choice answers

1.	(d)	16.	(a)
2.	(a)	17.	(b)
3.	(d)	18.	(a)
4.	(b)	19.	(c)
5.	(c)	20.	(c)
6.	(b)	21.	(b)
7.	(a)	22.	(d)
8.	(b)	23.	(d)
9.	(c)	24.	(b)
10.	(d)	25.	(a)
11.	(a)	26.	(b)
12.	(b)	27.	(b)
13.	(c)	28.	(c)
14.	(a)	29.	**(a)**
15.	(c)	30.	(b)

Chapter 4 – Craft theory

Short answer questions

1. Five different types of screw could be any from the following:
   - Countersunk
   - Raised head
   - Rounded head
   - Mirror screw head
   - Pan head
   - Dome head
   - Coach screw.

2. The Simmonds nut has a nylon insert which when fastened onto the bolt 'bites' down into the threads and lock onto them.

3. A PVC/SWA cable is terminated using the following method:

- Remove outer sheath for length needed.
- Measure approx 1½ times the length of the armoured gland cone and then remove armouring by cutting part way and snapping off.
- Place PVC shroud and back nut of the gland, open the armouring strands into a cone shape and attach the main body of the gland.
- Screw both parts together, with the armouring secured between the two parts.
- Remove the second outer sheath and leave at least 10 mm protruding past the gland.
- Attach to the electrical equipment using a lock nut and terminate.

4. Terminate a MICC cable using the following method:
   - Remove the outer PVC sheath, and slide the PVC shroud, gland nut, compression ring and gland body over the cable.
   - Remove the outer copper sheath to the length needed.
   - Screw on the nut using a pot wrench.
   - Fit the sealing ring and fill pot with insulating compound.
   - Crimp together using a crimping pot tool.
   - Apply coloured sleeving to the copper conductors and test the insulation of the cable.

5. A 90 degree bend in a length of conduit can be made using the following method:
   - Mark the conduit 200 mm from the fixed point
   - Place the tube in the former with the fixed point in the rear. In this position a square should form a tangent from the fixed point to the leading edge of the former.
   - If the remaining length is too long to down bend, deduct three times the outside diameter of the tube from the initial mark.
   - Place the tube in the former with the fixed point to the front with the mark at 90 degrees to the edge of the former.

6. The different materials used for conduit are steel and plastic.

7. There are three main types of cable tray coverings/materials. These are:

- Hot dipped galvanised – common and suitable for most environments.
- Plastic coating – either polyethylene or PVC against chemical contamination.
- Stainless steel – for special applications, such as food or marine.

8. There are seven light switch terminals in an intermediate circuit: three on each 2-way switch and four on the intermediate switch.

9. The live conductors are terminated into the same fuse or mcb, the neutrals are connected together in the neutral block and the cpcs are connected together into the earth terminal block.

10. There are three terminals used in a junction box: one for the live conductors, one for the neutrals and one for the cpcs.

Multiple choice questions

1.	(c)	14.	(d)
2.	(a)	15.	(a)
3.	(c)	16.	(b)
4.	(d)	17.	(c)
5.	(c)	18.	(d)
6.	(c)	19.	(c)
7.	(a)	20.	(b)
8.	(d)	21.	(b)
9.	(c)	22.	(a)
10.	(c)	23.	(b)
11.	(b)	24.	(d)
12.	(c)	25.	(c)
13.	(b)		

Chapter 5 – Statutory regulations and codes of practice

Short answer questions

1. BS 7671 are regulations developed to cover all aspects of the installation process and to take account of new equipment and its usage in the electro technical sector. Complying with them will also lead to compliance with the Electricity at Work Regulations 1989.

2. The special locations referred to in BS 7671 are:
   - a bath or shower
   - swimming pools and basins
   - rooms and cabins containing sauna heaters
   - construction and demolition site installations
   - agricultural and horticultural premises
   - conducting locations with restricted movement
   - electrical installations in caravan/camping parks
   - marinas and special locations
   - exhibitions, shows and stands
   - solar photovoltaic (PV) power supply systems
   - mobile or transportable units
   - electrical installations in caravans and motor caravans
   - temporary electrical installation for structures, amusement devices and booths at fairgrounds, amusement parks and circuses
   - floor and ceiling heating systems.

3. IEE Guidance note 7 also covers medical locations.

4. 'Absolute' means that the safety or protective measure must be carried out regardless of economic cost or difficulty. 'As far as is reasonably practicable' means that the risk of danger is assessed against the cost, time, trouble and difficulty in taking steps to reduce the danger and a decision is made regarding what is needed or not depending on the circumstances.

5. 'Statutory' means it is the law and as such criminal proceedings can be brought against anyone contravening the contents of the legislation.

Multiple choice questions

1. (a)
2. (d)
3. (b)
4. (a)
5. (b)
6. (b)
7. (a)
8. (c)
9. (a)
10. (b)
11. (a)
12. (b)
13. (d)
14. (c)
15. (b)
16. (a)

Chapter 6 – Earthing and protection

Short answer questions

1. Overcurrent can be subdivided into two categories based on its cause. These causes are: overload due to abuse by the consumer or overload due to bad design of wrong modification by the installer.

2. The advantages of the BS 3036 fuse include:
   - low initial cost
   - it is easy to see when the fuse has blown
   - low element replacement cost
   - no mechanical moving parts
   - easy storage of spare fuse wire.

3. The following correction factors need to be applied:
   - ambient temperature
   - grouping factors
   - thermal installation
   - BS 3036 fuse
   - MICC cable.

4. Advantages of the BS 88 HBC fuse include:
   - no mechanical moving parts
   - no weakening with age
   - operation is very rapid under fault conditions
   - difficult to interchange the cartridge, as different ratings are made to different sizes.

   Disadvantages of the BS 88 fuse include:
   - it is very expensive to replace
   - stocks of these spares are costly and take up space
   - care must be taken when replacing them to ensure that the replacement fuse has the same rating and the same characteristics as the fuse being replaced.

5. Earth fault protection can be provided either by a circuit breaker or a fuse.

6. An RCD continuously compares the current in the phases and neutral conductors. This should be equal at all times. In a fault situation, some current will flow to earth, unbalancing these conductors. In these circumstances, an RCD activates and disconnects the circuit.

7. Exposed conductive parts are those parts of the electrical system which can be touched under normal operation but, under fault conditions, can become conductive and a potential hazard.

8. The formula used for finding the fusing factor is:

$$\text{Fusing factor} = \frac{\text{Fusing current}}{\text{Current rating}}$$

9. Voltage drop is calculated using the following formula:

$$\text{Voltage drop (VD)} = \frac{\text{mV/A/m} \times \text{Ib} \times \text{L}}{1000}$$

(or $\text{mV/A/m} \times \text{Ib} \times \text{L} \times 10\text{-3}$)

Voltage drops because the resistance of the conductor becomes greater with the length of the cable. Appendix 4 of the BS 7671 gives a table of values for cable voltage drop in millivolts per ampere per metre (mV/A/m). This is multiplied by the circuit's design current (Ib) and the length of the cable in metres (L) and divided by 1000 to give the total voltage drop for a circuit.

10. Z_e is the loop impedance external to the installation. Z_s is the total fault loop impedance.

Multiple choice questions

1.	(c)	**16.**	(c)
2.	(d)	**17.**	(c)
3.	(b)	**18.**	(c)
4.	(b)	**19.**	(b)
5.	(b)	**20.**	(b)
6.	(a)	**21.**	(b)
7.	(d)	**22.**	(c)
8.	(b)	**23.**	(b)
9.	(a)	**24.**	(b)
10.	(b)	**25.**	(b)
11.	(a)	**26.**	(c)
12.	(b)	**27.**	(d)
13.	(d)	**28.**	(d)
14.	(b)	**29.**	(c)
15.	(c)		

Chapter 7 – Lighting

Short answer questions

1. The light emitted by the mercury gas discharge, which is mainly ultraviolet, is converted to white light when it strikes the phosphor coating.

2. The three factors to be considered when choosing different fluorescent tubes are:
- lamp efficacy
- colour rendering
- colour appearance.

3. Lamp efficacy means the efficiency of a lamp, i.e. how much light is produced for a given input power. This is expressed in lumens per watt (lm/W).

4. The choke produces a high voltage when it is open circuited under load – this high voltage causes the tube to 'strike' or switch on. The choke also limits the current to a predetermined value.

5. The five advantages that high frequency fluorescent circuits have over standard circuits are:
- higher lamp efficacy
- first time starting
- noise free
- the ballast shuts down automatically on lamp failure
- no stroboscopic effect.

6. The stroboscopic effect is caused by rotating machinery being illuminated from a single source. This makes the machinery appear to slow down, stop, or even change direction. The following actions can help prevent this:
- Fitting tungsten lamps locally to lathes, etc. will lessen the effect.
- Connecting adjacent fluorescent fittings to a different phase reduces the effect as each phase flickers at a different time.
- Twin lamps can be wired to a lead-lag circuit.
- Using high frequency fluorescent lighting reduces stroboscopic effects by 60%.

7. Four advantages of a GLS lamp are:
   * comparatively low initial costs
   * immediate light when switched on
   * no control gear
   * can be easily dimmed.
   One disadvantage of a GLS lamp is its low efficacy compared with other types of lamp.

8. When installing tungsten halogen lamps the lamp should not be touched with the fingers as this will cause failure. The linear type must be installed within 4° of horizontal to prevent failure.

9. The four advantages tungsten halogen lamps have over GLS lamps are:
   * increased lamp life (up to 2000 hours)
   * increase in efficacy (up to 23 lumens per watt)
   * reduction in lamp size
   * can be designed to work at extra low voltages.

10. The following are all types of discharge lamp:
    * low-pressure mercury vapour
    * high-pressure mercury vapour
    * low pressure sodium
    * high pressure sodium.

11. The following calculation will need to be used:

$$E \text{ at centre of bench} = \frac{2500}{25} = 100 \text{ lux}$$

$$\tan \theta = \frac{1}{5} = 0.2; \text{ then } = 11.3°$$

and $\cos = \cos 11.3° = 0.9806$ and $(\cos 21.8)^3$
$= 0.9429$

$$\text{Therefore } E = \frac{2500 \times 0.9429}{25} = 94.29 \text{ lux}$$

Multiple choice questions

1.	(b)	12.	(d)
2.	(d)	13.	(a)
3.	(c)	14.	(d)
4.	(d)	15.	(b)
5.	(c)	16.	(c)
6.	(c)	17.	(b)
7.	(b)	18.	(b)
8.	(c)	19.	(b)
9.	(b)	20.	(c)
10.	(d)	21.	(d)
11.	(a)	22.	(b)

Chapter 8 – Electrical science

Short answer questions

1. Any three electrical components from the following can be named:
   * room thermostat
   * hot water thermostat
   * pump
   * programmer
   * diverter valve
   * zone valve
   * fused spur
   * multi-way connection box.

2. Maintained lights are continuously lit and are both the main and emergency light. Non-maintained lights are separate from the main light and only operate when the main light fails.

3. The three general types of fire alarm named as stated in BS 5839 are type M, L and P.

4. The three parts of the fire triangle are oxygen, fuel and heat.

5. A weekly inspection of a fire system could be one of the following:
   * Check panel key operation and reset button.
   * Test fire alarm from a call point (different one each week).
   * Reset fire alarm panel.
   * Check all call points and detectors for obstruction.
   * Enter details of test in logbook.

6. It is important to ensure the exposed and extraneous conductive parts are bonded to earth so that the parts are all at the same potential and, if a fault develops and they became 'live' then the protective device or devices would operate.

7. The heater coil around the bi-metal strip heats up as current flows to the hotplate. When the temperature is reached then the bi-metal strip bends and opens the contacts supplying the hotplate. When the heater coil cools down then the bi-metal strip returns to its original position and closes the contacts and hence re-supplies the hotplate. This continuous switching on/off maintains a constant hotplate temperature.

8. A multiplexer produces multiple images more clearly than a quad processor.

9. Perimeter protection is the protection of the property by detecting an intrusion before the intruder enters the premises. Space protection is designed to detect an intruder after they have entered the premises.

10. A xenon light continues to flash after the sounder has stopped to warn the owner of the building that there has been an alarm condition and to be aware of possible intruders still on the premises.

Multiple choice questions

1.	(c)	**9.**	(c)
2.	(b)	**10.**	(a)
3.	(b)	**11.**	(b)
4.	(c)	**12.**	(d)
5.	(a)	**13.**	(d)
6.	(c)	**14.**	(b)
7.	(d)	**15.**	(c)
8.	(b)		

Chapter 9 – Inspection, testing and commissioning

Short answer questions

1. The sequence of testing for a small installation is as follows:
   - Safely isolate the installation.
   - Test for continuity of circuit protective and bonding conductors.
   - Test for continuity of ring final circuit (if applicable).
   - Carry out an insulation resistance test.
   - Test the polarity.
   - Carry out an earth electrode test (if applicable).
   - Carry out an earth fault loop impedance test.
   - Carry out functional testing (including testing any RCD).

2. Instruments required for test procedures are as follows:
   - Voltage indicator and proving unit.
   - Low ohms meter/insulation resistance tester.
   - Earth fault loop tester.
   - RCD tester.

3. The general characteristics of the supply that are required before testing begins are the:
   - nominal voltage
   - nature of the current and the frequency
   - prospective short circuit current at the origin
   - external earth fault loop impedance
   - type and rating of the over current protective device.

4. The principle means of protection against direct contact are: insulation, barriers and enclosures, obstacles, placing out of reach.

5. The single signatory form is used when the design, installation and inspection and testing is the responsibility of the same person. The multiple signatory form is used when the design, installation and inspection and testing are the responsibility of different persons.

6. The test method used to confirm continuity of supplementary bonding , assuming safe isolation, is as follows:
   - Use test method two, the long lead method.
   - Select a low ohms meter.
   - Confirm instrument functions correctly.
   - Record long lead resistance (or null tester).
   - Disconnect supplementary bonding at each end.
   - Measure end to end resistance of bonding.
   - Deduct resistance of test leads.
   - Compare with requirements (not more than 0.05 ohms).
   - Reconnect bonding.
   - Enter measured reading onto test result schedule.

7. The steps involved in confirmation of ring final circuit conductors are:
   - Interconnect P1 and N2 and P2 and N1 and test at all sockets.

- Interconnect P1 and CPC2 and P2 and CPC1 and test at all sockets.
- Restore installation, compare readings and record on test schedule.

The two items confirmed at the same time are polarity and the R1 + R2 value of the circuit.

8. (a) The reading is acceptable as it is above 0.5 M-ohms, which is above the minimum requirements of BS 7671.

   (b) As a low insulation resistance reading may be evidence of a latent fault, a reading between 0.5 and 2 M-ohms should be investigated.

9. Reasons for the necessity of a Periodic Inspection Report include:
   - licensing authority requirements
   - legislation requirements
   - compliance with BS 7671
   - change of occupancy
   - change of use of premises
   - after any significant alterations or additions
   - any major change of electrical loading
   - where there is reason to believe there has been damage to the installation.

10. Indirect contact is contact with conductive parts not intended to be live, but made live by a fault. The principle method of protection is by Earthed Equipotential Bonding and Automatic Disconnection of Supply (EEBADoS).

Multiple choice questions

1.	(c)	16.	(b)
2.	(c)	17.	(c)
3.	(a)	18.	(a)
4.	(a)	19.	(d)
5.	(c)	20.	(a)
6.	(b)	21.	(a)
7.	(a)	22.	(a)
8.	(b)	23.	(a)
9.	(d)	24.	(c)
10.	(b)	25.	(a)
11.	(a)	26.	(b)
12.	(c)	27.	(b)
13.	(a)	28.	(b)
14.	(d)	29.	(d)
15.	(c)	30.	(d)

Chapter 10 – Fault diagnosis and rectification

Short answer questions

1. The complete sequences for testing isolation can be found on pages 262 and 263 in Chapter 10.

2. An off load device is not usually operated when the system is in use, only after it has been switched off from the source. It is then switched off and the installation in question can be worked on for either fault diagnosis or general maintenance. An on load device is used to break the circuit under load but in the case of MCBs much higher levels of fault current. Switches are on load devices but cannot be used for isolation.

3. The categories of fault are:
   - position of faults
   - operation of protective devices
   - transient voltage
   - insulation failure
   - plant, equipment or component failure
   - faults caused by abuse, misuse or negligence
   - prevention of faults by regular maintenance.

4. Review drawing based on actual installation layouts. Figure 10.3 is a good indicator of quality.

5. (a) Circuits are divided into smaller circuits to avoid danger and minimise inconvenience in the event of a fault and to facilitate safe operation, inspection, testing and maintenance.

   (b) The technique used in Figure 10.3 is the operation of each circuit breaker or fuse individually.

   (c) A fault at A1 or B1 in Figure 10.3 would be most likely. A failure of units at A, B or C would be unlikely.

6. (a) An overload is an overcurrent occurring in a circuit which is electrically sound. Examples of this are:

- multi-adaptors used in socket outlets causing the rated load of the socket to be exceeded
- unauthorised extending of existing circuits
- incorrect selection of protective device by not taking into account high inrush currents.

(b) A short circuit is an overcurrent resulting in a fault of negligible impedance between live conductors. Examples of this are:

- insulation breakdown due to a variety of causes, such as age and mechanical damage
- severing of one or more live conductors in an enclosure
- bad workmanship during installation, such as incorrect polarity, not discovered during testing or energised before testing.

(c) An earth fault is a fault current that flows to earth. Examples of this are:

- insulation breakdown due to a variety of causes, such as age and mechanical damage
- incorrect polarity and not tested or not discovered due to incorrect test methods
- bad workmanship during installation, such as allowing copper strands to be exposed and in contact with earth.

7. (a) The must common faults in luminaries are:

- lamp expired
- starter expired
- choke of ballast break down
- capacitor break down.

(b) The most common faults in flexible cables and cords are:

- poor terminations to accessory
- wrong type of cable used
- incorrect size of conductor selected
- incorrectly installed.

8. The logical sequence for fault diagnosis and rectification is as follows:

1) Identify the symptoms.
2) Gather information.
3) Analyse the evidence.
4) Check supplies.
5) Check protective devices.
6) Isolate and test.
7) Interpretation of information and test results.
8) Rectify the fault.
9) Carry out required installation testing.
10) Restore the supply.
11) Carry out functional testing.

9. Three ways of obtaining information whilst investigating a fault are as follows:

- Inquiry – asking the operator or user of the faulty equipment what the problems are is an obvious first step. If technical specifications are needed then inquiries can be made to the REC.
- Investigation – if required a certain amount of investigation can be carried out, using great care and ensuring safe isolation procedures have been carried out.
- Measurement – using a low ohm meter or an insulation resistance tester can give valuable indicators as to the type and position of the fault.

10. A typical company contingency plan when called out to an unfamiliar installation could be as follows:

- Signing in.
- Wearing identification badges.
- Identifying and locating supervisory and key personnel.
- Locating key data and drawings.
- Liaison with customer before commencing work.
- Insisting on following safe isolation procedures.

Multiple choice questions

1.	(a)	**16.**	(c)
2.	(a)	**17.**	(a)
3.	(c)	**18.**	(b)
4.	(b)	**19.**	(b)
5.	(c)	**20.**	(d)
6.	(c)	**21.**	(c)
7.	(a)	**22.**	(a)
8.	(d)	**23.**	(d)
9.	(c)	**24.**	(a)
10.	(d)	**25.**	(d)
11.	(d)	**26.**	(d)
12.	(a)	**27.**	(b)
13.	(d)	**28.**	(a)
14.	(a)	**29.**	(d)
15.	(c)	**30.**	(c)

Chapter 11 – Electrical machines and motors

Short answer questions

1. The most common method for reversing a d.c. motor is by reversing the connections to the armature. A d.c. can also be reversed by reversing the supply to the electro magnets.

2. In an a.c. motor the field coil is wired in series with the armature. This type of motor has a high starting torque and good speed control characteristics. This means it is capable of starting heavy loads.

3. A d.c. generator has a commutator. An a.c. generator uses slip rings.

4. Synchronous speed is the speed at which the rotating magnetic field rotates in a three phrase motor. It is dependent upon the frequency of the supply and the number of pairs of poles in the motor.

5. Faraday's Law describes when a conductor cuts a magnetic field or is itself cut by a magnetic field, leading to an e.m.f. being induced in the conductor. The magnitude of this e.m.f. is directly proportional to the rate at which the conductor cuts the magnetic field or the rate at which it is cut by it.

6. A single phase motor can be 'fooled' into thinking a rotating magnetic field exists by causing a phase shift between the start and run windings. This is usually done by making one or the other more resistive, inductive or capacitive than the other one.

7. A DOL starter works by connecting the supply to the contactor coil after the start button is pressed. This closes the contact on to the terminals and switches the three phrases through to the motor windings.

8. An automatic star/delta starter can be hand operated or automatic, A start button is pressed and the main and star contactor energise together, connecting the motor windings in star, to accelerate the rotor from standstill. After a pre-determined time, the electronic timer de-energises the star contactor and energises the delta one, once the rotor has reached a steady speed. The motor is then connected in delta configuration.

9. The speed of a series motor can be controlled by connecting a variable resistor in parallel with the field winding. In a shunt motor, the same effect can be reached by connecting a variable resistor in series with the field winding. In both cases the field current is altered, thus the strength of the magnetic field and the speed.

10. A VFD has an a.c. supply fed into its converter which changes it into d.c. This is then fed into a constant-voltage d.c. bus where it is smoothed out. This d.c. voltage is then fed into an inverter where it is changed back into a.c. using an insulated bipolar gate transistor, which creates the variable voltage and frequency output to the motor.

Multiple choice questions

1.	(a)	**13.**	(b)
2.	(c)	**14.**	(c)
3.	(d)	**15.**	(b)
4.	(b)	**16.**	(c)
5.	(c)	**17.**	(a)
6.	(c)	**18.**	(d)
7.	(a)	**19.**	(a)
8.	(c)	**20.**	(b)
9.	(c)	**21.**	(d)
10.	(d)	**22.**	(b)
11.	(b)	**23.**	(a)
12.	(c)		

Chapter 12 – Electronics

Short answer questions

1. The diagrams for these can be found on the following pages:
   a) Figure 12.27 (page 336)
   b) Figure 12.19 (page 332)
   c) Figure 12.18 (page 331).

2. The two types of resistor are fixed and variable. A fixed resistor cannot be changed mechanically but can be affected by temperature or other effects. Variable resistors have some means of adjustment, such as a spindle or slider.

3. (a) $500 \, \Omega + 5\%$
   (b) $43000 \, \Omega$ or $43 \, K\Omega + 10\%$
   (c) $69000000 \, \Omega$ or $69 \, M\Omega + 2\%$.

4. A cadmium sulphide film in a light resistor is stored inside a clear window on the resistor. When light is shone on the film the resistance varies, reducing as the light increases.

5. The capacitance of a conductor relies on:
   a) the areas of the conducting services facing each other
   b) the separation of the plates (the closer they are the higher the charge that can be stored)
   c) the dielectric, or spacing material used.

6. Materials are made suitable for conduction by adding an impurity to the material in a process called doping. This can be done in two ways:
   a) pentavalent – contains five valence electrons (e.g. arsenic) providing a surplus negative charge
   b) trivalent – contains three valence electrons (e.g. aluminium) providing a surplus positive charge.

7. A zener diode is designed to operate in the reverse breakdown region of a p–n junction without destruction. This is achieved by controlling the doping level during manufacture. When reverse biased a zener diode acts as a short circuit when the voltage reaches the diode's reverse breakdown voltage, limiting the voltage to a known value.

8. To operate a transistor requires:
   • a thin base
   • few majority carriers in the base
   • a forward bias in the base–emitter junction and a reverse bias in the base–collector junction.

9. The three main series of transistor codes used in the UK are:
   • Codes beginning with B (or A) – the first letter indicates silicon (B) or germanium (A). The second letter indicates type: low power audio frequency (C), high power audio frequency (D) or low power high frequency (F). The rest of the code identifies the transistor and is determined by the manufacturer.
   • Codes beginning with TIP – this stands for Texas Instruments power transistor. The letter at the end identifies versions with different voltage rating.
   • Codes beginning with 2N – 2N identifies the part as a transistor and the rest of the code identifies the particular transistor.

10. A smooth supply can be created through three methods:

- Capacitor smoothing – a capacitor connected in parallel across a load, charges the capacitor when the rectifier allows a flow of current and discharges when the rectifier voltage is lower than the capacitor. It is most effective under no load conditions.

- Choke smoothing – an inductor in series with a load, the changing current through the inductor will induce an e.m.f. in opposition to the current that produced it, which will try to keep the current steady. The heavier the rate of change in the current, the more it will be smoothed.

- Filter circuits – these combine both techniques.

Multiple choice questions

1.	(d)	**11.**	(c)
2.	(c)	**12.**	(b)
3.	(c)	**13.**	(c)
4.	(a)	**14.**	(a)
5.	(c)	**15.**	(b)
6.	(c)	**16.**	(b)
7.	(b)	**17.**	(d)
8.	(c)	**18.**	(c)
9.	(a)	**19.**	(c)
10.	(d)		

Index

A

a.c. (alternating current) 75, 82, 84–9,
93, 300, 323
  motors 93, 294, 305–6
  rectification 346–8
  speed control of machines 311–12
access equipment 52–3
accidents 40, 46, 47, 61–2, 170
  see also PPE; safety; working at
height
ACOPs (approved codes of practice)
48, 156
actual speed (motors) 305
adiabatic equation 180–1
alarm sounders 206, 217
alarm systems 332
  fire alarms 115, 204–8, 334
  intruder alarms 216–17, 334
alternating current *see* a.c.
alternators (alternating current
generators) 95–6, 292–4, 294–5
aluminium 74, 110
ambient temperature 177
ammeters 90
amperes 71, 73, 76
antistatic precautions 286
approved codes of practice
(ACOPs) 48, 156
arcing 265, 270, 287
armature 294, 295, 296
asbestos 40, 62
(asynchronous) single-phase
induction motors 300–5
atoms 73, 74

B

backup batteries 202–3, 207, 208, 287
bad earths, results 163
ballasts (chokes) 188, 189, 190, 191,
276
bar charts 26, 27, 28
basic protection 228, 232, 236
baths, locations containing 144,
145–8
batteries 77–8, 287, 346
  for backup 202–3, 207, 208, 287

bi-metallic strips 189, 190, 191, 212
bipolar transistors 335–43, 344
bolts 107
British Standards (BS) 154, 202
BS 7671 Requirements for Electrical
Installation (IEE Wiring
Regulations 17th Edition/The
Regulations) 12, 28, 140–50, 222,
223, 270, 271
Building Regulations 144
building services 9, 10
burglar alarm systems 216–17, 332,
334

C

cable couplers 149
cable ladders 129
cable trays 128–9
cables 10, 113–16, 228, 272–3
  for computer installations 116
  core colours 111–13, 277
  fibre optic 116, 286
  for fire alarm systems 207
  flexible 113, 193, 232, 277–8
  grouping 177
  for immersion heaters 209
  installation methods 176
  insulation 111–13, 118, 178
  interconnections 120–1, 152, 231,
272–3
  multicore 131–3
  protection of 118
  seals and entries 274
  selection 175–81, 267
  single core 130–1
  sizes 131, 134, 135
  terminating 119–20, 121–2, 272,
273
  thermal insulation 178
  transmission cables 93
  see also insulation
calibration of instruments 242, 243,
283
cameras for closed circuit television
214–15
capacitance 87–8, 324, 325, 328
capacitive circuits 287

capacitive reactance 88
capacitor start-capacitor run
motors 304
capacitor-start motors 301–3
capacitors 87–8, 88–9, 189, 323–30,
347
  coding 327–8
carbon filament lamps 187
career development 8–9
cartridge tools 106
ceiling fittings 117–18, 193
certification and reporting 251–5
changing demand 7–9
charging capacitors 329, 330
checklists
  for inspection 236–9
  for instruments before
testing 282–3
chemical hazards 61–2
chips 345
choke smoothing 347
chokes (ballasts) 188, 189, 190, 191,
347
circuit boards 276
circuit breakers 134, 152, 170, 171,
173, 235, 275
  see also MCBs; RCBOs; RCDs
circuit diagrams 20, 77
circuit protective conductors (cpc)
165, 168, 180–1, 234, 244
circuits 80–2, 266
  d.c. circuits 80–2, 85, 323
  filter circuits 348
  for fire detection and alarm
systems 204, 205, 207
  isolation 61, 153, 230
  lighting circuits 130–3
  logic gate circuits 340–1
  radial circuits 135
  ring circuits 134
  spurs 135, 281
civil engineering 9
clearing up 29, 40
clients 13, 21, 28, 252, 256, 275
closed circuit television and camera
systems 214–15

coding/colour banding
  capacitors 327–8
  resistors 321–2
  transistors 341–2
colour codes, cable insulation 111–13, 277
colour rendering 189, 192
commissioning 223–4, 228, 240–3
communication 6, 31–2
communications, electronic 10, 24–5
commutators 95, 294, 295
completion dates 8, 28
component failure 269
compressed air, safety 106
computer systems 10, 24, 208, 268, 287
conductors 74–5, 110–11, 228, 231
  continuity testing 234, 244–6, 265, 280
  safety 152, 153
conduit 122–6, 130
connecting transistors 342
connections 120–1, 152, 231, 272–3
construction industry 9
construction site installations 148–50
construction stage 15–18
contactors 84, 275–6
continuity 272, 273
  testing 234, 244–6, 265, 280
continuity of supply 284
contractors 14
  other contractors 28, 30, 230
contracts 6, 13, 14, 15, 284, 285
  of employment 2
control equipment, faults 274, 275
control panels 205, 217
cooker thermostats and controllers 212–13
copper 75, 110
cords, flexible 113, 193, 232, 277–8
core colours 111–13, 277
correction factors 177, 178–9
cosine rule 195
costs 14, 28, 283
coulombs 76, 77
CPA (critical path analysis) 26–7, 28
cpc (circuit protective conductors) 165, 168, 180–1, 234, 244
critical path analysis (CPA) 26–7, 28
current 71, 75, 76–7, 80–1, 85, 95
  amplification 338–9
  induced 305
  measuring 90
customers 13, 21, 28–9, 252, 256, 275
cycles 84–5, 85, 87, 293

D

dangerous substances 7, 41, 46, 155–6
Dangerous Substances and Explosive Atmospheres Regulations 2002 (DSEAR) 46, 155–6
data cables 116
Data Protection Act 1998 2–3
data storage 24–5, 287
d.c. (direct current) 75, 82, 93
  circuits 80–2, 85, 323
  conversion of a.c. supply to 346–8
  generators 95–6, 294
  motors 295–6
  speed control of machines 311
deadlines 8, 28
deliveries 23, 28
demand, changes in 7–9
design 7, 13–14, 24, 269, 271
design current 176
design data 280
diacs 334
diagrams 18, 19–20, 21, 26–7, 280
dimmer circuits 334
dimmer controls 193
diodes 331–2, 346–7
direct current see d.c.
discharge lighting 188–92, 193
discharging capacitors 329, 330
discrimination 3, 4–5, 175
diseases, work-related 46, 47
disposal of waste 7, 59
diversity 181, 193
documentation 22–4, 25–7, 222–3, 228, 229–30
domestic heating programmers 200–1
double insulated equipment 152
down time 283–4
drawings 13, 14, 18, 21, 24, 25, 28, 280
DSEAR (Dangerous Substances and Explosive Atmospheres Regulations 2002) 46, 155–6
duty holders 150–1, 154

E

earth electrode resistance testing 241, 248–9
earth faults 267, 268
earth leakage 170
earth-fault loop impedance 180
earth-fault loop impedance testing 234, 235, 241, 249–50, 251, 282
earth-fault loop path 162, 164–5, 280

earthed equipotential bonding and automatic disconnection (EEBAD) 169, 232
earthing 122, 152, 193, 208, 228, 232, 286
  purpose 162–5
  systems 165–8
EAW (Electricity at Work) Regulations 1989 42, 150–4, 222, 230, 262, 271
eddy currents 128
EEBAD (earthed equipotential bonding and automatic disconnection) 169, 232
efficacy of lamps 186, 187, 189, 191, 192
effluents, disposal of 59
electric shock 55, 58–9, 143, 162–3, 169, 235
  protection against 39, 93, 146, 147, 164, 180
electric showers 210
electrical contractors 12–13
Electrical Installation Certificates 226, 251, 252–3, 256
Electrical Installation Minor Works Certificates 251, 254–5
electrical safety 55–8
  see also safety
electrical symbols 18–19
electricity 74
  distribution 94–5
  generation 94
  transmission 93, 94
Electricity at Work (EAW) Regulations 1989 42, 150–4, 222, 230, 262, 271
Electricity Safety, Quality and Continuity Regulations 2002 43, 223
electro-static discharge 286
electromagnetic induction 78
electromagnets 78, 83
electromotive force (e.m.f.) 77–8, 95, 292–4, 347
electron theory 73–4
electronic communications 10, 24–5
electronic devices 276, 286–7
electrons 73–4, 75, 76–8, 81, 84, 286, 330–1
electrotechnical industry 7–9, 9–13
email 24, 25
emergency lighting 202–3
e.m.f. (electromotive force) 77–8, 95, 292–4, 347
employees' responsibilities 38, 40, 41
employer structure 12–13

employers' responsibilities 38, 40, 41, 44, 46, 47, 50, 59
employment contracts 2
employment legislation 2–5
EMS (environmental management systems) 6–7, 60
enclosures 118, 169, 233, 264
energy 69–70, 71
entries 274
environmental legislation 7
environmental management systems (EMS) 6–7, 60
environmental safety issues 59
equal opportunity 3
equipment 28, 44, 143, 152, 274
    for distribution of electricity on sites 149
    failure 269
    for hazardous areas 156
    safety 40, 55, 58, 143
    test equipment 58, 240–3, 264, 282–3
    for working at height 52–3
equipotential bonding conductors 234
estimates 14, 22
European Standards (EN) 6–7, 18–19, 140, 156–7, 202
excavations 53, 61
explosive atmospheres 46, 61, 152, 154–7, 286
extension leads 278
external influences 175

F

facilities of workplaces 43
Faraday's Law 292
fastenings 106–10
fault protection 228, 232, 236
faults 175
    diagnosis 266–83
    rectification 279–83
    repairs 283–4
FETs (field effect transistors) 344, 345
fibre optic cables 116, 286
field windings 294, 295
    see also induction motors
filter circuits 348
fire detectors 115, 204, 205, 206
fire extinguishers 51
fire hazards 162, 163
fire safety 50, 50–1, 115, 118, 228
fire-alarm systems 115, 204–8, 334
Fire-tuf/FP200 cables 115, 122, 207, 274
first aid 45, 58–9

fixed capacitors 324–5, 325–6
fixed resistors 318, 318–19
fixing devices 108–10
fixings 106–10, 123–4
flash point 156
Fleming's rules 292
flexible cables and cords 113, 193, 232, 277–8
floorboards 116–17
flow charts for isolating electrical supplies 56–7
fluorescent lamps (low pressure mercury vapour lamps) 188–92, 192, 276
force 66, 71
forces 67–9
FP200 cable 115, 122, 207, 274
friction 69, 75, 286
functional testing 281–3
fuses 127, 134, 135, 152, 170–2, 178, 267, 275
    immersion heaters 209
    ring circuits 134
    withdrawal 262, 263, 264
fusing factor 174

G

Gantt charts 26
gases 40, 154–7
gears 68
general lighting service (GLS) lamps 186–7, 192, 334
generation of electricity 94
generators 95–6, 162, 208
    Fleming's right hand rule 292
    simple d.c. generators 294
GLS (general lighting service) lamps 186–7, 192, 334
good earth paths 164
gravitational potential energy 69–70
gravity 66
'grounding' 286
grouping of cables 177
GS 38 (Guidance Note 38, HSE) 264, 283
Guidance Notes (IEE) 140, 251

H

hand tools 102–5
handover to client 256
HASAWA (Health and Safety at Work Act 1974) 41, 47, 48, 150, 229, 230, 286
hazardous locations 45, 152, 154–7, 286

hazardous substances 44, 46
hazards 61–2
health and safety 40, 47–8
    legislation 41–7
Health and Safety at Work Act 1974 (HASAWA) 41, 47, 48, 150, 229, 230, 286
heat generation by cables 177, 178–9
heating
    programmers 200–1
    space heating 210–11
    water heating 208–10
high-pressure mercury vapour lamps 192
high-pressure sodium lamps 192
hot water systems 208–10
    programmers 200–1
HSE (Health and Safety Executive) 11, 24, 46, 48, 58, 154
    GS38 264, 283
Human Rights Act 1998 3–4

I

ICs (integrated circuits) 345
IEE Guidance Notes 140, 251
IEE On-site Guide 118, 119, 123, 126, 141, 222, 228, 251
IEE Wiring Regulations 17th Edition see BS 7671
ignition energy 156
ignition sources 156
ignition temperature 156
illuminance levels for emergency lighting 203
illumination 194–5
immersion heaters 134, 208, 209
impedance 88, 164, 175
    earth-fault loop impedance 180, 234, 235, 241, 249–50, 251, 282
incandescent lighting 186–8, 192
inch control 308, 309
inclined planes 68
induced current 305
inductance 86–7, 88
induction 286
induction motors 296–306
inductive reactance 87
inductors 86–7, 88, 330, 347
information
    fault diagnosis 278–9, 280
    storage, use and retrieval 24–5
initial inspection 223–4
inspections 143, 272, 274, 277
    checklists 236–9
    documentation 222–3

initial 223–4
    periodic 143, 224–7, 251, 252
    process of 228–39
    requirements 231–3
    results 280
    schedules 251, 252, 253
inspectors 224, 282
installation techniques 116–29
installations, testing 143–4
instrumentation faults 276
instruments 58, 90–1, 240–3, 264,
    282–3
insulation
    cables 111–13, 118, 178
    failure 268, 269
    inspecting 228, 232
    thermal 178
insulation resistance, testing 235,
    241, 246–7, 281
insulators 74, 75–6
insurance 60
integrated circuits (ICs) 345
intermediate switching 131, 132–3
Internet 24
interpretation of test results 280–1
intruder alarm systems 216–17, 332,
    334
inverse square law 194
inversion 346
ions 73
ISO 14001 6–7, 60
isolation 222, 230, 233–4
    of circuits 61, 153, 230
    devices for 150, 265
    by earthing 162
    of electrical supplies 55–7, 61,
    233–4
    of equipment 153
    immersion heaters 209
    minimising disruption 233–4, 285
    safe 262–4
isolators, testing 235
IT equipment 10, 24, 208, 268, 287

J

JIB (Joint Industry Board) 55–7, 262
joint boxes 133, 135, 272
joints 120–1, 152, 231, 272–3
junction boxes 133, 135, 272

K

kinetic energy 70
kitchens 144

L

labelling 229, 262, 263
lamp dimmer circuits 334
lamp dimmer controls 193
lamp fittings/caps 188
lamp holders 234, 247
lamps see lighting
laws see legislation
lead-lag circuits 191
leading errors 91
LEDs (light-emitting diodes) 332
legal responsibility 284
legislation 229
    data protection 2–3
    disability 3
    discrimination 2–3
    employment 2–5
    environmental 7
    fire safety 50
    health and safety 41–7
    see also HASAWA
levers 67
lifting see manual handling
light bulbs see tungsten filament
    lamps
light dependent resistors 323
light levels in different environments
    215
light-emitting diodes (LEDs) 332
lighting 186–92
    circuits 130–3, 193, 248
lightning protection 162, 168
lightning strikes 269
limitation of test instruments 282–3
line-earth loop see earth-fault loop
liquid petroleum gas (LPG) 61
live working 262, 265
    see also faults
locking 153, 222, 230, 262, 264, 265
    devices 107–8, 264
logic gate circuits 340–1
logical approach 279–80
loss of supply 267, 307
low pressure mercury vapour lamps
    (fluorescent lamps) 188–92, 192,
    276
low-pressure sodium lamps 192
LPG (liquid petroleum gas) 61
luminaires 203, 276, 277
luminous flux 194

M

magnetic fields 292–5, 305
    see also motors
magnetism 82–4, 95

maintenance 9, 10, 207–8, 269, 284,
    285
    for prevention of faults 266, 271,
    283, 285
making good 118, 285
management 6, 22–4, 26, 28
manual handling 19, 23, 46, 53–4
manuals 19, 23, 280
manufacturers' information 19, 23,
    26, 231, 280
mass 66, 70, 71
materials 23, 28, 59, 271
    conductors 74–5
    insulators 76
MCBs (miniature circuit breakers)
    135, 170, 186, 209, 264, 267
measurement
    electrical quantities 90–1, 278
    illumination 194
measuring devices 105
mechanical advantage 69
mechanical integrity 272, 273
mechanical power 70
mechanics 66–70
MICC (mineral insulated copper
    cable) 115, 121–2, 126, 135, 207,
    274
miniature circuit breakers (MCBs)
    135, 170, 186, 209, 264, 267
molecules 73, 74
motion detectors 215, 216
motors 96, 294–5
    a.c. motors 93, 294, 305–6
    d.c. motors 295–6
    Fleming's left hand rule 292
    induction motors 296–306
    slip 305
    speed 305
    starters 307–10
    uses 299, 301, 302, 303–4, 304
    windings 306–7
multicore cable 131–3

N

National Grid 93, 94
neon lamps 192
neutral conductor 152, 166–7, 167–8,
    170, 193, 275
noise 45
non-live tests 280
number codes, resistors 321

O

occupations 9
off-load devices 265

ohmmeters 240–1, 243–4, 244–5, 282
Ohm's law 80, 81, 82, 91
on-load devices 265
one-way switching 130, 131
operating devices 265
other contractors 28, 30, 230
oven thermostats 213
over voltage, damage to electronic devices 286–7
overcurrent 170–4, 267, 268, 307
overhead lines 168
overhead working 40, 52–3
overloads 170–4, 267, 268, 307

P

parallel circuits 81
passive infrared (PIR) sensors 215, 216, 332
PAT (portable appliance testing) 60
p.d. (potential difference) 71, 74, 77, 78, 81, 162, 323
periodic inspection 143, 224–7, 251, 252
periodic testing 224–7, 233–4, 279
permanent magnets 82–3
permanent split capacitor (PSC) motors 303–4
personal protective equipment see PPE
petrol filling stations 157
phase angle 86, 88
phasors 86, 87
photoconductive cells 334–5
PIR (passive infrared) sensors 215, 216, 332
plans 14, 24
plant 28, 269
plastic (PVC) conduit 126
PME (protective multiple earthing) 167–8
polarity 268, 328
    testing 234–5, 247–8, 281
pollution 7, 41, 59
portable appliance testing (PAT) 60
portable appliances and equipment 60, 278
potential difference (p.d.) 71, 74, 77, 78, 81, 162, 323
potential energy 69–70
power 71
    a.c. circuits 88–9
    d.c. circuits 82, 85
power factor 86, 88, 89, 176
power ratings, resistors 244
power tools 55, 61, 105

power triangle 89
PPE (personal protective equipment) 7, 38–40, 45, 53, 61, 62, 117, 118, 153
preferred values, resistors 319–20
prefixes for SI units 72–3
preparing for inspection 229–30
printed circuit boards 286
programmable logic control 340–1
programmers 200–1, 209
project management 28
project roles and responsibilities 13–18
prospective short circuit current (PSCC) 174
protection of cables 118
protective conductor 166–7, 273
protective devices 170–4, 228, 232, 247, 275
    earthing and 162, 163, 168, 232, 267, 268
    faults and 175, 266, 267–8, 273, 276–7
    rating 176, 267
    speed 180
    see also circuit breakers; fuses
protective equipment 152
    see also PPE
protective multiple earthing (PME) 167–8
PSC (permanent split capacitor) motors 303–4
PSCC (prospective short circuit current) 174
pulleys 68–9
PVC insulated cables 114, 116, 247
    PVC/copper cable 114, 135
    PVC/PVC cables 114, 119, 121, 274
    PVC/SWA/PVC cables 114, 119, 121
PVC (plastic) conduit 126

Q

qualifications 9
quality systems 5–7

R

radial circuits 135
range of test instruments 282–3
RCBOs (residual current circuit breakers with overload protection) 170
RCDs (residual current devices) 55, 134, 151, 170
    testing 235, 250–1, 281

record keeping 266
rectification 346–8
reference methods 176
The Regulations see BS 7671
regulations see legislation; standards
relationships
    customers 28–9
    other contractors 30
    team working 31
relays 84
remote control signals 332
remote start/stop control 307, 308–9
replacements 283
reporting and certification 251–5
reports 23–4, 32
residual current circuit breakers with overload protection (RCBOs) 170
residual current devices (RCDs) 55, 134, 151, 170
    testing 235, 250–1, 281
resistance 71, 73, 74, 75, 76, 78–80, 80–1, 88, 164
    circuits with too much 163
    heat and 86, 276
    measuring 91
    see also resistors
resistivity 71, 79
resistors 80–2, 85, 318–23
    coding 321–2
    testing 243–4
responsibilities 13–18, 271
    for certification and reports 251–2
    duty holder 150–1
    employees' 38, 40, 41
    employers' 38, 40, 41, 44, 46, 47, 50, 59
    legal 284
    for PPE 38
restoration of supply 265
reverse polarity 235
rewiring 116–17
ring circuits 134
ring final circuit conductors, testing 145–6, 281
risk assessment 28, 39, 40, 49, 54, 285, 286–7
roles 13–18
rotor 295, 298–9, 300, 305–6
routine checks 227

S

safe working 40, 262–5, 280
safety 24, 28, 29, 55–62
    batteries 287
    capacitors 324

commissioning 223–4
compressed air 106
during inspection 230
of equipment 55, 58
fibre optic cabling 286
fire safety 50, 50–1, 115, 118, 228
lamps 188
live working 262, 265
manual handling 46, 53–4
PVC adhesive 126
tools 40, 55, 102, 103, 104, 105–6
working at height 52–3
working in excavations 53
see also BS 7671; electric shock;
HASAWA; health and safety; HSE;
inspection; PPE; safe working;
testing
safety equipment 7
safety signs 38
scaffolds 52–3
schedule of test results 251, 254
schedules 13
schematic diagrams 20
screws 106–7
seals 274
security alarm systems 216–17, 332,
334
SELV (Separated Extra Low Voltage)
93, 232, 236
semiconductors 193, 330–1
sensors, passive infrared (PIR) 215,
216, 332
Separated Extra Low Voltage
(SELV) 93, 232, 236
sequence of control 19
sequence of testing 233, 234
series circuits 80–1
series-wound universal motors 295
service manuals 19, 23
shaded-pole motors 204
short circuits 127, 170, 174, 175, 267,
268
showers 210
locations containing 144, 145–8
shut down of IT equipment 287
SI units 66, 69, 70–3
simmerstats 212
simple alternators 292–4
simple circuits 80–2
simple d.c. generators 294
simple machines 67–9
sine waves 84–5, 86, 87, 293
single core cable, lighting
circuits 130–1

single-phase a.c. synchronous
motors 306
single-phase (asynchronous)
induction motors 300–5
site documentation 22–4
site safety 51–5
slip calculations 305
smoothing 347–8
socket outlets 134, 135, 234, 247, 268,
274
bathrooms 147–8
construction sites 150
solenoids 84, 86
solid state devices 276
space heating 134, 210–11
special locations 144, 145–50
special precautions 286–7
specialist areas 10
specifications 13, 14, 15, 28, 223, 280
speed control 311–12
split-phase motors 300–1
spurs 135, 281
standards 5–7, 12, 28, 29, 154, 202,
270, 271
see also BS 7671
standby/backup power 202–3, 207,
208, 265
starter circuits 188, 189–91
starters, motors 307–10
states of matter 74
static electricity 286
stator 295, 296–7, 297, 300, 305–6
steel conduit 122–6
storage
of information 24–5, 287
of materials 59
storage batteries 287
street lighting 192, 215, 223, 334
stroboscopic effect 191
structural engineering 9
supply
continuity 284
failure 267, 307
isolation 55–7, 61
support organisations 11–12
surge protection 268
suspension heights (cables) 113
switches 78, 84, 134, 232, 274
faults 275–6
testing 234, 235, 247, 248
transistors as 339–40
switchgear 274, 275
switching, lighting 130–3
switching devices for construction
sites 150

symbols
electrical 18–19
SI units 70–2
synchronous a.c. induction motors
305–6
synchronous speed (motors) 305

T

team working 31
telecommunications cables 116
tendering 8, 14–15
terminals 273
terminating cables 119–20, 121–2,
272, 273
test equipment 58, 240–3, 264, 282–3
test lamps 240, 262, 263, 264, 265
testing 143–4
continuity testing 234, 244–6, 265,
280
documentation 222–3
fault protection 236
fire alarm systems 207–8
functional testing 281–3
instruments for 58, 240–3, 264,
282–3
interpretation of results 280–1
periodic 224–7, 233–4, 279
polarity 234–5, 247–8, 281
procedures 234–6, 243–51
RCDs 170, 235, 250–1, 281
safe working during 280
sequence 233, 234
transistors 343
thermal constraints 180–1
thermal effects 232
thermal insulation 178
thermistors 322–3
thermostats 200, 264
immersion heaters 209
ovens 213
three-line (phase) distribution 94–5
three-phase a.c. synchronous motors
305–6
three-phase induction motors 296–9,
307–8
three-phase supply 266
thyristors 333
timers 200–1, 209, 264
TN earthing systems 166–7, 193
tools 28, 55, 61, 102–5
safety 40, 55, 102, 103, 104, 105–6
torque 296, 298, 299, 301, 302, 303,
304
trade unions 5, 11, 141
training 6, 8, 11, 44, 46, 271

transformers 86, 92–3, 162, 169, 276, 346

transient voltages 268–9

transistors (bipolar) 335–43, 344
coding 341–2

transmission of electricity 93, 94

triacs 333

tripping of circuit breakers 173

tripping time 235

trunking 126–8, 130

truth tables 340–1

tungsten filament lamps (GLS) 186–7, 192, 334

tungsten halogen lamps 187, 192

two-way switching 130–1, 132

U

underfloor heating 148, 211

understanding the installation 278–9

unearthed appliances 162–3

Uninterruptible Power Supply (UPS) 208, 287

unions 5, 11, 141

units
illumination 194
SI units 66, 69, 70–3

UPS (Uninterruptible Power Supply) 208, 287

V

value codes, resistors 321

variable capacitors 326

variable resistors 318, 319

velocity ratio 69

voltage 75, 77–8, 80–1, 85
amplification 338–9
detectors 240, 262, 263, 264
measuring 90
National Grid 94
reduced 152

voltage drop 179

voltmeters 90

W

warning labels 262, 263

warning notices 229

waste 7, 59

water heating 208–10
programmers 200–1

weather 39, 43, 152

weight 66

wet locations 144, 145–8

wiring
construction sites 150
fire alarms 207

wiring diagrams 20

work done (mechanics) 66–9, 70

working at height 40, 52–3

working environments 41, 43, 45

working in excavations 53

working in isolation 59

working overhead 40, 52–3

'working voltage' 324

written communication 24, 31–2

Z

zener diodes 332, 334

zoning
for fire detection 205
hazardous areas 155–6
wet areas 145–6